THE POLITICS OF EUROPEAN INTEGRATION IN THE TWENTIETH CENTURY

THE POLITICS OF EUROPEAN INTEGRATION IN THE TWENTIETH CENTURY

DAVID ARTER

Professor of European Integration
Leeds Metropolitan University

Dartmouth

Aldershot • Brookfield USA • Hong Kong • Singapore • Sydney

Published by
Dartmouth Publishing Company Limited
Gower House
Croft Road
Aldershot
Hants GU11 3HR
England

Dartmouth Publishing Company
Old Post Road
Brookfield
Vermont 05036
USA

A CIP catalogue record for this book is available from the British Library

Library of Congress Cataloging-in-Publication Data
Arter, David
    The politics of European integration in the twentieth century / by David Arter.
        p.   cm.
    Includes bibliographical references and index.
    ISBN 1-85521-216-1 (hbk). – ISBN 1-85521-255-2 (pbk.)
    1. European federation.   2. Europe–Economic integration.
I. Title.
JN15.A76   1993
321'.04'094–dc20   93-18110
                                                                         CIP

Printed in Great Britain at the University Press, Cambridge

ISBN 1 85521 216 1 hbk
ISBN 1 85521 255 2 pbk

Contents

List of Tables and Maps

Tables

Maps

Acknowledgements

There is a story about a phone-in on Radio Yeravan in the Soviet Republic of Armenia in November 1990 during the presidency of Mikhail Gorbachev. Questions were put to the local Communist Party boss, vetted, processed and the responses duly broadcast a week later. 'Comrade, which came first, the hen or the egg?', one listener had the temerity to inquire. The statutory week elapsed and then the answer came back in the familiar, flat and somewhat irascible tone of the party chief. 'Which came first, the hen or the egg?', he read out the question again. 'Comrade, your question is irrelevant', he retorted, brusquely. 'Earlier we had both'! Gorbachev's brand of 'liberal communism' had brought *katastroika* and, it seems, not a little nostalgia for earlier times. One year later, Gorbachev had gone, Armenia was a member of the Commonwealth of Independent States (CIS) and times were, if anything, even harder. The capitalist–communist division had been replaced by simply a Europe of the 'haves' and a Europe of the 'have-nots'.

Broadly contemporaneous with the fragmentation of the Soviet Union, a civil war in Yugoslavia, occasioning appalling loss of life, marked the demise of a second communist federation. In the wake of the collapse of monopoly communism the 'successor states' of 1919–23 – the Baltics, Poland etc – have re-emerged as pluralist polities, whilst several 'losing nations' of the Great War – *inter alia* Croatia and Slovakia – along with those states whose sovereignty proved short-lived – Ukraine, Georgia etc – have reasserted their claims to statehood. All this has created a picture of centrifugalism and polarization in central and eastern Europe. Ironically, in the New Europe of post-1989 the 'peacemakers' in Brussels and Washington have been faced with similar problems of evaluating nationalist claims to those which confronted the celebrated peacemakers of Versailles in the New Europe of 1919.

If the road to Minsk and the creation of the CIS was largely unfamiliar to the general public – the national anthems of the gold-medallists of the member-states of the so-called 'Unified Team' at the 1992 Barcelona Olympics doubtless struck a strange if not necessarily discordant note – the road which led to the Maastricht summit of European Community (EC) leaders in December 1991 was mapped out in detail even in the popular press. Indeed, whilst disintegration appears to have been the dominant dynamic within the former communist bloc, significant progress towards integration has been made in Western Europe: Germany has been reunified, a European Economic Area (EEA) comprising nineteen states agreed and plans laid for the completion of economic and monetary union within the EC by 1 January 1999. The European Community appears to have become the major politico-economic power base on the continent, drawing more and more states into its magnetic field. Thus in spring 1992, Finland, in its seventy-fifth year of independence, became the first of the successor states of 1919–23 to apply for full membership, although a quarter of a century earlier it was not even a full member of the OECD.

This book is an analysis of European integration since the Great War. As such, it is a study which highlights the challenges of the past – the enduring bifurcation of the continent into an agrarian–industrial, communist–capitalist, rich–poor partition – and the lessons to be learnt from them for the Europe of the future. For example, the singular failure to integrate the economies of East and West Europe between the wars in the manner advocated by the Czech prime minister, Milan Hodža, or, indeed, to reintegrate the economies of the successor states of the Hapsburg and Romanov empires, viz. to harness the forces of political and economic nationalism in the inter-war period, contributed to the holocaust of Hitler and the Second World War. The eclipse of Europe, apparent to leading industrialists before the war, became unmistakable after it with the realities of US Marshall Aid.

Some time ago, an American academic visiting Leeds inquired whether it was the practice in our institution to hold meetings on Wednesday afternoons. When the response came back in the affirmative, he remarked: 'Hm, shame. Pity to spoil two weekends!' Many 'Wednesday afternoons' have retarded the progress of this volume and, for his patience and encouragement in its completion, I am grateful to my publisher, John Irwin. Pauline Spencer helped to strike the right balance when the pace of political change became vertiginous and David Bell helped on a number of specific matters regarding France and the European Community. My wife, Eeva-Kaisa, was, as always, supportive throughout. As to the rest of the family (an accountant, student and sixth-former respectively), inured to my perennial scribal endeavours and displaying a monumental disregard at the conclusion of the present work, they served as a wholesome reminder of the essential truth for authors of the Danish proverb, 'Not every cock that crows heralds a new day' – or in the 'hen-and-egg' parlance of the Yeravan dialectics, 'Not every hen that clucks lays an egg'!

David Arter
August 1992

Introduction: Another 'New Europe'?

It is better to go into Europe tipsy than in a drunken stupor

Janusz Rewinski – Polish Beer Lovers' Party
October General Election, 1991

The champagne – if not Polish beer – flowed freely and a mood of historic intoxication was created in Paris in November 1990 when the 35 members of the Conference on Security and Cooperation in Europe (CSCE) signed a Charter for the New Europe. There was agreement that this momentous gathering marked the end of an 'era of confrontation in Europe' and signalled a new epoch of 'democracy, peace and unity'. Indeed, the labour pains in Paris were shortly to give birth to an infant post-communist, post-Cold War Europe that might yet be the child of a United States of Europe.

The main features of the scenario which has unfolded since May 1989, when television cameras were invited to the Hungarian borders to film soldiers removing barbed wire and demolishing watch-towers, are familiar, although it is worth recounting the scale and significance of the main developments.

First, there has been the disintegration of the Soviet empire in Eastern Europe and the collapse of the Warsaw Pact as a military alliance. The autumn revolutions of 1989, which saw the breaching of the Berlin Wall and culminated in the shabby execution of the Ceauşescus on Christmas Day that year, were in part facilitated by Gorbachev's readiness to observe what Gennardy Gerasimov referred to as 'the Sinatra doctrine' – namely, that the satellite states could now 'do it their way'. As formally expressed by Gorbachev at the Council of Europe in July 1989: 'The political order in one country or another changed in the past and may change in the future. This change is the exclusive affair and choice of the people of that country. Any interference in domestic affairs and any attempt to restrict the

1

sovereignty of states, both friends and allies or any others, is inadmissible.'[1] Notably, the same week in June 1989 that the Chinese leadership sent troops into Tiennamen Square, Moscow refrained from similar action when the Communist Party agreed to share power with Solidarity in Warsaw.

Second, in the aftermath of the abortive hardline coup on 19 August 1991, there has been the accelerated disintegration and ultimate collapse of the Kremlin-dominated Soviet Union. The abolition of its central power structure and vanguard of the proletariat, the Communist Party – shortly after Gorbachev's return from house arrest in the Crimea – accompanied by wholesale de-Leninization, did nothing to stem the powerful centrifugal forces released in the republics. The Baltic states of Latvia, Lithuania and Estonia quickly regained independence; then, following an overwhelming pro-independence vote in a referendum in Ukraine on 1 December, a Commonwealth of Independent States (CIS), initially comprising the Russian Federation (under President Boris Yeltsin), Byelorussia (later named Bielarus) and the Ukraine was formed, boasting 73 per cent of the population and 85 per cent of the total industrial production of the former USSR.

Third, and broadly contemporaneous with the collapse of the Soviet Union, a second Communist federation, Yugoslavia, disintegrated into civil war. By summer 1992, the independence of Slovenia, Croatia and Bosnia had been recognized in the West (EC recognition of Macedonia was blocked by Greece) and Slovenia had also asked to join the European Community. The scale of the violence, the size of the displaced population (no less than two and a half million refugees) and the horrors of 'ethnic cleansing' committed by both Serbs and Croats turned towns like Vukovar, Karlovac and Sarajevo into household names. Indeed, the failure of repeated peacekeeping missions and the refusal of international bodies to intervene militarily to bring the situation under control – in this, the Bosnian Muslims have suspected a 'conspiracy against Islam' – have heightened the risk of more general war developing across the whole of south-eastern Europe. The 'New Europe' will not, of necessity, be a peaceful Europe.

Fourth, the reunification of the two Germanies brought the former German Democratic Republic (East Germany) into the European Community and marked a unique fusion of market-economy and command-economy systems. Despite the problems of integrating the old Soviet and Western partitions, the re-emergence of Germany, coupled with the collapse of the Soviet Union and its empire of satellite states, have radically reshaped the balance of power in central and eastern Europe.

A fifth critical development has been the end of an extended period in which the European continent was dominated by military and ideological conflict between two (largely) extra-European superpowers, the United States and the Soviet Union. In a real sense, the Paris gathering of the CSCE states in November 1990 marked the peaceful conclusion of what Patrick Brogan has called 'The Fifty-Years War'. In the changed climate of detente and arms reductions, the role of the American-dominated NATO (North Atlantic Treaty Organization), as both a military and political alliance, has been called into question, particularly in view of Franco-German proposals for a European army under the direction either of the European Community (EC) or the Western European Union.[2]

Finally, there has been the significant deepening and widening of West European integration, reflected in the May 1992 agreement linking the EC and European Free Trade Area (EFTA) states in a European Economic Area (EEA) which will form the largest free trade region in the world; the progress of the 12 EC states (or, at least, 11 minus the UK) on economic and monetary union made at the Maastricht summit on 9–10 December 1991; as well as the growing list of states applying for membership of the EC.

Sweden is a case in point. A Conservative Party (*Moderaterna*) poster during the 1988 general election campaign declared, 'Sweden needs Europe more than Europe needs Sweden'. Then, however, the ostensible stumbling-block to a formal application was the nation's traditional policy of neutrality. At a press conference on the night of the Social Democratic victory in September 1988, the prime minister, Ingvar Carlsson, categorically ruled out a formal application until after the September 1991 election at the earliest.[3] In the event, when the Cold War security system collapsed and precipitated a reappraisal of traditional conceptions of neutrality, Sweden joined the queue of applicants three months *before* the general election. When a bourgeois coalition won power, the Conservative foreign secretary stated publicly that 'neutrality' was no longer an adequate term to describe the foreign and security policies which Sweden wished to pursue within the European framework.[4]

It has become almost the conventional wisdom to assert that the demise of Moscow's authority has left the European Community as the most important political power base on the continent. Seven West European states have applied to join – Sweden, Austria, Finland, Switzerland, Cyprus, Malta and Turkey; more are set to apply – or, in the Norwegian case, reapply. In December 1991, the Visegrad Triangle of Czechoslovakia, Hungary and Poland gained associate status designed to produce closer politico-economic ties and the eventual creation of a free-trade zone with the EC; they may ultimately be followed by the former Yugoslav republics, Bulgaria, Romania, the Baltic States, Ukraine and possibly even Russia itself.[5]

In the build-up to the Maastricht European Council meeting, Frans Andriesson, the Dutch Vice-President of the European Commission, noted that a Community of 24 was on the horizon, whilst in *Belvedere* magazine, the President, Jacques Delors, wrote: 'We have to multiply the links and work out a new political and institutional programme for a structure comprising twenty-four or even thirty countries. There can be no Greater Europe without the Community, but neither can there be a future for the Community without development.'[6] Are we then moving towards what Winston Churchill described during the Second World War as a 'United States of Europe'?

In a much-quoted speech on 18 October 1989 at the College of Europe in Bruges, Delors urged the need for the European Community to respond to the 'acceleration of history'. His point is well taken, although it is pertinent to inquire whether the acceleration has been in forward gear, reverse or a combination of both? Indeed, a central theme of this volume is that the New Europe of Paris 1989 has the decidedly familiar look of the New Europe created by the peacemakers in neighbouring Versailles in 1919. The challenges of uniting Europe today, it is suggested, are similar in many ways to those of the inter-war years and it is imperative to learn and learn from the lessons of history. It is these historic challenges which provide an important focus for the book since, taken together, they have informed a significant part of Europe's recent past and the manner of their resolution will determine a good deal about the Europe of the 21st century. Five historic challenges warrant emphasis.

1   The disintegration of the Soviet empire in Eastern Europe and the subsequent collapse of two communist federations – the Soviet Union itself and Yugoslavia – have confronted the 'peacemakers' in Brussels and Washington with similar problems of evaluating and resolving nationalist claims to those faced by the celebrated peacemakers of 1919–23.
2   The collapse of the Soviet empire in Eastern Europe has facilitated the re-emergence of the 'successor states' of 1919–23 and resurrected problems of national integration which were petrified for half a century under monopoly communism.
3   The re-emergence of the successor states as pluralist systems has raised afresh the spectre of the rampant economic nationalism that characterized the inter-war period and has pointed up the paramount need for the reintegration of the economies of the post-communist states.
4   The New Europe of 1989, like the New Europe moulded after the Great War, involves the challenge of sustaining pluralist democracy in states which had little or no democratic tradition at their inception and have little or no democratic tradition today.
5   The collapse of monopoly communism has revealed the continued existence of the 'two Europes' depicted by François Délaisy

in *Les Deux Europes* in 1924. As the Pole, Tadeusz Mazowiecki, the first non-communist prime minister in the Warsaw Pact, warned the CSCE summit in Paris: 'Our common future threatens to be shrouded by dark clouds caused by the resurgence of old conflicts, unless the division between the Europe of the haves and have-nots is overcome.'[7]

Jean Monnet, one of the pioneering figures of post-war West European integration, once remarked that Europe will not be built from crises, but from the sum of the resolution of these crises. It is contended here that the way Europe reacts to meet the historic challenges enumerated above will determine in large part the future of the continent in the decades ahead.

There is a passage from a popular contemporary Swedish song, quoted in the memoirs of the second post-war Finnish president, J.K. Paasikivi, which serves as an admirable ode to the wisdom of hindsight:

Jag fattar inte snart
men det är så underbart
att efteråt är allt så klart

'I didn't catch on quickly,' it goes, 'but it really is remarkable how afterwards everything is so clear.'[8] Beforehand, of course, there is copious room for speculation – as to whether, for example, a European confederation of 40 or more nations will emerge, stretching beyond the Urals, and having responsibilities ranging from security policy to human rights and the environment.

The task at hand is not prognostication – forecasting the precise course of European unity – nor is it primarily prescription – laying down a particular institutional framework within which to develop a United States of Europe. Rather, the aim is essentially diagnostic; that is, to undertake a systematic examination of the factors and forces of integration and disintegration in the New Europe of post-1989 in light of the lessons of the recent past.

The first three chapters analyse the New Europe of 1919–23, a period when the forces of disintegration were in the ascendancy and when a concern to promote and protect national sovereignty was paramount. The challenges of integrating inter-war Europe are perceived from three overlapping perspectives.

1   The *domestic standpoint* which focuses on the task of national integration; that is, the vital need to reconcile state and society in the new regimes created out of the collapse of the former central and east European empires. The existence in several of the successor

states of numerically significant and geographically-concentrated ethnic minorities created conditions in which counter-nationalism could thrive. This territorial opposition, combined with various forms of ideological opposition to the new states, served to complicate the achievement of a democratic breakthrough – a shift to stable pluralist politics.

2   The *regional standpoint* which concentrates on the outcome of various schemes for integrating states linked by geography, history and demography and which possessed common cultural bonds. Proposals for unions of states in *inter alia* the Baltic, Balkans and Danube Valley are considered and the functional logic of *federalism* explored, both as an ideology and a structure for containing the strident politico-economic nationalism of the 'winning' nations and the counter-nationalism of the 'losing' nations of 1919–23.

3   The *pan-continental standpoint* which highlights a number of ambitious blueprints for uniting Europe, largely geared to meeting the growing economic challenge of the US. The fundamental rationale of such 'grand design' proposals was to create, and permit access to, wider markets.

On the threshold of the Second World War, however, the European continent was divided along an East–West axis into two regions, characterized by contrasting levels of economic and political modernization, which were non-integrated in the sense of lacking extensive mutual trade flows.

Chapters 4 to 8 analyse the progress of European integration, from the reassertion of the legitimacy of national self-determination by the Big Three at Yalta in February 1945 and the ruthless disregard shown for this same principle by the 'liberating' Red Army shortly afterwards, to the autumn revolutions of 1989 which marked the collapse of five decades of monopoly communism and the re-emergence of the successor states of 1919–23 as competitive systems. The ideological bifurcation of the continent, the origins and development of the capitalist–communist Cold War confrontation and the superpower domination of Europe are examined. So, too, is the course which West European integration charted, from the initial steps to form the European Coal and Steel Community in 1950 and the Rome Treaty founding the Common Market in 1957, to the subsequent descent of an economic iron curtain formed by rival (EEC–EFTA) trading blocs across Western Europe by 1960. Consolidated regional integration, which witnessed the expansion of the 'Six' into the 'Twelve' by 1986, was paralleled by signs of centrifugal pressures within several states of the Soviet empire in Eastern Europe. The collapse of the Soviet Union itself, in the wake of the failure of the hardline anti-Gorbachev coup in August 1991, recast the post-war mould and, taken together with the civil war in Yugoslavia, accentuated the dichotomy between integration in the West and disintegration in the East.

The conclusion in Chapter 9 draws the main threads and themes of the book together and, based on the lessons of the past, looks to the future by asking whether events are leading towards a United States of Europe. Warning of the necessity to organize a cross-party 'Little Englander' front against the 'Euro-federalists', David Owen, in his valedictory Social Democratic Party broadcast in September 1991, declared that 'a United States of Europe is neither historically desirable nor politically wise'.[9] During a tour of the US, moreover, former Conservative prime minister Margaret Thatcher also inveighed against a federal Europe, claiming that the hope of creating an ideology of Europeanism – or what she called 'new European nationalism' – to replace individual national sentiment was 'a bureaucratic fiction'.[10] Significantly, both politicians equated a United States of Europe with the Western Europe of the EC and specifically opposed steps towards economic and political union discussed at the Maastricht summit.

A primary aim of this book, however, is to give the European debate width and historic depth: Europe is not synonymous with the EC and, as a new century approaches, it is essential to eschew parochialist in favour of broad-gauge attitudes to the complex challenges facing the continent. The canvas of this volume, therefore, extends from the Atlantic to the Urals and from the Arctic to the Adriatic. This is the New Europe of post-1989, a Europe impelled rapidly by the momentum of events towards a destination as yet unknown. Certainly it cannot be said today, as William Pitt is reputed to have remarked in January 1806, after Napoleon's victory at Austerlitz: 'Roll up that map of Europe; it will not be wanted these ten years!'

Notes

1   'Putsch sends shivers through the old bloc', *The Guardian*, 20 August 1991.
2   'Mais, pourquoi donc passer du Marché commun à l'Europe politique?', *Le Soir*, 7–8 December 1991, p.6.
3   David Arter (1989), 'A Tale of Two Carlssons: The Swedish General Election of 1988', *Parliamentary Affairs*, **42**, (1), 84–101.
4   Margaretha af Ugglas, 'Foreign Policy: New Patterns and Challenges', Address at the London Seminar on the Nordic Countries in Europe, 28 November 1991.
5   'Oekraïne wil toetreden tot EG', *Het Nieuwsblad*, 7–8 December 1991, p.8.
6   'Delors proposes a Greater Europe', *The Guardian*, 14 October 1991, p.8.
7   'East agrees to dissolve Warsaw Pact by 1992', *The Guardian*, 20 November 1990.
8   Cited by Paasikivi's successor, Urho Kekkonen, when justifying his conviction that the Social Democratic-Agrarian-Conservative Party cabinet under K.A. Fagerholm would fail because of the deterioration in Finno-Soviet relations in

autumn 1958, known as the 'Night Frost' crisis. See Urho Kekkonen (1976a), *Kirjeitä myllystäni 1956–1967*, Keuruu: Otava, p.66.

9   'Owen last word on federalists', *The Guardian*, 13 September 1991.

10 'EC finalises co-operation deals with the United States', *The Guardian*, 24 September 1991.

1 'The New Europe', 1919–39

Proportionately, there are more small states in Europe than in any other continent.

Thomas Masaryk, The Making of a State, p.370

The New Map of Europe

The 'New Europe' of the inter-war years was first and foremost a Europe of small nation-states. The collapse of the Hapsburg and Romanov empires and the defeat of the Hohenzollerns in Germany spawned a patchwork of 'successor states' in the broad zone of territory between Russia and Germany.

The overthrow of Czarist absolutism in Russia, the turmoil caused by the Bolshevik revolution of November 1917 and the subsequent Civil War created conditions which enabled a number of peripheral areas – Finland, Latvia, Lithuania, Estonia, Georgia and the Ukraine – to secede (in the case of the last two mentioned albeit only temporarily) and declare themselves independent. A measure of the size of the newly-sovereign polities can be gained from the fact that the combined population of the four Baltic republics numbered under eight million.

The dissolution of the Dual Monarchy in Austria–Hungary led to its territory being carved up between no less than seven states. New nation-states in the form of Poland, Czechoslovakia and Yugoslavia appeared; existing ones, such as Romania, acquired territory; the dismembered Imperial powers, Austria and Hungary, themselves became small states with about eight million people each. Only Poland, with a population variously estimated at between 27 and 32 million, was plainly not a small state and could reasonably aspire to play (and would, indeed, find it exceedingly difficult to avoid) Great Power politics.[1] In addition to the partition or 'Balkanization' of the Russian and Austro-Hungarian empires, the disposition of Ottoman territories meant that Greece in particular profited, whereas European Turkey was reduced to a small area surrounding Constantinople.

The economic wisdom of dissecting Europe was in hindsight extremely questionable. 'After an orgy of destruction multiplied by modern technology,' wrote Sally Marks, 'there remained an impoverished, small continent cut up into some thirty competing little states.'[2] But, especially for the younger generation of 1919, weaned on Ronald Burrows' and R.W. Seton-Watson's magazine *The New Europe*, it was the new Serbia, the new Greece, the new Bohemia and the new Poland – in sum, the new successor states – which inspired them and which they believed to be the justification of the suffering and victory in war.[3]

Inevitably, the peace conference was dominated by the victorious Allied powers of England (Great Britain), the United States of America, France, Italy and Japan – the 'Big Five' – whose principal concern was to devise arrangements that would ensure lasting peace and security. There were only seven small and medium-sized European Allies among the 32 states invited to the Paris Peace Conference beginning on 18 January 1919. As Harold Nicolson cryptically observed, moreover, 'the smaller powers were only admitted into consultation at plenary sessions (which were always of a formal, indeed farcical character) and thus spent much of their time in lobbying and grumbling'.[4] It was, in any event, difficult for the established members of the European state system and for old-school diplomats to get accustomed to the idea of a 'Balkanized Europe'; rather, they tended to view the new states primarily as a means of weakening the powers that had lost the war.[5] The reality was, of course, to prove very different. Germany was surrounded by weak states comprising German *irredenta* whose claims would no longer be ignored in Berlin (as they had before 1914 with a view to preserving Austria–Hungary).[6]

Writing in 1942, after the Fascist reduction of the successor states of central Europe, the former Czechoslovak prime minister, Milan Hodža, argued cogently that, whilst the freedom and security of individuals should be guaranteed by the state, the freedom and security of small nation-states could in turn only be guaranteed by their federation.[7] The functional logic of integrating the new states of central Europe was, by implication, overwhelming on both economic and security grounds.

There is, indeed, evidence that, as early as 1919, England and the US would willingly have acquiesced in arrangements for the creation of a federation of Danubian states though, according to the contemporary diplomat Charles Seymour, the suggestion would have been 'no more effective than a tenor solo in a boiler-shop. The nationalities would have none of it.'[8] Nonetheless, an important (if surprisingly neglected) strand in the fabric of inter-war history was the fitful and ultimately belated search for an acceptable form of organization incorporating the small and medium-sized states of central Europe which would boast all the advantages of the much-maligned Austro-Hungarian empire without most of its obvious social and political disadvantages. The various inter-war schemes for a confederation of Danubian states will be examined in Chapter 3, but first it is necessary to set the scene by examining the landscape of the New Europe between 1919 and 1939.

The First World War was a monstrous miasma which spread inexorably to four continents and spanned an interminable four years. It was, however, primarily a European war. The continent of Europe was the stage for the bulk of hostilities and it was on the western front that the detritus of trench warfare numbered millions of dead. It was the Somme – within earshot of the City of London – that proved for many to be their corner of a foreign field.

Ironically, after four years of enervating conflict, the exhaustion and collapse of Germany in November 1918 took the Allied and Associated powers by surprise and left them in a state of some disarray. True, when the peace conference opened, there were certainties to be faced: the Austro-Hungarian empire was a thing of the past; a civil war was raging in Russia for the ideological soul of the post-Czarist state, and a revolutionary tremor could be felt across much of Germany and central Europe. The nationalities, moreover, were literally on the march. Every peace settlement should perhaps be regarded, not as the consummation of a given victory, but as the foundation of a slow process of reconstruction.[9] However, the Allied troops were anxious to be demobilized and return home and there was the real fear, especially on the part of the British prime minister Lloyd George, that, unless a relatively speedy settlement was reached, the millions starving in central and eastern Europe would become easy prey to Bolshevism.[10] Time, in short, was against the Allies while the pressure of impatient publics added to the need for an expeditious settlement.

Yet there were clear differences of interest and principle separating the victorious powers. Crudely stated, the US, England and France sought peace and security, whereas Italy and Japan wanted to increase their power and possessions.[11] There were, in any event, differing conceptions among the three first-mentioned countries about the means by which security could be achieved. The US and, to a lesser extent, England believed, rather imprecisely, that peace could be predicated on the legitimacy of democratic institutions; the French, in contrast, worked for concrete guarantees against future German aggression. Indeed, for the dominant faction in France, led by prime minister Georges Clemenceau, the emergence of a network of successor states in central Europe constituted a major pillar in the construction of a security system designed to thwart a resurgence of German militarism and to act as a barrier to Russo-German collusion. Put simply, Clemençeau supported the territorial demands of the successor states, both to secure their friendship and, by apportioning them German territory, to ensure that they would remain in a state of hostility with Germany.[12]

So much was implicit in a memorandum drafted on 31 March 1919 by André Tardieu, a member of the French Chamber of Deputies. On instructions from Clemençeau he responded to a communiqué from Lloyd George in which the British prime minister put the case for leniency towards Germany and the need to formulate a peace treaty that would appear equitable to the major defeated power. Although Tardieu repeatedly disavowed punitive intentions with regard to France's old adversary, the sanctity of his cause – the well-being of the nascent successor states of central Europe – could scarcely disguise a concern to safeguard French security interests at Germany's expense. 'If in order to give these young nations [Poland, Bohemia etc.] frontiers which are essential to their national life, it is necessary to transfer to their sovereignty Germans, the sons of those who enslaved them, one may regret having to do so and do it only with measure, but it cannot be avoided.'[13]

In the case of the Sudetan Germans, the English in particular were hesitant about handing over to the rule of another people, and against their clear will, a population of over three million, comprising one-third of the total population of Bohemia-Moravia. After all, on 28–9 October 1918 the Germans had formed Councils in German Bohemia and German Moravia–Silesia which declared their wish to join German-Austria or, failing that, Germany. The Czech response was a refusal to negotiate with rebels.[14] But the economic as well as the strategic arguments were strong, and the fears of the peacemakers were lulled by a statement from the influential Czech lobbyist, Eduard Beneš, that 'it was the intention of the Czechoslovak government ... to make out of the Czechoslovak Republic a sort of Switzerland, taking into consideration, of course, the special conditions in Bohemia'.[15]

France was equally supportive of the new Poland (contrast Lloyd George's irritation at what he saw as Polish greed), as well as determined to prevent the proposed *Anschluss* between the rump Austrian state and neighbouring Germany. When German-Austria proclaimed her independence, she declared herself to be part of the German republic. At the insistence of the French, however, this action was nullified and, on the basis of Article 89 of the Versailles Treaty, Germany was obliged to acknowledge and respect the independence of Austria. Austria, in turn, was compelled, under vehement protest, to change her name from *Deutsch-Österreich* to *Österreich*.[16]

French support for the creation of a complex of buffer states against German aggression in central Europe did not, however, meet with universal domestic approval. Indeed, time was to show that there was much force in the minority critique expressed by Jacques Bainville that, whilst Germany was essentially preserved, Europe had been broken up (see Map 1.1, p.27). The balance of power which might have acted as a counterweight to a resurgent Germany, Bainville asserted, had not been restored.[17]

The Principle of National Self-Determination

The New Europe of small states had its basis in the doctrine of national self-determination, which held that no population should be subjected to foreign rule against its will. The principle of self-determination was clearly enunciated in the American President Woodrow Wilson's Fourteen Points, which were submitted to Congress on 8 January 1918.

Points 6–13 postulated that Russian territory be evacuated and Russia given an unhampered opportunity for the independent determination of her national policy; Belgium was to be evacuated and restored; France was to be evacuated, her invaded portions restored and Alsace–Lorraine returned to her; Italy's frontiers were to be readjusted along clearly recognizable lines of nationality; the peoples of Austria–Hungary were to be granted the freest opportunity for autonomous development (this was subsequently modified to provide for complete independence); Romania, Serbia and Montenegro were to be evacuated and their occupied territories restored; the Turkish portions of the Ottoman empire were to be assured a 'secure sovereignty', whilst the subject nationalities were to be allowed the 'absolutely unmolested opportunity for autonomous development'. Finally, an independent Poland was to be created, including territories inhabited by indisputably Polish populations.

When the four Western leaders (Wilson, Lloyd George, Clemençeau and Orlando) converged on the highly intense atmosphere of Paris in January 1919, the validity of self-determination as the guiding *principe* in redrafting the map of Europe was not seriously questioned. Self-determination, moreover, was not to be merely a quixotic phrase, but rather was to serve as an imperative of action. Certainly if the post-Napoleonic Congress of Vienna in 1815 allowed its deliberations to be dominated by the twin theories of legitimacy and the balance of power, so there were delegates in Paris who held in private that the peace conference was unduly obsessed by the concept of nationality contained in the self-determination formula.

It is, of course, incontrovertible that defeat in war and the concomitant challenge to dynasticism contributed both to releasing and allowing expression to a vigorous strain of political nationalism across the entire European continent. Indeed, the peacemakers were obliged to adjudicate among a bewildering array of nationalist claims.

The Czechs, Slovaks and Croats all claimed the right to independence although, as Mirjana Gross has argued, a mass Croatian national consciousness seems to have developed only after the establishment of Yugoslavia and Serbian domination of the new Kingdom.[18] Sinn Fein election propaganda in December 1918 (the 'Coupon Election' on the mainland), however, alluded to the dubious nationalist demands of Yugoslavia and Czechoslovakia, referring to them as 'races infinitely less historical' than the Irish. 'The Czechoslovaks and Yugoslavs are younger than this ancient country by a thousand years', one poster announced. Another prominent one inquired, 'Why did they die?' – a list of Irish martyrs was appended – and retorted, 'They died to secure the liberation of the oldest political prisoner in the world – Ireland'.[19] When it was announced that the peace conference was concerned only with the minorities of defeated powers, Erskine Childers thundered in *The New Europe* of June 1919 that:

> Instead of being the pioneer of a new order, Great Britain is the most conspicuous and responsible upholder of an old order; not merely in the sense that Ireland is the only remaining subject nationality of those existing in the Europe of 1914, but in the ominous dynamic sense that this evil example survives to aid in perpetuating a whole system of vicious statecraft, breeding new Irelands – they are germinating under our eyes – and poisoning the politics of Europe and the world.[20]

Yet while some nations (or nationalist elements) were seeking either statehood or to extend the territorial boundaries of their new state by reference to ethno-linguistic claims, other peoples presented the peacemakers with a largely silent countenance. Having gained independence as a by-product of the Russian revolution, nationalist forces in Finland worked to incorporate the Finno-Ugric peoples of Russian Karelia into a 'Greater Finland', *Suur-Suomi*. In a telegram to his prime minister in November 1918, however, Rudolf Holsti, the Finnish ambassador in London, reported how American experts had stated that not only was the acquisition of Eastern Karelia complicated by the important Murmansk railway line, which lay within it, but that the local population had not expressed the wish to be merged with Finland.[21]

Similarly 'mute' were regions such as the semi-feudal Sub-Carpathian Ruthenia which formed part of the Hungarian partition following the 1867 *Ausgleich* and which, it appeared, was too backward to sustain nationalist sentiments. Bartha, writing in 1901, vividly portrayed the totally expendable and thoroughly exploited nature of the Ruthenian peasantry. 'The sovereign stag,' he wrote, 'should not be disturbed in its family entertainments ... what is a Ruthenian compared with it? ... only a peasant.'[22] On the uncertain national identity of the Ruthenes, Hugh Seton-Watson has commented, 'a few thought themselves Ukrainians, a few Russians, the rest accepted the Hungarians' designation of them as "Ruthenes"'.[23] In the case of the Ukrainians in East Galicia, their claim to form a nation-state was countered by the objection that the people were unripe for self-government and would be unable to maintain a state.[24]

The claims and counter-claims of putative nations to statehood raised the wider question of what the peacemakers believed legitimately bestowed rights of territorial sovereignty on groups. If the short answer was probably that, in principle, the state was to be rendered as far as possible coextensive with ethnic–linguistic frontiers, it is important to note that the Western leaders largely failed to comprehend the enormity and complexity of the nationalities problem. Poland illustrates admirably the tangled obscurities of the ethnographic map of central Europe after the Great War and places in context Wilson's subsequent admission to his closest confidant, Colonel House, that he had no prior conception of the extreme difficulties entailed in resolving the nationalities problems in the region. What, it might reasonably be inquired, were to be regarded (in the words of the Fourteen Points) as territories inhabited 'by indisputably Polish populations'?

Thus, in contrast to West Prussia and Posen, which had largely belonged to Poland until the partitions in the late 18th century, Upper Silesia had been separated from Poland for 600 years and in the Allenstein District of East Prussia there was a large Polish-speaking population which had never been directly under Polish rule. Unlike the majority, moreover, this area was Protestant. As Robert Lord has noted, these facts raised doubts about whether all the Poles in Prussia could fairly be treated the same way simply because they were Poles.[25]

In any event, at Lloyd George's personal insistence and in the face of French opposition, plebiscites were organized in Allenstein and Marienwerder – the latter Poland claimed on strategic and economic grounds (the shortest railway route from Danzig to Warsaw passed through Marienwerder) – and both areas ultimately opted overwhelmingly for Germany.[26] The problems of Prussian Poland bear witness to the wider point that such were the ethnic conditions moulded by centuries of history not lived under the aegis of the nation-state that any set of frontiers was bound to place or leave some national minorities under alien rule.[27]

This was undoubtedly the case, although when it came to redrafting the map of central Europe, some nations enjoyed a head start in the eyes of the Allies. Indeed, it is less to attribute venal motives to the Western powers and more to point up the exigencies of the war effort to note that, before the US entered hostilities in May 1917, the English and French had entered into secret agreements which directly violated the principle of self-determination. The territorial increment of these war-time agreements was far from exiguous. Promises were made to Italy regarding territories inhabited by Greeks, Slavs, Albanians and Greeks; to Romania regarding the incorporation of a substantial Magyar minority; to Japan concerning the Chinese province of Shantung, and to France in relation to areas claimed by the Arabs.[28] The notion of self-determination, in short, was compromised from the outset by prior commitments, born of an Allied concern to enlist associates and win the war.

Equally, the post-war map of central and eastern Europe owed much to force applied *after* the armistice with Germany. By March 1919, the Czechs had occupied the Sudetenland and German Bohemia, and two months later, Yugoslavia – until 1929 the 'Kingdom of the Serbs, Croats and Slovenes' – acquired Klagenfurt and southern Styria. The Poles, moreover, had taken eastern Galicia and aspired to reclaim all the territory lost by them in the 18th-century partitions.

The collapse of the German war effort also undermined the March 1918 Treaty of Brest-Litovsk, the 'forgotten peace', which was designed to create a number of German client states in the Baltic, Poland and the Ukraine and to confine Russia to her narrow ethnic frontiers.[29] The Ukraine was particularly attractive to the Germans who could use it as the granary for central Europe. Between 1918 and 1919, a series of nominally independent Ukrainian governments were formed although, as the German General Max Hoffman wrote, 'The difficulty in the Ukraine is simply that the central *Rada* [administration] has only our rifles behind it.'[30] Even so, when the Paris Peace Conference first convened, the outcome of the Russian civil war left the future of the Ukraine – subsequently annexed by the Bolsheviks – still in the balance. The pace of events and the fluidity of the situation facing the Allies warrant emphasis. None of the Baltic provinces, for example, contemplated or probably even desired complete separation from Russia during the months of provisional government which followed the overthrow of Czarism. Instead, it was the Bolshevik revolution which not only enabled, but in a real sense compelled, them to go further and demand complete independence.[31]

All in all, it is clear that, for the peacemakers in Paris, it was not a matter of applying the notion of self-determination dispassionately in a power vacuum. The Great Powers did not sit down with a blank sheet of paper at a drawing board, so to speak, to redraft the map of

Europe. Rather, they were confronted with a wide array of *de facto* claims and developments. The settlements of 1919–23 (see Table 1.1) cannot be comprehended except in a world of *realpolitik* in which considerations of expediency conflicted with decisions of principle. The fact is that, whilst some nations achieved independence, others had nationality – in the form of citizenship – thrust upon them. Armies, diplomacy and tactical opportunism all played their part, as did astute leadership and the effective marketing of claims. Czechoslovakia is a particularly instructive case study in state-building.

The Making of a Nation-State: Czechoslovakia

In his chapter, 'Truth and Legends about the Origin of Czechoslovakia', Joseph Kirschbaum quotes the British historian H.A.L. Fisher's celebrated maxim that 'Czechoslovakia is the only state in the world that owes its origin to propaganda'.[32] The creation of an independent Czechoslovakia out of the dismembered Austro-Hungarian empire undoubtedly owed little to the Wilsonian principle of national self-determination, still less to popular demands for national sovereignty. Rather, it was indebted to the enterprise of a number of émigré leaders in networking support for a Czech state on the international stage.

There was Voska's 80-strong Secret Service in the US, formed in 1914 (and two years later funded by the British secret service) which was designed to counter pro-Austrian and German activities in America;[33] the sedulous promotional activity of T.G. Masaryk among the American Slovaks and Czechs and the attendant flag-waving processions in national costume which drew the attention of the American public to the Czech movement for independence; the activity of several French Slavists like Milan R. Štefánik; and, not least, the endeavours of the Czechoslovak legions in France, Russia and Italy. As Masaryk has acknowledged: 'Without our propaganda abroad, without our diplomatic work and the blood of our Legions, we should not have achieved our independence.'[34]

This was particularly true because the Allies had not originally pledged themselves to the break-up of the Austro-Hungarian empire, merely promising the liberation of the Italians, Romanians and Southern Slavs. It was not until 12 June 1917, in response to Woodrow Wilson's request for an Allied exposition of their peace terms, that a commitment was made to the 'liberation of the Italians, Slavs, Romanians *and also Czecho-Slovaks* from foreign rule'. The word 'Czechoslovaks', it appears, was inserted into a completed draft largely at the behest of Eduard Beneš who argued that it was necessary in order to

Table 1.1   The Main Territorial Terms of the 1919–23 Settlements

28 June 1919 Treaty of Versailles (with Germany)

Alsace–Lorraine returned to France

The Saar placed under international control for 15 years, but France to control the coal mines

Kiel Canal and Rhine internationalized

Provision for a plebiscite in Northern Slesvig which in 1920 voted to join Denmark

Posen and a valuable part of Upper Silesia transferred to Poland and so, too, the so-called Polish Corridor, a strip of Prussian territory, giving her access to Danzig

Danzig granted 'free city' status under the control of the League of Nations

The East bank of the Rhine demilitarized (for 30 miles beyond the river) and the West bank occupied by Allied forces for 15 years

September 1919 Treaty of St Germain-en-Laye (with Austria)

South Tyrol and Istria forfeited to Italy

Slovenia, Bosnia–Herzogovina and Dalmatia ceded to new Yugoslav state

Bohemia and Moravia incorporated into the new Czechoslovakia

Galicia merged into the new Poland

Bukovina conjoined to Romania

November 1919 Treaty of Neuilly (with Bulgaria)

Western Thrace lost to Greece and small territorial losses to Yugoslavia also

June 1920 Treaty of Trianon (with Hungary)

Transylvania lost to Romania

Burgenland transferred to Austria

Croatia incorporated into Yugoslavia

Slovakia and Ruthenia built into Czechoslovakia

August 1920 Treaty of Sèvres (with Turkey)

Eastern Thrace passed to Greece

Greeks also to administer Smyrna for five years

Sèvres not ratified and replaced by 1923 Treaty of Lausanne

stiffen the resolve of the oppressed Hapsburg races; it also owed much to the good offices of the French prime minister Aristide Briand.[35]

The Allied reluctance to dismember Austria-Hungary needs emphasis and was the product of several factors. First, Britain, France and the US did not experience the same hostility towards Vienna as towards Berlin; Austria, in turn, declared war only upon Serbia, Russia and Belgium and let the other states declare war on her.[36] Second, the Allies generally regarded Austria as a counterpoise to Germany and as a safeguard against the 'Balkanization' of central Europe. Palacký's axiom that, had Austria not existed, it would have had to be invented, reflected the predominant Allied sentiment. Finally, in neutral America, the Slovaks and Ruthenes came under Magyar influence by the seductive argument that Austria–Hungary was a victim of Germany by whom she had been compelled to make war against her will.[37] This view of the German subjugation of Austria contributes, perhaps, to explaining why Wilson did not declare war on Austria–Hungary until 4 December 1917 – seven months after the American declaration of war on Germany.[38]

Moreover, despite the endeavours of expatriate groups like the Mid-European Democratic Union, whose aim was to submit to the American people a blueprint for a zone of small nations in central Europe, it appears that in neither the Czech nor Slovak lands was there strong support for, or even a clear conception of, an independent Czechoslovakia during the war. Throughout the hostilities, Bohemian politicians proclaimed their loyalty to the Austrian crown. In January 1917, the Czech group of deputies in the Austrian *Reichstag* emphatically rejected the Allied goal of liberating the Czechs, whilst the delegation of Czech Socialists attending the second Socialist International in Stockholm in June 1917 voiced the demand for 'an independent Czech state *within* a federated Austria–Hungary'.[39] Masaryk, to be sure, insisted that this was a tactical position designed specifically to counter the Austrian Social Democrats' reductionism in seeking to restrict the autonomy of the Hapsburg peoples merely to educational matters.[40]

Unlike the Bohemian provinces, Slovakia formed part of the Hungarian partition between 1867 and 1914; as István Deák has noted, a suspicious attitude towards Vienna and an attempt at Magyarization at home were the dominant themes of Hungarian politics.[41] Accordingly, the harsh repression of views that diverged from the Budapest line induced a general passivity among the Slovak political parties during the war. The Catholics in Andrej Hlinka's Slovak People's Party, together with the Slovak Socialists, were temporarily silenced – a silence broken only on 19 October 1918 when the People's Party delegate, F. Juriga, demanded a sovereign Slovak state with the right of representation at the Paris Peace Conference.[42]

In his study, *The United States and East Central Europe 1914–1918*, V. Mamatey argues persuasively that until 9 June 1918, when Wilson first received him, the American government was lukewarm towards Masaryk and his activities.[43] This is in line with Kirschbaum's view that the destruction of the Hapsburg monarchy was favoured principally by the French, especially Clemençeau, as a means of weakening Germany and gaining allies in central Europe. The lobbying of the Czechs and Slovaks abroad was successful, he concluded, only because their aims were compatible with the plan of destroying Austria–Hungary favoured by French politicians, the army and later, albeit reluctantly, by the US.[44]

That Wilson changed his mind regarding his initial concern to preserve Austria–Hungary cannot be in question. Precisely why he did so is less clear, although the Allied and particularly French view outlined above provide the backdrop. Certainly the impact of the propaganda of the American Czechs and Slovaks on the White House should not be exaggerated. Even among the Czechs and Slovak communities in the US there were those who distrusted the revolutionary character of the independence movement, whilst others were unashamedly pro-Austrian. The turning point for Wilson, however, was probably the Siberian 'Anabasis' in late May 1918 which saw Czech detachments marching from Tchelyabinsk to take a succession of Volga townships from the Bolsheviks and seize the Trans-Siberian railway before moving on to capture Vladivostok.

The Czech legion in Russia, comprising emigrant Czechs along with prisoners and deserters from the Austrian army, was originally formed to combat the Germans, not the Bolsheviks. Indeed, when in mid-April the initial skirmishes in Tchelyabinsk occurred, the troops were en route by rail to Vladivostok where they were to be transferred to France to bolster the fight against Germany. Although the British were committed to the view that the Czech legion could be deployed most effectively in Russia, Clemençeau was obsessed with developments on the western front and wanted the Czechs out of Russia. His argument was nonetheless a curious one: '50,000 Czechs in France, apart from their value as a fighting force, might produce a revolution in Prague.'[45] Whilst the actions of the Czech legions in Russia remain surrounded by certain ambiguities, the evidence nevertheless does not bear out Kavka's dogmatic claim that their ultimate goal was the occupation of Moscow.[46]

The Siberian Anabasis generated enormous enthusiasm in America for what Wilson's Home Secretary, F.K. Lane, described as the 'march of the Czechoslovaks across five thousand miles of Russian Asia – an army on foreign soil, without a government, without a span of territory that is recognised as a nation'.[47] Masaryk justly concluded that the Anabasis significantly influenced the political decisions of the

American government.[48] Shortly afterwards, on 30 June 1918 in Pittsburg (Pennsylvania), the 'Czechoslovak Convention' welded together the Czechs and Slovaks of America and guaranteed Slovakia an autonomous administration, assembly and courts in the new Czech state.[49]

If the acquiescence of the Slovaks in the new union is open to question and if there were elements who pushed for Slovakian independence, it is equally true that the autonomy of Slovakia, though written into the Pittsburg Pact, was flouted from the very beginnings of the Czech republic. In an attempt to prevent this, Hlinka went secretly to Paris in September 1919 to advocate international guarantees of self-government for the Slovak nation within Czechoslovakia. Apparently, however, the Czech delegation denounced him to the French authorities as a Hapsburg spy and he was forced empty-handedly to return to Slovakia where he was imprisoned by order of Prague.[50] The Croatian nationalist leader Radić, incidentally, had as little success when he tried to persuade the conference to hear the voice of independent Croatia.

Beneš, meanwhile, had successfully coaxed the peacemakers into accepting his thesis regarding the viability of a single Czechoslovak nation-state. The initial Allied recognition of the Czechoslovak National Council (which transformed itself into a provisional government) headed by Masaryk, Štefánik and Beneš, and the subsequent proclamation of the Czech republic, probably came as something of a surprise to most Czechs who had not mandated such developments. The émigré leaders had based their struggle for independence on the vigorous propagation of the notion of one Czech people; for Slovaks like Hlinka, this represented the triumph of myth over reality, the institution of a centralized state in violation of the Pittsburg Pact, precipitating a separatist movement.

A New Order

For an enthusiastic generation of young idealists like Harold Nicolson, the journey to Paris in January 1919 was undertaken with a view not merely to eradicating war, but to founding a New Order in Europe – an order that would provide the basis for lasting peace, justice and security. They were subsequently to discover, in the words of an increasingly frustrated Woodrow Wilson, that 'justice is not the first fruit yielded by the tree of knowledge, but the last'.

The map of the New Europe inevitably reflected the interaction of the personalities, prejudices and preconceptions of a Big Three who were closeted together for long periods in very much the style of modern summit conferences. For example, in his *Portrait of a Decision*,

Howard Elcock notes that Wilson was 'torn between his ideals and his hatred of Germany', adding that 'his principles were for use chiefly where the villainous Germans were not involved'.[51] Wilson evidently felt particular revulsion towards the Germans after the severe Brest-Litovsk treaty. His American delegation, moreover, lacked sustained unity. When the president was indisposed, Colonel House would deputize, occasionally exceeding his remit and even going behind Wilson's back. Clemençeau was primarily concerned to maintain Allied unity as a means of safeguarding French security and accordingly compromised more than the president and parliament would have wished and more than many historians have allowed. Lloyd George, whilst accepting that Germany should be adequately contained, also believed that moderation was the only way to secure a lasting peace. Yet the English and French prime ministers were faced with concerted domestic pressure to effect a punitive settlement. For many in Britain, Lloyd George's task was to make a Carthaginian peace, a goal supported by a profusion of inflammatory rhetoric in Lord Northcliffe's newspapers. Clemençeau, in turn, was the object of criticism from both the Head of State, Raymond Poincaré, and the Chamber of Deputies for his excessive moderation.

The New Europe that followed the Great War was to be a continent of largely small states grounded in the principle of national self-determination to which Wilson had given eloquent expression in his Fourteen Points. It was the new successor states which inspired readers of Burrows' and Seton-Watson's magazine The New Europe and which opened the door to the future. For the Allied leaders, though, the search for a lasting peace in Europe involved the more prosaic pursuit of territorial arrangements that would deter Germany from further aggression. It is in this light that the creation of a network of small buffer states should largely be viewed although, as it turned out, the balance of power necessary to prevent a resurgence of German expansionism was not achieved. Moreover the regional federation which Hodža and others later sought – and which might have constituted a powerful economic and security bloc in central Europe – failed to materialize, negated by the very nationalist forces that had propelled the successor states into existence.

The predominantly pragmatic (rather than principled) approach to the aspirations of small central European nations to statehood is well illustrated by the way revolts among the Austro-Hungarian peoples were encouraged, with a view to strengthening the Allied position during the war. The Czech National Council, set up under Masaryk in Paris in 1916, was recognized after the Brest-Litovsk treaty in March 1918 as the rightful organ of the Czech nation abroad in its search for independence. Furthermore, in the Pact of London in 1917, the Allies committed themselves to supporting a united state of Serbs,

Croats and Slovenes.[52] Military considerations also prompted the Allies to enter into secret agreements during the war which violated the self-determination principle. Ironically, Italy, one of the four leading Western Allies, auctioned her support in the war effort: this was bought at the 1915 Treaty of London at the price of part of the Austrian Tyrol, a frontier on the Brenner Pass and a number of Adriatic islands.

The New Order designed by the peace treaties of 1919–23 perpetuated old rivalries since the new states emerged as multi-ethnic polities in which many of the former problems of empire were revived in microcosmic form. To be sure, the sheer complexity of the ethnographic map of Europe made this almost inevitable. However, in seeking to quantify as a means of illustrating the minimal nature of ethnic strains in the new regimes, Winston Churchill's claim that the treaties condemned only about 4 per cent of the total European population to live under foreign allegiance does scant justice to the extent of minority problems in the inter-war years.[53]

Adapting Hugh Seton-Watson's typology, three types of ethnic minorities can be delineated.[54] First, there were *frontier minorities*, national minorities living in border regions, such as the Sudeten Germans, the Ukrainians in Eastern Galicia (part of Poland), the Albanians in the Kosovo region of Serbia and the Magyars in Slovakia. Next, there were *displaced or homeless minorities*, national minorities separated by great distances from their homeland as, for example, the Armenians found in some of the older towns of the former Ottoman dominions. A distinctive case here were the Jews who lacked a country of their own but were widely distributed across certain areas of eastern Europe. Finally, there were *minorities in areas of accentuated multi-ethnicity*. Regions comprising exceedingly mixed populations included the Banat, which embraced Romanians, Serbs, Hungarians, Germans and smaller clusters of Slovaks and Ruthenes; Transylvania, which mixed Romanians, Hungarians and Germans with smaller settlements of Ruthenes, Slovaks and predominantly town-based Jews; and Macedonia, which was populated by Serbs, Greeks, Bulgarians, Albanians, Turks and Vlachs.

Importantly, the peacemakers envisaged liberal provisions for the accommodation of national minorities whilst the League of Nations, conceived as a central instrument in maintaining the New Order, was to administer plebiscites in disputed ethnic territories. Yet the fact remains that if, in a strictly legal–constitutional sense, the physical boundaries of the new states of inter-war Europe were ratified by the Allies and *de jure* state-building was thus completed by international treaty, *de facto* state-building – legitimizing the new arrangements – had only just begun. This involved the not inconsiderable task of integrating the various nationalities, irrespective of their former status, living within the new territorial frameworks. The consequent challenge of national integration will form the subject of the following chapter. However, before that, one final point is in order.

The New Europe of 1919–39 was placed in the hands of an almost exclusively European management when, in March 1920, the Senate of the US Congress refused to ratify the Treaty of Versailles and, accordingly, America did not accede to the nascent League of Nations. Wilson's dilemma lay in Congress' total unwillingness to cede any of its sovereign decision-making power. It is significant that, at an earlier stage, the American President had been obliged to turn down a French request for a League of Nations General Staff on the grounds that Congress would perceive this as an attempt to usurp its right to declare war.[55] American non-participation devalued the League of Nations as an agency in the mediation of conflict. American isolationism also predisposed the West European Allies increasingly to view her as a rival, especially in the economic field. Above all, though, the New Europe was obliged to stand on its own feet without American participation in a novel international body designed in large part to secure the very map of Europe which, in the wake of the Great War, American President Woodrow Wilson had contributed so significantly to redrawing.

Notes

1 C.A. Macartney and A.W. Palmer (1962), *Independent Eastern Europe*, London: Macmillan, p.153.
2 Sally Marks (1976), *The Illusion of Peace: International Relations in Europe 1918–1933*, London: Macmillan, p.29.
3 Harold Nicolson (1964), *Peacemaking 1919*, London: Methuen, p.33.
4 Ibid., p.xxi.
5 Max Engman (1989), 'Finland as a Successor-State' in Max Engman and David Kirby (eds), *Finland: People, Nation, State*, London: Hurst, p.104.
6 J.M. Roberts (1967), *Europe 1880–1945*, London: Longmans, p.313.
7 Milan Hodža (1942), *Federation in Central Europe; Reflections and Reminiscences*, London: Jarrolds, p.171.
8 Charles Seymour (1921), 'The End of an Empire; Remnants of Austria-Hungary', in Edward Mandell House and Charles Seymour (eds), *What Really Happened at Paris*, London: Hodder & Stoughton, pp.89–90.
9 Nicolson (1964), op. cit., p.xvi.
10 Howard Elcock (1972), *Portrait of a Decision*, London: Eyre Methuen, p.322.
11 Nicolson (1964), op. cit., p.xiii.
12 Elcock (1972), op. cit., pp.320–21.
13 André Tardieu (1921), *The Truth about the Treaty*, London: Hodder & Houghton, pp.117–18.
14 Macartney and Palmer (1962), op. cit., p.117.
15 Ibid., p.122.
16 Ibid., p.116.

17   Gerhard Schultz (1967), *Revolutions and Peace Treaties, 1917–1920*, London: Methuen, p.224.
18   Cited in E.J. Hobsbawm (1990), *Nations and Nationalism since 1780: Programme, Myth and Reality*, Cambridge: Cambridge University Press, p.74.
19   Robert Kee (1976), *Ourselves Alone*, London: Quartet Books, p.51.
20   Erskine Childers (1919), 'Ireland: The International Aspect', in *The New Europe*, **X1** (138), 5 June, 180–84.
21   David Arter (1978a), *Bumpkin against Bigwig: The Emergence of a Green Movement in Finnish Politics*, Tampere: Tampere University, p.101.
22   Oscar Jászi (1945), 'The Problem of Sub-Carpathian Ruthenia', in Robert J. Kerner (ed.), *Czechoslovakia*, Berkeley: United Nations Series, p.196.
23   Hugh Seton-Watson (1977), *Nations and States*, London: Methuen, p.188.
24   Macartney and Palmer (1962), op. cit., p.141.
25   Robert Howard Lord, 'Poland', in House and Seymour (1921), op. cit., p.74.
26   Macartney and Palmer (1962), op. cit., pp.105–7.
27   Ibid., p.141.
28   Nicolson (1964), op. cit., p.xvii.
29   Antony Polonsky (1975), *The Little Dictators: The History of Eastern Europe since 1918*, London–Boston: Routledge & Kegan Paul, p.16.
30   Alfred Cobban (1969), *The Nation State and National Self-Determination*, London–Glasgow: Collins, p.214.
31   The Information Department of the Royal Institute of International Affairs (1970), *The Baltic States: A Survey of the Political and Economic Structure and the Foreign Relations of Estonia, Latvia and Lithuania*, Westport, Conn.: Greenwood, p.18.
32   Joseph M. Kirschbaum (1960), *Slovakia: Nation at the Crossroads of Central Europe*, New York: Robert Speller, p.86.
33   T.G. Masaryk (1927), *The Making of a State*, London: George Allen & Unwin, pp.241–4.
34   Ibid., p.265.
35   Ibid., pp.127, 264.
36   Ibid., p.244.
37   Ibid., p.245.
38   Ibid., pp.246–7
39   Kirschbaum (1960), op. cit., pp.89–90.
40   Masaryk (1927), op. cit., p.202.
41   István Deák (1965), 'Hungary', in Hans Rogger and Eugen Webber (eds), *The European Right*, Berkeley–Los Angeles: University of California, p.366.
42   Kirschbaum (1960), op. cit., pp.90–92.
43   Victor Mamatey (1962), *The United States and East Central Europe 1914–1918*, London: Macmillan, p.285.
44   Kirschbaum (1960), op. cit., p.92.
45   David Robin Watson (1974), *Clemençeau: A Political Biography*, London: Methuen, pp.321–4.
46   Frantisek Kavka (1960), *An Outline of Czechoslovak History*, Prague: Orbis, p.106.
47   Masaryk (1927), op. cit., pp.255–6.
48   Ibid., pp.255, 273.
49   Ibid., p.208.
50   Kirschbaum (1960), op. cit., p.97.
51   Elcock (1972), op. cit., pp.306–7, 321–2.
52   Ibid., p.12
53   Ibid., p.299.
54   Hugh Seton-Watson (1986), *Eastern Europe Between the Wars 1918–1941*, Boulder–London: Westview Press, pp.268–77.
55   Elcock (1972), op. cit., p.7.

Map 1.1   Europe 1919–23

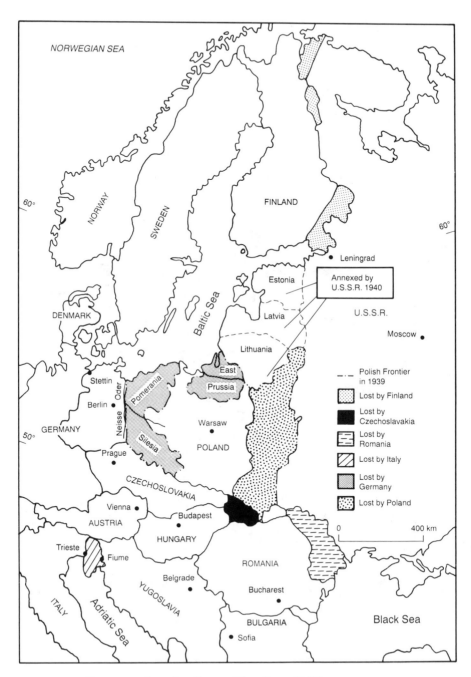

Map 1.2   Europe after the Peace Treaties, 1947

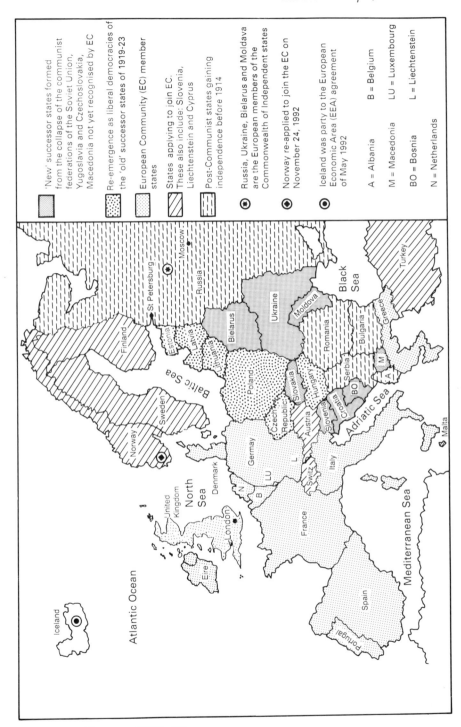

Key:

■ 'New' successor states formed from the collapse of the communist federations of the Soviet Union, Yugoslavia and Czechoslovakia, Macedonia not yet recognised by EC

▨ Re-emergence as liberal democracies of the 'old' successor states of 1919–23

▧ European Community (EC) member states

▨ States applying to join EC. These also include: Slovenia, Liechtenstein and Cyprus

▨ Post-Communist states gaining independence before 1914

⊛ Russia, Ukraine, Bielarus and Moldava are the European members of the Commonwealth of Independent states

◉ Norway re-applied to join the EC on November 24, 1992

◉ Iceland was party to the European Economic Area (EEA) agreement of May 1992

A = Albania   B = Belgium
M = Macedonia   LU = Luxembourg
BO = Bosnia   L = Liechtenstein
N = Netherlands

Map 1.3   Europe 1989–93

2 The Challenge of National Integration in the New Europe, 1919–39

The nationalism which drove the small states to oppress minorities was a form of emotional compensation for their own plight under their former rulers.

Karl J. Newman, *European Democracy Between The Wars*, p.67

Throughout 20th-century Europe, multi-ethnic and multi-cultural systems have been the norm, so that the embryonic states of the New Europe of the inter-war years were not exceptional. Nonetheless, the extent of the ethnic groups they incorporated warrants emphasis. In the new Poland, Poles constituted only 69.2 per cent of the population; in Romania, Romanians made up 71.9 per cent of all persons; in Czechoslovakia, Czechs and Slovaks comprised 65.5 per cent of inhabitants; and in Yugoslavia, Serbs, Croats and Slovenes numbered only 82.6 per cent of the total citizenry. Even in defeated Bulgaria and Hungary, national minorities made up 10 per cent of the overall population. Plainly, a multi-ethnic blueprint is not *ipso facto* unworkable, although the disintegrative force of counter-nationalism – based on geographically-concentrated linguistic minorities – is likely to be accentuated in polities such as the new successor states seeking to make the transition to pluralist democracy.

Counter-nationalism cannot, of course, be viewed in isolation from other anti-systemic factors complicating the task of national integration in the new states of 1919–1939. A wider conceptual framework is needed. Indeed, this chapter argues that a *sine qua non* of regime consolidation in emergent liberal democracies is the successful integration of political society – a pluralist organism containing a range of

31

competing groups and interests – and the state, i.e. the rules and structures relating to, and personnel of a central authority exercising sovereign powers over, a defined territorial unit.

In the case of the inter-war successor states, the challenge of national integration should be set against the backdrop of a political society shaped by the interaction of three main factors. First, as a concomitant of universal suffrage, there emerged a significant body of new and wholly inexperienced actors in the form of a mass peasant electorate. Second, as a by-product of the state-building process, an array of ethnic minorities ('losing nations') were included in the new states due to the imperialist designs of the 'winning nations'. In short, dominant and subject nationalities were created and earlier power relationships frequently inverted. Third, whilst the majority of 'losing nations' comprised peasants, there were also dispossessed elites (estate owners, factory owners and high-ranking officials) who had enjoyed privilege and power under the Hapsburg and Romanov monarchies.

In mobilizing, socializing and organizing mass electorates, recruiting a new class of political leaders and building a pro-system consensus, the nascent parties and party systems were cast in a paramount role as agencies of national integration. Equally, parties could serve as channels for the articulation of dissenting, anti-systemic sentiment; they could give expression to ideological and/or territorial opposition and, by extension, challenge the legitimacy of the ground rules of the new states. Thus it was that communist and several peasant parties, as well as counter-nationalist (separatist) groups challenged the foundations of state power in the successor regimes of inter-war Europe.

The Strength of Anti-System Ideologies in the Successor States – Communism and Peasantism

In several of the sovereign territories fashioned from the ruins of the Russian and Austro-Hungarian empires, indeed even in regions previously under the Hohenzollern crown, the first post-war decade was marked by a struggle for the ideological soul of the state in which two radical credos challenged the emergent order – communism and peasantism.

In the aftermath of enervating warfare, the successor states embarked on life in a debilitated economic condition. Factories were destroyed, stocks exhausted and communications badly disrupted; the land was stripped of livestock and devoid of fertilizers, and the population prey to disease and starvation. Revolutionary feeling, especially among the relatively small body of industrial workers, gorged on these privations and drew inspiration from the events in Russia, whilst a widespread revulsion against the reactionary character of the *ancien régime* attracted to the political left a greater proportion of recruits from outside its traditional working-class catchment than was generally the case in Western Europe.

The Challenge of Communism

In this radicalized post-war climate, communist movements sought to capture the state by force. There were abortive risings in Vienna (1919), Prague (1920) and Tallinn (1924); a short-lived Soviet republic was established in Budapest in March 1919 and, two years later, Georgia succumbed to Soviet communism.

In the Austrian capital in 1919, Red Guards and the Socialist and Workers' Council twice endeavoured to emulate developments in Moscow and Budapest although, in the event, the Social Democrats conspired to prevent the emergence of a separate communist party. In Prague, the Czech Communists under Šmeral organized a general strike in December 1920 which was designed to be the prelude to an attempted coup. It was suppressed three days later.[1]

In Estonia, the Communists gained 10 per cent of the seats in the National Assembly between 1923 and 1926 and, against the background of labour unrest, attempted an armed coup on 1 December 1924. Their target constituency was the urban working class, especially the Tallinn dockers, and the Russian-speaking inhabitants in the border areas from Narva to Petseri. Georg von Rauch has brought out the Russian influence in the insurrection and concluded that Zinoviev, the party secretary in Petrograd, was the leading spirit behind the Tallinn putsch.[2] Although the outcome of the events of 1 December demonstrated that the army and the majority of workers remained loyal to the regime, Estonian developments were greeted with alarm across Europe, reviving memories of the Soviet coup in Georgia in 1921 and abortive revolutions in Germany and Bulgaria in October 1923.

In late 19th-century Georgia, the dominant political element was the Menshevik (moderate) wing of social democracy which, feeding off a groundswell of agrarian discontent, aspired to build a socialist republic in which both workers and peasants would form the van-guard.[3] In fact, the Georgian case seems to underwrite the hypothesis that 'what looked like mobilising the masses in 1917–18 was social revolution, rather than national self-determination'.[4] Georgia wished to remain in post-Czarist Russia, but when at Brest-Litovsk Lenin surrendered part of its territory, it seceded to form a segment of a short-lived Republic of Transcaucasia; this, in turn, quickly split three ways into the autonomous states of Georgia, Azerbaijan and Armenia. As long as Civil War engulfed Russia, Georgia survived precariously as a sovereign state, but in 1921 the victorious Soviet forces annexed it without a struggle.[5]

The situation of acute social and economic distress which the Communists could exploit to good effect was graphically illustrated in Hungary, where on 21 March 1919 Belá Kun, the son of a Jewish, Kossuth-idolizing town clerk in Transylvania, set up a Soviet republic, modelled on Leninist lines. When Harold Nicolson arrived at the *Ostbahnhof* in Budapest on 4 April 1919, as part of an Allied mission led by General Smuts to fix an armistice line between Hungary and Romania, he reported 'Red Guards all along the platform with fixed bayonets and scarlet brassards'![6]

After the total collapse of the Dual Monarchy and the bloodless 'Autumn Rose' revolution of 31 October 1918, Mihály Károlyi headed a liberal–socialist coalition which boasted solid working-class support. Yet with the government unable to achieve peace or accomplish urgent social reform, the Communists in opposition ran a highly successful recruitment campaign directed at four main groups: workers in heavy industry (armaments, metal, etc.) in the Budapest area; the Budapest Soldiers' Council; former prisoners-of-war who, like Kun himself, had served in Russia; and the Association of the Unemployed. When Károlyi failed to secure a settlement with the Allies and resigned, the Communists and Socialists combined forces, the former bringing the promise (unrealized) of Russian military intervention against Romania, the latter keeping communication lines open to the West.

The Soviet republic was hardly guilty of inactivity: wage differentials between blue- and white-collar workers were abolished and there was a wholesale programme of nationalization. As Carsten has noted, 'government emissaries would enter houses and take inventories of all contents, warning the housewives not to touch anything because it was now national property'.[7] Kun's regime profited in no small measure from patriotic outrage at the Allied instruction to evacuate Transylvania. 'In a wave of abject submission,' one historian wrote, 'thousands of the bourgeoisie and aristocrats applied for admission to the party of the proletariat.'[8] Indeed, perhaps the greatest failure of the Soviet republic was its evident inability effectively to harness this nationalist backlash. By 1 August, after 133 days at the helm, 'Belá Kun had bolted'[9] and the Communist Party remained outlawed throughout the subsequent right-wing regency of Admiral Miklós Horthy.

Although only a brief interlude and not viewed as a serious threat by the Smuts mission, Kun's regime confirmed the worst fears in Western establishment circles of an insidious advance of Bolshevism across the continent. The 'Red Peril' seemed to be charting an inexorable course westwards – from the Russian revolution in St Petersburg, via the creation of Soviet republics in Hungary and Slovakia, to a Bavarian People's State (founded after King Ludwig's abdication in November 1918) and onwards to France where, at Tours in December 1920, a majority split from the Socialists (*Section Française d'Internationale Ouvrière*) to form the French Communist Party, leaving the Alsacian Jew, Louis Blanc, to guard *la vieille maison*.[10] Moreover, in distant view of a dismayed Westminster and Whitehall, the Red flag was run up over Glasgow's main post office, while workers' soviets were formed in the Glasgow and Belfast shipyards in 1919.

Western establishment concern with these developments was mirrored in the new successor states where there was little or no democratic tradition; mass electorates were largely uneducated and, accordingly, gullible when confronted by Red agitators; the region as a whole also lay appreciably closer to the revolutionary epicentre than Paris or London. The controlling bourgeois elites thus sought from the outset to preserve parliamentary democracy by proscribing both communist parties and their cover organizations; the result, at best, was that only a restricted form of pluralism was permitted.

In Yugoslavia, Minister of the Interior Drašković worked to ban communist organizations on the grounds that they sought to establish a dictatorship of the proletariat; however, in July 1921, he was himself assassinated by communists. This provided a ready pretext for a 'Law for the Defence of the State' which suppressed all communist groups, declared it a prisonable offence for state employees to strike, and authorized the government to dissolve all trade unions engaging in illegal activities. Communism was thus driven underground.[11]

In Estonia and Latvia, despite extremely liberal constitutional provisions, communist parties were proscribed from the outset on the (justifiable) suspicion that they were agents of the Comintern (the propaganda organization founded in Moscow in March 1919). This meant that the only way they could participate in elections was by operating under an assumed name. By this means, the Estonian Communists won five seats in the 100-member *Riigikogu* at the 1920 general election and, significantly, double that number three years later.

In Finland, the Red exiles of the 1918 Civil War, who founded the Finnish Communist Party in Moscow the following year, also used a cover organization to contest elections in the new republic. The Socialist Workers' Party, in fact, polled almost 15 per cent of the vote in 1922 and achieved a membership which was nearly 70 per cent of that of the Social Democrats.[12] The organizational infrastructure it established in the more industrialized areas of Turku, Vaasa and Western Kuopio undoubtedly served as a springboard when the Communist Party was again legalized in 1944. In a dramatic step in 1923, however, President K.A. Ståhlberg ordered the imprisonment of the entire Socialist Workers' Party's parliamentary delegation, the party's activities thereafter being closely monitored by the authorities. Ironically, the Communist threat was at its weakest when the radical rightist Lapua movement began vituperative attacks which, in 1930, led to a total ban on the Socialist Workers' Party. Its underground organization had already been smashed and that same year it surrendered control of the central trade union federation SAJ, *Suomen ammattijärjestö*.[13]

The general picture of official restrictions on communist activity varied significantly only in Czechoslovakia. After Šmeral's ineffectual coup, the Communist Party, which was never made illegal, sought (Euro-communist style) to accommodate itself within the Czech party system and remained throughout the inter-war republic a sizeable electoral force. In 1933, a group of 'moderate communists' merged with the Czech Social Democratic Party and participated in a coalition government under the Agrarian Jan Malypetr.[14]

As part of a general strategy of destabilizing bourgeois democracy, the communist parties sought to exploit fissures in the socio-ethnic fabric of the successor states and allied themselves with the stance of counter-nationalist and separatist movements. In the Polish Ukraine, it was the Communists alone who advocated secession, urging the case for a merger with the Soviet Union.[15] Elsewhere, communism was able skilfully to activate support across racial lines, whilst maintaining an appeal to the nationalist sentiment of individual ethnic minorities. This would partly explain the success of the Czechoslovak Communists, who emerged from the 1925 general election as the second largest parliamentary group, with 41 of the 284 delegates in the lower house in Prague. Equally, the Communists drew substantial support from the illiterate and impoverished landed population in Sub-Carpathian Ruthenia, where nationalist sentiment was weak.

At the Constituent Assembly elections in Yugoslavia in 1920, ethnic minorities were not allowed to establish parties and, consequently, voted *en masse* for the Communists who became the third largest group in the assembly. They were then summarily proscribed. The link between the Comintern and separatism in Yugoslavia was revealed in a bizarre episode in August 1923, when the highly disgruntled leader of the (non-Marxist) Peasant Party in Croatia, Stefan Radić, indicated during a visit to Moscow that his party was willing to adhere to the Third International and to a Common Front of all communists and dissatisfied peoples in the Balkans. The affiliation of the Croatian Peasant Party was endorsed by the Fifth Congress of the Communist International in 1924.[16] Although a tactical error on Radić's part, which he later acknowledged, the incident clearly illustrates

Moscow's willingness to befriend separatist causes with a view to undermining the new bourgeois regimes.

By the late 1920s, the communist parties in most of the successor states were banned and functioned at best from a base in exile. Typically, the central committee of the Estonian party was obliged to operate from the Scandinavian countries.[17] Defying the authorities, however, communists across central and eastern Europe organized in tightly-knit revolutionary cadres which pursued the overthrow of pluralist democracy with fanatical zeal. The underground nature of this activity is vividly documented in Gusti Stridsberg's autobiography *Menschen, mächte und ich* which records the schedule of an idealistic young Croatian communist called Stefan and the work she, Stridsberg (a lady of high aristocratic birth), undertook on his behalf.

There were highly risky assignments, such as the one in autumn 1932 which took her from Moscow to Yugoslavia (only Stefan Radić had previously survived such a trip) and involved depositing leaflets carried in a suitcase with a false bottom at the central railway station in Ljubljana and then delivering the left-luggage ticket to an address which she had memorized by heart. The leaflets appealed to intellectuals to work for the release of Yugoslavian political prisoners and to oppose King Alexander's authoritarian Serbian-dominated regime. Stefan was the organization secretary in an underground cell of the Yugoslavian communists based in Vienna, led by party secretary Gorkić – a man mentioned in Dedijer's book *Tito Speaks* – the whole operation being monitored by a member of the Russian embassy in the Austrian capital. Relations between Stefan and Gorkić deteriorated when the latter, in order to advance his career, painted an unduly optimistic picture of the revolutionary situation in Yugoslavia.[18] Stefan was ultimately misrepresented by Gorkić to Stalin and presumably liquidated in one of the dictator's many purges in the mid-1930s.

The Challenge of Peasantism

In considering the crucial task of national integration in inter-war Europe, a second (and lesser-known) anti-system ideology deserves emphasis. This was generated by the widespread discrepancy between the various levels of political and economic modernization in the successor states – the challenge of radical peasantism.

Briefly stated, the legitimization of the new regimes involved the bestowal at a stroke of full political rights on relatively backward societies consisting in the main of peasants and agricultural labourers. The regime-validation process also entailed the complementary enactment of land reform which, conceived as a measure of 'social engineering', sought to effect a fundamental redistribution of holdings. The twin innovations of universal voting and land reform generated obvious tensions between, on the one hand, a minority of social 'losers' – the large landowners, urban entrepreneurs and educated professional classes – and, on the other, the majority who gained from this change. Outside the relatively industrialized Czechoslovakia, that meant essentially the peasantry. In summary, the superimposition of mass democracy on predominantly rural societies undergoing radical land reform provoked a struggle for political and economic control in the successor states in which the peasants challenged the ruling hegemony of the established socioeconomic elites.

In several parts of the defeated empires, including those provinces previously subject to Hungarian and Czarist Russian rule (Slovakia, Croatia, Ruthenia and the Congress Kingdom of Poland), there was a notable lack of a democratic tradition so that the development of the pluralist structures of political parties and organized groups was badly retarded. Populist politics operated at best under duress and at worst underground. In those peripheral parts of the Czarist empire where democratic rights had been reluctantly conceded in the wake of Nicholas II's October Manifesto of 1905, they had been effectively withdrawn or negated by the time of the 1917 revolutions. Only in the former Austrian territories of the Bohemian provinces,[19] Slovenia and Galicia, along with the Grand Duchy of Finland, was there a democratic tradition that could be built upon in the post-independence period. Elsewhere, the need to integrate within a single state regions with sharply contrasting political and administrative backgrounds posed a further challenge to the new regimes. Olga Narkiewicz stresses this point with reference to the 'new Poland': the three parts of Poland which had been in different partitions had an almost autonomous existence, she notes, 'as though the empires to which they had formerly belonged were still there, even though their habitual markets, suppliers, legislatures and administrators had disappeared'.[20]

Traditional landholding arrangements mirrored the extent of social inequality in central Europe before the First World War. In Bohemia, for example, 43 per cent of all farms comprised less than half a hectare (under one acre) at the turn of this century,[21] and 0.1 per cent of the total number of landed proprietors owned no less than 35.6 per cent of the total surface area of the province.[22] The Schwartzenberg family alone owned one-third of the land.[23] In Hungary, there was a body of three million peripatetic, landless peasants – Hungarian agriculture was a monoculture which demanded vast quantities of seasonal labour – and *gesinde*, who were agricultural workers contractually hired (sometimes for life) to one estate.[24]

The mobilization of mass rural electorates, of course, demanded leaders and organizations. Notable figures emerged – Alexander Stamboliiski in Bulgaria, Antonín Švehla in Czechoslovakia and

Wincenty Witos in Poland. Several of them appeared publicly in rustic apparel. Witos, for example, was asked to form a government in 1920 largely on the basis of his personality, peasant garb and gruffness of voice – qualities which commanded widespread admiration among the peasants.[25] Often, there were several peasant parties within a single state. It was not until March 1931 that *Piast*, *Wyzwolenie* and the Peasant Party united as the Populist Party (*Stronnictwo Ludowe*) in Poland, although shortly afterwards Witos went into exile. Above all, the inter-war years were *par excellence* the heyday of Green politics, with agrarian–peasant parties from as far afield as France and Finland, Belgium and Bulgaria sending delegates to the regular meetings of the Green International which were convened in Prague beginning in 1928.

Underlying the ideology of the agrarian–peasant parties was a strong cultural antagonism towards the towns and the capital city in particular. As Rudolf Schlesinger has observed: 'The main sectional differences within the Central European democracies concerned the issue of town versus countryside.'[26] This anti-urban prejudice was in part a consequence of distance prior to the development of fast, modern transportation systems; importantly, too, it reflected a thoroughgoing mistrust of the manners and mores of the town. Ignorance and illiteracy compounded the peasants' perception of the town as an alien milieu, populated by vain, urbane and profane people – a place for bloated bigwigs, not for the sturdy bumpkin. Symptomatically, the Bulgarian prime minister and Agrarian leader, Stamboliiski, described the capital, Sofia, as 'a Sodom and Gomorrah' and the professional classes populating it as 'verminous parasites'.[27] All in all, the peasants regarded the national capital as an enclave city, harbouring hedonistic and sybaritic elites who lived an insidious existence on the back of the toiling classes in society.

Both before the First World War and, more significantly, after it, the imperial capital, Vienna, was viewed in such terms. Frederick Hertz cites the Czech Socialist paper *Delnicke Listy*'s description of Vienna in 1920 as a 'centre of profiteers, agents and wire-pullers, supporters of debauchery, pseudo-art and pseudo-literature'.[28] It was this type of antipathy to the old Hapsburg capital, especially in Czechoslovakia, which undermined Austrian schemes for a post-war federation of Danubian states.[29]

Broadly speaking, the greater the numerical strength of peasantism, the more radical its demands. In Romania in 1928, for instance, a merger of the Transylvania Party and Ion Mihalache's Peasant Party enabled Dr Julius Maniu's united Peasant Party to claim no less than 324 of the 387 legislative seats. In its most strident genus, peasantism was a revolutionary ideology incompatible with pluralist democracy. Particularly in the Balkans, as numerically the largest class, the peasantry was vested with the right to conquer the leadership of political society.[30]

Elsewhere, agrarian democracy, although institutionalizing rural–urban conflicts of interest, generally worked as a positive force for national integration. Agrarian parties represented an important component of inter-war governments in Czechoslovakia, Finland and the Baltic states and also dominated coalitions in Poland until 1926. Although industrialization was relatively little advanced in the successor states and the size of the factory working class accordingly small, an instrumental relationship between agrarian democracy and social democracy was vital to the stabilization of liberal politics. Indeed, in several of the new states of inter-war Europe, the achievement of Red–Green social democratic–agrarian democratic coalitions, or at least *ad hoc* legislative deals between the farmers and blue-collar workers at critical junctures, served to marginalize the threat of extremism on both left and right and to reduce the risk of descent into authoritarianism. Interestingly, the advent of recession led in 1933 to Red–Green bargains being struck in Denmark and Sweden too. In return for measures of agricultural protection, the farmers' parties supported Social Democratic welfare reforms.[31]

Territorial Opposition in the Successor States

From the outset, the successor states of 1919–23 embraced a measure of potential ethnic conflict which was perhaps an unavoidable consequence of the only partial application of the self-determination principle. Certainly E.H. Carr has insisted that ethnic hostility was inevitable: 'The movement which dismembered Austria-Hungary and created Yugoslavia and Czechoslovakia,' he posits, 'was bound to be succeeded by movements for the dismemberment of Yugoslavia and Czechoslovakia. Given the premises of nationalism, the process was natural and legitimate and no end could be set to it.'[32] Yet it is imperative to record that the peacemakers did envisage legal guarantees for the protection of national minorities.

The predominant model involved organizing the electorate along ethnic lines, with quota arrangements permitting the proportional representation of the nationalities in the central parliament. Each nationality, moreover, was to be allocated a cabinet seat and enjoy absolute cultural and religious autonomy.[33] The successor states, to be sure, accepted such provisions with the utmost reluctance. They could, after all, reasonably inquire why they should have to display magnanimity towards their minorities when such large West European states as France, England and Italy were not under a similar obligation.[34]

The treatment of ethnic minorities in the successor states varied considerably. Estonia built up a reputation for exemplary management. The 1920 constitution thus guaranteed racial minorities tuition in their own language and granted every citizen the right to declare which nationality he or she belonged to. Article 23, moreover, provided that individual Germans (1.5 per cent of the total population), Russians (8.5 per cent) and Swedish nationals (0.7 per cent) were entitled to address the central administration in their mother tongue. Furthermore, on 4 February 1925, a Law of Cultural Autonomy was adopted, permitting any minority numbering over 3000 persons to exercise cultural autonomy.[35] In Latvia, too, where ethnic minorities comprised 23.4 per cent of the total population in 1930 (Russians 12.5 per cent, Jews 4.9, Germans 3.7 and Poles 1.4), their position was generally favourable and, until 1929, they frequently had representatives in the cabinet. In Lithuania, in contrast, national minorities fared considerably less well.

In the former Hapsburg lands, the handling of national minorities has been the subject of widely differing interpretations. One view asserts that there was a policy of cultural imperialism which involved imposing Czech as the official language and requiring German and Hungarian officials to pass an examination in it.[36] The Germans numbered 22.3 per cent and the Magyars 4.7 per cent of the population in the republic in 1930.[37] Much animosity, it seems, was aroused by the so-called *hraničáři* or frontiersmen. These were Czech officials who could not speak German, but were assigned to purely German-speaking areas and brusquely repulsed all attempts to conduct official business in that language.[38] Karl J. Newman contends that there were also attempts to place Czechs in key positions in Slovakia (the official statistics on nationalities do not distinguish Czechs and Slovaks).[39]

In sharp contrast, Joseph Roucek, whilst conceding that the Pittsburg Agreement on the creation of a Slovak assembly was not implemented, nonetheless concludes that the Czech minorities problem was much less serious than German and Magyar propaganda led others to believe.[40] The same author does, however, admit that the Poles used their superiority to suppress German influence in Upper Silesia, and that, after the 1934 German–Polish non-aggression pact, the government pursued its policy of imposing the Polish way of life with great fervour, especially on its western borders.

Territorial opposition was likely to be accentuated and problems of national integration compounded in the emergent regimes of interwar Europe when measures of radical restructuring exacerbated mutually reinforcing lines of class and ethnic conflict. Indeed, the new political elites appeared on occasions to implement land reform programmes consciously directed against the previously dominant nationality. Alexander Brož has noted, for example, that the German estate-holders in Bohemia – who had received their land from the Hapsburgs in return for services rendered during the Czech revolution of 1620 – were specifically targeted for expropriation.[41] No compensation whatsoever was allowed for those estates belonging to the former ruling house, together with land held by subjects of enemy states and persons deemed guilty of offences against the Czechoslovak nation. Significantly, 86.5 per cent of the expropriated land in Estonia belonged to the German Baltic barons, whilst in Latvia, a policy of no compensation for confiscation was adopted. Moreover, petitions on the compensation question presented to the League of Nations by the German Balts of Latvia (1925) and Estonia (1926) and by Polish landowners in Lithuania (1929) were all rejected on the grounds that agrarian reform constituted a social rather than a minority question.[42]

Deteriorating economic conditions undoubtedly activated underlying ethnic tensions. It was thus the German-speaking industrial workers in the Sudetenland, particularly hard hit by unemployment in the early 1930s, who turned an increasingly sympathetic ear to the panacea-peddling of Henlein's *Heimatfront*. The location of the national capital in a region populated by the dominant nationality could also give ethnic conflict a territorial dimension. Finally, the practice of administrative centralism, provided either by the constitution, as in the Czech case (which was modelled on the French Third Republic), or in violation of the constitution, as in Yugoslavia (which was formally a federal state), fuelled devolutionist and separatist demands. In this last context, the assassination in the national parliament *Skupština* in Belgrade of the Croatian nationalist and Peasant Party leader, Stefan Radić, marked the beginning of the end of liberal democracy in inter-war Yugoslavia.

Probably the most blatant form of minority oppression in the successor states was the widespread violation of Jewish rights. In Lithuania, the autonomous Jewish National Council, representing 7.5 per cent of the citizenry, was abolished by the Christian Democratic government in 1924 and, shortly after the establishment of the Valdemaras dictatorship two years later, there were reports of anti-Jewish pogroms. Notwithstanding the provisions of Poland's Minorities Treaty, moreover, Czarist laws limiting Jewish liberties remained in force in the former Russian partition, where 78 per cent of Jews were resident, until 1931. These same laws were invoked by a local official in November 1926 to invalidate the election of a Jewish mayor.[43] Relations improved somewhat after this incident, but as Macartney and Palmer conclude: 'Although anti-Semitism retreated under the surface, its latent strength hardly diminished, nor did Jews come appreciably nearer to real integration in the national life'.[44]

In the hands of xenophobic leaders, anti-Semitism involved an assertion of the claims of the nation – the 'winning nation' – against a powerful foreign elite which had controlled the state and monopolized strategic positions in the establishment. That the socioeconomic influence of the Jews was disproportionate to their numerical strength in the total population was beyond dispute. In Hungary, Jews made up one-quarter of the population of Budapest in 1920 – compared with 5 per cent in Berlin and 10 per cent in Vienna – but owned the mines, considerable sections of heavy industry and nearly all the newspapers in the capital city. They accounted for 70 per cent of journalists and were relatively numerous in other professions too. It was much the same in Romania between the wars, where Jews numbered at most 5 per cent of the overall population. The official *Bulletin périodique de la presse roumaine* published figures on 19 June 1937 which demonstrated that 80 per cent of textile engineers were Jewish, as were 70 per cent of journalists and over half the doctors in the Army Medical Corps.[45]

Against this backdrop, anti-Semitism had an obvious anti-capitalist appeal. It was no coincidence that the main body of support for Szálasi's Arrow Cross Party in Hungary derived from industrial workers, who in 1937 constituted up to half the party's membership.[46] Equally, anti-Semitism was strongly anti-communist. Belá Kun and his henchmen in the 133-day Soviet republic were, of course, Jews, the Jewish intellectualism of the Hungarian Soviet leaders clearly providing an ideal target for the disillusioned and weary working class. Furthermore, although the Romanian Communist Party was banned in 1924, one of the avowed objectives of the Iron Guard, founded in 1930 as the militant wing of Corneliu Codreanu's Legion of the Archangel Michael, was the struggle against communism. In Codreanu's view, communism was synonymous with Judaism.[47]

Anti-Semitism was not, of course, an exclusively inter-war phenomenon. A.I. Dubrovin's Union of Russian People (*Soiuz russkogo naroda*), founded in the aftermath of Nicholas II's October Manifesto in 1905, for example, sought to restrict Jewish representation in the *Duma* (national parliament) to three delegates. Russian entrepreneurs were also to be protected from the competition of foreigners and Jews. After Stolypin's dissolution of the second *Duma* and drastic reduction of the franchise, anti-Semitism became the URP's stock-in-trade.[48] However, after the Great War, anti-Semitism was exploited by extreme nationalist leaderships to consolidate the position of the 'winning nation'; by the late 1930s, under the growing influence and sometimes in the pay of Hitler, radical rightist groups engaged in increasingly strident action against Jewish minorities.

Summing up, the process of state-building in central and eastern Europe was conducted in multi-ethnic polities and typically witnessed the imperialist leaderships of the 'winning nations' – who were entrusted with the task of regime consolidation – building structures and pursuing policies which, to varying degrees, discriminated against minority nationalities. The result was the rise of separatist movements based on the 'losing nations'. In the 1930s, these separatist movements were targeted by Hitler and, in turn, assumed an increasingly fascist character and style of their own. Yet the inter-war years indicate that multi-national states were not necessarily riven, still less undermined, by ethnic conflict. As the Finnish and Czech cases illustrate, the party system and inter-elite cooperation could significantly further the task of national integration.

In Finland, the essential contours of the party system were moulded well in advance of the achievement of statehood; significantly, too, the 9 per cent Swedish-speaking minority had a record of active participation in building the constitutional framework of the newly-independent republic. Profiting from the relatively liberal conditions in the Grand Duchy, the ethnic minority evolved its own political party in the 1880s which forged a mass base following the introduction of universal suffrage (including women) in 1906. The national minority, moreover, shared with the Finnish-speaking majority a common history of resistance to Czar Nicholas II's programme of administrative centralism (Russification) before 1914; then, following the Bolshevik revolution in Russia, the bulk of the Swedish population fought with the Finnish bourgeoisie to defeat the Reds in the 1918 Civil War. The Swedes and Finnish conservatives subsequently lost their parliamentary battle for a constitutional monarchy – a German prince, Karl-Friedrich of Hesse, had agreed to assume the Finnish crown – when the German war effort collapsed and a majority of Finnish farmers (in the Agrarian Party) and workers (Social Democrats) favoured republicanism.[49] But the Swedish People's Party became a regular member of government coalitions in the 1920s.

In Czechoslovakia, the party system which evolved in the Bohemian provinces before the First World War provided the focal point for the cooperation of economic interests across ethnic boundaries shortly after independence. This can be seen in the merger of the Czech and Slovak agrarian parties in the early 1920s and the inclusion of ethnic Germans in the national cabinet in Prague in 1926. It is clear, moreover, that Sudeten-German social democracy often had much more in common with Czech social democracy than with the separatist German Nationalist Party; the Czech Social Democratic Party enjoyed better relations with its German sister party than with Dr Kramář's National Democratic Party (Czech imperialist), whilst relations between the German and Czech Catholic parties were also excellent. In both Finland and Czechoslovakia, moreover, the teething troubles of parliamentary democracy – problems of coalition-building, cabinet stability, etc. – were overcome (a Head of State with significant powers helped), the experience of democracy before independence providing the foundation on which to consolidate pluralist politics after it.

Elsewhere, new regimes lacking a democratic tradition quickly succumbed to the type of authoritarian government which had characterized the pre-independence period. Such was the case in Hungary (1920), Lithuania (1926), Yugoslavia (1929), Poland and Romania (1930) and Estonia and Latvia (1934). Autocratic monarchs (Alexander in Yugoslavia, Carol II in Romania) or right-wing military figures (Piłsudski in Poland, Voldemaras in Lithuania) retained at most the pretence of democratic practices; moreover, under the growing influence of Italian fascism, they began to advocate neo-corporatist solutions.

The failure of democracy in much of central and eastern Europe between the wars is striking. When held, elections were largely corrupt and citizens the object of coercion. In Romania, for example, a small pamphlet entitled *The Black Book of Elections Held in 1922 in the County of Arges* reveals details of brutal beatings, intimidation and fraud.[50] Ferenc Nagy (who was briefly prime minister after the Second World War) chronicles a similar tale of bribery, blackmail and physical violence at Hungarian elections in his *Struggle Behind the Iron Curtain*.[51] The electoral systems, moreover, were widely gerrymandered and the broad franchise demanded by the Allies cynically curtailed. In July 1921, Horthy, the Regent, appointed the former leader of the Anti-Bolshevik Committee in Vienna, István Bethlen, prime minister; Bethlen proceeded to abolish the wide suffrage introduced in Hungary under Western pressure in 1920. The new arrangements enfranchised only 27.0 per cent of the population – uneducated persons and those without a fixed residence were excluded – and reintroduced open balloting in county districts and smaller towns.[52] In Romania in 1926, an amendment to the law inspired by the Siccardi legislation in Italy, which had enabled Mussolini to consolidate his power base, gave disproportionate parliamentary strength (namely a bonus) to any party gaining 40 per cent of the vote.[53] Following Piłsudski's arrest of the parliamentary deputies in 1930, rigged elections also became the order of the day in Poland.[54]

Moreover, when in power, the right increasingly favoured institutions based on the corporate principle rather than the conventional territorial representation of the Western democracies. In 1926, for instance, Bethlen reconstituted the House of Lords so as to comprise all resident members of the Hapsburg dynasty, representatives of the higher nobility, clergy (including the chief rabbi), local government authorities, universities, trade, industry, agriculture and the professions, along with 44 members appointed by the Regent.[55] For rightist elements in opposition, too, the corporatist alternative was vigorously canvassed. Thus, in December 1926, Roman Dmowski, the National Democrats' leader, came out in favour of a 'Camp of Great Poland'[56] whose purpose was to organize the nation outside the conventional parliamentary channels rather than squandering time in futile deliberations in the *Sejm*.

Whilst a full analysis of the democratization process is contained in our concluding chapter, it is worth noting *en passant* that, in several of the new regimes, conditions scarcely appeared to favour stable Western-style pluralism. Thus the diffusion of *power resources*, which sociobiologists regard as an essential condition of effective democratization, was largely absent,[57] whilst the *socioeconomic structure* given prominence by political sociologists did not appear supportive either. Society, in short, appeared largely undifferentiated and dominated by a lumpen peasantry often lacking basic literacy and numeracy and, by extension, the resources to mobilize in pursuit of its own interests.

In inter-war Romania, for example, about 40 per cent of the population over seven years was illiterate, while the overwhelming body of economically active persons comprised scrapholders who survived by hiring themselves out as labourers and domestic servants. It was much the same story in Poland where, in 1921, 23.1 per cent of the population over the age of ten was illiterate. True, there was significant regional variation – from a low illiteracy rate of 4.2 per cent in the former Austrian province of Galicia to no less than 64.7 per cent in the former Congress Kingdom (the Russian partition). Across the region, moreover, excluding the large estates acquired from the German and Hungarian-speaking nobility, land reform never advanced beyond an initial stage and largely failed to create the prosperous agrarian middle class widely regarded at the time as a bulwark of democracy.[58]

National Integration in the Successor States: An Inventory

Although economic recession in the early 1930s clearly imposed enormous strains on the new regimes of central and eastern Europe, contributing to the rise of authoritarianism in several of them, liberal democracy collapsed in Poland, Lithuania, Yugoslavia, Hungary and Romania *before* the advent of global slump. The causes of the failure to consolidate liberal democracy thus appear to have been principally domestic: the challenges of integrating state and society were not effectively met and the new systems quickly became 'state-led societies' under the firm control of rightist elements.[59] A number of interrelated factors contributing to this democratic breakdown are enumerated below.

First, there was the creation at a stroke of mass electorates, divided along (often mutually reinforcing) lines of class, religion and ethnicity. If this created the phenomenon of *Verzuiling* - or 'pillarization' of political society - (depicted by Arend Lijphart *et al.*) in such small West European democracies as Holland and Switzerland, the politics of accommodation in the successor states was further complicated by another factor. This was the way universal suffrage was superimposed on systems whose territorial components had formerly come under differing rule, had exhibited contrasting political and administrative cultures and, in many cases, had possessed little or no previous history of representative democracy.[60] The result was the emergence of Sartori-style extreme multi-partism,[61] mitigated by the significant pro-system forces of agrarian democracy, social democracy and christian democracy, but embracing as well significant anti-system elements in the form of communist, peasantist and, not least, counter-nationalist movements.

The strength of counter-nationalism should not be underestimated. Whilst the 'winning nation' was well integrated into the state by the end of the 1920s, there appears to have been a general intensification of nationalist feeling among the ethnic minorities – particularly a rising younger generation – which betokened a lack of national integration. A sense of embitterment and disillusion on their part was inflamed by recession and rising unemployment. Indeed, using statistics on declared nationality, one authority has concluded that, although in some cases there was considerable pressure and temptation, 'cases of genuine assimilation among the minorities to whom the changed frontiers had brought a step down ... were extremely rare'.[62]

Second, the overarching elite cooperation between strategic party leaders, which would have served to offset the worst effects of deep-seated social division and the attendant proliferation of parties, was effectively vetoed by an inevitable lack of experience in the art of political bargaining and in the achievement of negotiated, compromise outcomes within the new rules of the parliamentary game. In consequence, the short-lived coalitions that were a feature of the transition to mass politics in many West European states between the wars became very much the norm in the successor states. In such circumstances, it was relatively easy for anti-system groups to discredit and destabilize pluralist democracy.

The exception was Czechoslovakia, where Pětka practices (coalitions of all five large parties) dominated the inter-war republic and where Red–Green cooperation, originating in the Vlastimil Tusar cabinet, formed in July 1919, helped to sustain multi-party politics in a way which was unique among the former Hapsburg territories. There were, however, 18 cabinets in Estonia and 16 in Latvia between 1920 and the coups in 1934; particularly in Estonia, governments were little more than executive committees at the mercy of a disparate and undisciplined assembly.[63] Subsequent moves under the dictatorships to introduce corporatist bodies reflected a wider fascist influence, but also mirrored a strong aversion to the perceived ineffectuality of a liberal-democratic parliamentary system.[64]

Third, the provisions of the new constitutions often appeared inappropriate in prescribing institutional arrangements that facilitated, rather than mediated, conflict. For example, although the widespread adoption of systems of proportional representation in the successor states was designed to permit the integration of ethnic and religious minorities, it served in practice as a vehicle for party fragmentation in the central assembly. In the Yugoslavian *Skupština* in 1920, there were seven sizeable groupings, ranging from the Slovenian Liberals and Clericals and predominantly Serbian-based Democrats and Radicals to a bloc of Montenegrins and Independents. In Czechoslovakia the same year, there were no less than four parliamentary Catholic parties (Czech, German, Slav and Magyar versions), whilst in the Polish *Sejm* in 1922 there were 14 groups, led by the National Christian Union. The situation in the Baltic states was much the same. In Latvia, no fewer than 28 parties were returned to the *Saeima* in 1925, partly because the province of Latgale had its own parties, but also because the party system was segmented along clear lines of nationality.

Crucially, too, in Austria, Poland and the Baltic states, the constitutional balance of power was modelled on the lines of the French Third Republic and thus favoured the legislature at the expense of the type of strong executive which might have been vital in a crisis-management role – in defusing tensions, interpreting indecisive elections and tiding the country over periods of government instability. Estonia was an extreme case of a deputy-centred system, since even the prime ministership was a rotational post.[65] It was perhaps not surprising, therefore, that strong executive figures emerged, often from outside the parliamentary arena, by negating the groundrules of parliamentary democracy. Ironically, the Czech constitution, which did vest the Head of State with relatively significant powers, imposed a unitary form of government in a way which did nothing to integrate the 'losing nations' into the state.

A final barrier to regime consolidation and the achievement of stable pluralist democracy in the successor states was the problem of integrating the economies of regions with differing imperial pasts and contrasting levels of economic development. Poland is a case in point. In the former Prussian partition of Poznan, the incorporation of a portion of Upper Silesia substantially enriched the nation's mineral wealth and meant that, by 1923, Poland ranked fourth in Europe as a producer of hard coal and fifth as an iron producer.[66] In these western areas, the biggest problem was that of livestock losses and the need to find new markets to replace the old German ones. In the former Russian partition in the east, in contrast, strip farming and the *Serwituty* (a relic of the feudal system) were typical. The differential economic modernization of Czechoslovakia could similarly be charted on a geographical continuum from west to east, encompassing the progressive agriculture and industry of the Bohemian provinces to the very backward agrarian conditions of Sub-Carpathian Ruthenia. When economic and ethnic peripheries coincided, the problems of national integration were, of course, likely to be accentuated.

All in all, national integration constituted a complex, multi-dimensional process in all the successor states. There was the widespread need for administrative and cultural assimilation; for the socialization and mobilization of new mass electorates; for the promotion of literacy and welfare programmes, and for the coordination and harmonization of the economies of the former partitions. The role of schools as instruments of integration needs emphasis, especially in promoting a desired concept of 'nation'. This was not always a straightforward business. E.J. Hobsbawm has recalled how, in an Austrian primary school in the mid-1920s, he was subjected to a new national anthem. This desperately sought to convince children that the new rump Austria was worthy of patriotic devotion – a task, he notes, not made easier by the fact that the only thing local people had in common was their overwhelming wish to join Germany.[67] Schools could also promote the integration of state and society by providing minorities with an education in their own language. Equally, there was the risk and, indeed, the reality of acculturation – that is, the imposition via the schools of the language and culture of the 'winning nation'.

Notes

1 Malbone W. Graham (1945), 'Parties and Politics', in Robert J. Kerner (ed.), *Czechoslovakia*, Berkeley: United Nations Series, p.152.
2 Georg von Rauch (1974), *The Baltic States. Estonia, Latvia, Lithuania: The Years of Independence 1917–1940*, London: Hurst, pp.111–17.
3 Hugh Seton-Watson (1977), *Nations and States*, London: Methuen, p.310.
4 E.J. Hobsbawm (1990), *Nations and Nationalism since 1780: Programme, Myth and Reality*, Cambridge: Cambridge University Press, p.130.
5 Seton-Watson, op. cit., pp.310–11.
6 Harold Nicolson (1964), *Peacemaking 1919*, London: Methuen, p.69.
7 F.L. Carsten (1972), *Revolution in Central Europe*, London: Temple Smith, p.242.
8 I. Deák (1974), 'Hungary', in Hans Rogger and Eugen Webber (eds), *The European Right*, Berkeley-Los Angeles: University of California; first paper edition 1966; 2nd printing 1974, pp.364–407.
9 Nicolson, op. cit., p.324.
10 Roy Jenkins (1974), 'Leon Blum', in *Nine Men of Power*, London: Hamish Hamilton, pp.29–59.
11 C.A. Macartney and A.W. Palmer (1962), *Independent Eastern Europe*, London: Macmillan, p.219.

12   Gary London (1975), *The End of an Opposition of Principle: the Case of the Finnish Socialist Workers' Party*, University of Helsinki, Institute of Political Science Research Reports No. 37, pp.4–5.
13   Jorma Kalela (1976), 'Right-Wing Radicalism in Finland during the Inter-War Period', *Scandinavian Journal of History*, **1**, 105–24.
14   Graham, op. cit., p.161.
15   Macartney and Palmer, op. cit., p.189.
16   Ibid., p.223.
17   Tönu Parming (1975), 'The Collapse of Liberal Democracy and the Rise of Authoritarianism in Estonia', in Richard Rose (ed.), *Sage Contemporary Political Sociology Series*, **1**, p.13.
18   Gusti Stridsberg (1963), *Viisi maailmaani*, Jyräskylä: Gummerus, pp.212–22.
19   Bruce M. Garver (1978), *The Young Czech Party 1874–1901 and the Emergence of a Multi-Party System*, New Haven and London: Yale University, pp.277–309.
20   Olga A. Narkiewicz (1976), *The Green Flag: Polish Populist Politics 1867–1970*, London: Croom Helm, p.169.
21   Österreichische statistik tabelle 11, Grössengliederung sämtlicher betriebe, Wien: 1909, p.2.
22   Geoffrey Drage (1909), *Austria-Hungary*, London, p.14.
23   Lucy E. Textor (1945), 'Agriculture and Agrarian Reform', in Kerner (1945), op. cit., p.219.
24   S. Pollard and C. Holmes (1971), *Documents of European Economic History 11: Industrial Power and National Rivalry 1870–1911*, London: Edward Arnold, pp.60–68.
25   Narkiewicz, op. cit., p.165.
26   Rudolf Schlesinger (1953), *Central European Democracy and Its Background*, London: Routledge & Kegan Paul, p.277.
27   Macartney and Palmer (1962), op. cit., pp.226–7.
28   Frederick Hertz (1947), *The Economic Problems of the Danubian States: A Study in Economic Nationalism*, London: Victor Gollancz, pp.65–6.
29   On the question of the Slavs' refusal to acquiesce in Austrian schemes for a Danubian confederation in 1919, see two articles by 'A French Contributor': 'The Question of German-Austria: The Birth of a New State' and 'The Question of German-Austria: Confederation, Re-Union or Independence?', *The New Europe*, **X1**, 15–22 May 1919, 135–6.
30   Nissan Oren (1970), 'Popular Front in the Balkans', *Journal of Contemporary History*, **5**,(3), 69–82.
31   David Arter (1991), 'One *Ting* Too Many: The Shift to Unicameralism in Denmark', in Lawrence D. Longley and David M. Olson (eds), *Two Into One: The Politics and Processes of National Legislative Cameral Change*, Boulder–San Francisco–Oxford: Westview, pp.77–142.
32   E.H. Carr (1945), *Nationalism and After*, London: Macmillan, p.24.
33   Albert M. Hyamson (1919), 'National Rights in the New States', *The New Europe*, **X1** (140), 19 June, 233–4.
34   Karl J. Newman (1970), *European Democracy between the Wars*, London: George Allen & Unwin, p.155.
35   Information Department of the Royal Institute of International Affairs (1970), *The Baltic States*, Westport: Greenwood, p.37.
36   Newman (1970), op. cit., p.155.
37   Joseph S. Roucek (1945), 'Czechoslovakia and her Minorities', in Kerner, op. cit., p.174.
38   Newman (1970), op. cit., p.156.
39   Ibid., p.171.
40   Roucek (1945), op. cit., p.131.

41 Alexander Brož (1919), 'Land Reform in Czechoslovakia', *The New Europe*, **XI** (136), 22 May, 137–9.
42 *The Baltic States* (1970), op. cit., pp.29–30.
43 Macartney and Palmer (1962),. op. cit., p.189.
44 Ibid.
45 Eugen Weber, 'Romania', in Rogger and Weber (1974), op. cit., p.529.
46 Deák (1974), op. cit., p.544.
47 Weber (1974), op. cit., p.544.
48 Hans Rogger, 'Russia', in Rogger and Weber (1974), op. cit., pp.490–91, 493–4.
49 Arter (1978a), op. cit., pp.91–123.
50 Weber (1974), op. cit., p.539.
51 Deák (1974), op. cit., p.375.
52 Ibid.
53 Weber (1974), op. cit., p.516.
54 Narkiewicz (1976), op. cit., p.203.
55 Deák (1974), op. cit., p.376.
56 Narkiewicz (1976), op. cit., p.199.
57 Tatu Vanhanen (1990), *The Process of Democratization*, New York: Taylor & Francis, pp.50–51.
58 Newman (1970), op. cit., p.33.
59 J.E.S. Hayward and R.N. Berki (eds) (1979), *State and Society in Contemporary Europe*, Oxford: Martin Robertson, pp.261–2.
60 Arend Lijphart (1968), *The Politics of Accommodation: Pluralism and Democracy in Divided Societies*, Berkeley: University of California. Henry H. Kerry, Jr. (1974), *Switzerland: Social Cleavages and Partisan Conflict*, Contemporary Political Sociology Series, 1, London: Sage.
61 Giovanni Sartori (1970), 'The Typology of Party Systems: Proposals for Improvement', in Erik Allardt and Stein Rokkan (eds), *Mass Politics; Studies in Political Sociology*, New York: Free Press, pp.322–52.
62 Macartney and Palmer (1962), op. cit., pp.240–41.
63 *The Baltic States* (1970), op. cit., p.43.
64 Thus, in January 1935, President Konstantin Päts announced the intention of replacing the national assembly with a system of corporate representation, and in March 1936 an Economic Council was created. Similarly, in Latvia a law was promulgated in January 1936 which set up a national Economic Council comprising representatives of the Chambers of Commerce, Industry, Agriculture, Labour and Artisans to deal in an advisory capacity with questions submitted to it by the government. *The Baltic States* (1970), op. cit., pp.50–56.
65 The Estonian constitution was formulated after a thorough study of those in France, Switzerland, the US and, especially, Weimar Germany. It owed its extreme democratic character partly to a natural reaction against the former Czarist regime and partly to a concern (reflecting the wider European mood) to prevent any kind of presidential absolutism. Ibid., p.41.
66 Francis Bujack (1926), *Poland's Economic Development*, London: George Allen & Unwin, p.59.
67 Hobsbawm (1990), op. cit., p.92.

3 'The Two Europes': The Challenges of Political and Economic Integration between the Wars

> It may be that in Paris we underestimated the importance of economics and allowed to lapse too easily such provisions as were devised to prevent the creation of economic barriers.
>
> Harold Nicolson, *Peacemaking 1919*, p.xix

After an intense debate, during which she threatened to withdraw from proceedings, Russia gained official recognition of the coexistence of two distinct economic systems – capitalist and communist – at the World Economic Conference held under the auspices of the League of Nations at Genoa in May 1927.[1] The ideological bisection of Europe into Western market systems and Eastern command economies, which dominated the post-Second World War era until the revolutions of 1989, was thus formally inaugurated. Yet considerably more apposite in characterizing the inter-war period were 'the Two Europes', *Les Deux Europes* depicted by François Délaisy in 1924 – the essentially industrial economies of the West and the preponderantly peasant farming systems of Central and Eastern Europe. Western Europe was first and foremost a producer and exporter of manufactured goods, whereas the Central and Eastern European region was principally a producer and exporter of agricultural commodities.

The Two Europes had been relatively well integrated before the Great War. Western Europe constituted the chief market for the agrarian products of Central and Eastern Europe, supplying it in turn with agricultural machinery, technology and railway equipment and providing much-needed capital. Four years of total, enervating warfare, however, led to wholesale dislocation and prompted 'the break-up of

Table 3.1   Europe between the Wars: A Select Chronology of Events

1917   (December) Revolt of Don Cossacks marked the beginning of a 2-year civil war in Russia.

1918   (November) Kaiser Wilhelm II abdicated and 'retreated' to the Netherlands.

1919   (January) Start of the Paris peace treaty deliberations.

1919   (March) Lenin formed Third International (Comintern) in Moscow with the objective of the global diffusion of communism.

1919   (March) Start of Belá Kun's 133-day Soviet Republic in Hungary.

1919   (July) Constitution of the German Weimar Republic approved.

1919   Mussolini founded the Italian Fascist Party.

1920   (January) Formal birth of the League of Nations with its permanent headquarters in Geneva, Switzerland.

1920   (March) US Congress refused to ratify Versailles Peace Treaty and, accordingly, opted out of the League of Nations.

1920   Little Entente between Yugoslavia and Czechoslovakia, principally designed to afford protection against Hungary. Romania joined the following year.

1921   Polish 'big power' aspirations led to her forces capturing Vilna in Lithuania. Following war with Bolsheviks, the Treaty of Riga drew the Russian–Polish border to the east of the Curzon Line.

1921   Franco-Polish defence alliance.

1922   Lithuania accepted a League of Nations ruling that Vilna should be retained by Poland.

1922   Treaty of Rapallo established economic and diplomatic relations between Russia and Germany and bestowed on the signatories mutual most-favoured-nation treatment.

1922   (December) Irish Free State came into existence with dominion status.

1923   (January) French and Belgium troops occupied the Ruhr in response to Germany defaulting on her coal deliveries.

1923   Hungary became a League of Nations member.

1923   (June) Bulgarian Prime Minister Alexander Stamboliiski murdered; abortive Communist rising in Bulgaria the following September.

1924   (January) Death of Lenin.

1924   (January) First Labour (minority) government formed in UK under Ramsay MacDonald.

1924   Franco-Czech alliance.

1924   France obliged to accept the Dawes Plan revising arrangements for Germany's reparations payments. American credit to provide for infrastructural development.

1924   France and UK recognized the Soviet Union.

1925   Appointment of Briand as French foreign minister with Stresemann as his German counterpart. French forces withdrew from Ruhr.

1925   Locarno Treaty. Germany, France and Belgium reaffirmed the inviolability of their frontiers (guaranteed by Italy and the UK) whilst Germany guaranteed the demilitarization of the Rhineland.

1925   Greece invaded Bulgaria but complied with the League of Nations insistence on withdrawal.

1926	(January) Mussolini assumed dictatorial power in Italy.
1926	Germany admitted to the League of Nations.
1926	(May) 9-day 'national (general) strike' in UK.
1927	Austria, Czechoslovakia and Hungary admitted to the 1926 International Steel Cartel.
1928	The Kellogg–Briand Pact, which renounced war as an instrument of policy (defensive war was excluded), ultimately approved by 62 states, including the US and USSR.
1928	(December) Stalin announced the first Five-Year Plan.
1929	King Alexander established a dictatorship in Yugoslavia.
1929	(October) Wall Street crash precipitated world depression and the end of US loans to Germany.
1929	Young Plan introduced further modifications (instalment payments until 1977) to German reparations and reduced the 1921 figure by almost 75%.
1929	Death of Stresemann.
1930	France evacuated the Rhineland.
1930	German Nazis became the second largest Reichstag party.
1931	Creation of the Spanish Second Republic.
1932	(July) Nazis emerged as largest party in Germany with 230 parliamentary seats.
1933	(January) President Hindenburg nominated Hitler as German Chancellor.
1933	(March) Enabling Act gave Hitler unbridled powers for 4 years.
1933	US recognition of the Soviet Union.
1933	Germany and Japan withdrew from the League of Nations.
1934	Soviet Union joined the League of Nations.
1934	Attempted Nazi coup in Austria: Dollfus, the prime minister, murdered.
1934	Hitler became German *Führer*.
1934	Balkan Pact. Greece, Romania, Yugoslavia and Turkey agreed to guarantee each other's frontiers.
1934	Assassination of King Alexander of Yugoslavia in Marseilles.
1935	Czech–Soviet Mutual Assistance Pact.
1936	Hitler occupied the Rhineland.
1936	(June) Inception of French Popular Front government under Léon Blum. Socialists and Radicals supported from opposition by the Communists.
1936	(July) Beginning of Spanish Civil War.
1936	(November) Germany and Japan signed Anti-Comintern Pact, later joined by Italy.
1937	New Irish coalition created independent state of Eire.
1938	(March) Hitler's troops captured Austria and completed *Anschluss* with Nazi Germany.
1939	(March) Nazis entered Prague, Czechoslovakia.
1939	(March) Franco dictatorship established in Spain.
1939	(April) Italian invasion of Albania.
1939	(August) Ribbentrop–Molotov, German–Soviet Non-aggression Pact.

one of the finest achievements of the 19th century European and world economy – a network of multi-lateral trade'.[2] The spirit of international free trade was overcome by nationalist attitudes and a concomitant concern to regulate and protect. High tariffs, currency and fiscal controls, exchange rate manipulation and increased state control of the economy were all features of the inter-war years. It may be said that siege warfare was replaced by siege economics.

The Two European Economies

For the West European Allies, continental export markets and established patterns of trade relations were severely disrupted in the 1920s by the beleaguered position of Germany, which was emburdened with reparations, with the effective withdrawal from economic circulation of the Soviet Union under Stalin, and with the high tariffs imposed by the successor states of Central and Eastern Europe. Significantly, Germany and Russia entered a 'marriage of economic convenience' at Rapallo on 16 April 1922 which consolidated their isolation from the mercantile mainstream (see Table 3.1).[3]

The wisdom of imposing on Germany a reparations levy of the magnitude of 6500 million pounds sterling was strenuously challenged by the contemporary economist and diplomat, J.M. Keynes, in his controversial polemic, *The Economic Consequences of the Peace* (1920). Keynes contended that this indemnity figure bore no relation to Germany's capacity to pay – in addition to these monetary obligations, Germany had lost a large part of her mineral resources, her fleet and the bulk of her merchant shipping – and would lead to severe disruptions in European trade. He concluded his critique of Versailles by proposing a Pan-European Free Trade Union under the supervision of the League of Nations.

Even when, in the wake of the French and Belgian occupation of the Ruhr in 1923, German reparations were regulated by the Dawes Plan (1924), the sizeable annual instalments could still only be paid by raising loans in the US. Moreover, whilst the Young Plan in 1929 further lowered the annual payments and, for the first time, set a finite period for their completion, this was not to be until 1988! The concern of successive Weimar governments to meet at least part of their obligations undoubtedly aggravated the slump of 1930–32, with its massive deflation and unemployment, and in turn opened the door to Hitler.[4]

For the West European states, the primary stumbling-block to the reincorporation of the Soviet Union into the continental trading system was an unwillingness legally to recognize a government which, under Lenin, had peremptorily repudiated Czarist debts to the West, nationalized foreign enterprises without compensation and professed a wholly alien economic philosophy. A modest Anglo-Soviet trade treaty was finalized in 1921, but hopes that a closer understanding would emerge from the Genoa economic conference in April 1922 – an outcome of Lloyd George's concern with the chaotic condition of European trade – were dashed by the Rapallo Agreement between Germany and the Soviet Union. It was another five years before, in the same city, the West uneasily recognized the cohabitation of competing economic systems.

The concerted programme of industrialization (backed by high protective tariffs) instigated by the farm-producing successor states of Central Europe did much to destroy the economies of the region and sever bonds with their former suppliers in Western Europe. The bridge between the Two Europes was clearly in need of repair and attempts were made at Ponteroso in 1921 and intermittently (and largely unavailingly) throughout the inter-war period to promote economic collaboration among the Hapsburg successor states.

Ironically, as the West European Allies faced a contraction in their continental exports, non-European competition in world markets increased substantially. The original industrial nations surrendered many of their traditional overseas manufacturing markets simply because, lacking West European supplies, the latter developed a capacity to manage without or devise alternatives to them. Above all, Western Europe confronted severe competition from America.[5] Indeed, although the Western powers invested extensively in Eastern Europe and exploited the mineral resources of the Danube valley, the rise in West European per capita income failed to keep pace with that in the US. Since domestic investment capital for modernization was also in short supply, Western Europe came to rely heavily on injections of US capital.[6]

The West European economies incurred extensive physical damage as a result of war. In the UK, for example, industrial plant was decimated and much of the surviving stock antiquated. Governments struggled to compete in the home, let alone the world, market. Furthermore, although by 1925 Western European production had returned to pre-war levels, the growth rate remained slower than on other continents. At the heart of the problem lay the fact that European domestic markets were proving too small to absorb the increasing production, but tariff barriers across the continent inhibited exports.

A novel feature of the West European economies between the wars was the existence of a pool of long-term unemployed at every phase in the trade cycle. Following a speculative boom ending in 1920, several states experienced a dramatic slump; although this was succeeded by a rapid recovery in output up to 1925 and a soaring boom to 1929, a hard core of unemployed persons persisted, especially in Germany and the UK. In part, this can be attributed to belated adaptation to structural change. Whilst over-expansion occurred in some sectors, there was a decline in traditional methods in others; this contributed to the classic mismatch between supply and demand and problems of structural unemployment.

In Central Europe, the main consequence of war and the nationalism it released was the destruction of the economic community formed by Austria–Hungary. The Hapsburg empire had comprised a cohesive economic unit boasting internal free trade, a common currency and a common customs tariff and had been self-supporting to a remarkable degree. The Allies were probably cognizant of the economic interdependence of the new states of the region. Certainly the commission working on the revised boundaries of Central and Eastern Europe recommended a supervisory agency to undertake the coordination role previously performed by the Dual Monarchy.[7] The peace treaties, moreover, provided for a degree of economic cooperation among the successor states.[8] But little of these proposals was implemented.

The immediate task of post-war reconstruction, therefore, was intertwined with the need to adjust national economies to frontiers which denied access to the wider imperial market and created 'macro-diseconomies of scale'.[9] This process of adaptation was complicated by the highly protectionist attitudes of inexperienced leaders for many of whom national glory appeared far more important than the economic welfare of the population. Castigating the political elite, Sidney Pollard has asserted that 'their actions in the economic field proved nothing less than disastrous and contributed materially to the poverty and depression of the inter-war years and the eventual descent of much of Europe into barbarism'.[10]

Initially, the attempt to restructure the new economies coincided with a period of considerable prosperity. The return to peace heralded an enormous demand for building and construction: railways, factories and public buildings had to be repaired and private dwellings erected. The increased consumption of electricity required the installation of power stations, whilst the spread of the motor car underwrote the need for the modernization and expansion of the road network. Behind high tariff walls, factories sprang up and new plant was introduced. Those countries exporting machinery and construction materials, moreover, attracted large foreign orders and accumulated substantial profits. There was also a brisk demand for arms and military equipment.[11] This was in part the product of tension and animosity between the new states, especially between Poland and Czechoslovakia; partly, too, it reflected Poland's aspiration to rank among the Great Powers.[12] (Thus the aim of the Polish imperialists in the old ruling class was to recreate Historical Poland, by which they meant the restoration of the frontiers of 1772 – frontiers which did not remotely correspond to ethnic boundaries. Accordingly, in April 1920, the Galician Petliura and Polish Marshall Piłsudski reached an agreement to create a federal state embracing Poland and the entire Ukraine which, if it had materialized, would have encompassed an area greater even than the Poland of 1772.) Ultimately, though, the economic bubble burst. Prosperity fired overspeculation, and demand proved to be short-lived. In the prosperous late 1920s, however, long-term weaknesses in the economic structure of Central and Eastern Europe attracted little attention.[13]

Thus land reform (conceived in large part as a measure of 'social engineering') had a generally limited economic effect and failed to secure the viability of the bulk of peasant farms or solve the problem of agrarian unemployment. Since the traditional outlet for emigrants to the New World was blocked by fresh American legislation, the problem of rural overpopulation intensified and made it impossible for families to produce cheaply for the market or to save enough to invest in modern machinery or even fertilizers. Poverty, in short, was endemic.

Equally, industrialization, designed in part to absorb the underemployment in the villages, largely failed to keep pace with population growth. Protected by high tariffs, industrial progress was quite rapid, especially in the backward Balkan states of Bulgaria and Romania. In Czechoslovakia, the most industrialized nation, moreover, GDP doubled between 1920 and 1929. But in view of their poverty, technical backwardness and small domestic markets, valuable resources were squandered developing hopelessly inefficient plants, heavily reliant on subsidies. This, in turn, denied citizens the benefits of cheap manufactured imports as well as preventing the modernization of agriculture.

Access to foreign capital was, of course, a prerequisite for industrial development and the Czechs in particular forged strong links with the world financial community.[14] Indeed, nearly all the Central and East European countries borrowed extensively from abroad, especially from Britain and America. The advent of the Great Depression, however, led to the withdrawl of foreign credits and to a flight of capital which threatened the stability of currencies and obliged the Danubian states to impose stringent currency controls and import restrictions. The nadir of economic nationalism was reached with the adoption of barter trade in which every country bought only as much as it sold to another country and so obviated monetary transactions.

Summing up, the inter-war period was one of economic disintegration in which the primacy attached to the nation-state in the political sphere was paralleled in the economic by an obsession with national self-reliance. Especially in the successor states, political nationalism spawned economic nationalism and a preoccupation with measures designed to achieve national self-sufficiency or autarky. Even in Western Europe, however, there was heightened post-war protection of the national economy in the international market-place, with tariffs in the 1920s settling well above pre-war levels.

Protectionism intensified during the Great Depression and reached its apogee in 1932 when, as each country frantically endeavoured to safeguard sinking domestic markets against foreign competition, a universal tariff war developed. The UK, for example, ended nearly a century of free trade by imposing a rate of 20 per cent on most manufactured imports and 10 per cent on most semi-manufactures and foodstuffs. A system of Imperial preference was also instituted. In the paralysed Central and Eastern Europe, barter trade arrangements soon became prevalent.

The collapse of the relatively cohesive European trade network before 1914 was mirrored in the multiplicity of currency arrangements which replaced the single gold standard of the pre-war monetary system. By the mid-1930s, there were five separate currency areas (excluding the Soviet Union), three of them based principally on Europe: the Sterling area, including Northern Europe and the Commonwealth; the Gold bloc of Western Europe, led by France, which was in the process of dissolution; and the Exchange Control Area of Central Europe, which was tied to Germany. The German economy and its satellites had in fact become virtually isolated from the rest of Europe.[15]

Though the Two Europes, the industrial West and agrarian East, had complemented each other before the war, the bridge between them, badly damaged by the policy in the successor states of industrializing behind high tariff walls, effectively collapsed in the 1930s when Central and Eastern Europe were priced out of their only market for agricultural produce in Western Europe. Their highly-priced agricultural surpluses could not compete in Western markets with American grain pouring into Rotterdam and this meant that, despite French loans at high rates, the successor states found it increasingly difficult to accumulate the foreign exchange required to purchase industrial surpluses from Western Europe. This led in turn to signs of stagnation in the West.

Finally, as the American economy boomed in the 1920s and began to eclipse Europe on the world's commercial stage, comparisons began to be made by European business leaders between the economic disintegration of their continent – with its highly parochial and protectionist attitudes – and the large, integrated and successful free trade area in America. These comparisons were to provoke ambitious proposals for a 'United States of Europe' capable of holding its own with the United States of America.

Pan-European Integration between the Wars

For leaders of the business lobby in the 1920s, the paramount logic of European integration was access to wider markets and, by extension, the opportunity to compete more effectively with America. Political nationalism had moulded a patchwork of small states whose domestic markets were insufficient to consume the output of mass production and which had raised tariff barriers in a way that seriously inhibited exports. Many industrialists would doubtless have concurred (at least in private) with the view of mid-19th century liberal economists that self-determination should be applied only to nation-states that are viable in an economic sense; they would have accepted Friedrich List's thesis in *The National System of Political Economy* (1885) that 'a small state can never bring to complete perfection within its territory the various branches of production'.[16]

The dysfunctional nature of this small state system in the 1920s prompted voices among the business community to call for European economic union. The International Steel Agreement of 26 September 1926 represented a significant landmark in European industrial cooperation. Conceived in the auspicious post-Locarno climate, it established a steel cartel embracing Germany, France, Belgium, Luxembourg and the Saar, with the aim of limiting production and raising prices. Similar cartels to control metals, chemicals, pharmaceuticals and munitions quickly followed and by 1927 Austria, Czechoslovakia and Hungary were admitted to the steel cartel which operated a single quota. In sum, most major continental steel producers (Britain and Poland decided not to participate) had been conjoined by international agreement.[17] Many in the cartel sought nothing more than to increase their profits. There were those, however, including the cartel's first chairman Emil Mayrisch, who hoped it would lay the foundation for a subsequent European economic union.[18]

Throughout the inter-war period, there were isolated individuals making radical European integration proposals, though the tangible increment as a result of these initiatives was only slight. A Danish Europeanist, C.F. Herfordt, for example, presented plans for a European Community (involving a customs union and common foreign, defence and economic policies) in two volumes entitled *A New Europe* (*Et Nyt Europa*), published in 1924 and 1926, respectively. Herfordt sought backing from the Danish political parties and indeed from the other Nordic governments for a joint Scandinavian initiative to promote his cause, but was met with general indifference.[19]

Perhaps the most vaunted broad-gauge integration scheme, however, emanated from the French foreign minister, Aristide Briand, who in August 1929 proposed a Federal Union of European States. Briand, along with Chamberlain and Stresemann, was one of the 'Locarno men' who were collectively awarded the 1926 Nobel Peace Prize. Indeed, at the Hague Conference in August 1929, when under pressure from Germany and England, Briand reluctantly acquiesced in the withdrawal of foreign troops from the Rhineland; it was in this context that, six days later, he issued a clarion call for European union.

Briand's Federal Union of European States was based on the absolute sovereignty of its members. The signatory governments would simply bind themselves to meet regularly to examine all questions of 'primary interest to the commonwealth of European peoples'. Briand apparently envisaged the union operating as an affiliate of the League of Nations which, by dint of its region-specific character, would be able to act quickly and decisively to preserve peace on the continent. His exhortation to action was unequivocal: 'Unite in order to live and prosper – that is the necessity which confronts European nations today.'[20]

There were nonetheless a number of ambiguities in his proposal. For example, how could a federal union – which necessarily involves an element of supranational integration – be predicated on the absolute sovereignty of participants? How institutionalized were arrangements to be in light of Briand's evident belief in the need for permanent legislative, executive and administrative organs? At times, moreover, Briand seems to have envisaged a European Common Market involving the free circulation of capital, goods and peoples, whilst at others he intimated that detailed economic proposals should be deferred to an unspecified later date.[21]

The backdrop to Briand's proposal revealed much about its true motivation since, behind the façade of camaraderie at Locarno, there lurked a spirit of bitter confrontation. On the one side, there was a frightened France, flanked by her Little Entente allies (Czechoslovakia, Romania and Yugoslavia) and Poland. On the other, there was Germany, potentially the strongest nation in Europe, which worked unremittingly to redress the balance of power created at Versailles. Briand therefore sought to impose political, economic and diplomatic shackles on German revisionism, to enmesh France's historic adversary in a European web of cooperation that would obviate a recurrence of military conflict between the two nations. The Federal Union of European States, in short, was perceived primarily as a means of providing for regional security.

After Stresemann's courteous response to it, Briand's plan remained under active consideration throughout the summer of 1930. When, on 14 September 1930, the Nazi Party gained 107 seats to become the second largest German party, however, the Assembly of the League of Nations – with rare insight – referred the Federal Union proposal to committee where it was quietly interred.[22]

The 'European ideal' then became the almost exclusive preserve of a number of visionaries based in Vienna and led by Count Richard Coudenhove-Kalergi, a Bohemian aristocrat and Czech citizen. Coudenhove's 1923 book entitled *Pan Europa* envisaged a loose political union of all (or most) of the states of the European continent and the establishment of a central organ of government having jurisdiction over them. Coudenhove's grand design, which drew inspiration from the confederal union of Swiss cantons, had a dual objective – the achievement of lasting peace and the generation of prosperity by means of a common market. In this last respect, the American model was also canvassed by proponents of European economic integration. At a Congress of the Federal Committee of European Cooperation at Madrid in May 1929, for instance, the French Minister of Public Works, Yves le Trocquer, lauded the US when arguing that the elimination of European customs barriers should be given the highest priority.[23]

By the late 1920s, there were branches of Coudenhove's Pan-European Union in Germany, France and England, whilst by October 1926 his movement had gathered sufficient momentum to stage a pioneering Pan-European Congress in Vienna, opened by the Austrian Chancellor. The leader of the Austrian People's Party also gave a speech of welcome, whilst Briand and several other prominent European politicians sent greetings. By no means everyone was sympathetically inclined. Mussolini was so hostile that he sponsored a journal entitled *Anti Pan-Europa*!

Coudenhove-Kalergi's blueprint for a 'United States of Europe' went unrealized. In the words of one of his foremost admirers, himself a leading American "Europeanist': 'The union of Europe continued to be a concept that appealed to scholars, philosophers and occasional politicians, as it had for centuries, but the masses of the people and the organs of popular opinion remained largely uninfluenced and uninformed.'[24] The comment was intended to describe the situation in the decade or so after the Second World War; it was, in truth, even more appropriate to the inter-war years.

Regional Integration in Inter-War Europe

Pan-European integration initiatives of whatever origin, then, went largely over the heads of ordinary people who identified at best with a nation-state. In essence, they felt themselves to be citizens of a particular country or, alternatively, a linguistic minority within a state and, especially in Central and Eastern Europe, the local economy and community also remained salient terms of reference. Even among governments and party leaders, a preoccupation with state-building and the protection of national sovereignty conspired to produce a myopic view of international cooperation. Common interests were either not seen or, if seen, not acted upon. In the case of the small successor states this was in one sense surprising since some form of union or federation, based on common bonds of language, history and culture, offered obvious benefits both in defending regional economic interests and in promoting collective security against an outside threat. In the inter-war period, several proposals for regional federations in the Baltic, Danube Valley and Balkans were in fact put forward.

Proposed Baltic Federation

Plans for a Baltic federation of the successor states of the old Romanov empire – the northern Baltic republic of Finland and the southern Baltic republics of Estonia, Latvia and Lithuania – were submitted to the Supreme Allied Council in Paris by the first Estonian foreign secretary, Kaarel Robert Pusta, as early as 1919, but they proved to be stillborn.[25] What did emerge on 17 March 1922 was the draft of a Warsaw Pact between Finland, Estonia, Latvia and Poland (constituted from the 19th-century Russian, Austrian and Prussian partitions) which provided for consultation in the event of an unprovoked attack on any of the signatories. In the event, this failed to gain the ratification of the respective national governments. Various other proposals for a regional security union circulated among the northern capitals at this time, the most ambitious of which was probably the Finn Rafael Erich's plan in 1925 for a Nordic defence alliance incorporating Finland, the small Baltic states (excluding Poland) and Scandinavia (Norway, Sweden and Denmark). Erich went even further to envisage a 'Nordic Locarno' which would have included the Soviet Union (a later version, to be sure, omitted Russia).[26] The security framework provided by the Locarno agreement, he contended, encompassed only Western Europe and hence there was a need for a complementary arrangement based on northern and eastern Europe. Opposition from the Soviet Union and a cool response from the Scandinavian states, however, prompted Finland's centre-right government under Kyösti Kallio to dissociate itself from Erich's plan.

The mid-1920s proved a turning-point in the search for a regional security system. The regular meetings of Baltic foreign ministers were discontinued in 1926 and in the 1930s, as the southern Baltic states succumbed to authoritarianism, Finland turned towards Scandinavia. It was in 1934 that the Finnish foreign minister first attended the Nordic foreign ministers' conference in Stockholm; in December 1935, Finland publicly declared her solidarity with the Nordic neutrals.

Superficially, the omens for a Baltic federation had looked relatively good. There was considerable hostility and suspicion towards the former Imperial master (especially in bourgeois circles) and, as small states wedged between the great powers of Russia and Germany, undoubted importance was attached to national security interests. Regular meetings of the Baltic foreign ministers were organized which affirmed a commitment to regional cooperation within the framework of the League of Nations. Yet a union of Baltic states was never really a feasible proposition.

First, the type of broad Baltic arrangement proposed by Erich was vetoed by the Scandinavians who were extremely reluctant to become embroiled in international politics. They did not believe their frontiers to be at risk and proceeded (albeit not without a measure of internal dissent) to instigate significant defence cuts.[27] From the outset they committed themselves enthusiastically to the League of Nations which they viewed both as an agency of peace and as a channel for small power influence on the world stage. In 1923, the Scandinavian states (who were regarded as a single bloc) were assigned one of the non-permanent seats on the Council, to be held on a rotational basis.

Second, a Warsaw Pact-based federation, along the lines of the abortive 1922 agreement, was ruled out principally by the fears of the small Baltic states that Poland would exploit the arrangement to create a new power bloc against Germany and Russia. There was concern, especially in Finland, not to become embroiled in a Soviet–Polish dispute, whilst after the occupation of Vilnius by Polish troops, Polish–Lithuanian cooperation was totally out of the question. In November 1923, a bilateral Latvian–Estonian agreement was reached which sought to keep the two states out of the clutches of the great powers; thereafter, the Latvian foreign secretary, Zigfrids Meierovics, urged acceptance of a Little Baltic community of Latvia, Lithuania and Estonia. But little was achieved, not least because of petty jealousies among the prospective partners.

Finally, the Soviet Union was understandably concerned to sabotage any incipient regional federation and to deploy accords with individual Baltic states, both as a buffer against the West and to offset its own isolationism. The approach to Finland illustrates the wider point. On the one hand, Finland was accused of interfering in the internal affairs of the Soviet Union when concurring with a League of Nations resolution urging a 'normalization of affairs' in Georgia (which the Red Army occupied in 1921).[28] On the other, the Soviet union produced a proposal for a regional non-aggression pact which was discussed with the Finns in March 1926. In the aftermath of Locarno, the

Soviet Union was clearly seeking to compensate for the diminished importance of Germany within its security system. Finland, however, remained intransigent, continuing to view Russia as the traditional enemy and as a constant threat to her independence. There was, in short, little attempt between the wars to acknowledge geopolitical realities by achieving improved relations with the Soviet Union.[29]

It was not only a common security system, but also significant economic cooperation which failed to materialize among the newly-sovereign Baltic states. During initial discussions, several statesmen were openly sceptical, believing that a regional economic bloc would be too small to have any significant influence on the world economy. Little, indeed, was achieved in marrying markets. True, on 5 February 1927, Estonia and Latvia signed a customs union treaty although, significantly, this was never put into effect.[30] Latvian manufacturers feared Estonian competition in certain product areas, whereas Estonia's leading commercial bodies were concerned that a large part of her imports would be diverted to Riga if there were close cooperation between the two states.[31] Curiously, although during the third Baltic Economic Conference on 16–17 June 1930, the Lithuanians and Estonians refused to enter a proposed Baltic Customs Union, they did express interest in the establishment of common shipyards and a common currency![32] All in all, as Edgar Anderson has noted: 'Each country wanted to develop its own resources to the fullest and feared the competition of its neighbours. They had not yet learned to co-operate, to share their resources and opportunities, and to help each other.'[33]

Proposed Danubian Federation

Initial proposals for a Baltic federation roughly coincided with the first post-war schemes for a Danubian federation comprising the successor states of the Austro-Hungarian empire, although the origins of this notion date back at least to the turn of the century. The growing fear of Russian pan-Slavism and a German '*Drang nach Osten*' (Drive towards the East) cast into sharp focus the importance of a strong Dual Monarchy in maintaining the existing balance of power in Europe; such fears also fired a number of proposals for strengthening the distinctively multi-racial empire by means of an internal reform programme.

In 1902, for example, Rudolph Springer (the pseudonym of the Austrian Socialist leader, Karl Renner) published *The Struggle of the Austrian Nations for the State* in which he sought enhanced popular legitimacy for the regime by devolving power to the nationalities. The idea was to create 'a commonwealth of national self-governments', with Vienna dealing only with essential federative functions such as trade and foreign relations.[34] In 1906, the Transylvanian Aurel Popovici outlined a constitution for a United States of Great Austria in his book *Die vereinigten Staaten von Gross Österreich*. This also proposed a federal framework as a means of accommodating the ethnic minorities of old Hungary. Popovici's scheme nonetheless retained exaggerated privileges for the monarch and German-speaking classes.

War and the collapse of the Hapsburg dynasty radically altered the situation, leading elements in the new rump Austria to work for the reintegration of the economies of the states founded from the ruins of the former empire. Twice in October 1918, the Austrian Social Democratic Party declared that it was prepared to negotiate on the formation of a Danubian federation.[35] If this could not be brought to fruition, there was consensus among the Austrian parties that they should seek a union or *Anschluss* with Germany. Indeed, this was widely regarded as the desired option. When Czechoslovakia categorically rejected any *Anschluss* and equally categorically opposed a new union with Vienna, the prospects of a federation of Danubian democracies quickly evaporated.

Instead, a limited security agreement in 1920 between Czechoslovakia, Romania and Yugoslavia, known as the Little Entente, was all that emerged. It was primarily a defensive alliance designed to maintain the new frontiers against the threat of Magyar irredentism, but did envisage consolidated commercial relations between member-states. Little was achieved, however, since the Little Entente *troika* were economic competitors. All were timber exporters. Moreover, whilst Yugoslavia and Romania sold grain for which there was no market in Czechoslovakia, they themselves did not constitute a sufficient market for the exports of a Czechoslovak state on whose territory was situated over two-thirds of the entire industry of the former Dual Monarchy. In any event, it quickly became apparent that economic nationalism and its corollary – the pursuit of autarky, which imbued the thinking and actions of the Little Entente states – would severely undercut any basis of mercantile cooperation among them.[36]

A heightened sense of isolation and vulnerability, reinforced by the effects of the Great Depression, predisposed Austria to resurrect the *Anschluss* plan, but in 1931 opposition from France and Czechoslovakia combined to torpedo a proposed customs union between Austria and Germany. True, the so-called Tardieu Plan the following year envisaged a preferential tariff – a 10 per cent customs reduction – among the Danubian states, but this could scarcely be considered a serious contribution to resolving the economic difficulties of the region.[37] At the heart of the Danubian dilemma lay the fact that the industrial states of Czechoslovakia and Austria, which contained influential farm-oriented parties, were unwilling to make concessions to the predominantly food-exporting countries of Romania, Hungary and Yugoslavia; whilst the latter, themselves seeking to develop an industrial base, opposed any concessions to the industrial exporting states.

The presentation of Milan Hodža's first Danube Plan in 1936 signified that the initiative on the formation of a regional federation had passed from Austria to Czechoslovakia. Hodža's aim was to create 'one single, great economic unit in Central Europe' – to create (in an acceptable form) an organization which would have all the economic advantages of Austria–Hungary without its obvious political and social shortcomings.[38] The Plan contemplated economic cooperation between, on the one hand, the Little Entente states and, on the other, Austria and Hungary, who from 1934 onwards were members (with Italy) of the Protocol of Rome. It was supported by Schusnigg in Austria together with elements of Slovakia, Hungary and even Poland. By 1936, moreover, Czech foreign secretary Beneš, always principally concerned to protect national sovereignty, had relented in his opposition to the idea. The Plan contained seven main points.

There was to be the phased abolition of tariffs leading to a single internal market, the abolition of quotas and the establishment of common credit arrangements. Agricultural production was to be regulated with an eye to marketing outlets and to cooperation forged in respect of basic industries and the provision of raw materials. A common system of communications (post and telegraphs) was to be set up, and legislation and administration coordinated, particularly with a view to protecting all nationalities. Foreign exchange policy was to be mutually aligned and, finally, there was to be a permanent Agricultural Bureau to coordinate Central European interests and to facilitate the marketing of agricultural surpluses in Western Europe. Hodža, in short, envisaged a common market – with a single currency and single external tariff – comparable to the one formed by the old Dual Monarchy. Its paramount objective was to reintegrate the economies of the region, whilst at the same time linking them, as predominantly agricultural producers, with the industrial consumers of Western Europe.

There was opposition to the Danube Plan from Nazi Germany where the press denounced it as 'an effort to surround Germany'; the Nazi threat, in turn, bred tensions within the Little Entente.[39] Matters were further complicated by the gulf between Hungary and the Entente over the position of the Magyar minorities in Czechoslovakia, Romania and Yugoslavia, as well as by Hungary's demand for military parity (she had already engaged in substantial rearmament) since the Entente made any deal conditional on a non-aggression pact. At a 'working coronation' – King George VI's – in London in May 1937, the Central European leaders made some progress, but the advent of Goga as Romanian prime minister that autumn effectively ended hopes of a *rapprochement* with Hungary or indeed any plans for economic cooperation in the Danube valley.[40]

The Ribbentrop–Molotov Pact of 23 August 1939 created a dramatically changed picture and convinced even those previously recalcitrant states that only through a form of union could their future independence be guaranteed.[41] It was not until 23 January 1942, however, that an agreement was reached between the Polish and Czechoslovak governments in exile in London to form the nucleus of a great Central European Federation. Matters falling within the federal orbit were to be foreign, military, economic, social and financial affairs, together with transport, communications and postal services. Hodža declared at the time that 'a federalised Central Europe is one of the absolute necessities of a new post-war order' although, as it happened, his Danubian federation plan was overtaken by events, in particular by the 'liberation' of the bulk of the region by the Red Army.[42]

Despite the broad foundation provided by Catholicism, by regional cooperation between the agrarian and social democratic movements and by a largely common history, culture and lifestyle, a Danubian federation did not materialize. Nationalism blinkered the view and there was a curious dearth of constructive ideas and symbols with which to mobilize popular enthusiasm for it.[43] Federation was in fact only intermittently on the region's political agenda – shortly after the First World War and, again, from the mid-1930s onwards. Austria's Danubian federation proposal in 1918 foundered for two main reasons. First, the cessation of hostilities brought a temporary respite from the longstanding regional concern about Russian and German expansionism and meant that there was no longer the need to incorporate Austria into an alliance system, whether military and/or economic. Second, there was the Czechs' vehement opposition to federation. Beneš depicted the former Hapsburg union as 'a system of exploitation' and emphasized that, having severed the umbilical cord, the new republic had absolutely no intention of entering a federation proposed (and possibly dominated) by the old Imperial power.

As to the failure of Hodža's first Danube Plan in 1936, several factors were relevant: the strategic opposition of the Axis powers; the way Britain and the other Western democracies discouraged the notion of a preferential system; and, above all, the strength of political and economic nationalism among the successor states. Most of the region viewed an economic union too much from the standpoint of power politics rather than from that of economics.[44] Hungary, for her part, used the minorities question as a pretext for blocking a federal arrangement. Significantly, the Sudeten German Party worked ruthlessly to undermine the Danubian federation plan, activating opposition to it among Hlinka's Slovak autonomists and even sending a delegation to the Hungarian cabinet to confirm that it was against any such development.[45]

In a wider sense, Hodža's Plan should be set in the context of a Central European economy totally becalmed by the stagnating effects of recession: it lacked both Western outlets for its overpriced agricultural surpluses and, as a consequence, the purchasing power to buy back consumer goods from the industrial nations of Western Europe. It was this vicious circle of non-integrated economic blocs which Hodža hoped to square by orchestrating the Central European economies in a Danubian federation. Impatient with several neighbouring states for dragging their heels, Hodža also indicted the Western powers in respect of their engrained parochialism in economic outlook. Claiming that Western Europe did not realize either after the war or in the 1930s the importance of building bridges between Délaisy's Two Europes, Hodža contended (harshly) that the main weakness of Versailles was the absence of any provision for Central European cooperation that would have served as a bulwark against aggressive German nationalism.[46] Implicit in this thesis was a recognition that regional cooperation was essential for reasons of common security as well as economic well-being. Indeed, he argued persuasively that 'the freedom and security of small nations can only be guaranteed by their federation'.[47]

Proposed Balkan Union

Plans for a union of Balkan states were no more successful than those put forward in the Baltic and Danube valley. They were indeed extremely short-lived and died with the political demise of the Bulgarian prime minister Stamboliiski in 1922. The latter, however, had apparently conceived of a union of southern Slavonia and Bulgaria into a federation of Serbs, Croats, Slovenes and Bulgars which was to be achieved, it seems, largely through the medium of the regional agrarian parties.[48] Once, when asked whether he was a Bulgarian or a Serb, Stamboliiski is reputed to have replied indignantly: 'I am neither; I am a south Slav'.[49] The south Slavs (Serbs), however, were too busy building a position of strength in Yugoslavia (the Kingdom of the south Slavs) to pay much heed to Stamboliiski, who tended to be viewed simply as an imperialist. Tito was viewed in a similar light when he revived the idea of a regional federation of Balkan states in the late 1940s (see Chapter 4).

Regional federations had a powerful functional logic in the Europe of the inter-war years, but this was *par excellence* a period of accentuated disintegration when the pre-1914 system of multilateral free trade gave way to a strident nationalist economics characterized by insularity and protectionism. The 'New Europe' of Versailles, of course, survived a mere two decades before the continent was engulfed in a holocaust still more terrible than the bloody legacy of the Somme. Would the latest carnage create a climate conducive to European union, or would the Two Europes resurface? Would nationalism concede pride of place to a new spirit of internationalism? Could arrangements be made to prevent renewed conflagration on the European land mass? Above all, would the nation-states of post-Hitler Europe cast off the bunker mentality of the inter-war years and place cooperation before unbridled competition?

Notes

1   Sally Marks (1976), *The Illusion of Peace: International Relations in Europe 1918–1933*, London: Macmillan, p.85.
2   Sidney Pollard (1974), *European Economic Integration 1815–1970*, London: Thames & Hudson, p.146.
3   The Rapallo Treaty bestowed on the signatories mutual most-favoured-nation treatment and saw Germany legally recognize the Soviet Union and cancel all her debts, on condition that Stalin did not compensate other claimants.
4   Pollard (1974), op. cit., pp.136–7.
5   Max Silberschmidt (1972), *The United States and Europe: Rivals and Partners*, London: Thames & Hudson, pp.122–9.
6   The war had a marked influence on the relative credit standing of the Western industrial states. Before 1914, Britain, France, Belgium and Holland, as advanced manufacturing nations, were exporters of capital. During the war, however, France, Italy and others became heavily indebted to the UK and US, whilst their loans to Russia had to be written off. France, in particular, became dependent on reparations from Germany so as to facilitate her loan repayments to the US.
7   Charles Seymour (1921), 'The End of an Empire: Remnants of Austria-Hungary', in E.M. House and C. Seymour (eds), *What Really Happened at Paris*, London: Hodder & Stoughton, pp.110–11.
8   Marks (1976), op. cit., p.22.
9   Alfred Zauberman (1976), 'Russia and Eastern Europe 1920–1970', in Carlo M. Cipolla (ed.), *The Fontana Economic History of Europe: Contemporary Economics*, Part 2, Glasgow: Collins/Fontana, p.593.
10 Sidney Pollard (1981), *The Integration of the European Economy since 1815*, London: George Allen & Unwin, p.64. Equally unequivocally, Frederick Hertz refers to the existence of 'a constant economic war of all against all' centred on the pursuit of self-sufficiency. See F. Hertz (1947), *The Economic Problems of the Danubian States: Study in Economic Nationalism*, London: Gollancz, p.56.
11 Hertz (1947), op. cit., pp.78–86.
12 Some areas taken away from Austria and Hungary had been claimed by more than one successor state and, as Macartney and Palmer note: 'friend grabbed from friend just as shamelessly as from enemy'. Thus the Czechs and Poles had vied for Teschen; the Serbs and Romanians for the Banat, and the Italians and Yugoslavs for Fiume. C.A. Macartney and A.W. Palmer (1962), *Independent Eastern Europe*, London: Macmillan, p.127.
13 Macartney and Palmer (1962), op. cit., pp.236–9.
14 This was the result of the close contact which existed between the highly cartelized Czech industry and international cartels. A. Zauberman (1976), op. cit., p.599.

15 Pollard (1974), op. cit., pp.148–51.
16 Quoted in E.J. Hobsbawm (1990), *Nations and Nationalism since 1780: Programme, Myth and Reality*, Cambridge: Cambridge University Press, p.31.
17 Since the US, the world's largest steel producer, consumed her own production, she was not a factor on European or world markets. Marks (1976), op. cit., pp.84–5.
18 Marks (1976), op. cit., pp.85–6.
19 Toivo Miljan (1977), *The Reluctant Europeans*, London: Hurst, pp.78–9.
20 'Briand on a Federal Union in Europe', *The Times*, 19 May 1930, cited in Richard Vaughan (1976), *Post-War Integration in Europe*, London: Edward Arnold, pp.11–12.
21 Marks (1976), op. cit., p.106.
22 Ibid., p.107.
23 Arnold J. Zurcher (1958), *The Struggle to Unite Europe 1940–1958*, Westport: Greenwood, p.173.
24 Ibid., p.6.
25 G. von Rauch (1974), *The Baltic States. Estonia, Latvia, Lithuania*, London: Hurst, p.107. Indeed, on 7 September 1917 in the Estonian provincial assembly *Maapäev*, Jaan Tönisson astounded colleagues by advocating a Northern Union embracing the Scandinavian states, Finland, Estonia, Latvia and Lithuania. A Baltic bloc of 30 million citizens, he contended, would be able to assert itself at the international level. See von Rauch (1974), p.31.
26 Juhani Mylly (1978), *Maalaisliitto ja turvallisuuspolitiikka*, Turku: Turun yliopisto, p.169.
27 True, in a speech at the end of 1923, the Swedish foreign minister, Carl Hederstierna, surprisingly mooted a Finno-Swedish defence alliance. He did not, however, inform his own cabinet about the contents of the proposal and the storm of protest that ensued, both from his ministerial colleagues and from the political left, ultimately forced his resignation. A more representative Scandinavian orientation was Danish foreign minister Peter Munch's *Projet danois de Désarmement* in 1922 in which he argued powerfully for a general 80 per cent reduction in arms production. See Bengt Owe Birgersson, Stig Hadenius, Björn Molin and Hans Wieslander (1981), *Sverige efter 1900*, Stockholm: Bonnier, p.105. Also, T.K. Derry (1979), *A History of Scandinavia*, London: George Allen & Unwin, p.316.
28 L.A. Puntila (ed.) (1978), *Valtioneuvoston historia 1917–1966*, Helsinki: Valtion painatuskeskus, p.387.
29 D.G. Kirby (1979), *Finland in the Twentieth Century*, London: Hurst, pp.106–7.
30 Edgar Anderson (1967), 'Towards a Baltic Union 1927–34', *Lituanus*, **13**(1), 8.
31 Ibid., 12.
32 Ibid., 13.
33 Ibid., 5.
34 M. Hodža (1942), *Federation in Central Europe: Reflections and Reminiscences*, London: Jarrolds, pp.44–5.
35 Hertz (1947), op. cit., p.64.
36 Schultz (1967), op. cit., pp.202–3.
37 Hertz (1947), op. cit., p.68.
38 Hodža (1942), op. cit., p.131.
39 K.J. Newman (1970), *European Democracy between the Wars*, London: George Allen & Unwin, p.181.
40 Hodža (1942), op. cit., pp.131–9.
41 J.M. Kirschbaum (1960), *Slovakia: Nation at the Crossroads of Central Europe*, New York: Robert Speller, p.82.
42 Hodža (1942), op. cit., pp.172–5.

43 Newman (1970), op. cit., pp.180–88.
44 Ibid., p.181.
45 Ibid., p.182.
46 Hodža (1942), op. cit., p.105.
47 Ibid., p.171.
48 Schultz (1972), op. cit., p.201.
49 Macartney and Palmer (1962), op. cit., p.174.

4

'The Fifty Years War'. The Origins of the Capitalist–Communist Division of Europe, 1945–53

Today, no move to unite Europe politically could penetrate the Iron Curtain. United Europe can only mean United Western Europe, a defensive bloc of Western States, clinging together to defend themselves against the further encroachment of the Communist Eastern bloc.

Freda Bruce Lockhart, 'Towards a United Europe?',
The Nineteenth Century and After, July 1947, p.13

Europe united in adversity to overcome the fascism of the Axis powers, but victory betrayed deep divisions among the Allies which precluded lasting European unity. The vision held up by the Resistance leaders, who met in July 1944, of a pan-European federal union transcending old national boundaries foundered on the rock of an ideological bifurcation of the continent into two hostile camps – a communist East and a capitalist West.[1] This was a division more deepseated and starkly etched than the sharp contrast in the level of regional economic development which underpinned Délaisy's *Les Deux Europes* in 1924. As Winston Churchill observed portentously during a visit to the US early in 1946: 'From Stettin in the Baltic to Trieste in the Adriatic, an iron curtain has descended across the continent.'[2] The defeat of Hitler, in short, presaged a further period of accentuated disintegration in Europe which was no longer to the same extent master of its own destiny.

Superpower Domination of Europe

By 1949 two superpowers, one wholly extra-European (the US) and the other only partially European (the Soviet Union), were established at the heart of Europe. The continent divided into superpower spheres of influence, the division of the German state into Eastern and Western halves both reflecting and reinforcing the tension of the incipient Cold War.[3] What resulted were clients of the US and satellites of the Soviet Union. True, with the advantage of hindsight, it might be asserted that, whilst the Second World War doomed Europe to division, that very division made for a period of stability which provided the springboard for peaceful change at a later stage.[4] But the mood in Western capitals at the time was tetchy and pessimistic and there was a growing perception of the menace posed by the 'Soviet colossus'.

Post-War Soviet Influence

The collapse of the Nazi *Reich* signalled the emergence of the Soviet Union as the dominant European power. Permitted a hegemony of influence over Eastern Europe by Roosevelt at the 'Big Three' summit at Yalta in February 1945 – regarded by critics as 'another Munich'[5] – the Red Army occupation of the region enabled Stalin quickly to convert this influence into the reality of power. True, the Big Three determined jointly to aid the liberated countries 'to destroy the last vestiges of Nazism and Fascism and to create democratic institutions of their own choice',[6] but a Soviet puppet regime was confirmed in Poland without elections[7] and, as the Soviet leader remarked to senior Yugoslav communists in April 1945, 'whoever occupies a territory also imposes on it his own political system ... as far as his army can reach'.[8] In December 1941, however, it was Hitler's armies which had reached to within a tram ride of the Kremlin, making the balance of power in Eastern Europe at that time look very different.

Ironically, Hitler's unprovoked invasion of the Soviet Union on 21 June 1941 – code-named Operation Barbarossa – in search of the *lebensraum* he envisaged in *Mein Kampf*, seems to have come as a greater shock to Stalin than to the West, which had repeatedly warned him of the German threat. It did, however, oblige Soviet communism to link arms with Western capitalism in order to protect Europe against Nazi expansionism. Military developments, therefore, reversed the situation which had existed on the eve of the Second World War when Stalin had shocked the West by entering into a non-aggression pact with Hitler – a highly improbable and opportunistic alliance of communism and fascism.

The Ribbentrop–Molotov Pact of August 1939, moreover, had contained secret articles which partitioned Eastern Europe into Soviet and German spheres of influence. For the Baltic 'successor states' of Finland, Latvia, Lithuania and Estonia, which were allocated to the Soviet sphere, this was to mean sharply contrasting fates. The southern Baltic republics were occupied by the Red Army and summarily annexed to the Soviet Union in July 1940. Finland's refusal to accede to Stalin's demands to consolidate his strategic–military position overlooking the Baltic, however, led to the Winter War of 1939–40, during which the Finns, acquitting themselves well in the frozen, forested terrain of the Karelian isthmus, held up a numerically vastly superior Red Army for nearly four months.[9]

The exploits of the silent Finnish ski-troopers against almost impossible odds were widely acclaimed in the West and for Churchill, who depicted the conflict as a struggle between freedom and tyranny, the Winter War provided both a 'cause' and a distraction for an anxious British public during the long months of the 'phoney war'. Only 14 months after the Finns' defeat, however, Stalin, 'the tyrant of the frozen North', was thrown together with his arch-critics, Churchill and Roosevelt, by the exigencies of a common struggle against Nazi Germany. Cooperation between the Soviet Union, Britain and the US was to prove both a notable and durable feature of the Second World War.

Thus in July 1941, Britain and the Soviet Union bound themselves not to engage in a separate peace with Germany – approximately 6000 British and 7000 American planes reached the USSR during the war – and in November 1943 Stalin, Roosevelt and Churchill met at Teheran to agree on the goal of an unconditional German surrender (the zonal occupation of Germany also dates back to Teheran).[10] The USSR, in its turn, lent support to the Atlantic Charter of August 1941 in which Britain and America renounced all claims to territorial gain and expressed the devout hope that after the cessation of hostilities 'all men in all lands would be able to live out their lives in freedom from fear and want'. Ultimately, victory was bought at the price of enormous Soviet loss of life – at least seven and a half million servicemen are estimated to have been killed – but, beginning with Marshall Zhukov's counter-offensive on the outskirts of Moscow in December 1941, the Red Army began to push the Nazis back. By Yalta, in February 1945, the Soviet Union was in military occupation of virtually the whole of Eastern Europe except Greece which was liberated by British forces. Table 4.1 summarizes the main events of the Second World War in Europe.

Unlike the radical revisions of the 1919–23 peace treaties, the territorial changes to the map of Europe after the Second World War were relatively minor. No new states emerged, although Iceland severed

Table 4.1   The Main Events of the Second World War in Europe

1939	(September) German invasion of Poland leading to capture of Warsaw.
1939	(September) Soviet Union responded by invading and quickly acquiring an eastern segment of Poland comprising the Ukraine and Byelorussia (nowadays Bielarus).
1939	(September) US President Roosevelt asserted his country's neutrality.
1939	(November) Start of Winter War between the USSR and Finland.
1939	(November) Britain stood to profit from the US Congress' decision to sell arms on a 'cash and carry' basis.
1940	(March) Finnish defeat in the Winter War led to the surrender of much of Karelia to Stalin. The Soviet Union was, in turn, expelled from the League of Nations.
1940	(April) Twin Nazi strike against Denmark (overrun in one day) and Norway.
1940	(May) Simultaneous German invasion of the Low Countries.
1940	(May) In UK, National Coalition formed under Winston Churchill.
1940	(June) France obliged to sign an armistice with Hitler: the North was directly ruled by Germany; the South was nominally run by the puppet Vichy regime under Marshal Pétain.
1940	(July) The Axis Powers (Germany, Italy and Japan) signed a 10-year military pact in Berlin pledged to building a New Order.
1940	(July) Soviet occupation of the Baltic states of Latvia, Lithuania and Estonia.
1940	(July) German occupation of the Channel Islands.
1940	(August) Hitler launched repeated waves of air attacks on Britain.
1940	(15 September) Decisive Battle of Britain day. Heavy German air losses.
1940	(October) Italy declared war on Greece.
1940	(October) Germany occupied the remnants of Romania (following concessions to the Soviet Union, Hungary and Bulgaria).
1941	(March) US Congress approved 'Lend-lease aid' from which Britain profited.
1941	(April) Hitler attacked Serbia and there was massive bombing of Belgrade. He quickly obtained control of most of the Balkans.
1941	(June) Start of Operation Barbarossa – Hitler's invasion of the Soviet Union.

1941 (July) Britain and the Soviet Union agreed not to make separate peace arrangements with Hitler.

1941 (August) Roosevelt and Churchill proclaimed the Atlantic Charter based on the principle of self-determination and of peoples living 'in freedom from fear and want'.

1941 (December) Soviet counter-offensive under Zhukov as the Germans reached the approaches to Moscow.

1942 (August) Hitler ordered the seizure of Stalingrad.

1943 (January) Casablanca meeting of Roosevelt and Churchill planned a combined Allied offensive against Germany leading to her 'unconditional surrender'.

1943 (February) German surrender at Stalingrad.

1943 (July) Allied amphibious operation to conquer Sicily, an objective completed within a month.

1943 (July) Deposition of Mussolini as Italian leader.

1943 (September) Unconditional surrender of Italy to Allies.

1943 (November) 'Big Three' (Roosevelt, Churchill and Stalin) summit at Teheran in Iran. Churchill's plan to invade Eastern Europe, so pre-empting Soviet control of the region, fails to get Roosevelt's support.

1944 (June) 'D-Day'. The Allied landings in Normandy (code-named Operation Overlord) under the command of Dwight D. Eisenhower.

1944 (Autumn) Bulgaria, Romania, the majority of Hungary and about half Poland 'liberated' from the Nazis.

1944 (October) Tito-led Communist Partisans joined Soviet troops in Belgrade.

1945 (February) 'Big Three' meeting in Yalta in the Crimea at which it was agreed that Germany was to be disarmed, demilitarized and divided into zones (partitioned). The Soviet Union was also to receive half Germany's reparations.

1945 (3 April) Hitler committed suicide.

1945 (April) Death of Roosevelt.

1945 (8 May) VE (Victory in Europe) Day.

1945 (17 July) Potsdam meeting of Stalin, Churchill (shortly to be replaced by Labour leader and new prime minister, Clement Attlee) and new US President Harry S Truman.

1945–7 Formulation of peace treaties with Germany's allies, Italy, Hungary, Bulgaria and Romania, and co-belligerent Finland.

its connection with the Danish crown to become an independent republic following a referendum in May 1944.[11] Germany, as the principal perpetrator of war, was partitioned by the Allies into four zones; there was to be joint control of Berlin; the Saarland, which had voted to join Germany in 1935, remained under French control (until 1959); the German population was effectively expelled from Pomerania and Silesia, which were to be administered by Poland; and the Soviet Union acquired the northern part of East Prussia on the Baltic.

Peace treaties with Germany's Allies – Italy, Bulgaria, Romania and Finland, a 'co-belligerent' – were completed by 1947, with each obliged to pay reparations (mostly to the USSR, Yugoslavia and Greece) and to disarm. In addition, Italy ceded the contentious Istrian peninsula to Yugoslavia, whilst disputed Trieste was made a Free State; Greece acquired the Dodecanese Islands; Romania ceded South Dobruja to Bulgaria, but regained Transylvania which Hungary had taken in 1940.

Above all, the peace treaties incorporated territory into the USSR which served to extend the boundaries of the Soviet Union westwards. In addition to the southern Baltic states annexed in 1940 (and not part of the peace treaties), the USSR acquired much of Karelia and the Arctic port of Petsamo from Finland; Bessarabia from Romania, Ruthenia from Czechoslovakia and territory up to the so-called Curzon line from Poland (the Oder–Neisse line set before the Polish gains of 1921). It was also agreed at Potsdam that the Soviet Union would be entitled to 35 per cent of all the equipment in the three western zones of Germany; in practice, she would also have a free hand in her own eastern zone.

From the early stages of war, well before the rapid Nazi assault on Russia had been repulsed, Stalin was concerned with securing adequate future protection against renewed German aggression. Accordingly, at a meeting with British foreign secretary Anthony Eden on 16–17 December 1941, the Soviet leader proposed that, in addition to a military alliance, there should be a second treaty with a secret protocol dealing in detail with Europe's post-war frontiers.[12] After prevarication from Eden and an insistence that the US be consulted and acquiesce in any territorial revisions, the meeting concluded less than harmoniously. It is doubtful, however, if either then or, indeed, for two decades after the war, the Allies fully grasped the extent of Soviet anxiety about the prospect of renewed German militarism.

It has become commonplace to criticize the British and Americans for making undue concessions to Stalin at Potsdam. However, by the end of 1945, there had been changes at the helm of both Western Allies. President Roosevelt, who died soon after Yalta, had been replaced by Harry Truman, whilst shortly after the Potsdam conference opened, Clement Attlee succeeded Churchill as prime minister following Labour's landslide at the polls. France, meanwhile, was placed on a 'subordinate-on-equal-footing', omitted from the Big Three at both Yalta and Potsdam, but invited by the final Yalta communiqué to occupy a zone of German territory.[13] De Gaulle, the prime minister and war-time Resistance leader, held the Americans culpable for excluding France; Stalin, though, was even less sympathetic to her cause. The upshot of developments was that, by the time the Potsdam conference began in earnest, Stalin was the only survivor of the original Big Three and could therefore, it is argued, get things very much his own way. Equally, the Western leaders had probably little realistic alternative than to confirm Soviet territorial claims that were based on *de facto* military possession. The Red Army, in short, had a telling say *in absentia* at Potsdam.[14]

The 'liberating' Red Army enabled Stalin to construct a Soviet empire in Eastern Europe which clearly violated the spirit of the Atlantic Charter and its central premise of national self-determination. Article Five of the Yalta Agreement stated that countries occupied by Germany were to have the opportunity of setting up governments of their own choosing although, in the event, Stalin blatantly intervened in the internal affairs of the East European states with a view to eliminating non-communist opposition. Poland, a dominant issue at Yalta and also on the Potsdam agenda, was a case in point.

Eden recognized at Yalta that free elections under international supervision were a *sine qua non* of an independent Poland. When the time came, however, Stalin categorically refused to allow Western participation in the supervision or even in the observation of polling. Moreover, whilst the extent to which Britain alone could influence developments was plainly very limited, the US appeared unwilling to deploy her considerable military strength even as a bargaining counter against Stalin. 'In a moment of unparalleled feebleness',[15] Roosevelt actually volunteered the information that American forces would leave Europe within two years! Moreover, despite the initial appearance of a more resolute stance towards Stalin, Truman did not significantly alter US policy on Poland, with the result that before Potsdam, Churchill was effectively obliged to recognize the Lublin Committee (of Communist-dominated Poles backed by Moscow) and withdraw recognition from the London government-in-exile.[16] In truth, Churchill himself had earlier been 'Poles apart'[17] from Mikolayczyk when, with a view to appeasing Stalin, he tried (unsuccessfully) to bully the leader of the Polish government-in-exile into accepting the Curzon Line as the basis of the post-war settlement of his country.[18] All in all, whilst Stalin's intentions were clear throughout, the Allies played into the Soviet leader's hands on Poland.

Throughout the region in the immediate post-war years, Stalin engaged in concerted action to suppress the 'bourgeois' agrarian parties which still enjoyed substantial support in the countryside. Maniu, the Romanian Agrarian leader, and Petkov in Bulgaria were arrested in 1947; in Poland the same year, Mikolayczyk was crushed in an openly rigged election whose fraudulence he denounced; and in Hungary, Belá Kovács, the secretary of the Small Holders' Party, was arrested by the Russians, ostensibly for participating in a counter-revolutionary conspiracy.[19] Only in Czechoslovakia were free elections held and there the Communists, profiting from strong-anti-Western sentiment, gained an impressive 35 per cent of the vote in May 1946. However, in the first post-war election to the Berlin City Council (*Stadtverordnetenversammlung*) contested across the capital on 20 October 1946, the Social Democrats (SPD) emerged as convincing victors with 48.7 per cent of the vote to 22.2 per cent for the Christian Democrats (CDU), whilst the United Socialist Party (SED), created in the Soviet zone on 22 April 1946 from a merger of Socialist and Communists and led by Otto Grotewohl, managed only 19.8 per cent.[20]

Perhaps the fate of the inter-war successor states of Central and Eastern Europe was effectively sealed when the US failed to back Britain's active policy of encouraging federations in the region. Both Churchill and Eden, concerned to learn the lessons of recent history, adopted Hodža's view of the importance of integrating the Danubian states into a federation *inter alia* as a bulwark against German and Soviet expansionism. The Foreign Office, indeed, exploited the presence of several exiled governments in London to encourage negotiations along these lines, particularly between Czechoslovakia and Poland. The conjoining of Yugoslavia and Greece was also considered possible. Churchill's own preference was for a Danubian federation based in Vienna and incorporating Austria, Hungary and southern Germany. Eden, for his part, believed that such an arrangement should embrace only Austria, Hungary and possibly some Slav territories. Significantly, however, neither Roosevelt nor his Secretary of State, Cordell Hull, was particularly attracted by the prospect of a Danubian federation.[21.]

Allied division was plainly evident at a tripartite foreign ministers' meeting held in Moscow in October 1943 when Eden outlined the three main strands of Britain's Central and East European policy. First, the Big Three (and, above all, the Soviet Union) should renounce unilateral action in any part of Europe. They should, in short, eschew any intention to create 'separate areas of responsibility', meaning spheres of influence. Second, the Big Three should give positive encouragement to the merger of the small states of Europe into larger, federal units provided that the latter were not directed 'at other states'. Third, a positive commitment should nonetheless be given to respect the independence and rights of self-determination of the small nations of Europe.[22] In his response, Hull demonstrated that he was a prisoner of White House orthodoxy: the broad principles of Big Three cooperation should be agreed first and specific questions later, he contended, intimating that the US did not wish to become embroiled in British schemes for Eastern Europe, particularly if they were likely to antagonize Stalin.[23] Significantly, Averell Harriman, who attended the Moscow meeting and was shortly to become the US ambassador there, was critical of Hull's approach, arguing that greater emphasis should have been given to extracting satisfactory assurances on Eastern Europe.[24]

Predictably, Molotov, who was at heart anxious to avert a second 'cordon sanitaire', expressed grave reservations about both the wisdom and propriety of encouraging federations at this juncture. It was extremely doubtful, he asserted (justifiably), whether the non-elected and highly provisional governments-in-exile had the authority to pursue such ventures, adding that the incorporation of the Axis states of Hungary, Bulgaria and Romania into new federations might incline the Allies (unjustifiably) to treat them better than other former enemies. Molotov's opposition and Hull's lukewarm attitude conspired on 21 October 1943 to administer a death-blow to Britain's supportive line on the post-war integration of Central and East European states. As Keith Sainsbury has observed: 'Hull had pinned his hopes to the belief that the USSR was more likely to behave well in Eastern Europe if her confidence was first won and her assent secured to the principle of post-war cooperation. By his lack of support for Eden, he had ensured that his policy would prevail.'[25]

Soviet opposition subsequently meant that Tito's ambitious post-war plan to integrate the communist states of south-east Europe into a Balkan federation proved stillborn – a casualty both of nascent democratic centralism (the satellite parties' obligation of absolute obedience to the will of the Kremlin) and, more particularly, Stalin's indignation at the temerity and insubordination of the Yugoslav Communist leader. Uniquely among the peoples of Eastern Europe, the Yugoslavs had liberated themselves in 1945 without the assistance of the Red Army. In 1943 the British, under the influence of a handful of agents of the Special Operations Executive based in Cairo, switched allegiance from the Serbian General Draza Mihailović who, in the mountainous regions north of Belgrade, was the first soldier in occupied Yugoslavia to raise an army against Hitler, to the communist Partisans under Tito. Well equipped with British guns, explosives and aircraft, Tito went on to impose communism at great cost to human life.

After the war, Yugoslavia was admittedly on fractious terms with Italy over Trieste, with Austria over southern Carinthia and with

Greece over parts of Macedonia. However, Albania, a main organizational base of the Partisans, was almost entirely under Tito's control and he, in turn, began actively to campaign for a Balkan federation beginning with the merger of Yugoslavia and Bulgaria. After tortuous talks, Tito and Dimitrov agreed at Bled in 1947 to work for the gradual federation of the two countries.[26] It was this development which prompted Stalin to mobilize the opposition of other Communist leaders in order to sabotage the whole idea.

Born of a flagrant flouting of the right of national self-determination and nurtured on the wholesale violation of human rights, the fledgling Soviet empire in Eastern Europe nonetheless could not be accused of snuffing out a tradition of pluralist democracy. True, the inter-war successor states re-emerged as 'people's democracies', not pluralist democracies, but liberal politics had succumbed to authoritarianism (in one form or another) across much of the region well before the Second World War. With the significant exception of Czechoslovakia, post-war communism was thus imposed on East European states which had little or no tradition of competitive politics. Importantly, too, the Soviet empire inherited all the socioeconomic and cultural cleavages which had made Western-style democracy so difficult to sustain in the successor states between the wars, especially under the impact of recession. The very elements which had contributed to deep-seated problems of national integration – that is, reconciling state and society – were now placed in a communist straitjacket. The challenge of monopoly communism would be to contain these elements as well as such 'counter-ideological' forces as ethnic nationalism and Catholicism based on them. Failure to do so would open the door to disintegrative tendencies in a Soviet empire based on enforced integration.

Post-War American Influence

On the other side of the Iron Curtain, the US emerged as the rival superpower, abandoning its isolationist tradition in favour of an active involvement in Western Europe and the fight against communism. If the beginnings of the Cold War in 1947–8 and the partition of Germany served to define Western Europe as a political region, they also underlined the fact that it was a bloc of relatively small states which, after five years of military conflict, depended heavily for its politico-economic survival on support from the US. Having rallied to defeat fascism, Europe was split by an ideological struggle between expansionist communism in the East and enfeebled capitalism in the West, with the Soviet and American superpowers committed to achieving diametrically opposed outcomes.

The initial American counter-offensive against communism came in the somewhat bombastic form of the so-called Truman Doctrine of 12 March 1947 which was, in turn, a response to Soviet infiltration into the eastern Mediterranean. President Truman promised US 'support for free peoples' (in this case, the Greek nationalists) who were 'resisting attempted subjugation by armed minorities' (Soviet-backed communists) 'or by outside pressure'. The American head of state made it clear that action would be taken to prevent Communist takeovers; he emphasized, for instance, that the US would not tolerate a Communist government in Italy following the April 1948 general election.

It quickly became clear, however, that military support would not be sufficient since the economic eclipse of Europe in the face of heightened American competition, which had already been evident to leading continental industrialists during the strongly protectionist 1920s, was now accentuated by the devastation of war. While the US consolidated her position as the leading capitalist nation, Europe's important export markets were in a state of dislocation, with national economies standing in need of wholesale reconstruction. Industrial production in France, Belgium and the Netherlands had sunk to 40 per cent and in Germany to 70 per cent of pre-war levels; in occupied Germany cigarettes and chocolate had become the only acceptable currency. The Economic Recovery Programme or Marshall Aid was designed to remedy this situation. It involved a commitment to grant aid in support of a cooperative European regional effort to achieve economic self-sufficiency. By 1949 US grants and loans had funded nearly two-thirds of the French and Italian deficits, half the British and two-fifths of the German. Indeed, without direct exports of US meat and grain, millions of Germans would undoubtedly have starved.

The Marshall initiative represented the search for a cure, rather than merely a palliative, and constituted implicit recognition of the inadequacy of the various piecemeal efforts that had preceded it. The US Congress had earlier voted *ad hoc* credits towards reconstruction in Europe. Between 1945 and 1947, 15 billion dollars were spent on the task. But even the 3.75 billion dollar loan exceptionally granted to Britain, together with the Export-Import bank credits allocated elsewhere, proved insufficient. Indeed, when total West European production fell from 83 per cent of 1938 levels in the last quarter of 1946 to 78 per cent in the first quarter of 1947, there was growing concern on both sides of the Atlantic that economic distress would provoke social and political breakdown and create a situation which the Soviet Union could exploit.[27] In particular, the US seems to have overestimated the fundamental strength of the UK economy.

Britain's debilitated economic position was clearly recognized by the Labour foreign secretary, Ernest Bevin, who is widely accredited with a central role in persuading the US to assume responsibility for Europe. Marshall's speech created relatively little stir in America, but Bevin enthused over it, mobilized French support and generated the momentum which led to the formation of the 16-nation Organization for European Economic Cooperation (OEEC) to administer reconstruction aid.[28]

Whilst welcoming and recognizing the paramount importance of recovery aid, Bevin and his senior civil servants nonetheless sought (unavailingly) to claim special status for the UK 'as a partner of the US in world recovery'. In talks with the Americans in London in June 1947, the foreign secretary argued that, if the UK were treated as 'merely another European country', it would play into Soviet hands: when America encountered the expected slump, the UK would be left helpless, out of dollars and unable to prevent command of the continent passing to the Russians. As Alan Bullock has noted, Bevin was caught in an obvious conflict between poverty and pride. The British were financially dependent on the Americans for their economic survival, yet wanted to be treated as an equal partner in dispensing aid to the Europeans.[29] The Americans, however, doggedly insisted that it was to be a European programme and that no special positions could be accorded.

From an American viewpoint, the economic reconstruction strategy for Western Europe rested on at least two basic propositions. First, there was a recognition that the long-term US objective of a global trading system could not be achieved without a prosperous and stable Europe. Second, there was the obvious realization that the US had a vested interest in reviving the economies of Western Europe, since the region afforded a valuable trade outlet for American raw materials and export markets for its consumer goods. 'Let us admit it right off,' noted Will Clayton, a former cotton entrepreneur who became an assistant economic secretary at the White House, 'Our objective has as its background the needs and interests of the US. We need markets, big markets in which to buy and sell.'[30]

There could, of course, be little doubt that in the longer term an effective reconstruction programme would be counter-productive to US commercial objectives because of the inherent conflict between a cohesive West European trading bloc and the goal of global free trade anchored in institutions like the International Monetary Fund (IMF) and the General Agreement on Tariffs and Trade (GATT). Both were inaugurated in 1944, largely at the behest of the Americans. Yet those Americans who did perceive that an Economic Community in Western Europe would inevitably act as a factor of negative integration in world markets doubtless regarded this as a problem that could safely be deferred, being strictly subordinate to the immediate need to shore up the West European economies against incipient collapse.

There was an appreciation of the risk that parlous economic conditions might well nurture political extremism and consolidate the Communists' challenge to Western pluralist democracy. The functional political logic of economic recovery aid – its role as a weapon in the anti-communist armoury (which already contained the Truman Doctrine and was shortly to include the North Atlantic Treaty) – was therefore important to a US Congress accustomed to underwriting the nation's traditional policy of isolationism.

Truman subsequently asserted that the Marshall programme would go down in history as one of America's greatest contributions to the peace of the world. 'I think the world realizes that without the Marshall Plan it would have been difficult for Western Europe to remain free from the tyranny of communism,' he insisted.[31] At the time the President impressed on Congress that the programme was to be implemented in the expectation that European recovery would be substantially completed in about four years. Moreover, he noted that the estimated cost of 17 billion dollars represented only 5 per cent of the sum expended to defeat the Axis powers and would constitute only 3 per cent of gross national income during the time the programme was in effect. It was, he implied, a sound commercial as well as political investment.[32]

Marshall for his part emphasized the way economic aid would serve to spare America involvement in another war on the European continent. In his presentation to the US Senate Committee on Foreign Relations on 8 January 1948, he claimed that, without aid, 'the vacuum which the war created in Western Europe will be filled with the forces of which wars are made'; he maintained that, whilst dollars will not save the world, the world could not be saved without dollars.[33]

From a West European perspective, Marshall Aid was necessary to restore economies which simply did not have the capacity to restore themselves. They were all plagued in varying degrees by the disruption to trade patterns between Eastern and Western Europe, as well as by the loss of reserves and earnings from foreign investment and invisibles. Whilst there was a glaring need for American imports to facilitate rebuilding, there was also a patent inability to pay for them by exporting their own goods. Furthermore, although astute commentators recognized the stimulus to economic integration which recovery aid might provide, few believed in sustained collaboration without it.[34]

To counter allegations that it was principally designed to contain communism, the architects of the Marshall programme felt it tactically prudent to offer recovery aid on a pan-European basis. Clearly, though, the regional cooperation envisaged by Washington included only Western Europe. It was not expected that the Soviet Union would embrace Marshall Aid since, had it done so, Congress would have been extremely unlikely to have sanctioned it.[35] Predictably, Stalin refused to permit Poland or Czechoslovakia to participate in the programme and by 1949 had countered with a package of Soviet economic assistance to its satellite states – so-called Molotov Aid.

Whilst there was unquestionably more to American recovery aid than the containment of communism, it did constitute part of an emerging response to what citizens on both sides of the Atlantic viewed as a looming communist menace. Congress would not have approved it on any other basis; the same was equally true of the North Atlantic Treaty which incorporated Western Europe into a complementary security system. A leading proponent, Dean Acheson (who was strongly supported by Senator Vandenberg), described the treaty as 'the most important step in American foreign policy since the promulgation of the Monroe Doctrine'.[36] In Truman's view it represented another step towards achieving the military and economic strength necessary to negotiate with the Soviet Union as equals. In his daughter's opinion, experience had taught Truman that 'force – equality or superiority of force – was the only thing the Russians understood'.[37]

In essence, the North Atlantic Treaty of April 1949 and its derivative, the North Atlantic Treaty Organization (NATO), involved the US and Canada entering into a military arrangement for the mutual defence of Western Europe against communism. NATO, in short, formed part of the wider US design for the global combat of communism and signalled an American commitment of nuclear strength to Europe.

If the first Western security bloc proposal came during the war from a prescient General Smuts, who canvassed it as a counterpoise to the Soviet Union, the bulk of Western Europe in 1945 viewed a trans-Atlantic defence partnership as principally a means of containing any future resurgence of German militarism. In France in particular, the overriding objective of post-war foreign policy was security and the construction of a network of guarantees against her historic adversary. Accordingly, France vetoed all proposals to set up a centralized German authority, even the ministries of Finance, Communications and Foreign Trade provided for by the Potsdam agreement.[38] The thrust of the Anglo-French Treaty of Dunkirk in March 1947, providing for mutual defence, was also anti-German, its timing reflecting the growing French conviction that Franco-Soviet collaboration to curb Germany was already a dead letter.[39] Even the Brussels Treaty of March 1948, in which the Benelux countries adhered to the Dunkirk agreement, provided for collective protection against renewed German aggression although, significantly, the participants were already contemplating the need for adequate defence provision against the Soviet Union. Signed only a month after the Communist coup in Czechoslovakia, the Brussels Treaty was directed 'against any and all aggression', a turn of phrase suggested, it seems, by the US.[40]

It was the attritional Berlin blockade of 1948–9, however – in providing inescapable evidence of Western military weakness in Europe – that acted as the decisive spur to American involvement in a West European security system. The lopsided US-dominant character of the Euro-Atlantic relationship, however, owed more to circumstance than prior design. In effect, it was determined largely by the absence of any realistic alternative. Two concrete proposals canvassed in the US proved flawed and unworkable. The one, favoured by senior army strategists, argued for a build-up of Western military forces in Europe. This was effectively ruled out by the frailty of the regional economies and the political impossibility of rearming West Germany. Indeed, many considered the nascent Atlantic Alliance to be the real framework for containing Germany. It is doubtful, in any event, if Congress would have been willing to subsidize a build-up of US, still less West European, forces. The second proposal favoured a unilateral American guarantee to Western Europe, along the lines of the 19th-century Monroe Doctrine. This was not found convincing on either side of the Atlantic nor a likely credible deterrent against Soviet aggression.

Significantly, however, when the North Atlantic Treaty was signed, the US and West Europeans were not ready to envisage a structured and continuing Euro-Atlantic relationship. There was deep prejudice among sections of Congress about 'entangling alliances' and NATO was violently attacked by Senator Robert Taft (who was opposed to giving military assistance to Western Europe) and Forrest Donnell of Missouri, the latter because it might needlessly involve the US in war.[41] True, the very creation of NATO reflected a growing awareness of Cold War realities among both public and Congressional opinion. In 1947 neither the US nor Western Europe had been ready for a security alliance. But in its original conception – before the Korean War substantially altered things – the North Atlantic Treaty provided only a modest amount of conventional military aid. Rather, the aim was to neutralize the Soviet threat psychologically and counterbalance it militarily by placing the protection of Western Europe in the hands of US nuclear power. American nuclear strength, in short, was used in an explicitly political role, and relatively few Europeans appear to have objected to being taken under America's military wing.[42]

While the 'New Europe' which inspired Seton-Watson between the wars was a Europe of newly-created small states, the collapse of the German Reich led to a continent dominated by two superpowers – the US and the Soviet Union – and to a post-war Europe divided between their respective spheres of influence (see Table 4.2). The latter acted as magnetic fields, pulling the European states one way

Table 4.2   The Making of Cold War Europe

1946   (February) Winston Churchill's portentous 'Iron Curtain' speech in US.

1946   (December) United Nations (UN) recommended diplomatic boycott of Spain.

1947   (May) Italian Communists (PCI) excluded from governing coalition by Christian Democratic (DCI) leader, de Gasperi, under pressure from the Vatican and Washington.

1947   (July) US Marshall (reconstruction) Aid offered to Europe on a pan-continental basis.

1947   (September) Reorganization of the Lenin-founded Third International as the propagandist Cominform.

1947   (October) In the spirit of the Truman Doctrine, American intervention in Greece against Communist guerrillas.

1947   (November) Thorez called a revolutionary general strike in France, backed by the communist-controlled trade union federation CGT.

1948   (February) Communist coup in Prague, Czechoslovakia.

1948   (March) Soviet withdrawal from the Allied Control Council in Berlin.

1948   (April) Comfortable Christian Democratic victory in 'bridgehead' Italian general election.

1948   Stalin began the Berlin Blockade.

1948   (June) Tito's Yugoslavia broke with Moscow and Cominform.

1948   (June) 6 Western states, the US, UK, France and Benelux bloc announced their decision to create a new federal state of West Germany.

1949   (January) Foundation of the Soviet-controlled Council for Mutual Economic Assistance (COMECON).

1949   Molotov Aid offered to the East European 'satellite' states.

1949   (April) North Atlantic Treaty leads to the formation of NATO. The US and Canada entered a military alliance for the defence of Western Europe against Communism.

1949   (May) Stalin abandoned the blockade of landlines to Berlin.

1949   (September) Explosion of the first Soviet atomic bomb.

1950   First Soviet note to the West proposing a united, neutral but armed Germany.

1951   West Germany permitted its own foreign ministry.

1952   (March) Second Soviet proposal to establish a united Germany through free elections. It was to be non-aligned and outside NATO and the incipient Warsaw Pact.

1953   Death of Stalin.

1953   10-year US–Spanish treaty of military cooperation and economic assistance.

or the other. Thus, although Ireland, Sweden and Switzerland remained non-NATO neutrals, their basic 'Western' orientation was clearly reflected by participation in the Marshall Aid programme. Regional collaborative initiatives, independent of superpower networks, were unavailing and largely overtaken by events. For example, talks were mooted by Sweden on a Scandinavian Defence Union – a neutral but armed alliance pursuing a policy of non-involvement backed by the capacity to repel intrusion. Although gaining strong Danish support in January 1948, the talks collapsed a year later when Denmark and Norway opted for NATO and Finland signed a Treaty of Friendship, Cooperation and Mutual Assistance with the Soviet Union in April 1948.[43]

Of the post-war West European states, only Spain was beyond the diplomatic pale, so to speak, inasmuch as it was the only continental state which London and Paris excluded from the list of those invited to the Marshall Plan conference in July 1947. Attitudes towards Franco's authoritarian regime in Spain in fact pointed up clear differences between the US and her main West European allies, Britain and France. Immediately after the war, the Americans desired to maintain relations with Spain, not least to safeguard against the concealment of both Germans and German assets,[44] but on 12 December 1946 the newly-formed United Nations Organization recommended, and the US observed, a diplomatic boycott.

In 1948, however, Franco sent out his former foreign secretary, José Félix de Lequerica, to woo the Americans and on 30 March 1948 the House of Representatives voted by 149 to 52 to back an amendment proposed by O'Konski from Wisconsin to include Spain in the Marshall programme. Concerned that Western Europe should itself administer recovery aid, Truman insisted that the amendment be dropped, although as Max Gallo has observed, 'Franco could rest assured that the United States could no longer remain unfavourable to him. It was just that they could not yet show their favour openly.'[45] Certainly Republican Party delegates continued to canvass Spanish participation in the aid plan; they argued, too, that in view of its strong army, well-located airfields and strategic defence position – in addition to Franco's exemplary anti-communist record – Spain should form part of the emergent Western security system. When in October 1948, however, Senator Gurney, chair of the Senate Armed Services Committee, visited Franco and openly pronounced in support of renewed diplomatic relations, there were hostile reactions in London and Paris.[46]

The intensification of the Cold War worked to Franco's advantage and brought Spain some way in from the diplomatic cold. Thus when the explosion of a Soviet atomic bomb in September 1949 occasioned a reassessment of the strategic position, an increasing number of US politicians perceived the advantages to be gained from taking up

Franco's offer of bases. Interestingly, on 21 February 1949 the *New York Herald Tribune* referred to Spain as a country boasting law and order, in pleasant contrast to the industrial conflict afflicting France and Italy.[47] Formal negotiations on the establishment of US military bases commenced in 1951 and two years later a ten-year treaty of economic assistance and military cooperation was realized.[48] True, (essentially) left-wing opposition in Western Europe kept Spain out of NATO, but the American pact greatly strengthened her political and diplomatic position. By 1965 Washington had provided 1.8 billion dollars in military assistance.

Throughout Western Europe, the scale and scope of government grew after the Second World War as cabinets assumed responsibility for orchestrating reconstruction with the help of Marshall Aid. There was institutional recognition of this evolution of the state towards economic management in countries like Holland, with the revival of the 45-strong Social and Economic Council, first set up in 1919 – on which there was equal representation of government, industry and trade unions – [49] and France, with the creation in 1946 of the *Commissariat du Plan*, inspired by Jean Monnet's blueprint on indicative planning. Everywhere, moreover, rationing provided a daily reminder of increased government control. Times were hard for the peoples of Europe: on the western side of the Iron Curtain there was the risk that economic distress might nourish a subversive strain of political extremism.

'Imperialist' versus 'Anti-Imperialist' Europe

With the intensification of the Cold War in 1947–8, the existence of sizeable West European communist parties provided the Soviet Union with a strategic power base. Via the machinery of the old Third International (reorganized as the Cominform in September 1947), these parties were exhorted to exploit the conditions of economic dislocation in order to undermine capitalism and bourgeois democracy. The three states in the geographic periphery of pluralist democracy – the liberal democratic frontier stretching from Finland in the north, to Czechoslovakia in central Europe and to Italy in the south – seemed particularly vulnerable, since their communist parties represented both a significant electoral factor and a potential instrument of destabilization, once Stalin had opted for a subversive course.

Precisely how much of a threat Western European communism posed to the parliamentary democracies of the continent in the late 1940s must inevitably remain an open question, although three points warrant elaboration. First, there is evidence, especially in Italy, of an internal division within the communist movement between Tito-style revisionism (with a preference for a national route to communism) and hardline Stalinist loyalism (which supported the Cominform's revolutionary agenda). Second, it appears that in Finland there was a tactical split among the hardliners over the timing and, by extension, the viability of a planned armed coup. Finally, it is clear that American initiatives, both Marshall Aid which was particularly effective in France, and the Truman Doctrine implemented against the Communist guerrillas in Greece in 1947, enjoyed some success in countering the threat of West European communism.

By summer 1948, the balance sheet showed that one of these peripheral democracies (Czechoslovakia) had dipped into the red, so to speak, whilst the others remained, however precariously, in the (bourgeois) black. Czechoslovakia succumbed to a Communist coup in February 1948, followed by 20 years of neo-Stalinist authoritarianism under Anton Novotny. Accordingly, Austria (although subjected to a Four-Power Occupation until 1955) became the outpost of liberal democracy in central Europe and there communism made virtually no headway, even in the eastern Soviet zone. Finland survived the 'danger years'[50] including strong rumours of a Communist coup in April 1948. Following this the Communists entered an 18-year period in the political wilderness, finally broken by the attainment of a left-wing majority at the polls in 1966. Between 1966 and 1983, the Finnish Communists regularly participated in government in a way that was unique in Western Europe.

In Italy, the Communists (PCI) and Socialists (PSI), with a combined 31 per cent of the vote, were trounced by the Christian Democrats, who polled a record 48.8 per cent at a 'bridgehead' election in April 1948, watched by the Western world with a mixture of anxiety and apprehension. Truman insisted that the US would not tolerate a communist government in Italy. On 15 March 1948 the US State Department announced that all economic aid would stop if the Communist–Socialist alliance won the elections; Americans of Italian extraction were urged to write to their relatives in Italy to stress this very point. Elsewhere, the British Labour Party worked behind the scenes to support Giuseppi Saragat's group of breakaway socialists (shortly to become Social Democrats) who left Pietro Nenni's PSI over its policy of cooperation with the Communists. The combined left lost its position as the leading electoral force. Indeed, despite party secretary Enrico Berlinguer's efforts in the 1970s to engineer an 'historic compromise' between the Communists and Christians, the PCI has not participated in government since being evicted from power by the DCI prime minister, Alcide de Gasperi, at the behest of the US and Vatican in May 1947. Considering that Tito and Yugoslavia broke with Moscow the following year, it seemed that, by the beginning of

1949, Stalin's ideological offensive against the West was on the retreat.

In the vanguard of the underground resistance to fascism, it was as leading patriotic parties that the West European Communists prospered at the polls following the restoration of parliamentary democracy in 1945–6. This was something Stalin clearly recognized. Interviewed in *Pravda* on 13 March 1946, the Soviet leader observed that the Communists' influence had grown because they had demonstrated themselves to be 'trusty, fearless, self-sacrificing fighters against the fascist regimes for the liberty of the peoples'.[51] As such, the Communists achieved (often) unsurpassed results in the immediate post-war years, as the Scandinavian states demonstrate. In Denmark, the DKP, profiting from extensive Social Democratic defections, gained 12.5 per cent of the vote in October 1945, compared with 2.4 per cent in 1939;[52] in Norway, where future West German Chancellor, Willy Brandt, had been prominent in the resistance, the NKP polled 11.9 per cent in the same year as against a mere 0.3 per cent in 1936;[53] and even in neutral Sweden the Communists managed 10.3 per cent in 1944, the first and last time the party managed double figures. In Finland, the armistice with the Soviet Union in September 1944 led to the renewed legalization of the Communist Party which, operating as part of the front organization, the Finnish People's Democratic League (SKDL), gained 23.5 per cent of the vote in 1945; then, following defections from the Social Democrats, it became the largest parliamentary party shortly afterwards.[54]

After the war, the West European communist parties pursued a so-called 'Popular Front' strategy based on strengthening collaboration with the other 'progressive' forces – mainly Socialists and Christian Democrats – that had developed during the resistance. To achieve their aim of participating in government as a means of achieving desired objectives, they devised programmes to appeal to a broad spectrum of industrial workers, small farmers, small entrepreneurs, white-collar workers and intellectuals.[55] Significantly, in two of the West European frontier states, Finland and Italy (as well as in France), numerically strong communist parties were involved in tripartite coalitions between 1945 and 1947. In Finland, the triangular agreement drawn up in April 1945 between the Communists, Social Democrats and Agrarians was a rather bland document, since the Agrarians apparently succeeded in scotching the original commitment of the two leftist parties to nationalize the banks, insurance companies and large firms.[56] Similar friction between socialists and non-socialists meant that the record of tripartism in France and Italy was also not particularly impressive – especially in the field of economic management – although in both countries a new constitution was enacted during this period and, in France, some of the social provisions of the

Resistance Charters were implemented. But the main point is that post-war West European communism, in its pre-Cominform manifestation, worked to achieve radical change by cooperating in cabinet with other reformist groups. Indeed, Stalin's offensive against Western 'imperialist forces' (including social democracy), launched in September 1947, split the West European communist parties and, particularly in Italy, revealed the existence of strong 'collaborationist' tendencies.

Remarkably, although de Gasperi, the Christian Democratic leader, precipitated a crisis which led to the DCI's exclusion from office in May 1947, the Communists continued until 31 January 1948 to lend the government intermittent support from an opposition base in the Constituent Assembly. It could equally well have mobilized a well-equipped irregular army of about 170 000 guerrilla veterans against the parliamentary system.[57] After a very disappointing showing at the polls in April 1948, moreover,[58] the PCI still eschewed the 'irresponsible opposition' and 'politics of outbidding' which Giovanni Sartori (drawing on the Italian experience) has associated with 'anti-system' parties.[59] Even at the height of the Cold War between 1948 and 1953, the PCI voted against only one-third of the government's proposals.[60] As Donald Blackmer has noted: 'Beneath the aggressive facade of the Cold War, which obliged the PCI to attack the parliamentary illusions and foolish hopes of political alliances with non-socialist parties, the party was in fact struggling to keep alive the essence of its earlier strategy.'[61] When obliged to define its basic line, it simply asserted its continuing commitment to the struggle for peace and independence, the validity of the constitution and the need to promote the national economy and, by extension, workers' living standards.

It was in the field, however, that the PCI's split over its future strategy was perhaps most evident. The 1948 election defeat led Giorgio Amendola, who was responsible for the PCI's southern organization, to give support to a 'Movement for the Rebirth of the South' (which also included non-communist 'progressives') in an attempt to broaden the Communists' support base in the *Mezzogiorno*. This fundamentally 'popular front' strategy was vigorously opposed and ultimately overturned by Pietro Secchia, the PCI's deputy leader, who sought to sabotage it by sending a large number of cadres (*costruttori*) from the north and centre to the south to help create a 'Leninist organization' there.[62]

In the Finnish case, the split in the ranks did not so much align Tito-style revisionists favouring a national road to communism against hardline loyalists committed to 'anti-imperialism' as involve a disagreement among the hardliners themselves over the timing of armed revolution. Following alarmist rumours of a Communist coup, President Paasikivi put the army and the Helsinki police force on full alert in April 1948. If a coup was indeed planned, it proved stillborn, but three points would seem to be in order.

First, there were elements in the Finnish Communist Party between 1944 and 1948, the so-called 'rifle group' (*kiväärilinja*), along with a substantial number of grassroots members and supporters, who did favour the creation of a socialist state by revolutionary means and who were inspired by the developments that produced the Communist coup in Czechoslovakia in February 1948. Second, the line which officially prevailed was ultimately that counselled by those émigré Finnish communists who returned from Moscow after the armistice, among them Armas Äikiä, Inkeri Lehtinen and Tuure Lehén who had been 'ministers' in the puppet Finnish government which Stalin created in the Karelian border town of Terijoki shortly after the outbreak of the Winter War in November 1939.[63] They contended that attempted military action would provoke civil war – irrespective of the response of the army – and, as a corollary, the possible intervention of the Soviet Red Army with the obvious attendant risk to Finnish independence.[64] Third, there is an outside possibility that rumours of an impending coup signified an intended act of revenge on the part of the Communist Interior Minister, Yrjö Leino, who had lost favour with his own party and the Soviet Communists.[65] The Finnish Communists had evidently received a note from the Soviet party in March 1946 criticizing Leino for not rooting out 'fascists' from the police force and indicating their intention to remove him from office after the completion of the Treaty of Friendship, Cooperation and Mutual Assistance with the Soviet Union in April 1948. As in Italy, support for the Finnish Communists fell back at the polls in 1948, leading to the party's dismissal from government. In both cases, moreover, the Communist coup in Czechoslovakia in February 1948 did nothing to enhance their electoral cause.

Czechoslovakia had a good deal in common with Finland in the years preceding the Communist coup in February 1948. In both cases, an exposed geopolitical position in the direct firing line between fascism and communism had dictated the need for an uncompromising *realpolitik*. In 1943 the exiled Czech leader Beneš enlisted Soviet aid against a Nazi force which, ironically, four years earlier had established a 'protectorate' in Bohemia with Stalin's acquiescence (following the August 1939 Ribbentrop–Molotov Pact). In Finland, the sequence was reversed; in 1944, President Risto Ryti reluctantly enlisted Nazi aid against the Soviet Union in an attempt to reclaim those areas of Karelia lost in the Winter War of 1939–40. In the event, both countries ceded territory to the Soviet Union.

Both Czechoslovakia and Finland boasted a history of regular, free elections and stable multi-party politics between the wars and, accordingly, a tradition of pluralist democracy which could (and would) not easily be erased. Both states entered the post-war period headed by non-socialist presidents – Paasikivi (1946–56) in Finland and Beneš (1945–8) in Czechoslovakia – acutely aware that building relations of mutual trust with the Soviet Union was essential to their survival as independent nations. However, whilst for strategic reasons Finland declined the offer of Marshall Aid (though profiting indirectly from Swedish participation), Beneš made the serious tactical error in July 1947 of entering into negotiations on the Marshall programme; this Stalin refused to countenance.

Following free elections in 1945, moreover, both countries acquired communist or neo-communist prime ministers at the head of coalitions which contained non-communists. In Finland, Mauno Pekkala, a People's Democrat (formerly a Social Democrat) was by no means revolutionary at heart; Klement Gottwald, by contrast, was a hardliner loyal to Stalin.[66] Both states also had communists in the key post of Interior Minister. Leino received a parliamentary vote of no confidence on 22 May 1948 and, when dismissed by Paasikivi, proceeded to call for a 'revolutionary' general strike which proved unavailing. Nosek, however, consolidated his support among the Czech secret service by dismissing eight senior officials and replacing them with his own sympathizers. This in turn prompted the ruling National Socialist Party to demand that the prime minister rescind the dismissal order; when he refused, 12 non-communist ministers – though, significantly, not Social Democrats – resigned from office. This marked the first step in the Communist seizure of power.

Both states were involved in extensive resettlement programmes immediately after the war. In Czechoslovakia, sizeable parts of the Sudetenland were vacated following the expulsion of the ethnic German population; in Finland, new homes had to be found for the *exode* of Karelians dispossessed by the Winter War. The displaced Karelians were predominantly small farmers who had supported the Agrarian Party and retained their partisan allegiance when relocated on land partitioned from larger holdings in central-southern Finland. In Czechoslovakia, the Communists claimed credit for the expropriation of Sudeten German property and allocated the best land to those members of the Czech corps who had fought with the Red Army. However, the party was also active in recruiting support from among those (largely poor) southern Bohemians who had been enticed to take up holdings in the evacuated areas.[67]

Finally, in both states there was a marked decline in Communist support as the 1948 general elections approached. The Czech Communists had polled a notable 35 per cent in May 1945, trading off strong pro-Soviet sentiment (understandable in view of the Red Army's liberation of Prague) and equally strong anti-Western sentiment (understandable in light of the perceived 'sell-out' of the Anglo-French 'appeasement' policy). Less than three years later, however, the Communists seemed to be heading for defeat and loss of office. They clearly lost a modicum of support as a result of bearing responsibility for an exceptionally severe food crisis in 1947, along with Stalin's refusal to allow the Czechs the Marshall Aid that would have made a signal contribution to alleviating the situation.[68]

When the showdown came, two factors appeared decisive in the outcome. One, the Communists had actively targeted support in the trade unions, army and police and could also mobilize large numbers of workers (armed or otherwise) to back their bogus claims. Two, on 19 February 1948 there was a strategically-timed visit from the Soviet Deputy Foreign Secretary which was widely held to imply at least the possibility of Soviet intervention. Confirmation that the Czech coup was inspired by the Kremlin, albeit carefully planned in Prague, came with a vigorous smear campaign against 'Czech bourgeois reactionaries' in the Soviet press. On 23 February 1948 the police dispersed student demonstrations with gunfire and launched a series of attacks on the National Socialist Party leadership. The following day the Social Democratic Party headquarters were taken by force. By 25 February pressure on the reluctant Beneš had yielded all the important cabinet posts to the Communists except the foreign secretaryship which Jan Masaryk retained. On 10 March, however, he died in mysterious circumstances following a fall from his office balcony.

Summing up, the Communist take-over in Czechoslovakia in February 1948 had a seismic effect on Western opinion, ostracizing the Communists in the eyes of mainstream voters. The party's patriotic halo faded fast and increasingly communism became synonymous with the dark menace of Stalinist designs on Western Europe. The party systems of the region polarized into non-communist and communist forces and pivoted on a clearly demarcated pro-system, anti-system axis. Hard on the heels of the events in Prague, the Soviet destruction of the Allied Control Council in Germany in March 1948 served to reinforce anti-communist animosity among the broad mass of people. Three further factors also appear to have been salient in sustaining parliamentary democracy in Western Europe at this time.

First, there was the influence of American interventionism in the spirit of the Truman Doctrine. This hardened the anti-communist resolve of the other parties and largely dictated the timing of the Communists' removal from power. In Italy, for example, de Gasperi would probably have preferred to postpone a confrontation with the Communists, but in May 1947 succumbed to strong pressure from inside his party and from the Vatican and Washington to exclude them.[69]

Next, the Socialist majority dissociated itself from the destabilization strategy of the post-Cominform Communists and worked strictly within the constitutional rules of parliamentary democracy. When Maurice Thorez, using the instrument of the Communist-controlled trade union federation CGT, called a revolutionary general strike in France in November 1947 following the Communists' dismissal from government, it was firm action from the Socialist-led cabinet which did much to protect the embryonic Fourth Republic until Marshall Aid arrived. With rumours of a coup rife, the government recalled 80 000 men to the colours on 28 November to maintain order and plug gaps in vital sectors of the economy created by the walk-outs.[70]

Third, the post-war conditions of extreme economic hardship rendered a concerted working-class attempt to overthrow the system problematic. When Thorez called a strike in the coal mines in autumn 1948 in protest against the American recovery programme, over 80 per cent of the miners returned to work within two months simply because they could not afford to stay out any longer.

Incidentally, Tito's acrimonious break with Cominform in June 1948 was viewed as a significant breach in the united front of advancing communism and tended to confirm the impression that by 1949 the 'Red peril' had, at least temporarily, been halted. Tito's ambitious plans for the creation of a regional bloc of Communist states – a Balkan federation – beginning with the merger of Yugoslavia and Bulgaria, were clearly interpreted by Stalin as a challenge to his supremacy in Eastern Europe and he vetoed the project.[71] Yugoslavia was isolated from the Eastern bloc, subjected to a complete economic blockade by the Soviet Union and its satellites and prevented from joining the Council for Mutual Economic Assistance (COMECON) founded in January 1949.[72] When the Yugoslav leader was reluctantly obliged to turn to the West for commercial dealings, this was hailed as a significant rent in the Iron Curtain.

In several West European states, the economic reconstruction process was complemented by measures of political engineering designed to restore parliamentary democracy as a stable form of government. This task involved the search for constitutional structures that would facilitate policy-making, whilst protecting the political process from the extremism that had blighted its existence between the wars. There was, however, absolutely no guarantee that parliamentary democracy would succeed; ultimately, in fact, elite attitudes would be crucial to its consolidation. In France and Italy, where the immediate threat of communism had been repulsed, there were grounds for cautious optimism by 1949; in Germany, the other 'aborted democracy', the situation remained fluid.

Germany – a Microcosm of Cold War Europe

For really the first time since 1814, Germany had been devastated by war. However, the immediate fate of the principal vanquished power after the defeat of fascism was unique. It did not cease to exist as a result of annexation; nor was it obliged to accept terms stipulated by the victors whilst retaining its own government. Rather, Germany continued to exist but, by engaging in a joint military occupation, the victorious powers assumed both the internal and external sovereignty of the nation.[73]

It is doubtful if, when the hostilities ceased, either superpower had a clear conception of Germany's future, and certainly no serious thought was given to the option of partition. At Potsdam the Allies had agreed that Germany should be treated as a single economic and administrative unit during the occupation period and that, as far as possible, uniformity of treatment was to be accorded to all German peoples. In practice, the one tangible agreement at Potsdam concerning reparations – namely the agreement that, in addition to those in its own zone, the Soviet Union would be entitled to a further 10 per cent of the reparations taken by the Western Allies – implied the continued division of Germany. This is not to say that the reparations deal was explicitly designed to divide Germany; certainly, the American Secretary of State, James Byrnes, may well not have realized its significance in this regard.[74] Stalin paid lip-service to the need to treat Germany as a single economic unit (minus the territory and nine million Germans to the east of the Oder–Neisse line which he had arbitrarily transferred to Poland) since this enabled him to make reparation claims on the Western zones and would also facilitate a voice in future German arrangements, particularly in respect of his proposal for the internationalization of the Ruhr. But the differences separating the views of the Americans and British on the side and the Russians on the other were evident to both at Potsdam.

Ironically though, it was France, only recently readmitted to the Big Power fold and allocated only a small occupation zone, that scuppered the central machinery for managing a single German economy as envisaged by the Big Three at Potsdam.[75] In October 1945, France thus used her veto in the Allied Control Council to defeat a proposal to create five central administrative departments, insisting that the Rhine and Ruhr (which she wished to see dismembered from Germany) should not fall within the purview of a central bureaucracy. In de Porte's judgement, this represented a missed opportunity – probably the best, possibly the only realistic opportunity – for the war-time Allies to work towards the creation of a united, neutral Germany.[76] Certainly although the British in particular had initially favoured promoting a single German economy and encouraged cross-zonal trade, there was growing impatience by early 1946 with the lack of consensus among the occupying powers on how the Potsdam formula on economic unity was to be implemented. On the British side, indeed, at least three factors militated towards an early acceptance of the East–West division of Germany as permanent and the adoption of a policy of working to integrate the Western zones.

First, there was the impossible financial burden involved in supplying the British zone indefinitely. The British zone, which included the Ruhr, was highly industrialized, urbanized and overpopulated, produced barely half its own food before the war and could not survive except as part of a larger economic entity. Second, there were obvious humanitarian considerations and the need for action to counter the prevalent hunger and despair. In March 1946, for example, the ration of daily calories was cut to a mere 1015 in the British zone. Finally, there was the political need to develop a model for stable Western-style democracy to convince the Germans that their future did not lie in the embrace of the Soviet Communists.[77]

A significant change in the American mood can be dated to the Paris meeting of the Council of Foreign Ministers in May 1946 at which Molotov avoided a definitive response to a US draft treaty proposing a four-power, 25-year guarantee of German demilitarization. Byrnes' reaction was to quicken the pace by stating that, until the other powers were prepared to treat Germany as a single economic unit, the US would suspend further deliveries of reparations. Behind the scenes, the US mooted the idea of merging the British and American zones;[78] the subsequent bizonal agreement, approved by the Attlee government on 25 July 1946, entailed a three-year plan to make West Germany self-sufficient by the end of 1949.[79] By September 1946, moreover, the US had openly committed itself to the expeditious establishment of a provisional West German government, had repudiated any notion of hiving off the Rhine and Ruhr and had stated categorically that, as long as there was an occupation army in Germany, American forces would be part of it.[80] During 1947, moreover, it was clear that US/UK cooperation would proceed with or without the dilatory French.

The Communist coup in Czechoslovakia in February 1948 and the Russian withdrawal from the Allied Control Council the following month, however, convinced the French Foreign Office that France could no longer resist Anglo-American plans to create a West German government ('trizonia'). By the end of April 1948 a comprehensive set of proposals was ready for ministerial assent. In June 1948, after further French hesitation,[81] six Western states – the US, UK, France and Benelux countries – announced their decision to establish a federal West Germany and, shortly afterwards, introduced currency reform to consolidate the economic recovery of the embryonic state.

The Soviet reaction was to proceed with a currency reform not only in its zone, but also in the whole of Berlin which, because of its location (it was argued), constituted the focal point of the economy of the region. When the Allies introduced the new West German currency, the *Deutschmark*, into West Berlin – though ostensibly designed to complement rather than replace the eastern currency, the *Ostmark* – the stage was set for the Berlin blockade.

The Berlin blockade could well have led to a Third World War; instead, it became a cameo of the wider Cold War confrontation developing between the capitalist and communist worlds and contributed significantly to the final East–West division of Germany in 1949. The blockade began in June 1948 when Stalin ordered the closure of all road and rail links between the Western zones of Berlin and the incipient West German state. The retaliatory Allied airlift ensured that the Western areas of the city received adequate food, raw materials and fuel at a time when, at the beginning of the operation, stocks in the Western sectors were sufficient to provide food for no more than 36 days and coal for the power stations for no more than 45. It was a massive undertaking. In all, the airlift supplied two and a half million people for 11 months with a daily average which rose from 1404 (American) tons in June to 4641 in September and, courtesy of an extremely mild winter, 5436 the following February. By April 1949, loads reached 7845 tons a day.[82]

The airlift was a triumph of Anglo-American collaboration – the British contributed one-third of the flights – although it seems that Foreign Secretary Bevin played a notable early role in stiffening the resolve of those wavering politicians in Washington who instinctively preferred a policy of non-involvement, whilst at the same time containing the bellicosity of such key US militarists as General Lucius Clay who wanted to bludgeon his way up the *autobahn* to Berlin. Indeed, in Bevin's view, the cause of intermittent tension between the two partners during the course of the protracted airlift was the American tendency to want to bring the Berlin issue to a head and to rush things.[83] In return for American participation, US B29 bombers carrying atomic bombs were allowed bases in the UK. Since the Soviet Union was prevented from exploiting its military superiority on land by the US nuclear supremacy in the air, the Berlin blockade became a battle of nerves which tested Western resolve to the limit. The nature of the stakes in this trial of strength, however, was well captured by Bevin when he insisted that 'the abandonment of Berlin would mean the loss of Western Europe'.[84]

Events in the autumn of 1948 served further to consolidate the division of Berlin. The Soviet authorities and their instrument, the Socialist Unity Party (SED), instigated a campaign of intimidation and physical violence against the civilian population in the city. In

September the Berlin city council was dispersed when Communist crowds stormed the *Stadthaus* (located in the Soviet sector), obliging the Social Democratic-led body (elected in October 1946) to remove to the Western zones. When, shortly afterwards, the Soviet flag was ripped down from the Brandenburg Gate following a mass meeting at which speakers denounced the Communist attempt to impose its will on Berlin, Russian troops fired into the crowd. The situation appeared to be escalating to the point at which the occupying forces would be engaged in open hostilities.[85] Elections for a new Berlin Council were fixed for 5 December, but on 30 November the Communists rallied their support at the city opera house, voted the old (All-Berlin) council out of existence and replaced it with a new one dominated by Communists. Although the SPD won a comfortable victory in the Western zones, Walter Reuter assumed the office of mayor in a deeply divided city. Ultimately, only a matter of days after the West German Constituent Assembly had completed its work in May 1949, the Russians called off the blockade. The two Germanies had become a reality.[86]

Much has subsequently been made of a Soviet proposal in March 1952 (expanded in May the same year) to establish a pan-German government through free elections and to rearm the reunified German state outside the two security systems, NATO and the Warsaw Pact (the latter was formalized in May 1955). Stalin's Warsaw Programme of June 1948 had contained essentially the same proposal.[87] However, whilst conceding that Stalin's 1952 blueprint for a neutral, but united and armed, Germany was perhaps not given the attention it deserved either in West Germany or by the Western Allies, Walter Laqueur insists that its primary intention was to retard the progress of the Federal German Republic (West Germany) towards political, economic and military integration with the West.[88] It was undoubtedly interpreted in the West as a Soviet attempt to destroy the European Defence Community (EDC) scheme which was ready for signing and would incorporate a rearmed West Germany. The Soviet proposal was consequently dismissed.[89] Laqueur adds that, since there is no evidence that Stalin ever seriously considered dispensing with the Ulbricht regime in the German Democratic Republic (GDR), his proposal on German unity is unlikely to have been genuine. Had there been any substance behind it, he concludes, the idea would have been reintroduced in modified form at a subsequent date, but it never was.[90]

Although US policy towards Germany was not clearly formulated in 1945, it became apparent by the Paris meeting of Foreign Ministers in May 1946 that the Americans were not willing to contemplate the creation of a united Germany under conditions that would be conducive to its domination by the Soviet Union. The US, backed by Bevin and the British, would in no circumstances risk leaving the door open to the *Finlandisierung* of Germany – that is, the process of 'adaptive acquiescence' to Soviet pressure leading to an erosion of sovereignty and a reduction in status to that of a Soviet puppet regime.[91] In short, partition of the country and the historic capital, Berlin, was seen in the West as the only realistic solution in the circumstances and as a by-product of Cold War antagonisms. A representative view is that of Laqueur; 'With the outbreak of the Cold War, the division of Germany became an established fact. It is impossible to point to any single event which made it final; the Prague coup, the Berlin blockade and the elimination of non-communist parties and their leaders in Eastern Europe all hastened it.'[92]

An alternative 'revisionist' interpretation, however, holds that it followed from the premise that a united Germany should not be exposed to the risk of Soviet domination, that a necessary condition of unification was the incorporation of Germany as an integral element into a united Europe. The US, it is held, failed to perceive the essential connection between German integration and wider European integration. More specifically, four substantive propositions lie at the heart of the revisionist critique of American post-war foreign policy.

First, there is the charge that the West spurned opportunities to unite Germany and so forced Stalin's hand in East Germany and Eastern Europe. Much would doubtless be made in this context of the French veto in the Allied Control Council in October 1945 of the central economic machinery proposed for managing Germany as a single unit; of Bevin's rebuttal of Molotov's plan for a united German state outlined at a Foreign Ministers' meeting on 10 July 1946; and particularly of the Allied failure to respond to Stalin's 1952 proposal for a neutral, united and armed Germany.

Second, there is the claim that the Truman administration's policy of containment of the Soviet Union together with its commitment to restore the economic and military strength of the West as a means of achieving that goal ultimately led it to lose sight of the supreme objective – the peaceful conclusion of the Cold War. From as early as 1945, it has been argued, Truman was biding his time, waiting for the opportunity to fire the type of broad anti-communist salvo subsequently contained in the Truman Doctrine of March 1947.[93] Active intervention against revolutionary change, it has further been contended, characterized US policy well before the Truman Doctrine and was anchored not only in 'dollar diplomacy' – the search for raw materials and markets – but also a 'moral mission' to stamp out political heresy.[94]

Third, it is alleged that the US and her Western Allies misunderstood Stalin's fundamental conservatism and pragmatism as well as his acute awareness of Russian weakness. Thus, whilst the traditional view emphasizes the fact that by the end of the war the Red Army had reached a line running from Lübeck to the Adriatic and was only prevented from moving into Denmark by the British under Montgomery,[95] the alternative perspective emphasizes how Russia was limited in both its objectives and means in the immediate post-war months. The Soviet Union did not attempt to interfere with the Berlin airlift, it is maintained, and ended the blockade when it was overtaken by events.[96]

Finally, it is argued that the establishment of two Germanies and the incorporation of the Federal Republic into the Western security system served to legitimize the presence of Soviet troops in Eastern Europe. Ultimately, the West came to have a vested interest in tolerating the post-war division of Germany and Europe as an alternative infinitely preferable to a military showdown with the Soviet Union.[97]

Whilst not enough is known about post-war Soviet policy towards Germany to determine how great an opportunity was missed, it is extremely doubtful whether the emergence of a united, neutral and non-communist Germany could have formed part of a Europe united in any significant sense of the term. More likely, a united Germany would have comprised at best part of a wedge of neutral states, along with Austria and Finland, that would have served as a 'Cordon Stalinaire' between Soviet Europe and the West and, for geopolitical reasons, would have been subject to extensive Soviet influence.

Plainly US policy contributed in a measure to, rather than being simply a reflection of, the divisions that quickly surfaced between the victorious Allies. Interestingly, however, by the time of Marshall's recovery aid speech in June 1947, enlightened opinion in Britain (not to mention politicians and military strategists) clearly perceived the deep division which already cut Europe into two. In a discerning article in July 1947, entitled 'Towards a United Europe?', Freda Bruce Lockhart expressed considerable doubt whether receipt of Marshall Aid could be extended much beyond the Western bloc. 'Europe today *is* arbitrarily divided,' she concluded, 'and the recent Soviet moves in Hungary, Romania, Bulgaria, Poland, Austria and Slovakia to reinforce the rigid structures of the Eastern bloc [by creating satellite states] have emphasised the impossibility of obtaining Soviet co-operation in a United Europe.'[98]

Both at the time of the Berlin blockade and throughout the subsequent Cold War years, however, there were ordinary citizens in the West who retained loyalty to the Soviet Union as a war-time ally. There was, for example, the father of the poet and literary critic, Jacques Darras. Darras' father fought in the infantry in 1940, was demobbed by Pétain, later arrested by the local Pétainist mayor and, as a prisoner of war, was sent to a German labour camp in Silesia. At the end of the fighting, Darras' camp was behind Russian lines and it was the Red Army that liberated him.[99] 'Liberator', to be sure, quickly turned into oppressor: it was the *de facto* control of much of Eastern Europe by the Red Army which the Western Allies felt so powerless to challenge and which contributed much to shaping the capitalist–communist division of Europe after the Second World War.

Notes

1 Resistance leaders meeting in July 1944.
2 Henry Pelling (1974), *Winston Churchill*, London: Macmillan, p.565.
3 John H. Backer (1978) *The Decision to Divide Germany: American Foreign Policy in Transition*, Durham, N.C.: Duke University.
4 Alpo M. Rusi (1991), *After the Cold War*, New York–Prague: Macmillan, p.12.
5 Rudolph A. Winnacker (1969), 'Yalta – Another Munich?', in Robert A. Divine (ed.), *Causes and Consequences of World War II*, Chicago: Quadrangle Books, pp.237–48. In fact, Winnacker's analysis is generally sympathetic to Roosevelt.
6 Ibid., p.241.
7 G.F. Hudson (1969), 'The Lesson of Yalta' in Divine, op. cit., pp.225–36.
8 Winnacker (1969), op. cit., p.239.
9 Geoffrey Cox (1988), *Countdown to War: A Personal Memoir of Europe 1938–40*, London: William Kimber, pp.139–53. Also, Martti Julkunen (1975), *Talvisodan kuva: Ulkomaisten sotakirjeenvaihtajien kuvaukset suomesta 1939–40*, Helsinki: Weilin & Göös, pp.62–76.
10 Winnacker (1969), op. cit., p.240.
11 Iceland had been a sovereign state in personal union with Denmark since 1918 (when it received its own national flag) and largely autonomous since 1914. Sigurdur A. Magnusson (1977), *Northern Sphinx: Iceland and the Icelanders from the Settlement to the Present*, London: Hurst, pp.139–41.
12 Stalin wanted *inter alia* Poland to be expanded westwards at Germany's expense; Austria to be restored; the Rhineland and possibly Bavaria to be detached from Germany; the Baltic states to be recovered; and the right to establish bases in Finland and Romania. William Lafeber (ed.) (1971), *The Origins of the Cold War 1941–47*, New York: John Wiley, pp.36–40.
13 Lois Pattison de Ménil (1977), *Who Speaks for Europe? The Vision of Charles de Gaulle*, London: Weidenfeld & Nicolson, p.29.
14 Thus Winnacker has remarked that: 'To accomplish the proposed political objective of liberating the border states in Eastern Europe, final success would have had to be achieved before October 1944. At that time, Soviet troops were outside Warsaw and in control of most of Romania and Bulgaria. It is doubtful that the Western powers could have met this time schedule' (Winnacker (1969), op. cit., p.247).
15 David Carlton (1981), *Anthony Eden: A Biography*, London: Allen Lane, p.253.
16 Ibid., pp.225–32, 245–7; 251–8.
17 Lord Moran (1966), *Churchill: The Struggle for Survival 1940–65*, London: Constable, pp.199–200.
18 Stanislav Mikolayczyk (1948), *The Pattern of Soviet Domination*, Maston: Sampson Low, pp.104–13.
19 André Fontaine (1965), *History of the Cold War*, London: Secker & Warburg, p.327.
20 *Chronik der Deutschen* (1982), Dortmund: Chronik Verlag, p.935. The CDU revived in Berlin in May 1945 and was not affected by the East–West split until December 1947. Wulf Schönbohm (ed.) (1980), *Programm und Politik der Christlich*

Demokratischen Union Deutschlands seit 1945, Bonn: CDU-Bundesgeschäftsstelle, pp.18–22.

21 Keith Sainsbury (1986), *The Turning Point*, Oxford: Oxford University Press, pp.15, 24, 27–8, 45.

22 Ibid., 83–8.

23 Ibid., p.89.

24 Ibid., p.48.

25 Ibid., p.90.

26 Fontaine (1965), op. cit., p.346.

27 A.W. DePorte (1979), *Europe between the Superpowers*, New Haven and London: Yale University Press, p.133.

28 Roy Jenkins (1974), *Nine Men of Power*, London: Hamish Hamilton, pp.77–8.

29 Alan Bullock (1983), *Ernest Bevin: Foreign Secretary 1945–51*, London: Heinemann, p.415.

30 Quoted in Michael White and Will Hutton, 'An altruism fuelled by fear', *The Guardian*, 2 September 1991, p.21.

31 Harry S Truman (1956), *Years of Trial and Hope: Memoirs*, Volume 2, New York: Signet, p.144.

32 Ibid., pp.138–43 which describes the content of Truman's message to Congress on 19 December 1947 in which he sets out the part the US should play in a European recovery plan.

33 Richard L. Watson Jr. (1965), *The United States in the Contemporary World 1945–62*, New York: Free Press, p.62.

34 Freda Bruce Lockhart (1947), 'Towards a United Europe?', *The Nineteenth Century and After*, July, 14.

35 In any event, at a foreign ministers' conference in Moscow in April 1947, Marshall discovered that his audience 'was coldly determined to exploit the helpless condition of Europe to further communism rather than co-operate with the rest of the world' (Fontaine (1965), op. cit., p.327).

36 Margaret Truman (1979), *Harry S Truman*, London: Hamish Hamilton, p.406.

37 Ibid., p.407.

38 As de Gaulle noted in his *Memoirs*: 'The abolition of a centralised Reich. This, in my opinion, was the first condition necessary to prevent Germany from returning to its bad ways.' Cited in de Ménil (1977), op. cit., p.327.

39 During an eight-day trip to Moscow in December 1944, de Gaulle had sought (and reached) a bilateral agreement with Stalin on Germany which, he hoped, would afford him extra diplomatic leverage in dealing with England and the US. In the wider historical perspective, he was also searching for reassurances against the possibility of future 'Rapallos'. However, it quickly became apparent that the 1944 Franco-Soviet defence treaty was stillborn. DePorte (1979), op. cit., p.138; de Ménil (1977), op. cit., pp.26–31. On the Dunkirk Treaty, see Duff Cooper (1954), *Old Men Forget*, London: Hart-Davis, pp.374–84.

40 Fontaine (1965), op. cit., p.356.

41 Margaret Truman (1979), op. cit., p.406.

42 DePorte (1979), op. cit., p.140.

43 Neil Elder, Alastair Thomas and David Arter (1982), *The Consensual Democracies? The Government and Politics of the Scandinavian States*, Oxford: Martin Robertson, pp.205–6.

44 J.W.D. Trythall (1970), *Franco: A Bibliography*, London: Rupert Hart-Davis, p.201.

45 Max Gallo (1973), *Spain Under Franco*, London: George Allen & Unwin, p.185. It seems that at the very time he was opposing Spanish involvement in the Marshall Plan, Truman hinted to Martin Artajo, the Spanish foreign minister, that the American government would have no objection to Spain receiving a loan from private American banks.

46   Bullock (1983), op. cit., p.619.

47   Gallo (1973), op. cit., pp.188–9.

48   Although this did not constitute an official military alliance at the NATO level, it provided for the construction of three major Strategic Air Command bases in Spain under joint Hispano-American sovereignty, a large US naval base on the south Spanish coast and sizeable economic aid for both the armed forces and the domestic economy. See Stanley G. Payne (1968), *Franco's Spain*, London: Routledge & Kegan Paul, p.38.

49   D. Coombes and S. Walkland (1980), *Parliaments and Economic Affairs*, London: Heinemann, pp.193–5.

50   More than 400 organizations were proscribed in accordance with Article 21 of the 1944 Armistice. A senior National Coalition (Conservative Party) figure has revealed how he felt the Communists would willingly have worked to include his party on the list of banned organizations. Hannu Rautkallio (1978), 'Kokoomuksen kujanjouksu', *Suomen Kuvalehti*, **49**, 8 December, 70–74.

51   Lafeber (1971), op. cit., p.143. In France, where after the Constituent Assembly elections in October 1945 they became the largest party, the Communists had been the most cohesive of the many resistance groups, although their principal organization, *Front National*, kept itself to itself. Particularly in the rural areas, the Communists were the sole resistance fighters during the Occupation. They also enjoyed much success in recruiting from the ranks of organized labour. H.R. Kedward (1985), *Occupied France*, Oxford: Basil Blackwell, p.57.

52   In Denmark, which Hitler overran in 24 hours, the Communist Party was banned during the Occupation. Although many of its active members were imprisoned, others eluded the authorities to work tirelessly in the resistance movement – the Communist organ *Land og Folk* was first published illegally in 1941 – and it was as a leading resistance party that the DKP was represented on the Danish Council of Liberation (*Danmarks Frihedsråd*) and the subsequent Liberation Cabinet. 'Udrensning hos kommunisterne', *Nordisk Kontakt*, 2/90, 24–6.

53   Willy Brandt (1978), *People and Politics*, London: Collins, pp.164–5. Willy Brandt (1971); *In Exile: Essays, Reflections and Letters 1933–1947*, London: Oswald Wolff, pp.159–99.

54   Mauno Pekkala, an SKDL member, became prime minister of a broad left-centre Government of National Unity in March 1945 although, according to a long-serving Agrarian minister, he was 'a patriot and far too indolent to effect a revolution!' David Arter (1978b), 'All-Party Government for Finland?', *Parliamentary Affairs*, **XXXI** (1), 73.

55   John Logue (1982), *Socialism and Abundance: Radical Socialism in the Danish Welfare State*, Minneapolis: University of Minnesota Press, p.75.

56   Pentti Sorvali (1975), *Niukkasesta Kekkoseen*, Helsinki: Kirjayhtymä, p.212.

57   Wolfgang Berner (1979), 'The Italian Left, 1944–1978: Patterns of Co-operation, Conflict and Compromise', in William E. Griffith (ed.), *The European Left: Italy, France and Spain*, New York: D.C. Heath, p.18.

58   François Borella (1979), *Les partis politiques dans l'Europe des Neuf*, Paris: Editions du Seuil, pp.158–9.

59   Giovanni Sartori (1990), 'A Typology of Party Systems', in Peter Mair (ed.), *The West European Party System*, Oxford: Oxford University Press, pp.331–5.

60   Donald L.M. Blackmer (1975), 'Continuity and Change in Post-War Italian Communism', in Donald L.M. Blackmer and Sidney Tarrow (eds), *Communism in Italy and France*, Princeton: Princeton University Press, p.49.

61   Ibid., pp.47–8.

62   Grant Amyot (1981), *The Italian Communist Party*, London: Croom Helm, pp.47–8.

63 Hertta Kuusinen (1984), 'Viimeinen valovoimainen kommunisti', *Suomen Kuvalehti*, **21**, 25 April, 76–8.

64 Lauri Haataja (1985), 'Tie helvettiin on laskettu ns objektiivisilla tekijöillä', second part, *Suomen Kuvalehti*, **28**, 12 July, 29.

65 'Oliko kaappaushuhu Leinon kosto?', *Helsingin Sanomat*, 17 January 1986, p.13.

66 As the foreign editor of *Le Monde* noted at the time: 'He could be moderate or fierce as the Soviet interest demanded'. Fontaine (1965), op. cit., pp.341–2.

67 Jan Sejma, a high-ranking Communist who defected to the West in 1968, has related how, having got a house and farm in the evacuated Sudeten area, he was approached to join the party. 'We filled in our application form for membership, my father with some misgiving,' Sejma notes. 'However, he duly hung a portrait of Stalin on the wall to join those we already had of Christ, the Madonna and President Beneš.' Jan Sejma (1984), *We Will Bury You*, London: Sidgwick & Jackson, p.16.

68 The pretext for the coup came when all the non-communists, except the Social Democrats, resigned from Gottwald's cabinet over Nosek's dismissal of senior secret service officials. The Communists, using typically extremist rhetoric, accused the bourgeois parties of working systematically to replace Gottwald's government with one of a reactionary, anti-democratic character.

69 Berner (1979), op. cit., p.18.

70 Fontaine (1965), op. cit., p.337.

71 Ibid., pp.345–7.

72 Bullock (1983), op. cit., p.700. The Soviet Union also withdrew its support on the question of Trieste and Yugoslavia's claims against Austria.

73 Alfred Grosser (1964), *The Federal Republic of Germany: A Concise History*, New York: Praeger, pp.3–4.

74 Bullock (1983), op. cit., pp.28–9.

75 France was invited to join the European Advisory Commission (Anthony Eden's brainchild) in November 1944 – it was this body that agreed the zones of occupation – but was not represented at Potsdam, although assigned a small occupation zone and, by extension, a seat on the Allied Control Council.

76 DePorte (1979), op. cit., pp.144–6.

77 The British foreign secretary, Ernest Bevin, certainly recognized that the danger from Russia was at least as great as from a revived Germany and that the worst possible scenario would be 'a revived Germany in league with or dominated by Russia'. Bevin ultimately favoured the reconstitution of Germany as a loose federation with a central administration handling only such matters as were necessary for economic unity. He believed this was the best safeguard against the Communists extending their power if they gained control of the centre. Bullock (1983), op. cit., pp.265–8.

78 Ibid., pp.269–71, 282–3.

79 Agreements setting up five bizonal agencies were signed during autumn 1946. Both the US and UK were anxious to avoid any suggestion of a political union between zones which might obstruct a provisional pan-German government. Accordingly, the five agencies were established in different cities and no coordinating agency was created in case it might be mistaken for an embryonic government. A bizonal legislature was not set up either.

80 Bullock (1983), op. cit., p.309.

81 The governing Socialists (SFIO) favoured another approach to Stalin, whilst Bidault and the Catholic MRP were concerned about an adverse reaction from de Gaulle and the Communists. Bullock (1983), op. cit., pp.565–7.

82 P. Brogan (1990), *Eastern Europe 1939–1989: The Fifty Years War*, London: Bloomsbury, pp.24–6.

83 Bullock (1983), op. cit., p.634.

84   Ibid., p.588.
85   Ibid., p.593.
86   Michael Freund (1972), *From Cold War to Ostpolitik: Germany and The New Europe*, London: Oswald Wolff, pp.27–33.
87   Bullock (1983), op. cit., pp.692–3.
88   Walter Laqueur (1969), *Russia and Germany: A Century of Conflict*, London: Weidenfeld & Nicolson, p.277.
89   De Porte (1979), op. cit., pp.162–3.
90   Laqueur (1969), op. cit., pp.277–8.
91   Hans Mouritzen (1988), *Finlandisation: Towards a General Theory of Adaptive Politics*, Aldershot: Avebury, p.2.
92   Laqueur (1969), op. cit., p.277.
93   David Horowitz (1967), *From Yalta to Vietnam: American Foreign Policy in the Cold War*, London: Penguin, pp.70–78.
94   Gar Alperovitz (1970), *Cold War Essays*, New York: Anchor, pp.35–50.
95   Bullock (1983), op. cit., p.19.
96   Horowitz (1967), op. cit., p.79.
97   Rusi (1991), op. cit., pp.12–17.
98   Lockhart (1947), op. cit., 13.
99   Jacques Darras and Daniel Snowman (1990), *Beyond the Tunnel of History*, London: Macmillan, p.72.

5

A Region of Europe or a Western Europe of Regions? Post-War Integration, 1945–60

The name Europe distinguishes a continent or a civilisation, not an economic or political unit. ... The European idea is empty; it has neither the transcendence of Messianic ideologies nor the immanence of concrete patriotism. It was created by intellectuals and that fact accounts at once for its genuine appeal to the mind and its feeble echo in the heart.

Raymond Aron, *The Century of Total War* (Doubleday, 1954), p.313

Post-war conditions appeared conducive to the promotion of supranational cooperation, and significant progress was indeed made towards the economic integration of Western Europe in the 15 years after the collapse of the German *Reich*. In this, the Benelux states showed the way. The decision to pool their resources in a single economic unit, taken by the exiled governments of Belgium, Holland and Luxembourg, was implemented in 1946; two years thereafter, customs duties were abolished and a common external tariff instituted. The Benelux countries also established a small customs union within the wider customs bloc formed by the European Economic Community (EEC) which the 'Six' – the Benelux group plus France, West Germany and Italy – set up under the Treaty of Rome in March 1957. This Common Market marked a significant advance in the march of sectoral integration, following the first successful step taken in 1951 with the creation of a European Coal and Steel Community (ECSC).

Britain played at best a reactive, at worst a reactionary, role in the development of West European economic integration at this time. The British proposal for launching a West European Free Trade Area (WFTA) in 1957 was thus largely designed to sabotage the efforts of the Six, its failure resulting in an institutionalized division of Western

Europe into an 'inner Six' and 'outer Seven' (Britain, Norway, Denmark, Sweden, Switzerland, Portugal and Austria). Accordingly, the two Europes of East and West, defined and dictated by the Cold War, were augmented by two Western Europes – one based on the Common Market and the other on the European Free Trade Association (EFTA). In short, progress in integration spawned division and there were those, particularly in the US, who feared that an economic iron curtain had descended across Western Europe (see Table 5.1).

Table 5.1   West European Integration, 1945–60

1946   Benelux states created single economic unit.
1947   Formation of Uniscan as a deliberative forum for the British and Scandinavians.
1948   (April) Formation of the Organization for European Economic Cooperation (OEEC).
1949   (May) Foundation of the Council of Europe.
1950   West Germany admitted to the Council of Europe.
1950   (September) Creation of a European Payments Union (EPU).
1950   Start of Korean War. Invasion of South Korea by Communist government in North Korea.
1951   (March) Creation of the European Coal and Steel Community (ECSC).
1952   Formation of the Nordic Council.
1954   (August) European Defence Community (EDC) treaty ditched by the French National Assembly.
1955   (May) Agreement on a Western European Union (WEU) came into force.
1955   (July) US–Soviet summit at Geneva led to full Austrian independence.
1955   (October) Saar plebiscite. Overwhelming majority against severance from West Germany.
1956   (July) Egyptian President, Colonel Nasser, nationalized the Suez Canal.
1956   (October) Anglo-French invasion of Suez.
1956   (October) Soviet troops crushed Hungarian uprising in Budapest.
1957   British proposal for a West European Free Trade Area (WFTA).
1957   (March) Treaty of Rome created the European Economic Community (EEC) and European Atomic Energy Community (Euratom).
1958   De Gaulle became President of the new Fifth French Republic.
1959   (November) Stockholm Convention created European Free Trade Association (EFTA).

Several factors appeared *prima facie* to militate in favour of a climate of unity in Western Europe after the Second World War. First, Marshall Aid provided the resources with which to reconstruct the West European economies, while the establishment in April 1948 of the supervisory Organization for European Economic Cooperation (OEEC) appeared to offer a valuable institutional framework within which to further regional collaboration. The OEEC encased the West European recipients of Marshall Aid in much the same way as Molotov Aid was designed to cement together the East European 'satellite' states.

Second, the US was ready to 'invest' in building a stable, prosperous and united Western Europe, not least so as to enable the region to participate fully in the global trading system and thereby to close the 'dollar gap' (in the late 1940s, the dollar was the only acceptable international currency). In Washington, economic cooperation among the West European states was viewed as a *sine qua non* for regional recovery. Accordingly, at the Marshall Plan negotiations, the Americans urged the creation of a European Customs Union and, when this was rebuffed, they pressed for the establishment of area customs unions along the lines of the Benelux association of 1946. It has been argued that for the Americans involved in the Marshall Plan 'the goal was to refashion Western Europe in the image of the United States' and part of that image involved the formation of a large single market. William Diebold Jr., however, is careful to scotch allusions to the Americans possessing 'mega-designs' for Western Europe and instead emphasizes the acceptability of incremental gains in the supranational field. He adds that thoughtful Americans knew that whatever was to be lasting in European integration would have to be achieved by the Europeans themselves.[1]

Third, 'Europeanism', which at a minimal level may be defined as the commitment to move progressively towards West European unity, provided the region with both a cause and a counterpoise to the threat of Soviet imperialism. As a contemporary American diplomat insisted, the achievement of progressively greater West European unity became an ideology in a way in which 'Atlanticism', for all its importance, never did.[2] Europeanism also provided a valuable extramural focus for the constitutional (pro-system) parties of Western Europe in their struggle against internal communism – a struggle given immediacy by the Communist coup in Prague in February 1948.

In the last-mentioned context, the Council of Europe, founded on 5 May 1949 and which by the end of 1950 comprised 15 member-states, created what Jean Monnet described as a 'European climate' and became the inspiration for much of Europe's thinking about Europe.[3] Hence it was in the Consultative Assembly of the Council of Europe that the Schuman Plan, the European Defence Community and the European Political Community proposals (all discussed later in this chapter) were first officially formulated. As the Dutch foreign secretary noted at its seventh session in July 1955: the Council of Europe is 'the centre and framework of all efforts being made towards the unification and integration of Europe'.[4]

The Council of Europe and the Main Strands of 'Europeanism'

The Council of Europe was testimony to the collective propaganda efforts of a diverse body of private 'pro-Europe' organizations in the years following the Second World War. These included the United Europe Movement, the European Union of Federalists, the Economic League for European Cooperation, the French Council for a United Europe, the Socialist Movement for a United States of Europe and *Nouvelles Équipes Internationales*, the continental grouping of Christian Democratic parties. In December 1947, these groups coordinated their activities in an International Committee of the Movements for European Unity.[5]

The momentum was maintained by 'European-minded' parliamentarians in several West European assemblies, who canvassed the establishment of a provisional Council of Europe comprising representatives of the Marshall Plan countries. In March 1948, for example, a group of British MPs, backed by kindred spirits in France and the Netherlands, endorsed the idea of convening a constituent assembly of parliamentarians which would consider full federation together with a common citizenship, currency, defence force and foreign policy.[6] Subsequently, the International Committee convoked an unofficial Congress of Europe which met at the Hague from 8–10 May 1948 and pledged itself to work for a united Europe, a Charter of Human Rights, a Court of Justice and a European Assembly and to devise measures for attaining a full political and economic union 'open to all European nations democratically governed'.[7] On 28 January 1949, final agreement was reached on the foundation of a Council of Europe.

The Council of Europe's basic objective, as enshrined in Article 1 of its 5 May 1949 statute, was to provide for greater unity among its members through the 'discussion of questions of common concern and by agreements and common action in economic, social, cultural, scientific, legal and administrative matters'. A commitment was also given to the maintenance and further realization of human rights and fundamental freedoms. Indeed, all member-states were obliged to accept the inviolability of the rule of law and human rights (Article 3) and could be expelled for infringement of these fundamental obligations (Article 8). In terms of its institutional structure, the Council of

Europe was to comprise a ministerial committee meeting in private and a consultative body meeting in public. In the trenchant words of Paul Reynaud, a dedicated pro-European, the Council of Europe consisted of two organs: one, the Consultative Assembly, was in favour of European integration; the other, the Council of Ministers, was against it.[8]

The Consultative Assembly was distinctive on at least three counts. First, a system of proportional representation was adopted which allocated the highest number of seats to France, West Germany (admitted in 1950), Italy and Britain and, in practice, guaranteed them an absolute majority.[9] Second, delegates to the Assembly (an imcompatibility rule applied between the latter and the Council of Ministers) were nominated by the respective national parliaments, so freeing the Assembly – in principle at least – from a tight governmental rein. Third, delegates were to derive from all the parliamentary parties; only the Communists were excluded, ostensibly because of the disregard for the rule of law and human rights of their East European fraternal parties. Excepting matters of internal procedure, where a simple majority sufficed, all acts of the Consultative Assembly – 'recommendations' to the Council of Ministers, 'resolutions' addressed to its own committees as directives and 'declarations' geared to the world at large as expressions of opinion, preference or aspiration – required a two-thirds majority (Articles 29/30).

The Council of Europe stimulated valuable cross-national contacts between political parties and begot a class of Euro-MPs which developed broad representative duties. For instance, the European Coal and Steel Community's Common Assembly contained parliamentarians who also belonged to the Council of Europe's Consultative Assembly. Indeed, the Schuman Plan protocol in 1951 called for cooperation with the Council of Europe in two respects. First, reports from the ECSC's executive body (High Authority) and Common Assembly were to be transmitted to the Consultative Assembly. Second, the two assemblies were to hold a joint annual session at which the ECSC's record was to be debated. In fact, the Council of Europe wanted to go further and proposed formal votes at the joint sessions, along with joint sessions of the standing committees of the two assemblies. The ECSC's Common Assembly, however, rejected such steps, partly to exclude delegates from non-ECSC countries from meddling in its internal business, but also out of concern that the Common Assembly would lose much of its rationale if it became embroiled in cross-institutional consultation.[10]

For the Council of Europe's Consultative Assembly, the strategy of close alignment with the Schuman Plan assembly reflected the search for greater influence than it had procured under its own statute. Significantly, whereas the term 'union' was explicitly used in the resolution adopted by the Hague Congress of Europe in May 1948, the Council of Europe's statute referred only to 'economic and social progress through closer unity and association'. Indeed, the Council of Europe emerged as an institutional compromise which mirrored the contrasting approaches of minimalists, who had an essentially functionalist perspective on European integration, and maximalists, who espoused wide-ranging federation. These two main strands of Europeanism warrant a note of elaboration at this point.

For the *federalists*, the goal of regional integration involved nothing less than the construction of constitutional arrangements for a United States of Western Europe along the lines of the American model. This they desired either as an end in itself (for a variety of ideological and tactical reasons) and/or as a necessary condition for the realization of economic goals. The federalists regarded a maximum of central institutional development as self-evidently desirable. In Leon N. Lindberg's terms, it was a question of *integration as political unification*.[11]

Federal political union was to be achieved in the main by the vigorous and concerted lobbying of ministers and members of parliament. Over 1946–7, for example, Coudenhove-Kalergi surveyed West European parliamentarians with the question, 'Are you in favour of a European federation within the framework of the United Nations?' and received an overwhelmingly favourable response (over 90 per cent) from MPs in France, Italy, Belgium, Holland and Luxembourg. The ultimate problem (if not poverty) of this approach, however, was revealed in summer 1954 when the French National Assembly declined to debate the European Defence Community treaty – and so condemned the complementary European Political Community proposal – a fact which prompted Altiero Spinelli and the European Union of Federalists to call (in vain) for the organization of a European front of militant federalists to press *inter alia* for the immediate abolition of the nation-state![12]

The fundamental dilemma of this type of 'strong' Europeanism, according to Ernst Haas, was that it lacked the two necessary components of any ideology – a distinctive set of principles which in turn shape a detailed programme of action. He supports his view by referring to the way the 1948 Hague Congress reached agreement on only four main points: that Europe constitutes a cultural and spiritual unity; that the essence of politics is basic human rights; that economic progress can only be achieved through measures of sectoral integration; and that national sovereignty must be restricted insofar as is necessary to achieve the aims of social and economic betterment.[13] This very general postulation of European principles, however, did not permit the formulation of a detailed programme since there was no consensus on further particulars.

The *functionalists*, by contrast, adopted a more stealthy approach to federation. Theirs was a pragmatic, piecemeal strategy – 'a sort of bit by bit approach' – which eschewed broad paper schemes in favour of delegating specific functional powers to supranational authorities.[14] They contented themselves with incremental gains – federation by random improvization rather than wholesale innovation. Thus, at the birth of the European Coal and Steel Community, the Christian Democrats in *Nouvelles Équipes Internationales* advocated a step-by-step methodology, arguing that, in order to advance West European integration, a large economic area must be created within which goods, capital and labour could circulate freely. For the functionalists, the onus, in Lindberg's terms, was on *integration as economic unification*.

In the basic sense of a commitment to move progressively towards West European unity, Europeanism embraced both the federalist and functionalist approaches. Indeed, the concept of a united Western Europe provided the type of adaptable symbol which diverse partisan groupings, from Conservatives to Socialists, had little difficulty in embracing. Even anti-integrationists could often draw a European veil over their views so that opposition to sectoral unification could be paraded in European colours. It was in part the very malleability of the concept which led Haas ultimately to conclude that 'while the nuclei of various European ideologies can be isolated ... "Europeanism" does not provide a doctrine useful for the study of the integration process', in other words, the analysis of structured social action.[15]

It needs mentioning, finally, that the rationalization of trade and production, the achievement of a more efficient division of labour, the abolition of customs barriers and the establishment of supranational regulatory authorities were all goals of the inter-war 'Europeans'. The American federal structure, indeed, which appeared to provide case-study material illustrating the validity of the 'economies of scale' theory, had inspired Coudenhove and others between the wars, as it did Monnet, Philip and the post-war Europeans. The European 'productivity teams', which visited the US under the auspices of the Marshall Plan and strongly advocated American-style union, in essence revived the views expressed at the Congress of the Federal Committee of European Cooperation in May 1929.[16] In many ways, therefore, the post-war European movement recalled, extended and elaborated on the ideas of the pre-war period, with few long-range objectives added. The principal point of differentiation with the inter-war period, however, was that measures of economic integration were successfully implemented within six years of the death of Hitler. The European Coal and Steel Community was the first pioneering step in the process of conjoining sectors of national economies which culminated in the formation of the European Economic Community or Common Market in 1957.

Sectoral Economic Integration and the Schuman Plan

The European Coal and Steel Community (ECSC) was a truly novel development in West European integration, as simple as it was effective. Furthermore, despite the ECSC's overtly economic character and the national economic advantages each participant undoubtedly hoped to gain from it, political aims underlay French foreign minister Robert Schuman's blueprint, which viewed economic union as a stepping-stone to wider federal union. According to the original statement, 'the pooling of coal and steel production will immediately ensure the setting up of common foundations of economic development, the first step in the federation of Europe'.[17]

The ECSC was founded on 19 March 1951 when delegates from France, West Germany, Italy and the Benelux countries initialled the Schuman Treaty. The basic aim was to create a single market for coal and steel, to be achieved in two stages over a five-year transitional period. First, internal tariff barriers and other international restrictions, such as quotas and exchange controls that might affect the distribution of coal and steel, were to be removed. Second, a common customs frontier for these two primary products was to be established between the Six and the outside world. In order to guarantee that the common market became a free market, the Schuman Treaty empowered the ECSC to proscribe private cartels and private marketing arrangements.

Institutionally, the ECSC comprised a nine-member executive or High Authority, a deliberative organ or Common Assembly of 78 delegates, and a Court of Justice made up of seven judges elected for a six-year term of office. In addition and largely at the insistence of the Belgians, who were apprehensive about the coercive force of supranational authorities, a Council of Ministers was introduced, designed (through a veto provision) to preserve in some measure the principle of national sovereignty.

The ECSC was formed against the backdrop of a steel industry which, until the Korean War in 1950 stimulated demand for rearmament, had been reduced to a virtual standstill. Markets were drying up, producers were coordinating steps to promote the industry and a resurrection of the inter-war European steel cartel was seriously being mooted. Remedial action in the form of a cross-national steel authority embracing both steel-producing and steel-consuming states was canvassed by a variety of organizations. These included the European Movement's International Council at its Westminster Economic

Conference in April 1949; the Economic Committee of the Consultative Assembly of the Council of Europe in December 1949; and, early the following year, the Steel Section of the Economic Commission for Europe. The central thesis of these bodies was that a basic equilibrium in the industry could not be achieved by relying on the actions of individual national governments since their policies were usually characterized by indeterminacy. Nor should there be a reliance on private cartelization. Only the supranational integration of the coal and steel sectors would suffice to orchestrate recovery and facilitate subsequent prosperity.

In a classic analysis of the ECSC, it has been observed that 'each of the Six, for individual reasons and *not* because of a clear common purpose, found it possible and desirable to embark on the road of economic integration using supranational institutions'.[18] From the outset, in short, West European integration did not involve sacrificing national economic interests on the altar of Europeanism; rather, considerations of national economic gain provided the motor force which carried them down the road of West European integration. Thus in the French case, the ECSC offered the prospect of outlets for her expanding steel exports, along with guarantees of crucial imports of coking coal.

Unlike the Federal German Republic, France entered the ECSC negotiations from a position of relative strength.[19] Monnet's *Commissariat Général du Plan de Modernisation et d'Équipement* had contributed to stimulating an economic revival after 1947 centred on the coal and steel industries, which together absorbed no less than 30 per cent of Monnet Plan funds in the first five years of its operation. By 1949 French coal production exceeded the level of the late 1930s whilst, in the same year, crude steel output was at its highest for two decades and, in 1951, surpassed the pre-war record. France, it seemed, would need export markets to accommodate her increased output, especially if the new wide-strip steel mills were to operate at their optimal level.

Significantly, however, although her production was high, her equipment good and her output per manshift well above the European average, France needed to continue importing coal. Most notably, she lacked adequate supplies of coking coal which had largely been acquired from the Ruhr in a long-established pattern of French dependence. True, the French had hoped that the International Ruhr Authority would continue to provide access to German coal, but West German independence and the rise in Ruhr steel production squeezed this supply, making it conceivable that France would ultimately be able to procure coal only on terms that favoured the Germans.[20] The Schuman Plan, in short, held out the prospect of assistance both in terms of French steel exports and coal imports.

For Schuman and Monnet, its principal architects, the ECSC possessed a wider economic logic in that it would open up the highly protected French economy and, in the face of German competition, oblige her industry to modernize. Predictably, there was opposition from the business pressure group CNPF, and in 1951 the steel and metallurgical industries mounted a vehement anti-ECSC campaign. The steel cartels, however, inherited a bad reputation from the Third Republican days of the *Comité des Forges*, while Monnet and his supporters encouraged the creation of a countervailing association of users of steel products to put the pro-membership case. Moreover, coal and railways, previously allies of steel, were now nationalized and agriculture – hoping that the ECSC would set a precedent for preferential arrangements for foodstuffs – came down on Monnet's side.[21] In any event, Schuman stood firm and, with the support of the Socialist Party (SFIO) and centrist groups, the ECSC was ratified by a majority of 144 against opposition from the business wing of the Conservatives and outright condemnation from the Communists.

In American accounts, DePorte's in particular, it has become the conventional wisdom to regard the ECSC as being largely dictated by a French fear of German industrial domination. Accordingly, if some form of discriminatory containment (i.e. overtly punitive treatment) of the German economy was not feasible, indeed was likely to be counterproductive – and it was acknowledged in hindsight that the massive indemnity of 1919 had proved damaging to the whole continental trading system – France might seek to incorporate its core elements and place them, along with the key components of its own economy, under machinery of control external to both.[22] According to this view, Schuman himself conceded some years later that the High Authority's purpose was to enable West Germany to accept restrictions on the very sovereignty that was gradually being restored to it.[23] In fact, however, the French pioneers of the ECSC clearly recognized that the challenge from German industry could not be met by containment (at least in the middle and longer term), but only by enhancing France's own industrial competitiveness. Where the containment logic did have an application, to be sure, was in the defence policy aspects of the ECSC.

Indeed, despite the evident economic benefits of membership, it was the political logic of the Schuman Plan that was considered paramount in France. The ECSC offered first and foremost a means of providing security against a possible resurgence of German militarism, a role for supranationalism to which the Benelux leaders also subscribed. The aim was to pool the crucial raw materials necessary for waging war and to create 'European' machinery with which to control them. Since coal and steel were vital resources in armaments production, placing the entire Franco-German output under a common

High Authority, it was believed, would render renewed hostilities between the two historic adversaries materially impossible.[24] Interestingly, in response to a personal hand-delivered letter from Schuman on 8 May 1950, the Federal Republic's Chancellor, Konrad Adenauer, demonstrated that he well understood the force of French fears of renewed German aggression. Adenauer noted in his *Memoirs* that 're-armament always showed first in an increased production of coal, iron and steel. If any organisation such as he [Schuman] was proposing were to be set up, it would enable each country to detect the first signs of rearmament and would have an extraordinarily calming effect in France.'[25]

Jean Monnet's role in devising and promoting the Schuman Plan warrants emphasis. Having conceived of the venture, it took Monnet only three weeks in April 1950 to produce a plan which, although amounting to a mere 104 lines, enabled France to take the initiative regarding Germany and Europe.[26] Importantly, Monnet sought to launch the Coal and Steel Community before admitting Britain, and certainly conveyed the impression that he was seeking to cut the ground from under London's feet. Thus, although working hand-in-glove with Adenauer and informing the Americans in confidence about developments, Monnet did not consult the British before the initial Schuman Plan talks in London in May 1950. He then insisted that, as conditions for participating in negotiations, there should be acceptance of the principle of pooling coal and steel resources, along with the binding nature of decisions taken by the High Authority. Britain rejected these terms. Moreover, when his foreign minister, Robert Schuman, appeared willing to offer Britain concessions, Monnet promptly met Adenauer and agreed a joint communiqué which underlined the unanimity between the two countries on the principles of the French plan.[27] He also dispatched a note to the French government stating that 'to accept British participation' without the aforementioned terms would mean 'there would be no common rule and no independent High Authority, but only some kind of OEEC'.[28]

In contrast to Monnet, the French Socialists worked to accommodate the 'reluctant Europeans' across the English Channel. At its National Council meeting in 1950, the SFIO, whilst backing French negotiations on the Schuman Plan, stated that West European unity without British and Scandinavian involvement would be substantially devalued. There were, indeed, signs of frustration when the Labour government ruled out participation; an exasperated André Philip claimed that the real reason for Labour's recalcitrance lay in the government's wish to maintain Britain's position at the centre of the sterling area, in close conjunction with the Atlantic Community. But still the leading Socialists continued to seek British involvement in Europe. There was, indeed, a modicum of truth in one analyst's comment that 'the fact is that Continental supporters of supranational communities wanted British support on almost any terms. She was needed to umpire between France and Germany.'[29]

In West Germany, the Schuman Plan talks began with the country in the depths of a serious economic crisis and amid a mood of widespread fatalism concerning the prospects of recovery. Unemployment was high and housing in desperately short supply; in consequence, the governing Christian Democrats (CDU) under Adenauer had plummeted to an all-time abyss of 23 per cent in the opinion polls.[30] No sooner had a European Payments Union (EPU) come into existence in September 1950, moreover, than the economics minister, Ludwig Erhard, was obliged to acknowledge that West Germany had already expended its allotted credits on imports – mainly on food and supplies for industry – forcing him to turn cap in hand to the IMF for a special loan. Erhard admitted that 'it was a time when opinion seemed resigned to the ruin of West Germany ... opposition at home joined with international criticism'.[31] Unlike France, then, West Germany entered the Schuman Pool negotiations from a position of considerable economic weakness.

The invasion of South Korea by the North Korean communist government, however, signified a vital turning point. First, it pointed up the threat of communist expansionism and, by extension, the risk this posed to an undefended Federal Republic. Second, it rescued West Germany by stimulating global demand for precisely the industrial products that it was permitted and encouraged to supply. By May 1951, only two months after the finalization of the ECSC treaty, IMF loans and EPU credits were repaid and shortly thereafter the employers' organization and central trade union federation (DGB) reached agreement on the first pay rise since 1948.[32]

From the outset, Adenauer saw obvious advantages in the Coal and Steel Pool. In place of the International Ruhr Authority (1948–51), the Military Security Board and all the cumbersome paraphernalia of the Occupation, the ECSC opened up the prospect both of export markets for the crisis-ridden German economy and of the status of founder-member on equal terms with the French in promoting a pioneering measure of sectoral economic integration. Adenauer immediately agreed to enter the ECSC deliberations. 'I was able to react so quickly with regard to the Schuman Plan,' he wrote, 'because it was precisely the plan proposed to the then Reich government by two friends and myself in 1925, after the termination of passive resistance, when relations between France and Germany had reached a nadir.'[33] Adenauer was also convinced that, if the Schuman Plan was implemented, the Saar question would resolve itself.[34]

The status of the Saar was one of the chief stumbling-blocks to Franco-German understanding immediately after the Second World

War. At the Paris Conference of the American, British and French foreign ministers on 9–10 November 1949, France proposed that the Saar, which she wished to annex (and which in 1947 obtained its own constitution), should have separate representation in the Council of Europe. Britain and the US conceded the point, albeit with the caveat (not made public) that the Saar's accession to the Council of Europe was to be handled in connection with a German peace treaty. During Schuman's first official visit to Bonn on 13 January 1950, Adenauer underlined the importance of the Saar question and emphasized that, if developments were unfavourable, Germany's membership of the Council of Europe would be at risk.[35] The ECSC proposal, however, considerably eased Adenauer's position and allowed West Germany to take up the invitation to join the Council of Europe. Although it took until mid-June 1950 to carry the proposal through the Bundestag against Social Democratic opposition, this was a well-timed gesture of goodwill towards the nascent Federal Republic.[36]

Indicative of Adenauer's concern to transform West Germany from an economic pariah to a partner in the West European integration process was his 7 March 1950 proposal for the creation of a Franco-German economic union, something to which, it seems, Schuman, the French foreign minister, reacted favourably.[37] The Franco-German union, which Adenauer later specified might begin with a customs union, was propounded against the background of German mistrust of France over the Saar, its realization, indeed, being made contingent on the Saar's return to Germany. The Federal Chancellor insisted that for tactical reasons – namely to obviate the impression of creating a domineering Franco-German bloc – Britain, Italy, Belgium, Luxembourg and the Netherlands should be free to join. The fundamental logic of the economic union, like the ECSC proposal (which effectively subsumed it), was to satisfy French security demands whilst stemming the growth of German nationalism.[38]

Despite Adenauer's enthusiasm, there was opposition to the ECSC in West Germany. The Social Democratic leader, Kurt Schumacher, dismissed it as a capitalist conspiracy, a 'Europe Inc.', which consolidated employer and governmental power at the expense of the rights of organized workers.[39] The French 'profit motive', moreover, was apparent to many Germans, who were not enamoured with the imbalance of advantage that would plainly accrue from conjoining substantial areas of the two economies. A contemporary American observer captured this feeling admirably: 'Such slogans as "the Integration of West Germany into Western Europe" are interpreted by the Germans in their current mood as the granting of licence to France, Belgium and Switzerland to use German resources for their own benefit without corresponding benefits to Germany.'[40]

Significantly, Schuman first put the ECSC proposal to the UK, which turned it down,[41] a decision which the American Secretary of State, Dean Acheson, writing in 1969, described as 'the greatest mistake of the post-war period'.[42] The Dutch, after all, entered the negotiations on the proviso that they had the right to withdraw if the proposals proved unworkable, and it is difficult to see why the Labour cabinet could not have participated on the same terms. Equally, such were the differences between the British and French approaches that it is possible that, if the issue of prior commitment (an advance undertaking to accept the principle of the pooling of resources and supranational power-sharing) had not proved an insurmountable obstacle, something else would have.[43] Certainly Bevin was a sick man by this time and the way the Schuman proposals were sprung on him might conceivably have coloured his judgement. But there was in any event widespread scepticism in government circles about the viability of the French plan and her ability to realize it (something Monnet exploited in order to keep Britain out).

Stafford Cripps, for example, argued that far more was at stake for Britain than for Holland since Britain produced half the coal output and one-third of the steel of the Schuman Plan countries and depended on these twin resources for its position as a leading manufacturing nation.[44] How, he inquired, could the Labour government surrender control of these core industries without knowing more about what was being proposed? For instance, would the High Authority be empowered to close coalfields and steel works?[45] Behind Cripps' concern, there was also pressure from the trade union movement, which feared that the Schuman Plan would interfere with the already nationalized coal, electricity, gas and transport industries as well as complicate the process of bringing steel into public ownership which was then well underway. In the social policy field, too, the Labour cabinet tended to view harmonization with Continental practices as synonymous with a deterioration in standards and as posing a threat to the pinnacle of its legislative achievement – the creation in 1947 of a National Health Service.[46]

The Labour Party also opposed throwing in its lot with what it perceived to be an essentially Christian Democratic rather than Social Democratic Western Europe.[47] There was strong suspicion of the political complexion of the French and German governments and their links with heavy industry. Kenneth Younger, for instance, referred critically to 'the Catholic "black international" which I have always thought to be a big driving force behind the Council of Europe'.[48] There were in fact few people in Britain in 1950, Socialists or otherwise, who really believed that she should yield control of the two industries on which her industrial power had been built to a supranational body.

Indeed, the attitude of the post-war Labour governments towards the process of West European integration, like that of the entire establishment, was deeply mistrustful. The British orientation was nationalist rather than supranationalist; imperial rather than continental; trans-Atlantic rather than European. Britain still saw herself as a great power,[49] the head of a Commonwealth of Nations and the proprietor of a special relationship with the US. Accordingly, she adopted a benevolent, avuncular, but strictly abstentionist approach to Continental integration. She wished it well, but wanted no part of it. In the final analysis, British leaders, both Labour and Conservative, approximated the position of enthusiastic American proponents of European integration – they were advocating unity for somebody else.[50] As Churchill observed in the Schuman Plan debate in the House of Commons on 27 June 1950: 'I cannot conceive that Britain would be an ordinary member of a Federal Union limited to Europe in any period which can at present be foreseen'.[51]

British post-war foreign policy thinking, in short, was still dominated by a view of her strategic location at the intersection of three concentric circles – Transatlantic, Commonwealth and European. These extra-European commitments, it was inferred, meant that Britain occupied a different position from that of Continental countries, which in turn dictated a different approach to integration. It is probably fair to assert, moreover, that most Britons in the first post-war decade saw the European relationship as less important than American and Commonwealth connections.[52] Britain had relied heavily on the Empire for men and materials during the war, and it was in the Empire that the war had principally been fought. The popular image in the 1940s was thus one of the Commonwealth having fought heroically with the 'mother country', America and the Soviet Union to defeat Nazi Germany. Whilst the arrival of the Cold War led to the evaporation of much pro-Soviet sentiment in Britain, the Atlantic Alliance continued to be held in utmost reverence, the Labour leadership identifying itself almost completely with the American analysis of the international situation.

There were, to be sure, Labour 'Europeans', but they were badly divided. Both R.W.G. (Tim) Mackay in his book *Western Union in Crisis* and the Committee for the United Socialist States of Europe actively sought West European integration in ways which closely resembled those of the 'strong' Europeans on the Continent.[53] But, ultimately, Ian Mikardo was the only prominent member of the Keep Left faction to reject NATO and the American alignment in favour of West European integration conceived as the pillar in a 'third force' policy.[54]

The manifest opposition of the Scandinavian states to West European integration was grounded on two main concerns. First, there was the fear that economic union would create 'imported unemployment' in the sense that the high living standards in the region would induce an army of continental workers to flood north in a (vain) search for jobs.[55] Second, there was the risk of imported *immobilisme*. The likes of the French and West German federalists, it was insinuated, reflected traditions of political instability which distinguished Continental Europe from the 'political maturity' of the Anglo-Scandinavian democracies. Whilst the Norwegians, in particular, shared Britain's preference for NATO and the Atlantic Community, there was also a deep sensitivity among the small Nordic states to the loss of sovereignty inherent in supranational solutions. Non-alignment was, of course, a prerequisite of a Swedish policy of neutrality which was diametrically opposed to federal union. In all the Scandinavian states, emphasis was placed on the benefits of global free trade to systems like theirs with very modest domestic markets.

The basic political reflex of the Nordic states, then, was to work for solutions to concrete problems and to move gradually towards West European cooperation at the inter-governmental level. A good example of this was the Uniscan organization, formed in 1947, which provided Britain and Scandinavia with a forum in which to formulate and coordinate responses to the federalist initiatives of the Six. So, too, was the Nordic Council created following a Danish initiative in 1952, which acted as a consultative body for the parliaments of the region (Finland acceding in 1956).

True, there were proposals designed to achieve sectoral economic integration in the Nordic region which paralleled developments among the Six and were partly a response to the same external stimuli – Marshall Aid and the concomitant American pressure to set up customs unions. A Norwegian initiative in July 1947, aimed at expanding Nordic economic cooperation, led the Bramsnaes Committee in January 1950 to recommend a Nordic Customs Union. This was ultimately ruled out in summer 1959, however, when Norway herself refused to participate, insisting that her domestic industry was weaker than those of her neighbours and could not hope to withstand Danish and Swedish competition.

Three concluding remarks on the ECSC will suffice at this stage. First, the Schuman Pool was notably successful. By 1958, after only five years in actual operation, the international trade in steel within the ECSC area had increased by 157 per cent and steel output by 65 per cent. Second, despite this success, the ECSC was hampered by functional restrictions. Thus, in addition to the most rational distribution of production at the highest level of productivity in the field of coal and steel, the ECSC sought to achieve the wider objectives of promoting economic growth, full employment and increased living standards. But it was frustrated in its pursuit of these goals by the fact that it could not interfere with monetary and fiscal problems, taxes, wages and social security.[56] Finally, it is important not to exaggerate the socialization role of this first venture in West European integration. General awareness of 'European' developments was extremely limited. In an opinion poll in *Sondages* in 1955, 26 per cent of the French sample were in fact completely oblivious of the existence of the ECSC.[57]

Plans for West European Integration in the Security and Defence Sectors

A paramount *prima facie* function of West European integration in the aftermath of the defeat of Nazi imperialism was to serve as an instrument in the moderation and mediation of deep-seated regional antagonisms, especially the historic conflict between France and Germany, so reducing the risk of a recurrence of war. A united Western Europe would contribute to the attenuation of longstanding 'domestic quarrels' and provide an acceptable framework for integrating the nascent Federal German Republic into the Western alliance system.

The logic of supranational integration as a means of achieving lasting peace and security in Europe was far from novel, although the advent of the Cold War delimited the scope for its application to Western Europe. The provision of regional security was a vital covert factor in Aristide Briand's proposal for a Federal Union of European States in August 1929 and also underpinned Coudenhove-Kalergi's plan for a United States of Europe six years earlier. Moreover on 21 March 1943, with the outcome of the war still in the balance, Churchill proposed that a Council of Europe (and other appropriate organs) be created to prevent future aggression on the Continent. He restated his idea in a celebrated speech in Zurich in September 1946 in which he argued that 'the first step in the re-creation of the European family must be a partnership between France and Germany. In this way only, can France recover the moral leadership of Europe.' Churchill added that 'there can be no revival of Europe without a spiritually great France and a spiritually great Germany'.[58]

In his European integration thinking, however, Churchill desired more than the framework for a lasting Franco-German partnership. He aspired to the development of a regional security system, oriented towards the need for external protection rather than simply the obviation of renewed internal conflict. At the outbreak of the Korean War in 1950, when acting as a British delegate to the Council of Europe, Churchill proposed the formation of a 'European army', a force to assist in safeguarding the West against the threat of Stalinist expansionism. This would clearly indicate a second (and related) security function of West European integration – to serve as an instrument with which to counter the Soviet Union and the threat of international communism. Although the Council of Ministers dismissed Churchill's proposal on the grounds that it exceeded its remit, it was taken up by Maurice Schuman who outlined two main reasons for proceeding with the European army plan. First, there was the desire to meet the persistent American demand for West German rearmament, first voiced at a NATO meeting in 1950. Second, there was the view that French interests would be better served by an integrated European force, including Germany, than the revival of a separate national military force.[59]

In the event, two French security initiatives, loosely based on Churchill's 'European army' proposal – the Pleven Plan, which was presented to the French National Assembly on 24 October 1950, and the subsequent European Defence Community (EDC) – proved stillborn. The Pleven Plan, which envisaged the creation of a Continental force within NATO, provoked consternation and dismay in Washington and a critical reaction in both London and Bonn. In an attempt to seize the tactical initiative from the Atlanticists in the UK, the French minister of defence urged the formation of a European Ministry of Defence accountable to the Council of Europe; the appointment of a ministerial-level European Defence Council and the operation of a single European defence budget. Member-states would contribute units of their armed forces – merged at the lowest possible (probably battalion) level – which would constitute a European army. Significantly, whilst West Germany would be permitted to participate, the Pleven Plan ruled out a German national army or defence ministry.

The new Conservative government under Churchill refused to participate: a cabinet memorandum of 29 November 1950 stressed the prime minister's unwillingness to forfeit Britain's 'insular or Commonwealth-wide character'.[60] In fact, it tended to view the whole enterprise with much the same air of benevolent scepticism as characterized the previous Labour government's approach to the Schuman Plan. How could a European Defence Ministry and defence budget be set up, it was inquired, before a European government (i.e. a West European federation) had been formed?[61] In West Germany, reaction to the Pleven Plan was openly hostile. If German involvement was deemed so essential to the defence and security of the region, why was the Allied occupation not terminated and full national sovereignty restored as a gesture of good faith?

In France itself, the Pleven Plan's fate was complicated by a Soviet note, transmitted to the Western Allies on 3 November 1950, in which a four-power conference on Germany was proposed and support canvassed for a demilitarized and neutral state (embracing both federal and democratic republics). Unequivocal French opponents of

West German rearmament (especially the Communists), together with a broad spectrum of groupings eager simply to stall rearmament as long as possible, joined forces in arguing that the prospect of West Germans in arms had rattled the Russians and brought them to the conference table. If the West showed a reluctance to compromise, it was argued, the likelihood of East–West military conflict would be substantially increased.

Like the Pleven Plan, the primary objective of the French EDC proposal was to postpone an independent West German military, whilst appearing to respond to mounting American pressure for rearmament in the Federal Republic. Although contemplating the fusion of contingents at a level close to that of a full-strength division, the EDC did not offer West Germany equality of treatment, and it is clear that British involvement was designed principally as a bulwark against the threat of German rather than Soviet militarism. The idea was opposed by the German Social Democrats, who feared that tying West Germany closer to the Western alliance would jeopardize the prospects of ultimate reunification, but it was backed by Adenauer and the Christian Democrats who considered it (however falteringly) a step in the right direction. Britain rejected involvement on much the same grounds as it rejected the Pleven Plan. However, the EDC treaty was signed by the six member-states of the ECSC on 27 May 1952. Ironically, however, it was not ratified on home soil since in August 1954 the French National Assembly refused even to debate it. The EDC in short came to naught.

The problem was that most Frenchmen, including the EDC's instigators, believed intuitively that the only effective guarantee of their national security was German disarmament. There was some fear among moderates, too, that, without full British membership, the EDC might one day become a German trap for France.[62] Agreement on a form of British EDC association was reached in April 1954, but this did not satisfy the French. Deep divisions among the ruling Socialists over the EDC mirrored a wider split over the issue.[63] Whereas the EDC plan signalled the very rearmament of West Germany to which the majority of French Socialists were adamantly opposed, it also appeared to mark significant progress towards a supranational Western Europe which a majority of the party supported. Broadly, the *cédistes* favouring EDC held that a European army, organized into integrated units and with effective supranational machinery of democratic control, represented a decisive step *en route* to a united Europe. Socialist opponents of EDC countered that the whole project was simply a fancy dress in which to disguise German rearmament.[64]

In the event, an improvement in the climate of international relations facilitated a French exit from the EDC impasse. Thus the election in 1952 of Dwight D. Eisenhower as American president, replacing

Harry Truman, brought about a negotiated peace in Korea (which confirmed the *status quo ante* of partition along the 38th parallel), whilst the death of Stalin the following year betokened a somewhat more pragmatic and less overtly adversarial approach to superpower relations in the Kremlin. The Soviet acquisition of the hydrogen bomb, moreover, seemed to negate the American nuclear advantage and to contribute to a sense of stalemate between East and West. Against this changed backdrop, the EDC lost some of its urgency, allowing the French National Assembly, following the government's lead, to bury the whole thing.[65] Importantly, the EDC's demise signified the failure of the only serious attempt in the post-Second World War era to achieve a measure of regional integration in the security field, although a degree of inter-governmental cooperation was achieved in the subsequent Western European Union (WEU).

The WEU was launched at a nine-power conference in London in October 1954 and was facilitated by amending the 1948 Brussels Treaty which had created a joint command for certain British, French and Benelux divisions. Largely at Britain's instigation, German and Italian forces were now admitted to the Brussels arrangements and the WEU agreement came into force in May 1955. Although the WEU operated a joint command under NATO, it was based on an inter-governmental rather than a federal formula. There was no fusion of national forces to create a 'European army' and no federal organs to scrutinize and exercise fiscal and administrative control over a common defence budget. National armies were to be perpetuated and, significantly too, the German army was restored. The WEU did, however, preserve the principle of integrated *action* in the security area.[66]

Britain's role in the genesis of security arrangements in Western Europe in the early 1950s warrants emphasis. She declined membership of the EDC because of its fundamentally federal character, but then devised a substitute in the form of the WEU. This was not without its price since, under the WEU agreement, Britain pledged to station four divisions of her second Tactical Air Force across the Channel at all times, something which was widely regarded as a condition for French acceptance of German participation in the WEU. If Britain had entered into such an undertaking earlier, of course, the stillborn EDC might well have seen the light of day.[67]

In the event, the WEU came for long to occupy an uneasy, quasi-independent and largely inconsequential place between NATO and the European Economic Community (EC), enjoying at best ephemeral importance. To be sure, with the question of political union firmly on the West European agenda in the 1990s, the WEU's significance has grown. There has been a lobby, especially in France, advocating a role for the WEU in providing for a more independent regional defence strategy; in June 1991, the WEU undertook to investigate a possible rapid deployment force of its own, together with the establishment of a satellite data interpretation centre which would reduce Europe's dependence on US-supplied intelligence. The WEU stated that, although it would contribute to 'solidarity within the Atlantic alliance', it accepted that 'European political union implied a genuine security and defence identity and thus greater European [West European] responsibility for defence matters'.[68] Indeed, the Maastricht Treaty of February 1992 envisaged the WEU playing an integral role in the EC's commitment to define and implement a common foreign and security policy which might in time lead to a common defence (see Chapter 7). Nonetheless, the exponential process of sectoral integration which began in Western Europe with the creation of the ECSC in 1951 has not yet realized defence and security provisions and Churchill's 'European army' has not materialized. The abortive EDC helped indirectly to promote the integration of West Germany within the West European fold, but responsibility for West European security has continued to rest with the Atlantic alliance.

Growing resistance to this dependency pointed to a further function of West European integration and one closely associated with the collapse of the EDC, with the Egyptian President, Colonel Nasser's nationalization of the Suez Canal in summer 1956 and with the advent of de Gaulle as head of the new French Fifth Republic in 1958. Integration came to be viewed in some quarters as a means of creating a West European superpower which would act as a 'third force' and provide a counterpoise to the US and Soviet Union. The 'third force' notion was anchored in the belief that, in an age of superpower rivalry, the continuation of West European nation–states as purely sovereign entities would inevitably entail their relative and absolute decline. In addition to the constant menace of the Soviet Union, there was also a growing concern that the US and its leadership might well lead the world astray.

The Suez crisis was an important watershed in the post-war history of Western Europe. Nasser's decision to nationalize the Suez Canal so as to finance infrastructural development – a programme of public works from which Britain and the US had recently withdrawn investment – led to an ill-fated Anglo-French invasion in October 1956 which was roundly condemned by world opinion. The Soviet Union threatened actively to intervene in the area; the US, embroiled in a presidential election campaign and both suspicious and irritated by the timing of the Anglo-French expedition, refused any support; while the joint action provoked virtually unanimous opposition in the UN General Assembly and Security Council. Faced with such broad-based hostility, the British and French were left with little real alternative other than withdrawal.

The Suez débâcle was instructive on several counts but, from an integrationist perspective, the principal lesson of the whole unhappy episode was well captured by a writer closely associated with the European Movement during the war. 'For all but the Colonel Blimps, the diehard chauvinists and the professional patriots, the Suez affair and its aftermath offered the most convincing demonstration yet that the national state system of Western Europe was inadequate to protect Western Europe's interests.'[69] Ironically, however, the two countries involved in the Suez operation came to different conclusions.

For Britain, who took the lead in the withdrawal of troops, Suez indicated an obvious inability to sustain a major military undertaking on its own. Indeed, the slump in gold and dollar reserves and the resultant pressure to devalue the pound (which the action occasioned) were the primary reasons, according to Conservative prime minister Anthony Eden, for acceding to the UN resolution on withdrawal. However, although in the aftermath of Suez Britain's pretensions to great-power status were somewhat diminished, she continued nevertheless to be a 'reluctant European', preferring to place faith in a renewal of the 'special relationship' with the US.[70] For France, on the other hand, which had apparently been more prepared to defy world opinion and remain in Suez, the Middle East crisis made a strong case for seeking to disengage from the US superpower.[71] In French circles in particular, it was after Suez that the idea of uniting Western Europe into a 'third force' came of age.

However, de Gaulle's plan for West European political union (discussed in Chapter 6) and the complementary Fouchet Plan in 1962 were no more successful than the blueprint for a European Political Community (EPC) which was unveiled in 1953. A draft of an EPC treaty was adopted by the ECSC's Common Assembly on 10 March 1953; if ratified by the national assemblies of the Six, it would have involved the creation of a bicameral federal assembly with a directly-elected People's Chamber of 288 members. However, the fate of the EPC was closely intertwined with the concurrent European Defence Community proposal (the EDC had not been ratified by any national assembly when the draft EPC treaty was published) since its immediate purpose was to provide an instrument of democratic control for both the European Defence and Coal and Steel Communities.[72] When the EDC finally went down in the French National Assembly on 17 August 1954, the EPC inevitably sank with it.

All in all, expansive schemes for federal political integration in Western Europe in the two decades after the Second World War ran aground in precisely the way the inter-war proposals of Briand, Coudenhove and Herfordt had done. As a prescient French representative to the Council of Europe's Consultative Assembly, Paul Bastid, noted at the 1950 session; 'If Europe is to be made ... it will have to be by dint of random improvizations – it will not be a palace, but a conglomeration of sheds.'[73] Two new sheds which in time were to assume palatial proportions, however, were erected in 1957: the European Economic Community (EEC) and the European Atomic Energy Community (Euratom).

An Economic Iron Curtain Descends across Western Europe

When the EDC and EPC sheds were destroyed by the force of nationalist winds, the ECSC was left in the mid-1950s as the sole monument to West European integration. By then, however, an association agreement had been reached between Britain and the ECSC. The backdoor for this had been left ajar from the outset with the stipulation in Article 13 of the transitional convention that the ECSC's High Authority 'undertake negotiations with the governments of third countries and particularly with the British'.[74] The High Authority and the British mission in Luxembourg did in fact create a joint committee and a series of working groups. However, the critical development came in December 1953 when Monnet formally invited Britain to enter negotiations, leading to the possible removal of some barriers between the two markets and a procedure for common action.[75]

If Monnet had worked actively and single-mindedly behind the scenes to pre-empt initial British involvement in the ECSC, it was largely because he considered there was no real hope of convincing her of its merits and because he did not wish to risk allowing British recalcitrance to jeopardize the whole project. Monnet felt that at heart Britain's reluctance to commit herself to the Schuman Plan was largely dictated by a lack of confidence in the ability (or even will) of Western Europe to resist a possible Soviet invasion: 'Britain believes that in this conflict, continental Europe will be occupied, but that she herself, with America, will be able to resist and finally conquer.'[76] But although Monnet desired to write Britain out of the ECSC script in 1950–51, he envisaged a part for her at a later stage. Indeed, he strove to make the Schuman Pool successful since British sceptics would then be confronted with a fact of life and they were good, he believed, at facing facts.[77]

In truth, Britain's acquiescent response to Monnet's offer of negotiations was probably conditioned more by foreign than economic policy considerations. When Monnet was invited to London in April 1954, the EDC's future still hung in the balance. As Britain had already agreed to be associated with the EDC, it would have been curious not to have at least negotiated with the ECSC. In the event, the House of Commons approved an association agreement in February 1955, its most significant achievement being the steel tariff agreement between Britain and the Community which went into effect in 1958.[78]

It was in many ways ironic that, when Britain became an associate member of the ECSC, much of the momentum appeared to have gone out of West European integration. Yet only nine months after France rejected the EDC, the ECSC's Common Assembly called upon the foreign ministers of the Six to devise ways of proceeding with further measures of sectoral integration. This coincided with a similar initiative from the Benelux governments and support from Jean Monnet who had left the ECSC High Authority in November 1954 to work for integration in a private capacity, founding an Action Committee for the United States of Europe. The result was the Messina conference of June 1955 which proved to be a turning-point in the history of West European integration.

The significance of the Messina conference, though, was probably not evident at the time. As William Diebold Jr. has noted: 'Messina produced no sharp electric shock signalling a new determination to resume the process of uniting Europe.'[79] The process succeeded, he argued, not because radical new ideas were ventured but because the governments of the Six gave a small group of pro-integrationists the opportunity to devise and promote workable plans. In the build-up to Messina, several strands in the 'European debate' could be disentangled.

First, there were functionalists who pressed for an extension of sectoral integration to include the energy and transport sectors, organized either within the purview of the High Authority or as separate agencies linked to the ECSC. Opponents of this approach held that a multiplicity of self-contained communities, each the custodian of a particular producer interest, would serve as a motor force for economic disintegration. What was needed instead was overarching integration in the form of an all-embracing customs union or common market. Interestingly, the Benelux governments had shifted towards this holistic philosophy before Messina. Yet another group contended that major measures of economic integration would flounder unless a framework of monetary integration was provided to limit the damaging consequences of inflation and balance of payments problems. There were also advocates of a European currency commission, a federal reserve system and even a common currency who emphasized the importance of the coordination of national policies and the cooperation of the central banks.

In 1956, the inter-governmental committee of experts set up at Messina under Paul-Henri Spaak was completing its deliberations concerning the measures necessary to realize both a common market and integration in the transport, nuclear and conventional energy sectors. These proposals were debated at a special session of the

ECSC's Common Assembly in March 1956. In the same year international developments conspired to draw out the politico-economic identity of Western Europe and to underline the need for renewed forms of regional cooperation.

After a brief period of detente in the wake of the 1955 Geneva summit, which saw the withdrawal of Soviet troops and the achievement of full Austrian independence, Russia's intervention to crush the Hungarian uprising the following year served as a sharp reminder of the Kremlin's determination to maintain its hegemony over Eastern Europe. Almost simultaneously, the ill-fated Anglo-French Suez invasion led to the two West European allies being disowned by both superpowers and prompted France, in particular, seriously to question the Atlanticist orthodoxy.

The rise of African and Asian nationalism, moreover, which precipitated the end of the 'white man's burden' and the geographical retreat of the imperial West European nations back to Western Europe, also suggested a covert goal of integration – to compensate for the loss of empire whilst also seeking to provide the means for preserving colonial advantages. Regional integration would enable Western Europe to be more independent of colonial raw materials and markets, but also create a power bloc capable of exerting more effective political control over colonial territories. It was significant that, during the setting up of a Common Market, France persuaded the other members of the Six to assume joint responsibility for maintaining a flow of capital to her colonial possessions and to initiate steps to establish the framework of a customs union between these colonies and the metropolitan states.

If international developments tended to consolidate the regional identity of Western Europe, growing economic prosperity across the Continent – the advent of the 'you've never had it so good' years – created heightened materialist expectations and gave a new angle to the old case for integration. Building a regional economy of sufficient scale and with sufficient resources became necessary not only to compete with the US, but also to meet the demands of an expanding population for improved living standards.

Despite her recent ECSC association agreement, Britain declined an invitation to the Messina conference, as she had the Schuman Plan negotiations five years earlier. Much the same sceptical mentality obtained; in Whitehall, in particular, there was the confident expectation that nothing would come out of the Common Market initiative. The cabinet was, in any event, so badly divided over the EEC that by October 1955 there was serious talk of withdrawing the British delegate from the inter-governmental committee of experts, set up at Messina, that was working on a customs union proposal.

In at least one important respect – the extent of Franco-German reconciliation – the British government appeared culpable of under-estimating the likelihood of a successful outcome to the EEC delib-erations. The result of the October 1955 Saar plebiscite bore witness to a growing pragmatism on the French side. An overwhelming major-ity voted against severing the region from West Germany; France appeared to accept the verdict of the people, acceded in the resignation of Johannes Hoffmann, the Saar's prime minister, and fixed free elec-tions for December 1955.[80] This action seemed to go a considerable way to removing a longstanding bone of contention between West Europe's two historic adversaries.

Moreover, insofar as the British cabinet had a European policy – and it was subsequently admitted that it was difficult to bring any concerted attention to the question [81] – it was essentially limited and negative in character. Perhaps part of the blame for Britain's unimagi-native response to the EEC initiative should be laid at the door of Harold Macmillan who, as foreign secretary and later as prime minis-ter, failed to maintain his earlier enthusiasm for West European unity.[82] Certainly there was absolutely no question of Britain joining the Six in the post-Messina period. It was still widely believed that Com-monwealth obligations made it impossible for her to adhere to a tightly-drawn plan for a Common Market, with all its supranational apparatus.[83] As Macmillan observed: 'The weight of British opinion in the Government, in the Conservative Party, in the Opposition and in the Press was against our joining as a full partner in the Common Market.'[84]

Remarkably, on 27 March 1957, less than three years after the col-lapse of the EDC and EPC ventures, the Six signed the Treaty of Rome setting up a European Economic Community.[85] The EEC envisaged the elimination of national tariffs over a minimum transitional period of 12 years (the French, to be sure, were concerned that this was too precipitate) as a precondition for the development of a uniform com-mercial policy with a common tariff against external goods at its core. There was also provision for the harmonization of social legislation and public welfare policies and for overcoming artificial national restrictions on transport within the community. Above all, though, the Treaty of Rome contained a long-term political goal, since it averred to the desire 'to establish the foundations of an ever-closer union among the European peoples'.

In constructing a wider Economic Community, the ECSC experi-ence was instructive on several counts.[86] First, there was the adoption of the notion of a social fund to assist in the retraining and redeploy-ment of workers displaced by economic change, especially the aboli-tion of special tariffs. Next, there was a proposed European Investment Bank designed to promote a common investment policy. Using funds borrowed on the capital market, the Bank's aim was to provide top-up loans and guarantees for private enterprise development within the Community. Finally, the Common Market's operating authority was to be vested in a nine-member Commission with powers similar to the High Authority of the Schuman Community – an interesting example of institutional diffusion growing directly out of the process of sectoral integration. However, the Commission was to be subject to the direction of a Council of Ministers embodying the sovereign authority of each member-state.

At the Messina conference, plans were also laid for coordinating the development and utilization of atomic energy, and a treaty setting up a European Atomic Energy Community (Euratom) was approved alongside the Treaty of Rome. The Euratom treaty brought under a single jurisdiction all civil exploitation of nuclear energy, including the purchase and production of nuclear ores and fuel, and provided a guarantee of adequate supplies of fissionable materials to all authorized public and private users. Euratom was also to supervise the use of patents and discoveries relating to the exploitation of nuclear power, to implement central regulations protecting the public against radiation hazards, and to promote investment in research and development.

Unlike the EEC project, which was complicated by the interplay of powerful vested interests, both national and private, nuclear power was a relatively unploughed field lacking the customary array of competing organized groups. There was, therefore, greater freedom of elite manoeuvre in devising arrangements for Euratom than in the case of the Common Market. Furthermore, whilst there were considerable shortfalls of power supplies in Western Europe, the Suez crisis had underlined the way a dependence on Middle East oil carried with it considerable political risks. Yet if greater autonomy in the energy field was obviously desirable, it was equally clear that the extensive spending necessary to sustain an effective atomic energy programme was such as to prohibit any one nation going it alone. Orchestrated action was a precondition of success, whilst American support possibly settled any last-minute doubts. At the opportune moment, President Eisenhower announced that the US would assign substantial quantities of U-235 for sale or lease abroad – albeit for civilian requirements only – so ensuring that the availability of reactor fuel would not pose a problem. The Euratom project consequently progressed quickly and smoothly.

The British government's somewhat tardy response to post-Messina developments came in the form of a counter-proposal – Plan G or the Grand Design of October 1956.[87] Plan G was formulated on the assumption that the Six would succeed in forming a Common Market and was designed primarily to negate the advantages that were feared likely to accrue from it.[88] Britain, in short, was concerned about the implications of successful economic union and worked to sabotage the whole arrangement although, of course, presenting the aims of the Grand Design as consonant with those of the Six. Plan G contained the main guidelines of a West European Free Trade Area (WFTA) comprising the Six (regarded as a single unit), the UK and any other OEEC country wishing to join. It was to be an industrial free trade area, excluding agriculture, with tariffs progressively eliminated over a ten-year transitional period. In contrast to the nascent Common Market, WFTA members would retain their existing freedom of action with regard to tariffs affecting the rest of the world, subject, of course, to their GATT commitments. The WFTA proposal thus enabled Britain to safeguard her Commonwealth trade.

Plan G remained on the table when the Treaty of Rome was signed in March 1957 and, two months later, Britain received unofficial assurances that, as soon as the Common Market treaty had formally been ratified in the assemblies of the Six, there would be renewed discussions on WFTA.[89] Shortly after Reginald Maudling, the Paymaster-General, had been given special 'European' responsibilities in August 1957, however, it became clear that the WFTA negotiations would run aground if Britain maintained a completely negative stance on foodstuffs. Indeed, the Six insisted that, in return for the ultimate duty-free access of British manufactured goods into their markets, EEC agricultural goods should be granted easier entry into the UK.[90] Nonetheless, on 16 October 1957, the OEEC Council declared its determination to promote WFTA and Maudling was elected chairman of an inter-governmental committee appointed to undertake the negotiations. Even when the Common Market formally came into being on 1 January 1958, there was no sign of breakdown in the wider discussions.[91]

Yet at the beginning of March 1958, France proposed two substantive amendments to the WFTA blueprint which were wholly unacceptable to the UK. One, agreement between the Common Market and other OEEC countries was to be reached on an industry-by-industry basis; ailing sectors would have to wait until conditions and competition had been 'harmonized' before entering the free trade area. Two, Britain's preferential tariffs for Commonwealth countries were to be extended to a quota of continental European goods.[92] When Macmillan met the new prime minister, de Gaulle, in June 1958, he sensed a hardening in the French attitude, and at a Maudling Committee session on 14 November 1958 Jacques Soustelle announced independently of the other EEC members that France ruled out the possibility of forming a WFTA along the lines envisaged by London.[93] By March 1958, in fact, it was plain that agriculture was not the real stumbling-block in negotiations, but rather that France was opposed to the whole WFTA concept. A number of factors contributed to this.

First, there was growing anxiety in French industrialist circles at the prospect of facing competition not only from the West Germans but also from the British. Erhard, the Federal German representative on the Maudling Committee, in contrast, appeared inclined to accept the WFTA scheme as laid down in the British White Paper of February 1957. Second, France had succeeded in incorporating her colonial empire into the Common Market and did not wish to risk jeopardizing this special arrangement. Ironically, there was particular French opposition to a much-publicized proposal, emanating from John Diefenbaker's succession to the Canadian premiership in April 1957, for a British–Canadian free trade area, since this confirmed the French suspicion that WFTA would open the door to the rest of the world.[94] Next, French federalist opinion was more concerned with the political than the economic integration of Western Europe.[95] French anxiety was also aroused at Britain's announcement of her desire to reduce the number of her troops stationed in the Federal Republic under the Western European Union (WEU) agreement as part of her shift to a nuclear-based capability. But undoubtedly the principal cause of the collapse of WFTA was France's (justifiable) suspicion that Britain's primary motive in the free-trade initiative was to cancel out the threat posed to it by the embryonic Common Market.

If Britain almost certainly underestimated the determination of the Six during 1955–6 to advance towards a Common Market, she also seemed to overestimate her own bargaining strength during the WFTA negotiations. The initial exclusion of agriculture (Britain had relented on this by January 1958) was an obvious indication of Britain's inability and/or unwillingness to take a realistic view of the problems of Western Europe. Maudling's retention as the leading British spokesman, after his appointment as chair of the inter-governmental negotiating committee, was a bad tactical error too, since, in the eyes of the Six, it tended to confirm Britain's domination of the other 11 OEEC states in the whole EFTA enterprise. In any event, when the French pulled out, the WFTA enterprise was effectively dead.

The idea of a delimited West European free trade zone was not, however, buried with it and, on a Swedish initiative, the European Free Trade Association (EFTA) was established by the Stockholm Convention of 20 November 1959. EFTA provided for a ten-year period of trade liberalization among its seven members – Britain, the Scandinavian states, Austria, Portugal and Switzerland – leading to the complete abolition of tariffs by 1970. There were also special arrangements for agriculture and fish products.

Formed as a residual free trade area to counterbalance – or, in the British view, rival and outflank – the economic power of the Common Market, and facilitated by the routine consultations between the British and the Scandinavian states within the framework of Uniscan,

EFTA was viewed as an interim arrangement from which any member could withdraw at 12 months' notice. There was no long-term goal of economic integration, still less political federation. In EEC circles, EFTA tended to be regarded as principally 'for effect' – designed to oblige the Six ultimately to reconsider the error of their ways in rejecting WFTA and bring its members back to the conference table to negotiate a pan-regional arrangement of the inter-governmental kind that Britain desired. The fact that the smaller members gained disproportionate benefits from EFTA and that the main emphasis during the House of Commons debate on the Stockholm Convention was on the Common Market appeared to bear out the Six's view on British motives.[96] As for the small EFTA states, there was doubtless the feeling that, unless they came together on a temporary basis to match the unity of purpose demonstrated by the 'Little Europeans', they would find themselves highly disadvantaged if and when they sought bilateral trade arrangements with the Common Market.

Although a disparate economic grouping, the lowest common denominator among the 'Outer Seven' states was their preference for a free trade area rather than a customs union. In Switzerland, Austria and Sweden, a common tariff and the supranational arrangements necessary to administer it were held to be incompatible with the prerequisites of neutrality, whilst for Britain and Norway, there was a strong aversion to any economic association that might conceivably spawn political integration.[97] All the prospective EFTA countries except Austria and Portugal, moreover, were low or relatively low-tariff countries with industrial structures geared to the import of raw materials and semi-manufactures, either tariff-free or at minimal rates of duty. Portugal, a member of the so-called 'forgotten five', to be sure, argued 'special case' status and for a longer transitional period to free trade in order to accommodate her lower level of industrial development. Indeed, Austria was the only intending EFTA member to possess high tariffs, but she was less concerned with reducing them than with the political ramifications of opening her border to the economic might of Federal Germany.[98]

The propensity of some EFTA members to view the rump free trade zone as at best a short-term expedient – a last resort rather than a first option – is well illustrated by the case of Denmark, which was undoubtedly the most restless Outer Seven member. Unlike her Scandinavian partners, Norway and Sweden, Denmark regarded EFTA as a half-way house – a step towards a pan-West European solution – and the only alternative to economic isolation once it was clear that the domestic political climate effectively ruled out the EEC membership that Jens-Otto Krag had sought and been offered in 1957. From the standpoint of Danish agricultural exports, it was imperative that an 'economic iron curtain' did not descend between it and the nation's main customers; accordingly, Denmark consistently took the view that EFTA's primary role was to build bridges to the Common Market rather than promote measures of retaliation against it.[99]

By the late 1950s, Western Europe was truly at sixes and sevens,[100] with relations between the two trade blocs remaining strained for much of the 1960s. Moreover, American concern at the division into an Inner Six and Outer Seven – the way a region of Europe had become a Western Europe of regions – contributed to an initiative to restructure the OEEC so as to permit non-European members. A new designation, the Organization for Economic Cooperation and Development (OECD), was adopted; this reconstituted body assumed the wider remit of focusing on international problems of economic development. In fact, by giving the Common Market states a direct link to Washington, the OECD implicitly challenged the special relationship between Britain and America. From a high point in the 'special relationship' during the Churchill–Roosevelt era, the orientation of the US became progressively more 'European' as ECSC proved itself enormously successful and as the quickening pace of integration realized a Common Market. Indeed, the US consistently encouraged London to join moves to form this nascent economic union. When, in July 1961, Britain did apply for membership, however, she found that the French cock wanted to rule the roost.

Notes

1   William Diebold Jr. (1959), *The Schuman Plan: A Study in Economic Co-operation 1950–1959*, New York: Praeger, pp.424–5.
2   A.W. DePorte (1979), *Europe Between the Superpowers*, New Haven–London: Yale University Press, pp.223–4.
3   A.J. Zurcher (1958), *The Struggle to Unite Europe 1940–1958*, Westport: Greenwood, p.165.
4   Ibid., p.168.
5   Ibid., p.169.
6   Ibid., p.172.
7   Ibid., p.173.
8   Simon Serfaty (1968), *France, de Gaulle and Europe: The Policy of the Fourth and Fifth Republics Towards the Continent*, Baltimore: The Johns Hopkins Press, p.56.
9   The Bundestag vote on the German Federal Republic's membership of the Council of Europe took place on 15 June 1950. The Christians (CDU/CSU), Liberals (FDP) and German Party (DP) were in favour, whilst the Social Democrats (SDP), under Kurt Schumacher, and the Communists (KPD) were opposed. The bill was passed by 220 votes to 152. Konrad Adenauer (1966), *Memoirs 1945–53*, London: Weidenfeld & Nicolson, p.266.
10   Diebold Jr. (1959), op. cit., pp.637–8.
11   Leon L. Lindberg, (1963), *The Political Dynamics of European Economic Integration*, Stanford: Stanford University Press, pp.108–9, 289–90.
12   Ernst B. Haas (1968), *The Uniting of Europe: Political, Social and Economic Forces,*

1950–1957, Stanford: Stanford University Press, p.26. This plan was defeated in 1956 and the UEF split formally in 1957.

13 Ibid., p.27.
14 Ibid., p.24.
15 Ibid., p.28.
16 Zurcher (1958), op. cit., pp.173–4.
17 Diebold Jr. (1959), op. cit., p.13.
18 Haas (1968), op. cit., p.xix.
19 Diebold Jr. (1959), op. cit., p.17.
20 Ibid., p.18.
21 Philip M. Williams (1964), *Crisis and Compromise: Politics in the Fourth Republic*, London: Longman, pp.362, 379.
22 DePorte (1979), op. cit., p.222.
23 Serfaty (1968), op. cit., p.61.
24 Ibid., p.62.
25 Adenauer (1966), op. cit., pp.256–7.
26 A. Bullock (1983), *Ernest Bevin: Foreign Secretary 1945–51*, London: Heinemann, p.769.
27 Ibid., pp.778–9.
28 Ibid., p.780.
29 Zurcher (1958), op. cit., p.202.
30 Dennis L. Bark and David R. Gress (1989), *From Shadow to Substance*, Oxford: Basil Blackwell, p.264.
31 Ibid., p.267.
32 Ibid., p.268.
33 Adenauer (1966), op. cit., pp.262–3. Commenting on ECSC, Adenauer remarked that 'a community of European countries was to be created on the basis of complete equality, the only basis of a genuine community' (ibid., pp.339–40).
34 Ibid., p.264.
35 Ibid., pp.231–8.
36 Bullock (1983), op. cit., p.774.
37 J.K. Sowden (1975), *The German Question 1945–1973: Continuity in Change*, London: Cresby Lockwood Staples, p.140.
38 Adenauer (1966), op. cit., p.247.
39 Bark and Gress (1989), op. cit., p.270.
40 Charles P. Kindleberger (1987), *The Marshall Plan Days*, Winchester, MA: Allen & Unwin, p.8. Cited in Diebold Jr. (1959), op. cit., p.432.
41 Adenauer (1966), op. cit., p.383.
42 Bullock (1983), op. cit., p.783.
43 Diebold Jr. (1959), op. cit., p.54.
44 Ibid., pp.54–5.
45 Bullock (1983), op. cit., p.783.
46 Michael Newman, however, brings out the illogicality of their anxiety by noting that it was the constraining influence of the US, rather than Continental pressure to move towards integration which, if anything, hamstrung the Labour Party. American pressure for rearmament, for example, led to a reduction in welfare spending and the highly controversial imposition of NHS prescription charges. Newman (1983), *Socialism and European Unity*, London, p.137.
47 Edward Heath (1970), *Old World, New Horizons*, London: Atlantic Alliance, pp.19–20.
48 Bullock (1983), op. cit., p.789.
49 In the House of Commons on 16 May 1947, the Labour foreign secretary, Ernest Bevin, had insisted that 'his Majesty's government does not accept the view …

that we have ceased to be a great power, or the contention that we have ceased to play that role'. Cited in Newman (1983), op. cit., pp.122–3.

50 Zurcher (1958), op. cit., p.29.
51 Bullock (1983), op. cit., p.787.
52 Diebold Jr. (1959), op. cit., p.424.
53 Zurcher (1958), op. cit., p.34.
54 Newman (1983), op. cit., pp.143–7.
55 Toivo Miljan (1977), *The Reluctant Europeans: The Attitudes of the Nordic Countries towards European Integration*, London: Hurst, p.82.
56 Serfaty (1968), op. cit., pp.62–3.
57 Haas (1968), op. cit., pp.17–18.
58 Heath (1970), op. cit., p.14.
59 Zurcher (1958), op. cit., pp.82–3.
60 Bullock (1983), op. cit., p.787.
61 Ibid., p.816.
62 Zurcher (1958), op. cit., pp.113–18.
63 Thus the Communists and radical right opposed German rearmament in any circumstances, whilst the Radicals feared it would trigger a potentially lethal arms race between the two Germanies. The Gaullists accepted the EDC idea in principle, but nonetheless felt it would denationalize the French army and bring matters a step closer to a 'Europe of the technocrats'. Serfaty (1968), op. cit., pp.56–8.
64 Newman (1983), op. cit., pp.29–30.
65 The government was assisted in this task by statements from the American Secretary of State, John Foster Dulles, criticizing the 'dilatory manoeuvres' over the EDC, which certainly reduced the likelihood of the treaty being successfully steered through the National Assembly.
66 Zurcher (1958), op. cit., p.130.
67 Ibid.
68 John Palmer (1991), 'WEU treads path of independence', *The Guardian*, 28 June.
69 Zurcher (1958), op. cit., p.179.
70 DePorte (1979), op. cit., p.224.
71 Derek W. Urwin (1978), *Western Europe since 1945*, London: Longman, p.215.
72 Zurcher (1958), op. cit., pp.95–126.
73 Ibid., p.67.
74 Diebold Jr. (1959), op. cit., p.502.
75 Ibid., pp.505–6.
76 Bullock (1983), op. cit., p.788.
77 Diebold Jr. (1959), op. cit., p.505.
78 Ibid., p.508.
79 Ibid., p.644.
80 Harold Macmillan (1971), *Riding the Storm 1956–59*, London; Macmillan, p.70.
81 Ibid., p.69.
82 Nigel Fisher (1982), *Harold Macmillan*, London: Weidenfeld and Nicolson, p.311.
83 Macmillan (1971), op. cit., p.84.
84 Ibid., pp.70–72.
85 In the Federal Republic, the Treaty of Rome was the first major international agreement that had the unambiguous support of both the major parties, the Christian Democrats and Social Democrats. Bark and Gress (1989), op. cit., p.381.
86 Zurcher (1958), op. cit., pp.135–8,144–6.
87 Macmillan (1971), op. cit., pp.79–80.
88 Fisher (1982), op. cit., p.309.
89 Macmillan (1971), op. cit., p.435.
90 Ibid., p.438.

91 Ibid., p.440.
92 Ibid., p.441.
93 Lindberg (1963), op. cit., p.120.
94 Miljan (1977), op. cit., pp.119–24.
95 Fisher (1982), op. cit., p.309; Macmillan (1971), op. cit., p.441.
96 Urwin (1978), op. cit., p.261.
97 Miljan (1977), op. cit., p.145.
98 Ibid., pp.144–9.
99 Ibid., pp.163–4.
100 Urwin (1978), op. cit., p.261.

6 The 'Six' becomes the 'Nine'. The Accession of Britain, Denmark and Ireland to the European Community in 1973

C'est très simple. Maintenant, avec les six, il y a cinq poules et un coq. Si vous joignez (avec des autres pays), il y aura peut-être sept ou huit poules. Mais il y aura *deux* coqs.

French Minister of Agriculture to Christopher Soames, January 1963. Cited in Harold Macmillan (1973), *At the End of the Day*, London: Macmillan, p.365.

Prima facie support for Haas' hypothesis that 'the geographical as well as functional dimensions of integration tend to expand as new sectors are added'[1] may be found in the way the consolidated integration achieved by the Inner Six in building a Common Market served to attract, first, members of the Outer Seven and, ultimately, a wider nexus of European states into its magnetic field. In particular, Britain's decision in 1961 to apply to join the Six confirmed that the EEC would become the politico-economic centre of an integrating Europe and attract peripheral states into its orbit. Fellow-EFTA states Norway, Denmark and Ireland lodged requests for membership at the same time. Indeed, the economic iron curtain which descended across Western Europe in 1959 had been largely drawn back by 1973 when Britain, Denmark and Ireland became full members of the Community and when the remaining EFTA states (Switzerland, Sweden, Austria, Portugal, Norway, Finland and Iceland) were linked to the EEC through free-trade agreements in industrial goods.

When Haas wrote *The Uniting of Europe* in 1958, he appeared to regard the process of European integration as inexorable and exponential and to overlook the fact that 'a de Gaulle could thrust a stick in the spokes of the European bicycle'.[2] Indeed, the first section of this chapter considers the 'rough ride' which Britain's first two applications to join the EC (the acronym EEC was dropped in 1968) received from the French president. There follows an analysis of a proposal for Nordic economic cooperation – the so-called Nordek scheme – mooted by Denmark following the impasse in West European integration created by de Gaulle's rejection of Britain's second EC application in 1967. Next there is a discussion of the expansion of the 'Six' into a Community of Nine in 1973 and, finally, attention is given to the referenda decisions as a result of which Norway opted to stay out of and Britain to stay in the EC.

Britain Applies to Join the Common Market

On 27 July 1961 Harold Macmillan's Conservative government approved a British application to join the Common Market. At least four considerations seemed to have underpinned the change of heart. First, there was growing anxiety that the economic rift between the two Western Europes would engender deepening political divisions. Second, it was believed that the economic prosperity accruing from membership would contribute to maintaining British influence in the Commonwealth – an influence increasingly dependent on its supply of capital, aid and technical expertise. Third, Britain hoped that participation in the Common Market would bestow enhanced political influence on Britain, not only on the European continent, but in her dealings with the US and developing countries.[3] Finally, there was an instrumental 'if you can't beat 'em, join 'em' element in the calculus. Britain had patently failed through WFTA to impede the process of sectoral integration among the 'Six', which was moving from strength to strength, although Macmillan tried on several occasions, in private conversation with de Gaulle, to persuade the French president to ditch the Rome Treaty in favour of a free-trade zone. Only when these efforts failed did the British prime minister, with strong backing from Washington, turn to the Common Market.

In analysing de Gaulle's peremptory 'non' to Britain's first application to join, it is important to grasp, on the one hand, the French president's highly utilitarian approach to economic integration and, on the other, his passionately-pursued vision of a politico-strategic bloc of continental states acting as a 'third force' against superpower domination. Ironically, de Gaulle was as reluctant as Britain to pool sovereignty in economic affairs – integration was viewed as a recipe for a nation in eclipse – and his followers repudiated almost every 'European' step taken by the governments of the Fourth Republic, as late as July 1957, reaffirming their opposition to the proposed Treaty of Rome.[4] Indeed, a central premise of *gaullisme* was opposition to supranationality which was regarded as surrendering decision-making power to authorities run by technocrats who were in practice responsible to no one.[5] De Gaulle's 'conversion' to the EEC, therefore, was strictly limited to a perception of its value as a vehicle for accelerating the renewal of French industry and, more importantly, diffusing the costs. In May 1962, indeed, he observed baldly that, had it not been to France's obvious advantage, the Common Market would not have come into being.[6]

De Gaulle plainly believed, moreover, that Britain's inclusion in the Common Market before a Common Agricultural Policy (CAP) had been formulated would almost certainly undermine French chances of pressurizing the other members of the 'Six' into making the concessions it wished. Britain was hardly likely to sacrifice the benefits of low food prices and Commonwealth preferences in order to purchase French surpluses at inflated prices within a Community-backed agricultural market. Ultimately, though, these were mere bread-and-butter matters alongside the main meat of Gaullist foreign policy – the creation of the type of 'Third Force Europe' which the French president had originally envisaged in his celebrated Bar-le-Duc speech on 28 July 1946 and which was reflected in its essentials in the Fouchet Plan of 1962.

At Bar-le-Duc, de Gaulle depicted Western Europe as a distinct geopolitical region, burying the hatchet of history and moving forward in union to create a powerful counterpoise to the two emergent superpowers. 'The nations of the ancient West,' he wrote, 'which have for their vital arteries the North Sea, the Mediterranean, the Rhine, geographically situated between the two masses, determined to maintain an independence that would be dangerously exposed in the case of conflagration, physically and morally linked to the massive effort of the Russians, as well as the liberal impulse of the Americans ... what weight they would carry if they succeeded in combining their policies, despite grievances exchanged from age to age!'[7] On assuming the highest office, de Gaulle's distinctive mission was thus to seek to persuade the states along the Rhine, the Alps and Pyrenees to form a political, economic and strategic bloc. This was to be a West European bloc in full control of its destiny and no longer a mere pawn on the chess-board of superpower politics. In prompting the cause of political unity, in short, de Gaulle viewed France's role as *l'élément moteur* of a West European region commanding an authoritative voice in world affairs.

In the event, the Fouchet Plan was scuppered by Dutch concern that, without British participation in the proposed union, the smaller states would be controlled by a Franco-German power axis. In early 1962 de Gaulle, not to be denied, put forward his proposal for 'FRALIT' – a union of France, West Germany and Italy – although Italy soon opted out.[8] He did, however, gain the consistent support of West German Chancellor Adenauer, and when both the Fouchet Plan and FRALIT had been abandoned, de Gaulle sought to proceed bilaterally with Bonn. The Franco-German treaty of 22 January 1963 was doubtless especially satisfying to de Gaulle since the regional cooperation and consultation between the two governments that it envisaged involved no element of supranationality whatsoever.[9] However, this policy of bilateral cooperation was, in fact, doomed from the outset by the Federal Republic's obsession with her security needs and the view that the French simply could not assume the role played by the US as principal custodian of a West German state whose intentions provoked considerable suspicion in the Kremlin.

When the Macmillan government applied to join the Common Market in July 1961, it faced opposition from the farmers, the Commonwealth, Conservative backbenchers and, of course, the French. Only French antipathy could not be overcome. Admittedly, the farmers remained at best sceptical, but Commonwealth misgivings were finally eased at a London meeting of Commonwealth prime ministers in September 1962, and at the Conservative Party conference the following month, only about 50 delegates supported the Turton/Walker Smith amendment opposing British membership.[10] There was, as noted, a powerful irony in the French opposition, since de Gaulle contemplated precisely the loose-knit inter-governmental cooperation that Britain advocated, although he did not want Britain to be part of it. For the Général, it was a question of *L'Europe à l'anglaise sans les Anglais*.[11]

When Macmillan met de Gaulle at Château de Champs in June 1962, he detected two main elements in the General's aversion to Britain in Europe.[12] First, it would fundamentally alter the character of the Community. The EEC had developed into a congenial club – not too big, not too small – under French hegemony, but if the British, Norwegians and Danes *et al.* were involved, its personality would be radically different.[13] Second, de Gaulle believed that, in addition to her Commonwealth allegiances, Britain would always be too intrinsically bound up with the Americans and, by dint of this predominantly Atlanticist orientation, would be at best a second-rate European state. Britain's 'Atlanticist heresy' was shared in varying measure by all the 'Six'. There was also concern that an enlargement – a 'widening' rather than a 'deepening' of the Community in the jargon of the 1990s

– would further reduce the Common Market's unity of purpose and open the door to its domination by the US.[14]

De Gaulle's opposition in principle to British membership was apparent during a tense encounter with the British prime minister at the Château de Rambouillet on 15 December 1962. Summarizing his impressions, Macmillan noted that: 'The Five had independently rejected the "Plan Fouchet" – so he [de Gaulle] had now lost interest in Europe. He rejected Europe. He would substitute a French hegemony of the Six and wanted no new members.'[15] Subsequently, de Gaulle did nothing to discourage the myth that his decision to veto the British application – announced at a press conference on 14 January 1963 – was provoked by the Nassau Conference of 18–21 December 1962 at which Macmillan succeeded (with difficulty) in securing agreement from US President John F. Kennedy to supply Britain with American Polaris missiles (to replace Skybolt). But the Rambouillet record clearly demonstrates that de Gaulle was immutably opposed in principle to British accession.[16]

After de Gaulle's veto, attention shifted to Bonn, where the Franco-German treaty preparations were under way. Monnet urged Adenauer not to sign unless de Gaulle lifted his veto; the Federal Republic's foreign minister, Gerhard Schroeder, exerted pressure on the Chancellor to use his leverage with de Gaulle to help Britain; Kennedy also intervened. But it was all to no avail.[17] However, the rupture in negotiations with London in January 1963 may well have temporarily weakened the EEC; in Monnet's view, the French veto deprived the European Community of the extra dimension that could have made it the equal partner of the US.[18]

By June 1964 and the eleventh meeting of The Action Committee for the United States of Europe, Monnet observed that 'with no political plans and no hope of rapid enlargement, the Community was stagnating'.[19] Harold Wilson's new Labour government, he noted, had only a slender parliamentary majority – which seemed likely to delay the possibility of fresh negotiations – and in the US, President Lyndon Johnson, who succeeded after Kennedy's assassination in November 1963, appeared preoccupied with domestic problems (and, of course, Vietnam) and showed little interest in Europe. Monnet might also have touched on the way West Germany's enthusiasm for integration seemed to have cooled in direct proportion to her need for it. By the mid-1960s, the Federal Republic was Western Europe's leading creditor, her celebrated 'economic miracle' threatening to disrupt the balance in, and French domination of, the Community.

De Gaulle's nationalism and his opposition to supranationalism nonetheless remained unrelenting. When in 1965 the President of the Commission, Walter Hallstein, announced proposals to vest the Community with its own resources – levied mainly from the external tariff and intended primarily to finance the CAP – de Gaulle excoriated the Commission as 'a mostly foreign technocracy determined to trample on democracy in France'[20] and also condemned the proposed shift to majority voting in the Council of Ministers which was due to be implemented in January 1966. The prime minister, Couve de Murville, restated the main lines of his nation's objections in the Council of Ministers on 30 June 1965 and France then pursued an 'empty chair' strategy, virtually withdrawing from the EEC for six months. Significantly, the price of accommodation was acceptance of the unanimity rule in the Council of Ministers where vital national interests were involved.

In contrast to the stagnation which Monnet bemoaned within the 'Six', there were those on the British left at the time who detected a Gadarene rush of their compatriots to join the Common Market. For example, Douglas Jay, the Secretary of State at the Board of Trade during the first (and most of the second) Wilson government, identified three main factors in the British establishment's change of heart.[21] First, he claims that the Conservative Party viewed membership as an ideal opportunity to shift to indirect, consumer-based taxation, especially food taxes (along the continental model) and, under the guise of European unity, to halt the redistribution of incomes through direct progressive taxation. Second, it was believed in City circles, he contends, that the free movement of capital and the enhanced competition this implied would serve to 'discipline' the trade unions, put paid to strikes and restore the bargaining power of employers. Finally, Jay attaches much importance to the conversion of the Foreign Office to the pro-Market case and the way, under the influence of Con O'Neill (who moved to the Foreign Office after a period as ambassador to the EEC in Brussels), Michael Stewart, the foreign secretary, was won over. Significantly, he notes, a 'European Integration Department' was set up in the Foreign Office long before parliament or cabinet approved membership of the EEC. Jay's account also attests to the influence of the propaganda activities of the European Movement which enlisted widespread support 'in high places' in Britain.

In singling out the main adverse effects of British membership as higher food prices, a less favourable balance in manufactured goods and a budget deficit, Jay claims that Whitehall demonstrably misjudged the strength of Britain's bargaining position.[22] The French, he insists, wanted to sell Britain expensive food she did not want, whilst the West Germans wanted to sell her industrial goods she did not need. The French clearly understood this, but the Foreign Office equally clearly did not.[23] In a powerful summation of his hostility to the Common Market, Jay concludes: '… to swallow the Rome Treaty and the CAP, food taxes and all, would be to abandon my lifelong belief in redistribution of wealth by progressive taxes from the rich to the poor; in free imports of food; in law-making as well as government by elected authorities; and in international organisation rather than regional blocs. To sacrifice all this would be to go back on 1689 and 1832 as well as 1846 and 1945.'[24]

On the face of it, the Wilson cabinet's decision on 9 November 1966 to conduct a 'probe' of Common Market capitals was not designed to 'sacrifice all that', but simply to engage in a fact-finding mission aimed at revealing more about the operation of the EEC. Summing up at a cabinet conference on Europe at Chequers on 22 October, the prime minister thus insisted that there was no question of negotiating with the 'Six', at least before the outcome of the Kennedy Round of trade negotiations in GATT, and expressed his opposition to the foreign secretary George Brown's suggestion that Britain should come out publicly in favour of the Treaty of Rome. He articulated particular concern about the Community's agricultural policies and the free movement of capital, but also believed 'Europe' wanted to know where 'that other fellow Wilson stood'. If de Gaulle inquired about the Treaty of Rome, the prime minister added, assurances should be given that, provided that our reservations could be met, acceptance of it would not be a sticking-point.[25] In retrospect, however, it is likely that the primary objective of Wilson's Common Market 'probe' was to buy time so that a major policy reversal would not look so glaring. Wilson himself came under pressure from George Brown to join, when the eclipse of the latter's Department of Economic Affairs led him to seek another 'grand design', and he was possibly fearful too of a hostile press campaign from the Daily Mirror Group headed by the avid 'European' Cecil King.[26] Certainly when the EFTA prime ministers assembled in London on 5 December 1966 there was undoubted disappointment at the direction events were taking.

That direction was sharply reversed the following year, however, when de Gaulle delivered his second 'non' to British entry into the Common Market. It is just possible, to be sure, that opportunities were missed during the 'probe' for the achievement of an agreement that would have accommodated British interests better than conventional EEC membership. On 24–5 January 1967, when Wilson and Brown met the French President, de Gaulle, it appears, spoke elliptically of 'something entirely new' tailored to suit Britain's needs.[27] But on 16 May the Général convened a press conference at which he summarily ruled out British membership on terms other than wholesale surrender; a formal French veto on the Wilson government's EEC application followed on 27 November 1967. When *Agence France Presse* requested his view of developments, Monnet asked dolefully: 'In what kind of society are we living if the Six are to reject without debate the request of a great democratic country, massively backed by its elected representatives, to join in the building of Europe?'[28]

For the Général, there was still one European 'joker' to play before the political cards were put away and he retired to Colombey-les-deux-Églises. It came on 4 February 1969 when de Gaulle invited the British ambassador, Christopher Soames, to a private luncheon meeting and talked freely about his dissatisfaction with the EEC and his desire to negotiate with Britain about its enlargement. De Gaulle apparently envisaged the Community evolving into a wide free-trade area, including Britain, Ireland and Scandinavia, in which each country would be at liberty to make separate arrangements on the exchange of agricultural produce. Political cooperation would focus on a Big Four inner council of Britain, France, West Germany and Italy. The independent Europe de Gaulle evidently contemplated – and which was strongly reminiscent of his 'Third Force' proposals of 1946 onwards – would, of course, have threatened NATO's role,[29] although an act of collective withdrawal was never made explicit.[30] Having discussed the matter with Soames, de Gaulle mooted secret bilateral talks with Britain on a wide range of economic, monetary, political and defence issues to ascertain whether mutual differences could be resolved. He sought a gesture from London indicating the desirability of such talks.[31]

Although expressed only verbally, there were several contemporary observers who believed that de Gaulle's initiative was a serious one and that Britain bungled the whole '*affaire Soames*'. Indeed, in the eyes of one leading anti-marketeer, the rejection by a muddled government of de Gaulle's 'new and wonderfully far-sighted offer to Britain' was 'as catastrophic a blunder as Chamberlain's rejection of Roosevelt's offer in 1938'![32] Whilst the cabinet was kept largely ignorant, moreover, the prime minister seemed both overtaken and deflected by events.

In order to avoid the subsequent charge that Britain had been colluding to destroy the Common Market, Wilson (who was due to visit Bonn on 12 February 1969) was counselled and, indeed, felt obliged to inform the West German Chancellor, Kurt Kiesinger, of the Paris talks. Britain's Western European Union partners and the American President, Richard Nixon, were also notified. Not surprisingly, he was accused by the French of 'diplomatic terrorism'.[33] On his return to London, moreover, Wilson discovered that the Foreign Office had sent a full transcript of the de Gaulle–Soames meeting to a number of embassies, without authority from either the prime minister or cabinet.[34] Following reports of the Soames conversation in *Le Figaro* and two other French newspapers on 21 February, Wilson agreed to release a full account to the British press. The French were incensed by this and both de Gaulle and Soames felt their confidence had been betrayed. The British had not so much trumped de Gaulle's 'European' card as disingenuously shown her own hand to other

(EEC) players. As French foreign minister Michel Debré noted (changing metaphors), the matter was now buried: 'The book had been opened in good faith on 4 February and closed on 22 February.'[35]

Although twice spurned by de Gaulle, Britain's overtures for Common Market membership forced the hand of several of her EFTA partners. Denmark, who was concerned to protect her agricultural exports against a possible Anglo-French deal on farm products, decided to apply for membership in 1961 and Ireland and Norway followed suit. True, Swedish criticism of the impending desertions from EFTA led in June 1961 to the London Agreement. Those states seeking to accede to the EEC committed themselves to maintain solidarity with EFTA during the negotiations and not to enter the Common Market until a satisfactory solution for the remaining Outer Seven states had been found.[36]

Interestingly, although de Gaulle's first veto of British membership in January 1963 effectively grounded the applications of the other EFTA states, six months later de Gaulle personally offered the Danish prime minister, Jens-Otto Krag, EEC membership (full or associate). Krag, though, immediately consulted with Macmillan and the outcome was a strong declaration of solidarity with Britain and EFTA. Whether de Gaulle's offer was genuine or not or simply an attempt to split EFTA was ultimately less important than the fact that the Danish government's strategy was based on concurrent entry with Britain; this, coupled with the strength of anti-Market sentiment, meant there was insufficient time to change direction and proceed with unilateral accession without causing serious domestic ructions. Denmark immediately followed Britain in renewing her application for EEC membership in 1967, but when de Gaulle vetoed this second attempt to join, Denmark looked around for regional alternatives and revived the Nordic Common Market project.

The Nordic Common Market (Nordek) Proposal

When a Nordic Customs Union (Nordek) treaty was ready for signature on 24 March 1970, Western Europe appeared on the verge of fragmenting into mutually exclusive and competing economic regions. Disintegrative tendencies were seemingly in the ascendancy. Relations between EFTA and the EEC were strained; the creation of an enlarged Community incorporating Britain, Denmark, Ireland and Norway had twice been ruled out by de Gaulle; also, with the impetus towards West European integration (at least temporarily) halted, a Nordic Customs Union was on the threshold of completion.

Several conditions appeared conducive to Nordic integration. The region comprised small states for whom a prerequisite of sustained growth was access to the wider market that a customs union could provide. They could also boast a post-war record of cooperation and consultation through Uniscan, as members of EFTA (which Finland joined with associate status in 1961), and as partners in the inter-parliamentary Nordic Council, which in 1954 succeeded in achieving a pioneering labour market agreement. There was also a basic cultural homogeneity in the Nordic region – common bonds of language and history – although, as Hodža's stillborn Danubian Federation proposal in the 1930s had demonstrated, cultural identity is no guarantee of collective action towards economic integration. Calculations of national advantage are likely to be far more important. There were, in any event, several imponderables regarding a Nordic customs union.

These included the response of Britain and remaining EFTA states (which turned out to be favourable); the issue of future relations with the Common Market, if and when the opportunity for membership arose; and the question of whether the protected Nordic market would be large enough to facilitate sustained growth. Memories doubtless lingered, too, of the protracted saga of the original customs union proposal which Norway finally wrecked in 1959 with the argument that her industry would not be in a position to compete effectively with that of Denmark and Sweden. It would also be crucial to take security policy considerations into account. The construction of supranational management structures could not be allowed to compromise Swedish neutrality or, by provoking a hostile Kremlin reaction, threaten Finland's position. Finally, there was a strong convention in the region that each state should take the interests of the others into account and that, in the absence of consensus on collective action, each state should go its own way.

Nonetheless, when de Gaulle vetoed Britain's second EEC application, the Danish non-socialist coalition under Hilmar Baunsgaard felt the time was ripe to resurrect the Nordic Common Market proposal. The Nordek blueprint involved the creation of a customs union embracing all sectors of trade, industry and agriculture, supervised by a number of common institutions and including a central investment bank. In resuscitating the customs union project at a Nordic Council meeting in February 1968, Baunsgaard acknowledged that the timing owed much to de Gaulle's 'non' to Britain which also left Denmark's bid to join the EEC high and dry. It was in this context of deadlock on the enlargement of the Community that Baunsgaard's foreign minister noted that: 'The Nordic countries could try and make a constructive contribution during the stalemate in European market integration efforts which has occurred against Denmark's will and desire.'[37]

The inter-governmental negotiations were completed within two years and agreement on a broad framework for Nordek's activities took no time at all. The Nordic states explicitly affirmed their continuing obligations as EFTA members and left the door open for Iceland – which was in the process of preparing an EFTA application – subsequently to join Nordek. Regional integration should not prevent the parties from later participation in an expanded EEC, nor should it constrain the Nordic aim of fostering Third World trade or frustrate their ultimate goal of global free trade. Finally, an economic union should not jeopardize foreign and security policy arrangements in the region. The 'Nordic balance', in short, should not be disrupted.[38]

It is plain that, during the greater part of the Nordek negotiations, Finland did not believe that the other participants would have an early opportunity of joining the EEC, at least on remotely acceptable terms.[39] Indeed, the impasse created by de Gaulle largely dictated Finnish tactics, since for security reasons it was imperative that, from the Soviet viewpoint, the nascent Nordek treaty should not be tarred with the Common Market brush. The Finns were probably gambling on an expeditious *dénouement* of negotiations and the approval of a Nordek treaty before Denmark and Norway re-entered direct negotiations with the Community. De Gaulle's resignation in April 1969 significantly increased the risk of Nordek being overtaken by events, however, as neither Denmark nor Norway had disguised the fact that they viewed the Nordek negotiations in large part as a stepping-stone to an accommodation – ideally a pan-Nordic accommodation – with the EEC.[40] The Hague summit of the 'Six' on 1 December 1969, at which it was agreed to deal promptly with a third British application for membership, tolled the death-knell for Nordek.[41] On 3 December the Finnish cabinet requested a postponement of an intergovernmental conference scheduled for the middle of the month; in a brief communiqué it noted, rather obliquely, that 'European integration has progressed to a stage at which attitudes to Nordek might well be influenced'.[42]

The Finnish government was in fact split between Mauno Koivisto, the Social Democratic prime minister, who initially wished to press ahead with Nordek, and Ahti Karjalainen and Paavo Aitio, representing the Centre and Communist parties, who did not. In defence of his line, Koivisto quoted Baunsgaard and Per Borten, the Norwegian prime minister, to the effect that the Hague talks had not altered their positive stance towards Nordic integration. Support for Baunsgaard's continuing commitment might perhaps be found in his subsequent suggestion of a SCANDEK customs union – Nordek minus Finland – although this was not countenanced by Borten or the Swedish premier, Olof Palme.[43]

Foreign secretary Karjalainen's desire to retard the Nordek process was founded on concern about a hostile Kremlin reaction to any formal Finnish association with a customs union essaying future links with the EEC. Karjalainen apparently gained President Urho Kekkonen's acquiescence in deferring a decision on Nordek until after the March 1970 general election. Nordek's highly sensitive political character, the foreign secretary concluded, stemmed from the Soviet suspicion that the whole enterprise represented a 'backdoor into the EEC'.[44] Karjalainen's tactical caution on the Nordek question and the centrol role of anticipated reaction in his analysis should be viewed against the background of his extensive contacts with Soviet diplomats in Helsinki and, as a corollary, his heightened anxiety about the strained state of Finno-Soviet relations.

Nonetheless, he clearly discerned possible grounds for believing that the Kremlin's attitude towards Finland had become increasingly hawkish since the fall of Khruschev. His evidence, though both subjective and anecdotal, constituted, in his judgement, a case for a detrimental change in the nuance, if not (as yet) the substance, of relations between the two countries. A number of factors, he contended, had cumulatively and adversely coloured the Soviet view. First, there was Soviet displeasure at his own United Nations speech in October 1968 in which Karjalainen had urged all nations to respect the territorial sovereignty of others and condemned the use of force, both in connection with the Warsaw Pact invasion of Prague (August 1968) and American involvement in Vietnam. Second, there were indications of Soviet irritation at the Finnish government's decision in 1968 to proceed to seek full OECD membership (it had previously enjoyed observer status). Finally, Karjalainen intimated that Kekkonen's initiative in May 1969 to organize a European Security Conference in Helsinki (originally a Soviet proposal emanating from the 1950s) was designed in no small measure to defuse the build-up of backstage Finno-Soviet tension. When, following Soviet President Podgorny's visit to Helsinki in October 1969, the official communiqué omitted the traditional reference to Finnish neutrality (a routine insertion ever since the return in 1955 of the annexed Soviet naval base at Porkkala in south-west Finland), there did indeed appear to be something in Paavo Aitio, the Transport Minister's, view that a hard illiberal line was emerging in Moscow.[45]

It is quite possible that Karjalainen's contacts with senior Soviet diplomats in Helsinki led him unwittingly to exaggerate Soviet hostility to Nordek. The reservations of individual diplomats did not necessarily reflect the official Kremlin line. Certainly the fact that Kekkonen felt able to proceed with Nordek, albeit in the face of a change of heart from Koivisto, appears to dash the persistent myth that the Finnish president was prevailed upon during a hunting trip to the Soviet Union to disengage his nation from negotiations. Equally, Kekkonen's policy rested on maintaining the rigid distinction between regional integration through Nordek and wider West European integration based on the EEC, which he recognized Moscow regarded with extreme mistrust.

The President's strategy was based on four main considerations.[46] First, Finland could not be involved in the Common Market as a full or associate member, either directly or through Nordek. Second, the expansion of the EEC to incorporate part of the Nordic region was not in Finland's interests. Third, Finland should continue with the Nordek negotiations but, in the event of a proposed Nordek member commencing negotiations on EEC membership, Finland should reserve the right to discontinue the Nordek talks until such time as any outcome regarding the EEC was clear. Finally, if the country in question proceeded to join the EEC, the Nordek project should be shelved: if they did not, negotiations could be resumed where they had left off. Kekkonen concluded that it was crucial that blame for the possible collapse of Nordek should not subsequently be laid at Finland's door: 'Culpability must be made to rest with the nation that chose the EEC before Finland'![47]

In accordance with Kekkonen's tactics, Finland requested a declaration of non-intent from her Nordic partners regarding Common Market negotiations, a move which permitted further progress on Nordek. When Koivisto met Kekkonen on 23 March 1970, a treaty merely awaited the formalities. Differences between the president and prime minister, however, continued, with Koivisto proposing that Nordek should go unratified. Kekkonen, for his part, believed that Finland should press ahead, not because he thought a regional common market would materialize, but because it would leave Finland in a strong tactical position when (as appeared inevitable) Denmark applied to join the EEC. The president emphasized that the final Nordek document incorporated a clause enabling Finland to withdraw the same day as another signatory state sought accession to the Common Market. Koivisto nonetheless held firm, insisting that it would be 'dishonest' of Finland to proceed in the circumstances.[48] Consequently, when senior diplomats convened in Copenhagen on 24 March 1970 to undersign the Nordek treaty, Koivisto sent dramatic countermanding instructions. The Finnish premier subsequently justified his action by reference to the intransigence of the Communists in the cabinet and the confused post-election situation in which setbacks for the coalition parties had necessitated a reshuffle of the governing pack that might take weeks.[49] A 'caretaker government', it was implied, did not have the authority to sign the Nordek treaty.

If the domestic political situation in Finland dealt it the final blow, Nordek was, in truth, overtaken by events external to the region in much the same way as the first Nordic customs union proposal had been effectively subsumed in the wider negotiations on WFTA (1957–

8) and the ultimate formation of EFTA in 1959. It is highly probable that for the Finns, the Nordek initiative was less about the economics of regional integration – the advantages of a pan-Nordic market – than the politics of regional integration and the imperatives of a *Westpolitik* that sought to extend contacts to another Western organization following the nation's recent accession to the OECD. Equally, in view of Finland's exposed geopolitical position, it was vital that Nordek should remain strictly independent of the Common Market so as not to jeopardize the nation's assiduously pursued *Ostpolitik* of maintaining relations of mutual trust with her superpower neighbour. The future expansion of the EEC envisaged in the Werner and Davignon reports (see Chapter 7) inevitably aroused Soviet suspicion and rendered it essential for Finland to dissociate herself from any approaches to the Common Market, particularly from the Nordic NATO members, Norway and Denmark. It was against this changed backcloth, and with Denmark having made no secret of her intention to reapply for EEC membership, that Finland ultimately declined to underwrite the Nordek treaty.[50]

For Denmark, like Finland, political rather than economic considerations were uppermost during the Nordek negotiations. Admittedly, regional integration and the concomitant protection of markets – if not necessarily the creation of a protected market – possessed strong appeal. Significantly, trade liberalization within EFTA had led to a steep growth in Danish industrial exports to the Nordic countries which, indeed, provided their main outlet at the time of the Nordek talks. But it was the politics of extra-regional economic integration – that is, future approaches to the EEC – that dominated Danish thinking, with the result that Nordek tended to be viewed, like EFTA, as little more than a temporary expedient and a pathway *en route* to the Common Market. For Denmark, Nordek thus served the purpose of strengthening bridges to the Nordic region before the magnetic force of the EEC drew her inexorably further away from her regional neighbours. It was in this tactical context that Miljan has argued that Denmark 'made it clear that it did not matter much whether the formation of Nordek was successful of not, as long as the exercise was carried out'.[51]

The 'Six' becomes the 'Nine'

Changed political circumstances in the course of 1969–70 facilitated a third (successful) British application to join the Common Market. First, there was the resignation of de Gaulle in April 1969, directly after a referendum on 'the creation of the regions and the transformation of the Senate'. De Gaulle's proposal – to set up regional councils, partly constituted along corporatist lines, and to downgrade the Senate to an essentially consultative role – was rejected by 53.2 per cent of French voters. Having made the outcome a matter of confidence, de Gaulle promptly relinquished the presidency;[52] in Philip Goodhart's felicitous phrase, 'a President who lives by the referendum must ultimately die by the referendum'.[53] He was succeeded in June 1969 by former prime minister, Georges Pompidou.

Second, the grand coalition of Christian Democrats and Social Democrats, which was formed in the German Federal Republic in 1966, gave way in October 1969 to a Social Democratic-led government under the enthusiastic pro-European Willy Brandt. For Brandt, the European Community was not to be viewed as merely an economic marriage of convenience (à la de Gaulle), but rather as a major force for peace and security on the continent.[54] In addition to enjoying a strong personal relationship with Pompidou, Brandt was instrumental in fostering crucial direct links between Heath and Pompidou in early summer 1971.[55]

Next, the technical questions associated with a third British application had been well aired in advance and solutions proposed. Thus, at its meeting in Brussels on 15 July 1969, the Monnet Action Committee reviewed the conclusions of four commissioned studies undertaken by independent experts into the problems of British membership: Guido Carli, the Governor of the Bank of Italy, on monetary questions; Lord Plowden and Karl Winnacker of Hoechst industries on technology; Edgard Pisani on agriculture; and Walter Hallstein on institutions.[56] The problems associated with British entry, it was concluded, could be resolved. Indeed, at the Hague summit of the 'Six' in December 1969, it was agreed to resume negotiations with Britain.

Finally, there was the election in June 1970 of a Conservative government under Edward Heath who, of course, had been the chief EEC negotiator for Harold Macmillan in 1961–2. The Common Market was not a contentious election question in 1970.[57] Earlier that year, an NOP poll found that the EEC ranked as only the eighth most important issue among voters and that a majority of persons were, in any event, unsympathetic to membership. Between April and July 1970 there was only about 20 per cent support for applying to join, compared with 60 per cent of respondents who opposed such a move. The Conservative manifesto, moreover, merely stated that 'our sole commitment is to negotiate' and not to enter the Common Market without the 'full-hearted consent of parliament and people'. The Labour Party was internally divided to an extent which prompted the leadership to play down the significance of its policy of applying for membership.[58] Once elected, however, Heath wasted no time. Negotiations on British entry into the Common Market lasted from late summer 1970 to the signing of the Treaty of Accession on 22 January 1972.

Third British Application to Join the EEC

A crucial factor in the success of the third British application was the attitude of Pompidou, whom Heath first met in May 1971 and with whom the Conservative prime minister established a good rapport. Unlike his predecessor, Pompidou saw a deal with Britain as advantageous to the French, for two major reasons. First, he perceived, along with the anti-Marketeers in Britain, that London was ready effectively to capitulate on all the essential EEC questions – including the Common Agricultural Policy – and that accession was therefore in France's economic interests. There was a recognition on the president's part that, in the case of the longstanding French opposition to British membership, 'ill-humour', in Monnet's words, 'had overruled reason and even self-interest'.[59] Shortly after the first Heath–Pompidou meeting, moreover, it became evident that a majority in France agreed: 55 per cent of a national sample held that British entry would be in France's interest, compared with only 17 per cent who believed it would not.[60]

Second, Pompidou regarded a revival of the Anglo-French *entente cordiale* as a vital counterweight not only to the resurgence of German economic power, but also to the successful West German initiatives towards a *rapprochement* with East Germany and the Soviet Union. True, in the build-up to the Paris summit of Common Market leaders in autumn 1972, Pompidou made much rhetorical play of his support for a (West) European confederation, intimating that economic and monetary union would serve as insurance against any drift to Atlanticism following British entry into the market.[61] But, in reality, Pompidou's *Westpolitik* and his support for Heath's third application for British membership were motivated first and foremost by concern about the success of Brandt's *Ostpolitik*.

In contrast, Pompidou's decision, announced at a press conference on 16 March 1972, to hold a referendum on British entry was motivated almost solely by tactical domestic considerations.[62] There was the desire to demonstrate his independence from hardline Gaullists – the likes of Michel Debré (who regarded Britain as an outpost of the US)[63] and Pierre Messmer[64] – by using the irreproachable Gaullist device of the referendum. There was a concern, too, to appeal to the ardent pro-European centrists with a view to facilitating their participation in government. Pompidou also sought to drive a wedge between the Socialists under François Mitterrand and the Communists led by Georges Marchais who were divided on the issue, but nevertheless planning electoral cooperation and a *programme commun* for the 1973 general election. Finally, Pompidou wanted to strengthen France's diplomatic hand at the Paris summit scheduled for autumn 1972. In this latter objective, he patently failed, since a minority of only 36.1 per cent of the registered electorate favoured the enlarged Community. Whilst 67.7 per cent of French voters on 23 April 1972 supported the expansion of the EEC, a turnout of 60.7 per cent represented the highest abstention rate in any national election since the war.

After a six-day parliamentary debate, the vote on 28 October 1971 on 'the principle of British membership' of the Common Market, on the basis of the arrangements which had been negotiated, split both major parties in the most dramatic circumstances. Opening the House of Commons debate, the Foreign and Commonwealth Secretary, Sir Alec Douglas-Home, noted prophetically: 'The European Economic Community will be a magnet for EFTA and other countries. It will go on and become more prosperous and neither Europe nor the world will wait for us any longer.'[65] Not everybody was convinced by any means, however, and indeed there were dissidents on both sides of the House. A leading Conservative anti-Marketeer, Sir Robin Turton, argued that Britain's role in the world was something much wider than an inward-looking community, whilst his backbench party colleague, Sir E.E. Bullus, claimed the terms were demanding, excessive and more in line with the crippling reparations required of a country defeated in war.[66] The Tory anti-Marketeers had in fact formed themselves into a faction, the '1970 Group', which they registered with the Whips and which met as a dining club about three times a year under Sir Derek Walker-Smith. Anybody who expressed opposition to EEC entry was eligible to join; at its height it boasted a membership of about 56 MPs.[67]

On the Labour side, David Owen, a member of the so-called 'Gang of Four' that in 1981 broke with the Labour Party and ultimately set up the Social Democrats, insisted that Britain would be better placed to exercise an influence for good in international and East–West relations within the Community than outside it.[68] In the event, 69 pro-Market Labour MPs, including (in addition to Owen) Roy Jenkins, Shirley Williams and William Rogers – the other members of the Gang of Four – defied a three-line whip and supported Heath, whilst 39 Conservative anti-Marketeers voted against the prime minister and with the Labour opposition. Twenty Labour MPs abstained, giving Heath a majority of 112 (356 votes to 244) on the principle of membership.

The anti-Marketeers, however, continued their fight into 1972 and, accordingly, a long parliamentary struggle ensued over the European Communities Bill (ECB) which contained the negotiated terms. The Heath government's position was seriously endangered by the Labour Party's decision in autumn 1971 to oppose the proposed terms of entry – during the three-day Second Reading debate, not one Labour MP rose to support the bill[69] – which meant that the government could no longer rely on the support of cross-voting from the Opposition benches. Since the 'Group 70' was still active in canvassing anti-Market support among the Tories and since a number of hardliners like Enoch Powell simply could not be 'whipped' into line, Heath adopted a two-pronged strategy for getting the ECB through parliament. First, a number of Tory anti-Marketeers came under pressure from their constituency organizations to toe the party line, with the implicit sanction of de-selection if they refused.[70] Second, as the Labour Party's decision to oppose the existing terms of entry turned the ECB's passage into a straight fight between the two leading parties, Heath could reasonably expect that considerations of party loyalty would prevail in the anti-Market camp. In order to emphasize the point, he was counselled into turning the Second Reading of the ECB into a vote of confidence in the government – defeat would mean a dissolution of parliament.

Despite these tactical endeavours, the result of the Second Reading of the ECB on 17 February 1972 turned out to be an extremely close call for the government. Heath contrived a majority of only eight votes (309–301); 15 Tories voted against the Bill – the first time in post-war history that a group of backbenchers had entered an Opposition lobby against a Conservative government on a vote of confidence.[71] Five more Conservatives abstained, as did five Labour MPs. Indeed, as Philip Norton has stressed, if the Heath government had not attracted the 'support' of five Liberals and the five Labour abstainers, it would have gone down to defeat.[72] Thereafter, notwithstanding vigorous opposition – Powell, for example, voted against his own government on no less than 80 occasions[73] – the ECB completed its remaining stages in the House of Commons unamended and was given a Third Reading on 13 July 1972.

Two final points on British membership need emphasis. First, despite the three-line whip on opposing the Tory terms of entry, the Labour Party remained deeply split on the EEC issue. The factionalism in its ranks (both reflecting and exacerbating existing left–right divisions) did not lead to fragmentation in the sense of the formation of breakaway groupings. But as Peter Byrd has noted, by summer 1975 the Labour government found itself in the anomalous position of entering the referendum campaign (on the renegotiated terms of British membership) opposed by a majority of its MPs, by party conference, by a revitalized National Executive Committee (NEC) and by the Trades Union Congress (TUC).[74]

Second, Britain became the only member-state to join the enlarged Community in January 1973 which did not hold a referendum on the question of accession. Moreover, there is no reason to suppose that the outcome would necessarily have been favourable as most of the electorate was ignorant of, and essentially hostile towards, the EEC. Indeed, notwithstanding the intensive campaigning of the pro-Market European Movement, which distributed 6.5 million items of literature over the second half of 1971,[75] an NOP poll in July 1971 found that only 13 per cent of interviewees knew which countries belonged to the EEC, while 40 per cent were unable to cite any of the principal issues involved in membership.[76] Understandably, perhaps, the decision of the Labour Party leadership and annual party conference to reject the terms of British entry meant that, in contrast to the majority of Conservative voters which favoured membership, Labour voters became increasingly antagonistic. Furthermore, the absence of a referendum frustrated the opportunity for a full popular debate; partly in consequence, the question of EEC membership lacked voter saliency. True, on 4 February 1970 a cross-party, extra-parliamentary 'Common Market Safeguards Campaign' had been founded (it was dogged by inadequate funding) to mobilize electoral opposition to British membership, but, ironically, several of its leaders concentrated their energies over summer 1972 not on the 'battle in Britain' (which after the enactment of the ECB seemed lost) but on the anti-market campaigns in Denmark and Norway where referenda were shortly to be held.[77]

Danish Application to Join the Common Market

Throughout this period Denmark had been the most restless EFTA state, fearing the ramifications for her agricultural exports of a permanent economic iron curtain descending across Western Europe.[78] An optimal scenario thus involved conjoining West Germany and Britain, her two leading customers, in a trade bloc of any kind as long as it included farm products. Indeed, when the EEC reached agreement on the fundamentals of the CAP during 1961–2 and, in addition, the Macmillan government shifted from free trade to 'Community', Denmark ended its earlier vacillation and submitted a formal EEC application, along with Britain, on 10 August 1961.[79] She followed Britain in renewing this application in 1967 but, after de Gaulle's second veto, proposed the reactivation of the Nordic Common Market proposal (Nordek) as a stop-gap measure.

In submitting a third application in tandem with Britain, the Danish Minister of Economics and Market Relations accepted that the intensification of cooperation in the monetary, economic, industrial and technological fields would be essential. He eschewed the need for a transitional period and underlined the way Denmark had been 'restructuring' – modernizing her economy since the late 1950s in readiness for membership.[80] Unlike the stumbling-block of fisheries in the cases of Britain and Norway, there appeared to be no major obstacles for Denmark to surmount during the EEC negotiations. The importance of the enlarged Common Market for Denmark, moreover, could be gauged by the fact that it stood to account for no less than 47 per cent of her imports and 42.1 per cent of exports on 1970 figures.[81] Yet despite the imposing economic arguments favouring membership, Denmark remained an 'equivocal European', working to protect and promote her fundamental interests, but not at the expense of a substantial loss of sovereignty, still less a commitment to any future political union.[82]

Denmark's third EEC application was submitted by the same non-socialist coalition – the first since before the First World War – under Baunsgaard that had taken the initiative on Nordek. However, the decision ultimately to submit the whole membership question to a popular referendum stemmed from the opposition-based Social Democrats, for whom three tactical calculations were germane. First, it was hoped that the promise of a referendum would neutralize the EEC as an election issue at the polls in September 1971 (it failed to do so). Next, it was hoped to minimize the loss of anti-Market Social Democratic votes to the strongly anti-EEC Socialist People's Party (SPP). It was significant that among those who joined the SPP before 1971 only 2 per cent mentioned opposition to the Common Market as their primary reason, whereas this figure rose to 19 per cent in 1971 and 45 per cent among those who joined in 1972.[83] Finally, the Social Democrats sought via the referendum commitment to buy time with which to undermine the anti-Market campaign.[84] In the event, both left-wing parties gained ground at the 21 September election, with the result that a Social Democratic minority cabinet, backed by the SPP (albeit not crucial EEC questions), led Denmark into the Common Market referendum of October 1972.

The intensive, at times even bitter, six-month referendum campaign generated unprecedented interest among the citizenry. A measure of the perceived importance of the EEC question – in contrast to the situation in Britain – can be gained from the fact that over 60 per cent of voters claimed to have seen all or at least most of the Common Market broadcasts of the five major parties. Even bearing in mind the existence of only one television channel, this would seem to disprove theories of selective exposure to arguments.[85] Equally, there was remarkably little shift in people's basic attitudes to the EEC over the course of the campaign[86] and their reasons (both for joining and staying out) also remained largely stable.[87]

The campaign also mobilized pressure group activity, although to widely varying degrees. For example, the relatively highly politicized blue-collar unions participated extensively on both sides of the argument. The 260 000-strong General and Semi-Skilled Workers' Union

(DASF) was especially prominent in opposing membership despite the fact that the central labour federation (LO) to which it belonged was in favour. Other sectional organizations (like the pro-Market agriculture, fisheries and craft unions) were less involved, and the white-collar organizations virtually dormant.[88] The leading anti-Market group was the cross-party 'People's Movement against the European Community' which attracted a broad spectrum of Social Democrats, Radical Liberals, radical leftists, students, environmentalists and rural nationalists, also receiving support *inter alia* from the anti-Market lobby in the UK.

Although opinion polls in the 1960s had indicated safe pro-Market majorities, opposition to Danish membership rose as the moment of truth approached. By the end of 1971, opposition had climbed to 30 per cent. In the event support had dropped to around 40 per cent;[89] 36 per cent of the electorate ultimately voted against entry on a 90.1 per cent turn-out. This vastly exceeded the figure (at most 20 per cent) which could have been expected on the basis of routine popular support for the anti-Market parties. At the final *Folketing* ballot on 8 September 1971, no less than 141 parliamentarians had voted 'yes' (the Conservatives and Liberals *en bloc*) and only 34 voted 'no'. Significantly, whilst two members abstained and two absented themselves, four Radicals, one Greenlander and as many as 12 Social Democrats opposed membership. Indeed, like its fraternal party in the UK, the Danish Social Democrats were divided on the EEC issue. Moreover, in the wake of Denmark's third application, a sizeable pro-Market majority was replaced by a clear partisan plurality against joining. Then, following the September 1971 general election, the anti-Marketeers formed their own faction within the Social Democrats' *Folketing* group – a unique phenomenon in the party's history.[90] (A maverick anti-EEC faction also emerged within the Radical Liberals' parliamentary group.) Yet over the course of the campaign, a clear Social Democratic majority against membership was converted into a narrow majority in favour of accession.[91]

The Common Market remained a live issue in Denmark, both inside and outside parliament, well after the October 1972 referendum. Significantly, the cataclysmic general election in 1973, in doubling the number of parties, revived the parliamentary fortunes of two anti-EEC parties (the Communists and Justice Party), whilst opinion polls conducted across the Community in the mid-1970s showed that Denmark was consistently the most negative in its attitude towards 'Europe'.[92] Moreover, until the outcome of the British referendum of 5 June 1975 there was a feeling that perhaps Denmark's EEC fate had not finally been sealed. In 1975 there was in fact a *Folketing* majority in favour of a new Danish referendum on whether to stay in the EEC should Britain reject the renegotiated terms[93] – which, in the event, she did not.

'The People's Movement against the European Community', however, continued its work and, at the first direct elections to the European Parliament in Strasbourg in June 1979, it achieved a remarkable result. Although Denmark's turn-out of 47.8 per cent was the second lowest behind the 33 per cent in the UK – itself a fair reflection of the general lack of enthusiasm for the Common Market – the anti-EEC alliance obtained no less than 32 per cent of the vote.[94] In 1984, too, when the participation level rose to 52 per cent, the electorate returned four People's Movement delegates (one-quarter of the Danish allocation to Strasbourg) on a 20.9 per cent vote, making anti-Marketeers the second largest Danish group in the European Parliament! Finally, although at the Strasbourg elections of 15 June 1989 the turn-out in Denmark dropped to a nadir of 46 per cent[95] the People's Movement succeeded in preserving its four seats, albeit on a somewhat reduced poll of 18.9 per cent.[96]

Three further EEC-related referenda have been held within the realms of the Danish kingdom since 1972. The first in Greenland in 1982 concerned leaving the EEC; the next in 1986 related to Danish approval of the Single European Act; the last, on 2 June 1992, was a national ballot on ratifying the Maastricht Treaty on European Union.

Granted Home Rule status by the Danish crown following a devolution referendum on the island on 17 January 1979, Greenland canvassed and gained Copenhagen's assent to an early referendum – held on 23 February 1982 – on continuing membership of the Common Market. To the question: 'Do you wish Greenland to remain in the EEC?', 12 615 voters or 52 per cent of the 74.9 per cent who turned out to cast a ballot said 'no', compared with 46.1 per cent who favoured the status quo of membership. Subsequently, there was unanimous acceptance of the referendum result in the regional assembly *Landsting*, although the opposition-based Atassut Party emphasized that its acquiescence was not *ipso facto* to be construed as approval of Greenland's decision to leave the EEC.[97]

Two primary anxieties dominated the Greenlandic anti-Market lobby, led by the left-centre Siumut Party, during the 1982 referendum campaign. First, concern had developed among the 50 000 Inuit-speaking Eskimo population that unduly generous fishing rights were being granted to West Germany around the Greenlandic coast. Second, the indigenous, nomadic Inuit lifestyle appeared threatened by the (voluntary) EEC seal import ban which was ruining the market for pelts.[98] The chair of the regional government, Jonathan Motzfeldt, also emphasized the future importance Greenland would attach to cooperation with the Inuit populations in Alaska and Canada.[99] In October 1972 there had been a massive 'no' to the EEC in Greenland:

70.2 per cent of the electorate on a low 56.0 per cent turn-out had opposed membership, compared with 29.3 per cent in favour. Ten years later it became the first region to leave the European Community, formally parting company on 1 January 1984. The Faeroe Islands, incidentally, which since 1984 have also enjoyed Home Rule status under the Danish crown, had no need to do the same because they were not incorporated into the EEC in 1973. A member of EFTA, the Faeroes left in 1973 when Denmark joined the Common Market but ultimately achieved a free-trade agreement with the EEC.[100]

A second national EC referendum in Denmark was called for 27 February 1986 by a minority non-socialist coalition under Poul Schlüter when, on 14 January that year, the leading opposition party, the Social Democrats, declared that they intended to vote against acceptance of the Single European Act.[101] Since the Radicals had already decided to oppose the EC reform package, because of the inclusion of the European Political Community (EPC) treaty, the traditional cross-party consensus on foreign policy was shattered. The Schlüter government used the referendum as a tactical weapon against a refractory *Folketing* majority as an alternative to calling a general election, leading to accusations of its use of Gaullist methods.[102]

As Torben Worre has noted, the 1986 referendum on approving the Single European Act – like the one in 1972 – was at heart a question of Denmark's membership of the European Community.[103] The central thesis of the opposition groups, that the reform package would set in train an accelerating process of political union, had a remarkable impact on the electorate; no less than 75 per cent of voters were in agreement – 57 per cent of those who favoured the package and virtually all those who rejected it. However, despite the manifest Danish aversion to integration, the spectre of political union failed to deter enough voters – in contrast to the Maastricht referendum of June 1992 – and 56.2 per cent favoured signing the Single European Act.

The victory for approval was largely the result of the deep division on the reform package among the Social Democratic electorate and a correspondingly lower turn-out on the 'no' side than among voters of the governing parties.[104] In fact, the volatility of Social Democrats on the issue was exceptionally high; it has been estimated that at least one-quarter of SDP voters changed their minds in the last weeks of the campaign.[105] In 1972 support for Common Market membership was higher in the middle-class areas of Greater Copenhagen than its working-class districts and relatively greater in the small towns and rural localities than in the capital, its suburbs and cities of more than 10 000 people.[106] The same was broadly true in 1986 and although the turn-out at 75.4 per cent was significantly lower than in 1972, support for increased European integration exceeded 75 per cent of voters in parts of Western Jutland,[107] but fell below half in Greater Copenhagen.[108] Reflecting on the 1986 referendum on the Single European Act, one expert concluded; 'Danish membership of the European Community is reaffirmed and will remain indisputable for many years to come.'[109] The third national EC referendum in Denmark in June 1992 on ratifying the Maastricht treaty on European Union, however, dramatically questioned such a judgement (see Chapter 7).

Ireland's Accession to the Common Market

Much as in Denmark, the main thrust of the pro-Market lobby in Ireland was that, if Britain joined, it would be virtually impossible for her to remain outside the EEC. Unlike the mainland, both the two main parties – the governing Fianna Fail under *Taoiseach* Jack Lynch and the main opposition Fine Gael – favoured membership, as did the vast majority of farmers. Ironically, despite following closely on Britain's coat-tails, one of the prominent pro-EEC arguments was that membership would serve to weaken Ireland's strong UK orientation in trade, loosen the ties apparently binding the two countries in a special relationship and give the Republic wider options. It was also believed (mistakenly) that London could not continue to deal with Northern Ireland as if it were simply a domestic family matter.[110] To the charge that EEC membership would involve a significant loss of sovereignty, the government insisted that 'such limitations on national freedom of action which membership of the Communities will involve will be more than counterbalanced by the influence which we will be able to bring to bear on the formulation of Community policies affecting our interests'.[111]

In the event, Ireland became the only neutral member of the Common Market. Her accession represented a significant step in the integration into the West European mainstream of a small polity of 3.4 million inhabitants which had for long isolated herself diplomatically through the pursuit of policies rooted in political and economic nationalism. Under a Fianna Fail hegemony of power (the party dominated government between 1932 and 1972), Ireland sought to achieve economic independence, that is to say self-sufficiency (autarky), behind high tariff protection walls. On the international stage, a foremost symbol of her sovereignty and independence lay in the active promotion of military (armed) neutrality. Thus, during the Second World War, Ireland was neutral and, indeed, remained inviolate albeit, in no small measure because this suited the Anglo-American alliance and constituted a benevolent neutrality from the British and American viewpoints.[112] Primarily dictated by pragmatic considerations, neutrality did not enjoy unanimous cross-party support in the Dail; significantly, there were several politicians who publicly indicated their acquiescence in any move to establish US military bases in Ireland for the duration of hostilities. Furthermore, as Raymond Raymond has shown, although the civil service seems faithfully to have implemented the policy laid down by the governing Fianna Fail, the main opposition Fine Gael was unenamoured of neutrality.[113]

Whilst a founder-member of the OEEC and Council of Europe, Ireland declined to join NATO in 1949. She felt unwilling to associate herself through NATO with an Imperial power in Westminster which maintained an arbitrary partition of Ireland.[114] In addition to the financial burden of membership, Ireland also feared a loss of independence resulting from the growing harmonization of the foreign policies of the NATO states.[115] The government confronting the NATO decision, moreover, was a heterogeneous grouping of Fine Gael, *Clann na Talmhan* (Agrarians), the Labour Party and the republic socialist *Clann na Poblachta* which spent much of its time trying to deny Fianna Fail issues – first and foremost the question of NATO membership – which could be used as the basis of a vote of no confidence.[116] Ireland did not become a member of the United Nations until 1956, her initial application being vetoed by the Soviet Union ostensibly on grounds of Ireland's neutrality during the war. Indeed, as Basil Chubb has observed, Ireland was simply not involved with what was going on in Europe or beyond until well after the Second World War;[117] in this sense of diplomatic isolationism, at least, there were obvious parallels with Spain.

Yet already by the 1940s, there was a growing readiness in some circles to re-examine old assumptions.[118] Neutrality, in particular, came increasingly to be viewed as a matter of political expediency rather than high principle. A split in fact emerged between the 'ideological neutrals', who regarded neutrality as an immutable symbol of national independence, and a body of 'pragmatic neutrals' willing to subordinate or abandon neutrality when circumstances so dictated. In any event, Ireland's participation in UN peacekeeping operations and her position 'as an ex-colonial and impeccably non-colonial country that was equally impeccably anti-Communist made Ireland *persona grata* with Western and emerging countries alike'[119] and gave her increased scope for diplomatic activity.

Although Britain effectively kept Ireland out of EFTA in 1959 – arguing that the industrial free-trade area was intended only for advanced economies, entailed no development fund and excluded agriculture[120] – Ireland lodged a first application to join the Common Market, alongside the UK, in 1961. At this time, three-quarters of her exports went to Britain and half her imports derived from the same source, making it imperative that Ireland should not remain outside any initiatives that might jeopardize her commercial relations with London. In addition to holding up the spectre of further years of isolationism, the pro-Marketeers argued that participation in the CAP would provide guaranteed and remunerative outlets for Irish farm produce and end a long period of exploitation at the hands of Britain's cheap food policy. Since 25 per cent of the national income derived from agriculture which, in turn, accounted for 36 per cent of the economically active population, such considerations were of supreme importance.[121] Compared with these harsh economic realities, the ardent pro-Marketeers regarded all else as of secondary concern. Indeed, on the basis of the advice submitted by the Department of External Affairs, it appears that, had NATO membership been a prerequisite of Irish membership of the EEC, the prime minister, Sean Lemass, would have accepted this condition – bitter though it would have been – and tried to take his Fianna Fail party and the country with him.[122]

De Gaulle's veto of Britain in January 1963, of course, temporarily put paid to Irish hopes of Common Market membership; in the ensuing stalemate, she again turned her sights towards London. In 1966 the Anglo-Irish Free Trade Area was formed – envisaging the removal of industrial tariffs over a ten-year transitional period – and EFTA membership was even considered.[123] The following year, Ireland joined Britain in making a second (unsuccessful) application to join the Common Market. By the time negotiations on Ireland's third application began in June 1970, the government had adopted a less parochial approach towards the Community, emphasizing its commitment to the broad political objectives of membership. Only thereafter did it strive to protect basic economic interests *inter alia* by working to secure transitional arrangements for Anglo-Irish trade, safeguards for sensitive industries, protection against dumping and incentive schemes to attract industrial investment to her backward regions. The pro-Market campaign, which was orchestrated by the Irish Council of the European Movement, benefited substantially from the support of the main opposition party, Fine Gael, although the ruling Fianna Fail was left to bear primary responsibility for defending a deal which, if it contained many positive aspects (especially concerning regional policy), fell short of expectations in relation to fishing.

Those opposed to full membership in the campaign leading up to the 10 May 1972 Common Market referendum were the Labour Party – which at its 1971 annual conference reversed its earlier position of lukewarm support – the Irish Congress of Trade Unions (which affiliated to the party in 1967), many small farmers in the West and the Official and Provisional Sinn Fein. Traditionally the smallest party of its kind in Western Europe, Labour opposed membership in terms of the threat it posed to national sovereignty, its harmful effects on price levels and the inability of the economy to absorb the farmers who would be displaced by the rationalization and amalgamation of holdings envisaged under the Mansholt Plan. There was also the likelihood of rising unemployment, which was viewed as an inevitable corollary of the long-term protection of much of Irish industry, especially consumer durables. Labour also attacked the government's apparent willingness to enter into future Community-based defence arrangements and generally stated its opposition in principle to what was viewed as the unbridled capitalism of the EEC. It concluded that associate membership would be more appropriate for a developing economy like Ireland's.[124]

It was, however, the fortunes of the hardline leftist opposition – the IRA and republican revolutionaries in Sinn Fein – which in many ways provided the primary focus of interest during the run-up to the referendum. With this first opportunity to gauge its electoral support south of the border since the Ulster crisis erupted in 1968–9, Sinn Fein seized the initiative from Labour with the instruction to vote 'no' in support of the internees in Long Kesh prison in Belfast.[125] The Labour Party indeed was obliged to spend much of the referendum campaign dissociating itself from extremist IRA rhetoric and posters exhorting voters not to 'let your children fight side by side with the British paras in NATO' and depicting a gangster-faced cigar-smoking German declaring, 'I want your daughter in the Ruhr.'[126]

In the event, the disparate anti-Market elements found it difficult to build a cohesive umbrella organization (even though, in July 1971, the Common Market Defence Campaign was launched), suffered from inadequate funding and went down to overwhelming defeat. On a turn-out of 71 per cent, 83 per cent of voters favoured Irish membership of the Common Market on 10 May compared with 17 per cent who were against. There was a pro-Market majority right across the country, although the affirmative vote was somewhat higher in the northern and western constituencies than in Dublin and the east. Partisanship was also notably high, with the bulk of the negative vote coming from Labour supporters. As to the significance of the result, Garvin and Parker have concluded that: 'The vote has variously been interpreted as a massive rejection of the IRA ..., a turning away from autarkic Gaelic nationalism, and as an acceptance of European perspectives. Perhaps it is best interpreted as a reflection of not only the economic, but also the political facts of life in Irish society.'[127]

Curiously, Labour largely failed to translate the threat to Irish neutrality posed by EEC membership into a potent campaign issue. To be sure, James Tully, the party's defence spokesman, contended that neutrality had both a history and symbolic importance which made the prospect of its imminent abandonment wholly unacceptable.[128] But advocates of membership argued the pragmatic line that neutrality might have to be adapted to changed circumstances; the enthusiastic pro-European Garret Fitzgerald asserted that bringing the defence question into the Common Market debate at all was a mischievous red herring.[129] In truth, with an overarching elite consensus behind membership on economic grounds, Irish neutrality was of necessity subordinated to 'bread-and-butter' considerations.[130] Whilst Swedish neutrality was perhaps 'determined by fundamental evaluations relating to security policy, not by economic interests',[131] the pro-Market lobby in Ireland never felt at liberty to take the same view.[132] This was not least because, unlike Sweden, Austria, Finland and Switzerland – in each of which agricultural exports amounted to less than 5 per cent of total national exports – agriculture constituted about 51 per cent of total Irish exports. Equally, the relative ease with which the question of neutrality was virtually neutralized during the 1972 referendum campaign probably reflected the lack of public sensitivity to any threat posed to it by the EEC. As one observer has noted: 'The Irishman talks about neutrality, not about security ... [but] he does not talk about it much and thinks about it even less.'[133]

A number of final points on Irish accession to the EEC are in order. First, as a new member-state, Ireland was generally concerned at the tendency of the larger Community countries, especially France and Germany, to resolve matters among themselves. This concern was particularly evident before the Bremen European Council in 1978 when the Fianna Fail government felt it was not properly briefed about Franco-German plans for a European Monetary System (EMS) – in which, incidentally, Ireland participated from the outset. Indignation at the behaviour of the larger states in fact led Ireland to seek (unsuccessfully) to organize an action group of small EEC states as a measure of protection against the politics of scale.[134]

Second, calculations of national self-interest dominated Irish approaches to European economic integration; when viewed in this instrumentalist light, there were both costs and benefits during the early years of Community membership. On the positive side, the remarkable transformation of Irish agriculture – reflected in a 35 per cent increase in the volume of farm output and a 75 per cent growth in farm incomes in real terms during the 1970s – was undoubtedly facilitated by Community funding. The problem lay not in the size of the CAP (from which Ireland profited enormously) but the inadequacy of industrial, regional and social policies. Also on the debit side, the fisheries issue isolated the Irish, with diplomatic protests following the introduction in 1977 of unilateral fish conservation measures. The European Court of Justice ultimately ruled that the Irish action was discriminatory.[135]

Third, although Common Market membership denoted a *de facto* loss of independence in foreign policy and led Ireland to adopt a 'European' stance on several international questions, she continued nonetheless to boast the status of a neutral country. At the time of the inaugural Conference on Security and Cooperation in Europe in 1975, Ireland even offered to act as a bridge to the EEC for the neutral and non-aligned (NNA) continental states, although the offer was not taken up.

Fourth, outright opposition to Irish membership of the Community was confined in the 1970s to the Irish Sovereignty Movement which argued, for example, that instead of being a sign of independence from the British pound, entry into the EMS constituted an act of subservience to the Western German *Deutschmark*. In the two decades that followed accession, however, the educated classes became gradually more 'European' and also increasingly secularized. In this respect, Charles Haughey's emergence as Fianna Fail leader in 1979 was aberrational since it represented something of a counter-cultural backlash and the reinstatement in power of the strict nationalist–Catholic value system of the de Valera era.[136]

Finally, as in other peripheral areas of the EC, Community membership did not prevent high levels of unemployment, massive government deficits and a slow rate of economic growth in Ireland during the 1980s.[137] Between 1980 and 1985 there was a 20 per cent decline in total manufacturing employment. Yet these economic difficulties were more the result of internal institutional and structural problems than a consequence of joining the EC. By the time of the referendum on the Single European Act in 1987 – which yielded a 2:1 majority in favour of ratification – a considerable balance of advantage had accrued to Ireland from Community membership.[138]

Norway Opts Out and Britain Opts to Stay In the Community

Norway Equivocates over EC Entry

In view of the special problems created by her geographical location and economic structure, the possibility of associate membership (the type of arrangement canvassed by the Irish Labour Party) was also debated in the Norwegian *Storting* in the early 1960s. Instead, however, in April 1962 Norway sought full EEC membership along with Britain, Denmark and Ireland – an application she renewed in 1967 and 1970. The crucial parliamentary votes in April 1962, July 1967 and June 1970 produced pro-Market majorities of 113–37, 135–13 and 132–17 respectively, hardly surprising, perhaps, given that her core industries of fishing, manufacturing and shipping rendered Norway more dependent on external markets than probably any other Nordic state. Nonetheless, the EEC was from the outset an emotive issue in Norway and one which mobilized significant sections of the citizenry.[139] For example, in response to active pressure from the agricultural lobby, the decision to reapply in 1967 contained an express commitment to attempt to safeguard Norwegian farming; the need to protect agriculture and fisheries was reiterated in 1970.[140]

The fundamental cross-party accord on the Common Market, which had survived for almost a decade, was suddenly dashed when, during a Foreign Affairs debate in November 1970, several Centre (formerly Agrarian) Party representatives articulated deep concern at the possible implementation of the Davignon and Werner reports, the latter incorporating a commitment to economic and monetary union. The Centre chairman and parliamentary group leader, Jan Austerheim, went so far as to insist on a judicial inquiry to assess the extent to which the Werner proposals were compatible with the Norwegian constitution.[141] It was internal Centre Party division over the EEC which indirectly led to the collapse of Per Borten's Centre-led coalition and its replacement in March 1971 by a Labour minority cabinet under Tryge Bratteli.

Ironically, in the summer months leading up to the September 1972 EEC referendum, the only solidly pro-Market party in Norway was the Conservatives, the largest non-socialist group in the *Storting*. The national conference of the Liberals and Christian People's Party both rejected membership although, in deference to the division in their ranks, members were permitted to campaign either for or against the Market. Significantly, Lars Korvald, the Christian leader, was one of two dissident members of the *Storting* Foreign Affairs Committee who could accept nothing more than an industrial free-trade agreement along Swedish lines, which would permit Norway to retain freedom of action in general political and economic matters.[142] Crucially, although the Labour Party's national organization campaigned for accession and, ultimately, prime minister Bratteli turned the EEC into a question of confidence (indicating that his government would resign if the voters rejected membership), the ruling party was split on the Common Market.

In January 1972, the anti-Marketeers founded the 'Labour Movement's Information Committee against Norwegian Membership of the EEC' with the aim of persuading party supporters to reject membership, whilst also assuring them that, by doing so, they were not reneging on the party's fundamental goals or placing their jobs or the country's security at risk. The existence of the Information Committee was in open violation of the Labour Party's rules and demonstrated the self-confidence of the internal opposition by early 1972.[143] In order to avoid a serious confrontation, the Information Committee was in fact given a latitude which proved almost impossible to restrict in the final stages of the campaign.[144] The Labour Party's 'elder statesman', Einar Gerhardsen, himself a committed pro-Marketeer, even declared publicly that loyal Labour supporters could vote against membership with a clear conscience.[145] If the Conservatives were the only uniformly pro-Market party, the only two *Storting* groups totally opposed to the Market were the Centre and Socialist People's parties, whilst both the government and three-quarters of parliament favoured membership.

Norway, however, became the only one of the small EFTA states seeking EEC membership along with Britain in 1971–2 in which the referendum result went against joining (see Table 6.1): 53.5 per cent of voters opposed accession compared with 46.5 per cent who favoured it. Admittedly, the gap between the two sides narrowed when the Labour Party machine cranked belatedly into action to campaign for membership. In September 1971, only 12 per cent of opinion poll respondents wanted to join the Common Market, 38 per cent were against and 50 per cent were undecided. Even among Conservatives, only 44 per cent supported membership.[146] Admittedly, too, only a minority of those entitled to vote opposed membership since the turn-out over the two-day poll (24–5 September) was a disappointing 77.6 per cent. Nor did Denmark's decision to hold its membership referendum after Norway do anything to assist the pro-Market cause. But the fact remains that, like the Maastricht referendum in Denmark in June 1992, the result of the EEC referendum in Norway in September 1972 marked a notable setback for the pro-Market majority in government and parliament.

Table 6.1   Referenda in the EFTA States on Common Market Membership, 1972–5

Date	Country	Per cent Yes	Per cent turn-out
10 May 1972	Ireland	83.1	70.9
24–5 September 1972	Norway	46.5	77.6
2 October 1972	Denmark	63.3	90.1
5 June 1975	Britain	67.2	64.5

In contrast to Ireland and Denmark, where a majority of voters in (virtually) all constituencies favoured membership, there were distinctive patterns of territorial opposition in Norway. In Ireland, both the governing Fianna Fail and the leading opposition party, Fine Gael, strongly supported membership, the only anti-Market publication being the fortnightly magazine, *Hibernia*.[147] Even in the Border counties of Cavan, Monaghan and Donegal, where IRA sympathy had been traditionally strong and where Sinn Fein had won seats at general and county council elections at the end of the 1950s, the pro-membership vote was well above the national average. In Denmark, too, the only areas to register an anti-Market majority were central Copenhagen and northern Århus – both predominantly working-class districts – and, of course, Greenland.[148] Yet in Norway, whilst there was a favourable majority in and around Oslo (in general, the larger the unit of population, the larger the pro-membership vote),[149] hostility to the EEC mounted proportionately with increasing distance from the national capital. Whereas in districts in the vicinity of Oslo the pro-EEC poll was 55 per cent, it dropped as low as 27 per cent in the outlying (farm–fishing) communes in the north.[150]

Patterns of territorial opposition largely mirrored the strength of class opposition to Common Market membership on the part of the Norwegian farmers and fishermen. Thus it has been estimated that only 20.9 per cent of the population in fishing communes voted in favour[151] and that altogether 85 per cent of Norwegian farmers and fishermen opposed accession in 1972.[152] Significantly, the Norwegian Farmers' Union had been vehemently opposed to the initial application in 1962 and maintained an equally hostile stance five years later.[153] In contrast to the confidence of Danish agriculture, the Norwegian farmers feared the penetration of domestic markets by foreign produce and the proscription of long-term government subsidies. As to the fishermen, the threat came from the common fisheries policy adopted by the 'Six' which opened up territorial waters beyond a three-mile zone to all member countries. The Norwegians did not regard the more favourable marketing conditions reputedly accruing from membership as remotely sufficient to offset the danger of the depletion of its stocks at the hands of foreign trawlers and the concomitant problems of redeployment and depopulation in the north and west of the country.[154] Indeed, the opposition of the farmers and fishermen, and the determination with which they pressed it, constituted the foremost explanation of the negative outcome of the Norwegian referendum on Common Market membership. It was their opposition which split Borten's non-socialist coalition – opposition from fishermen also divided the Labour Party[155] – and it was their opposition which formed the core of the popular resistance to the EEC. There were, of course, other reasons for the anti-Market majority, three in particular warranting emphasis.

First, there was the force of cultural nationalism and the wide appeal of the anti-Marketeers' slogan *selvrådett* – sovereignty – to a relatively young nation-state which had traditionally looked across the Atlantic to Britain and beyond to the US rather than south to continental Europe. Cultural nationalism espoused the values of the living national community, of tradition and the Norwegian way of

life as against the soulless supranationalism of Brussels and the re-
mote bureaucracy in charge of the EEC. There was much emotive
play on the negative implications of the internationalization of Norwegian society and the structural rationalization of its economy that
would necessarily follow membership. Typically, the anti-Marketeers
held that foreign books and papers would swamp the Norwegian
market; *riksmål* – Oslo Norwegian – would finally oust up-country
landsmål as the rural population was forced into the towns; and even
this standardized Norwegian would become a minority tongue spoken
by only four million of the Community's 250 million inhabitants.[156]
Foreigners, moreover, would flood north, buying up Norwegian lakes,
summer cottages and vast tracts of the deserted countryside.

Inevitably, this brand of cultural nationalism had sharply contrasting appeal. Voters speaking *landsmål* were, indeed, inclined to vote
'no'. So, too, were members of the numerous low-church Lutheran
revivalist movements – especially in the 'Bible Belt' of south-west
Norway – who rejected the secular–materialist value system of the
Common Market, with its emphasis on the 'quantity of life' rather
than a proper moral 'quality of life'. On the other hand, many of the
urban *riksmål*-speakers, especially the highly-educated, well-travelled
professional class which possessed a cosmopolitan outlook, supported
Norwegian accession. In general, 'the higher the level of education,
the closer in age to the middle years and the higher the income, the
stronger the support for membership'.[157]

Second, the domestic economic situation did not predispose citizens to view membership of the Common Market as a guarantee of
high living standards or as a necessary condition of long-term national
well-being. The pro-Marketeers' principal slogan – 'We cannot stay
outside' – lacked sufficient credibility. At a time when the average
Norwegian was more affluent than ever before and when oil was
being discovered in the North Sea, warnings about unemployment
and lower growth rates made unquestionably less impact than they
might have done a decade earlier.[158]

Finally, the anti-Market cause mobilized a younger cohort of educated Norwegians (students and academics) which, comprising a first
generation of townspeople, retained a strong emotive stake in the
countryside and was already engaged in a lively debate about the
future direction of Norwegian society. These young New Left radicals of the late 1960s challenged the high-technology, capital-intensive
route to the late 20th century charted by the industrial–business lobby
in Oslo and the south, championed the environment and decentralization, and defended the right of the citizen to make a living in his/
her own region. In the radical social and intellectual climate of the
time, the EEC thus became a juggernaut rolling inexorably towards a
centralized, federal European state in which the small Norwegian

nation and its people would have precious little influence. It was in order to prevent this doleful destiny that many educated younger persons adhered to the anti-Market movement. Indeed, as Hilary Allen has aptly concluded: 'It is a myth that the Norwegian establishment was overwhelmed by the periphery in September 1972 if the establishment is understood as extending beyond the narrow bounds of parliament and the central administration. The referendum was won by an alliance of the economic and cultural "periphery" – the primary sector and the rural conservatives – and important sections of the country's intellectual and political elite.'[159]

The Danish vote in favour of Common Market membership, only a week after the Norwegian rejection, left Norway as the only West European member of NATO (except Iceland and Portugal) outside the EEC. Moreover, following industrial free-trade agreements with the 'EFTA neutrals' – Sweden, Austria, Finland and Switzerland (see Chapter 7) – Norway became the only EFTA state as of 1 January 1973 not to boast a treaty regulating trade with the EEC. Since from April 1973 new uniform rules of origin were to be implemented, in regard to the EFTA bloc's trade both with the EEC and with each other, obtaining a free-trade agreement was clearly a matter of urgency.[160] Indeed, the aim of the numerically weak centre-based coalition under the Christian Korvald (which relied on anti-Marketeers and succeeded to power when Bratteli resigned) was to have a free-trade agreement ratified in time to join the other EFTA states in the first round of tariff reductions on 1 April 1973. True, the government had of necessity to secure terms which vindicated the anti-Marketeers' insistence that a free-trade agreement could protect Norway's vital economic interests as effectively as membership. But their target date was only narrowly missed and a free-trade agreement, unanimously agreed by the *Storting*, came into operation on 1 July 1973.

Curiously, the 'Nine' appeared not to display any perceptible ill-feeling towards a country which had only recently declined to join them. West Germany, in the form of Chancellor Willy Brandt (a volunteer in the Norwegian war-time resistance), was well disposed towards Oslo, and Denmark – the one Nordic member of the Community – was also active on Norway's behalf.[161] France, however, drove a hard bargain over aluminium. From a domestic viewpoint, the inherently difficult task of achieving an agreement reconciling the diverse interests of industry, agriculture and fisheries was partly off-set by the realization that there was simply no alternative to a free-trade arrangement. Whilst the minute Norwegian market was of minor importance to the 'Nine', access to the 350 million citizens in the enlarged Community was vital to Norway's export trade.

The acid test for an anti-Market cabinet would centre on the fish deal and here Norway requested the same treatment as Iceland, arguing that fishing was just as crucial to settlement and employment in large parts of Norway as in Iceland. It did succeed in getting most fish products included in the tariff reductions – the agreement stipulated very low tariffs for about four-fifths of Norway's exports of fish products to the EEC – although this excluded fresh fish and was contingent on Norway's maintaining her 12-mile fishing limit (concern having been aroused in September 1972 by the way Iceland had unilaterally extended her fishing limit to 50 miles).

Once the Norwegian free-trade agreement with the EEC had been ratified, the Labour Party committed itself not to reopen the question of membership (ironically, several polls now indicated a narrow majority in favour) during the next four-year legislative period, until 1978 at the earliest.[162] The aim was to attempt to neutralize the Community issue so as to allow time for the intra-party wounds it had inflicted to heal. At the same time in Britain, the leadership of a Labour Party equally divided over the EEC perceived the tactical gain in placing the Common Market on the political agenda for the February 1974 general election and committed the party, if elected to office, to stage a referendum on Britain's continuing membership.

Britain Holds Referendum on Renegotiated Terms

Despite Heath's manifesto commitment not to enter the Community without the 'full-hearted consent of parliament and people', Britain was the only one of the four EFTA applicants in 1970 not to stage a referendum on the question of membership. The call for a 'European-style' referendum was heard loudest in left-wing anti-European circles in the Labour Party and probably originated in an article written by Douglas Jay in *The Times* on 1 August 1970. A referendum commitment was adopted by the Labour NEC by the narrowest of margins (13–11) in March 1972, shortly afterwards by the Shadow Cabinet with an equally slender majority (8–6) and then, in September 1972, by the Labour Party conference. The price of the Shadow Cabinet's support for submitting the renegotiated terms to a referendum, however, was the resignation of Roy Jenkins and two other pro-Marketeers.

The Labour leader, Harold Wilson's ultimate acquiescence in the decision to place a set of renegotiated terms before the electorate was conditioned by two strategic calculations. First, he hoped to appeal to the anti-Market sentiments of voters: a Gallup survey on the eve of the February 1974 election indicated that 31 per cent of respondents wanted to leave the Common Market (compared with only 18 per cent wishing to stay in). Significantly, there was an even larger body of citizens (43 per cent) who wanted to remain in the Community but to renegotiate terms; it was this group which the Tory defector, Enoch Powell, exhorted to vote Labour. In announcing that he was not seeking re-election in Wolverhampton (refusing to be party to what he described as an 'essentially fraudulent election'), Powell added that he had cast a postal ballot for Labour as the only party offering an option on whether to continue in the EEC. (Powell later joined the Ulster Unionists and at the general election of October 1974 was elected as MP for South Down in Northern Ireland.)

Second, confronted with a party badly split on the Common Market, Wilson sought a way out of the impasse by delegating ultimate responsibility to the electorate. It was hoped that Labour would abide by the verdict of the people and that the whole troublesome question would be removed once and for all from the political agenda. As Monnet observed of Wilson's tactical sense: 'I had confidence in his skill and in nothing else'![163] The Common Market did not in fact play a major role in the February 1974 general election, although the Labour Party, which narrowly regained office, may have profited in the West Midlands from Powell's intervention. By the October 1974 election, which Wilson called with a view to consolidating his parliamentary majority, renegotiations were already in progress under the direction of James Callaghan, although no tangible results had yet emerged.

After a period of prevarication (indeed equivocation), Wilson finally announced on 23 January 1975 that a referendum on the renegotiated terms would be held the following June. The revised terms (affecting very little except New Zealand butter and Britain's EEC budget contribution) were published in a government White Paper in March and rejected by a 2:1 majority at a special Labour Party conference at the end of the following month. Faced by anti-Market majorities on the parliamentary backbenches, the NEC and in the TUC, Wilson bowed to the inevitable, abandoned the time-honoured convention of collective ministerial responsibility and granted dissident ministers licence freely to campaign against the Market. In the final analysis, 16 ministers came out in favour of continuing membership and six (Peter Shore, Michael Foot, Tony Benn, John Silkin, Barbara Castle and Judith Hart) against. It was this phalanx of left-wing ministers that had earlier organized 'Husbands and Wives' dinners – partners were invited to allay Wilson's suspicions and avoid the 'close marking' of civil servants – which provided a valuable opportunity for orchestrating anti-Market tactics.[164]

A three-week campaign was the prelude to the only national referendum so far held in Britain. Each household received three leaflets: one supporting a 'yes' vote from Britain in Europe; one urging a 'no' vote from the National Referendum Campaign (an umbrella for three anti-EEC organizations: the Safeguards Committee, the Anti-Common Market League and Get Britain Out); and one from the government recommending acceptance of the renegotiated terms. It may be, as many Labour anti-Marketeers believed, that the association in the electoral mind of Wilson and support for the revised terms was decisive. The pro-Market lobby also enjoyed much greater financial backing, private contributions to 'Britain in Europe' including almost every major firm on the Stock Exchange.[165]

The anti-Marketeers deployed three main arguments.[166] First, it was explained how the imposition of the CAP would increase food prices. The Safeguards Committee produced a pamphlet entitled 'The Common Market and Dear Food' which noted that, after less than one year in the Community, Britain had incurred an acute balance of payments deficit and claimed that this had built up before the Yom Kippur Arab–Israeli War and resultant oil-price explosion. Second, it was demonstrated how continuing membership would further erode Britain's already greatly diminished parliamentary sovereignty. The Safeguards Committee produced a pamphlet entitled 'The Common Market – The Way Out' which stated that, if the renegotiations proved unsuccessful, the UK should amend the European Communities Act and rejoin EFTA. Finally, much was made of the way the flood of imported manufactured goods from the continent would increase unemployment in Britain.

Table 6.2   **The Proportion of the Electorate Opposed to the Renegotiated Terms of British Membership of the EEC by 'National Groups'**

Nation/Region	Per cent against	Turn-out
Northern Ireland	47.9	47.4
Scotland	41.6	58.6
Wales	35.2	66.8
England	31.3	66.1

Source: Stephen L. Bristow (1975), 'Partisanship, Participation and Legitimacy in Britain's EEC Referendum', Journal of Common Market Studies, 14, 298.

There was a higher degree of popular mobilization at the EEC membership referenda held in 1972 in the three small states seeking accession than at the British referendum on the renegotiated terms three years later. A participation rate of 90.2 per cent in Denmark in October 1972 and 70.9 per cent in Ireland in May that year represented the highest turn-outs in any referenda in those countries, whilst the 77.6 per cent vote in the two-day poll in Norway in September, although approximately 5 per cent lower than in the two preceding general elections, was nonetheless the highest figure since the plebiscite on separation from Sweden in August 1905. Even in Britain, the turn-out of 64.5 per cent was only 8 per cent down on the October 1974 general election figure. The result – a 67.2 per cent vote in favour of the modified terms – constituted a comfortable victory for the pro-Marketeers.

True, support was 15 per cent lower in Northern Ireland and nearly 10 per cent lower in Scotland than the national average (see Table 6.2). Indeed, two or three Ulster constituencies and four in Scotland – three on Clydeside and one in Central Fife (in addition to Shetland and the Western Isles) – would almost certainly have shown anti-Market majorities.[167] However, small pockets of opposition to the EEC were largely concealed (as probably intended) by the county-level rather than constituency-level counting employed. Greater London, for example, was regarded as a single unit. In any case, as in Denmark and Ireland, there were strong links between partisanship, participation and support. The turn-out was highest in non-Labour, pro-Market counties and lowest in those where Labour was strong. Ultimately, however, none of the counties recorded a negative majority. Reflecting on the referendum result, Douglas Jay described it as 'an historic tragedy'. 'Had the "No" votes won', he exclaimed, 'it would have been the greatest triumph for genuine popular democracy, for the common people over the rich and selfish, in modern British history.'[168] But the 'no' votes did not win and Britain remained in the Community albeit, like Denmark, as something of a 'reluctant European'.

Notes

1   E.B. Haas (1958), *The Uniting of Europe*, Stanford: Stanford University Press, p.314.
2   Peter M. Leslie (1975), 'Interest Groups and Political Integration: The 1972 EEC Decisions in Norway and Denmark', *American Political Science Review*, **69**, (1), 74–5.
3   E. Heath (1970), *Old World, New Horizons*, London: Atlantic Alliance, pp.24–26.
4   S. Serfaty (1968), *France, de Gaulle and Europe*, Baltimore: Johns Hopkins Press, pp.134–5.
5   Ibid., p.78.
6   L.P. de Ménil (1977), *Who Speaks for Europe? The Vision of Charles de Gaulle*, London: Weidenfeld & Nicolson, p.181.
7   François Mauriac (1966), *De Gaulle*, London: Bodley Head, p.171.
8   De Ménil (1977), op. cit., p.77.
9   Serfaty (1968), op. cit., pp.131–2.
10 Harold Macmillan (1973), *At the End of the Day*, London: Macmillan, p.140.
11 Ibid., p.118.
12 Ibid., p.120.
13 The French Minister of Agriculture expressed this fear admirably to his British counterpart Christopher Soames in January 1963: 'It is very simple,' he asserted. 'In the present Six, there are five hens and a cock. If you [Britain] join, with the

others, there will probably be seven or eight hens, but also two cocks.' Macmillan, (1973), op. cit., p.365.

14 De Ménil (1977), op. cit., p.113.
15 Macmillan (1973), op. cit., p.354.
16 John Newhouse (1970), *De Gaulle and the Anglo-Saxons*, London: André Deutsch, pp.211, 227.
17 Ibid., pp.238–9.
18 Jean Monnet (1978), *Memoirs*, translated by Richard Mayne, London: Collins, p.467.
19 Ibid., p.479.
20 De Ménil (1977), op. cit., pp.481–3.
21 Douglas Jay (1980), *Change and Fortune: A Political Record*, London: Hutchinson, pp.424–9.
22 Ibid., p.358.
23 Ibid., p.353.
24 Ibid., p.361.
25 Barbara Castle (1984), *The Castle Diaries 1964–70*, London: Weidenfeld & Nicolson, pp.177–9.
26 Douglas Jay concluded; 'George Brown and ultimately Cecil King had pushed Harold Wilson into all this.' Jay (1980), op. cit., p.368; Castle (1984), op. cit., p.152.
27 Jay (1980), op. cit., p.375.
28 Monnet (1978), op. cit., p.488.
29 'Co-operation between sovereign states remained the basis of de Gaulle's European policy with everyone drinking from his own glass ... and taking whatever decisions he might think best for the country.' Monnet (1978), op. cit., p.485.
30 Newhouse (1970), op. cit., p.332.
31 Harold Wilson (1971), *The Labour Government 1964–70*, London: Weidenfeld & Nicolson, p.610.
32 Jay (1980), op. cit., p.431.
33 Newhouse (1970), op. cit., pp.337–41.
34 Jay, op. cit., p.433.
35 Castle (1984), op. cit., p.606. See, too, Uwe Kitzinger (1973), *Diplomacy and Persuasion*, London: Thames & Hudson, p.50.
36 T. Miljan (1977), *The Reluctant Europeans*, London: Hurst, p.167.
37 Ibid., p.102.
38 Birger, Hadenius, Molin and Wieslander (1981), *Sverige efter 1900*, Stockholm: Bonnier, p.275.
39 Mauno Koivisto (1978), *Väärää Politiikkaa*, Helsinki: Kirjayhtymä, p.36.
40 Indeed, at a Nordic prime ministers' meeting in Stockholm on 31 October 1969, Koivisto accused the Danes, Norwegians and, to some extent, Swedes of violating the spirit of the April 1968 conference which, he claimed, envisaged Nordek as a stable organization. Miljan (1977), op. cit., p.107.
41 'EEC: n ovet avautumassa', *Uusi Suomi*, 3 December 1969.
42 For his part, foreign minister Ahti Karjalainen remarked obscurely that 'the Nordek situation was unclear before the Hague summit and is even less clear now': 'Suomi ehdottaa Nordekin aikataulun siirtämistä', *Uusi Suomi*, 6 December 1969.
43 Koivisto (1978), op. cit., pp.58–9.
44 Ahti Karjalainen and Jukka Tarkka (1989), *Presidentin ministeri: Ahti Karjalaisen ura Urho Kekkosen suomessa*, Helsinki: Otava, p.168.
45 Ibid., pp.162–70.
46 Urho Kekkonen (1976b), *Kirjeitä myllystäni 2, 1968–1957*, Keuruu: Otava, pp.57–8.

47   Ibid., p.58.
48   Ibid., pp.121–2.
49   Koivisto (1978), op. cit., p.60.
50   Mauno Koivisto (1981), *Tästä Lähtien*, Helsinki: Kirjayhtymä, p.14; Urho Kekkonen (1980), *Tamminiemi*, Espoo: Weilin & Göös, p.99.
51   Miljan (1977), op. cit., p.109. According to a recent Finnish minister of education, Christoffer Taxell, the collapse of Nordek represented 'an historic opportunity lost'. At the time, the Swedish prime minister advised his Finnish counterpart that it was 'a perfect time to consolidate Nordic cooperation, a time which may never come again'. Since it was the Finns who appeared to have buried Nordek – contrary to the primary objective of Kekkonen's campaign plan – they became the target of extensive and, in the circumstances, somewhat disingenuous criticism, especially from the Danish government. It has indeed been suggested that the Nordek episode generated longstanding doubts among Danish politicians regarding Finland's Nordic solidarity – doubts which expressed themselves, for example, in the aftermath of the violence in the Lithuanian capital Riga in January 1991, when a small group of *Folketing* members urged that the Finnish delegates in the Nordic Council be replaced by representatives of the Baltic states. The Finns were criticized for their subservience to Moscow, their refusal to express joint Nordic support for the independence aspirations of the Baltic states and President Mauno Koivisto's view that events in the Baltic republics were 'an internal Soviet matter'. Christoffer Taxell, 'Nordek – Chansen vi missade', *Nordisk Kontakt*, 4/90, 17; Koivisto (1978), op. cit., pp.98–9; 'Danmarks Baltikum politik fremkaldes russisk protest', *Nordisk Kontakt*, 3/91, 25–8.
52   Vincent Wright (1978), 'France', in David Butler and Austin Ranney (eds), *Referendums: A Comparative Study of Practice and Theory*, Washington DC: American Enterprise Institute, p.143.
53   Philip Goodhart (1971), *Referendum*, London: Tom Stacy, p.14.
54   Willy Brandt (1978), *People and Politics: The Years 1960–1975*, London: Collins, p.497.
55   Ibid., pp.249–50.
56   Monnet (1978), op. cit., p.493.
57   Peter Bromhead (1970–71), 'The British Constitution in 1970', *Parliamentary Affairs*, **24**, (2), 104–11.
58   Peter Byrd (1975–6), 'The Labour Party and the European Community, 1970–1975', *Journal of Common Market Studies*, **14**, 470–71.
59   Monnet (1978), op. cit., p.496.
60   Michael Leigh (1975–6), 'Linkage Politics: The French Referendum and the Paris Summit of 1972', *Journal of Common Market Studies*, **14**, 159.
61   Ibid.
62   Wright (1978), op. cit., pp.139–67, especially 149–50.
63   Brandt (1978), op. cit., p.249.
64   Leigh (1975–76), op. cit., 162.
65   Philip Norton (1975), *Dissension in the House of Commons 1945–1974*, London: Macmillan, pp.395–6.
66   Ibid., p.397.
67   Philip Norton (1978), *Conservative Dissidents: Dissent within the Parliamentary Conservative Party 1970–74*, London: Temple Smith, pp.66–7.
68   Norton (1975), op. cit., p.397.
69   Ibid., p.405.
70   Norton (1978), op. cit., p.69.
71   Ibid., p.74.
72   Ibid.

73 Ibid., p.80.
74 Byrd (1975–76), op. cit., 483.
75 Jay (1980), op. cit., p.454.
76 Leigh (1975–76), op. cit., 471.
77 Jay (1980), op. cit., pp.450–95.
78 Certainly EEC agricultural policies had a greater effect on Danish farming than on farming elsewhere in Scandinavia. M. Donald Hancock (1972), 'Sweden, Scandinavia and the EEC', *International Affairs*, 48(3), 425.
79 Miljan (1977), op. cit., p.176.
80 Ibid., pp.179–82.
81 Alastair H. Thomas (1975), 'Danish Social Democracy and the European Community', *Journal of Common Market Studies*, 13(4), 461.
82 Svend Auken, Jakob Buksti and Carsten Lehmann Sørensen (1976), 'Denmark Joins Europe', *Journal of Common Market Studies*, 14(1), 1–36, especially 3.
83 J. Logue (1982), *Socialism and Abundance*, Minneapolis: University of Minnesota Press, p.223.
84 Miljan (1977), op. cit., p.183.
85 Peter Hansen, Melvin Small and Karen Siune (1977), 'The Structure of the Debate in the Danish EC Campaign: A Study of an Opinion–Policy Relationship', *Journal of Common Market Studies*, 15, 117–19.
86 Ibid., 105–6.
87 Ibid., 126.
88 Jakob A. Buksti (1980), 'Corporate Structures in Danish EC Policy: Patterns of Organisational Participation and Adaptation', *Journal of Common Market Studies*, 19 (2), 154.
89 Hansen *et al.* (1977), op. cit., 103.
90 Ibid., 104.
91 Nikolaj Petersen and Jørgen Elklit (1973), 'Denmark Enters the European Community', *Scandinavian Political Studies*, 8, 204. Even so, it has been estimated that perhaps half a million Social Democratic voters came out against the EEC. See John Fitzmaurice (1981), *Politics in Denmark*, London: Hurst, p.152.
92 John Fitzmaurice (1976), 'National Parliaments and European Policy-Making: The Case of Denmark', *Parliamentary Affairs*, 29(3), 281–92, especially 285.
93 Thomas (1975), op. cit., 468.
94 John Fitzmaurice (1980), 'Reflections on the European Elections', *West European Politics*, 3 (2), 230–41.
95 Hermann Schmitt (1990), 'The European Elections of June 1989', *West European Politics*, 13 (1), 116–23.
96 'Bunderekord ved EF-valget', *Nordisk Kontakt*, 9/1989, 29–32.
97 'Grønland ønsker at forlade EF fra 1984', *Nordisk Kontakt*, 8/1982, 578–9.
98 David Arter (1984), *The Nordic Parliaments: A Comparative Analysis*, London: Hurst, p.4.
99 Jørgen Holst Jørgensen, 'Grønlands neg til Ef', *Nordisk Kontakt*, 5/1982, 366–7.
100 Jógvan Sundstein, 'Faerøsk utilfredshed med EFs frihandelstilbud', *NK tema Integration* 1991 (Special theme issue of *Nordisk Kontakt*), 24–5.
101 Initially, the Social Democrats had been reasonably happy with the reform package, although they were concerned that the rules for promoting an internal market (which as an objective they supported) might prevent Denmark from implementing its own environmental and work environment policies. They were also opposed in principle to any expansion of the European Parliament's powers. Torben Worre (1988), 'Denmark at the Crossroads: The Danish Referendum of 28 February 1986 on the EC Reform Package', *Journal of Common Market Studies*, 26(4), 361–88, especially 369.
102 Ibid., 370.

103   Ibid., 373.
104   Ibid., 387.
105   Ibid., 380.
106   Kenneth E. Miller (1982), 'Policy-Making by Referendum: The Danish Experience', *West European Politics*, 5(1), 62.
107   'Et behersket ja til EF-pakken', *Nordisk Kontakt*, 31, 5/1986, 30–31.
108   The People's Movement against the European Community maintained its influence despite being denied the opportunity of putting its case at the final eve-of-poll debate on radio and television. After the referendum foreign minister Uffe Ellemann-Jensen was strongly criticized for deploying ministry officials to write his pro-Market propaganda speeches during the campaign. 'TV trodser ombudsmanden', *Nordisk Kontakt*, 31, 5/1986, 32.
109   Worre (1988), op. cit., 386.
110   Basil Chubb (1982), *The Government and Politics of Ireland*, Second Edition, London: Longman, p.332.
111   Ibid., p.333.
112   Ibid., p.329.
113   Raymond S. Raymond (1984), 'Irish Neutrality: Ideology or Pragmatism?', *International Affairs*, 60(1), 34.
114   Thus O'Corcora and Hill note that, 'It has repeatedly been made clear that its [Ireland's] neutrality is based on specific Anglo-Irish problems; there is no commitment to non-alignment in East–West relations'. Michael O'Corcora and Ronald J. Hill (1982), 'The Soviet Union in Irish Foreign Policy', *International Affairs*, 58(2), 266.
115   Ibid., 40.
116   Ibid., 37.
117   Chubb (1982), op. cit., p.330.
118   Raymond (1984), op. cit., 40.
119   Chubb (1982), op. cit., pp.330–31.
120   Trevor C. Salmon (1981), 'Ireland', in Carol and Kenneth J. Twitchett (eds), *Building Europe: Britain's Partners in the EEC*, London: Europa Publications, p.192.
121   Ibid., p.193.
122   Trevor Salmon (1982), 'Ireland: A Neutral in the Community', *Journal of Common Market Studies*, 15(3), 211. Also Raymond (1984), op. cit., 40.
123   Salmon (1981), op. cit., pp.194–5.
124   Andrew Orridge (1977), 'The Irish Labour Party', in William E. Paterson and Alastair H. Thomas (eds), *Social Democratic Parties in Western Europe*, London: Croom Helm, p.167.
125   Ronan Fanning (1972), 'Europe, the Irish and the IRA', *Spectator*, 3 June, 849–50.
126   Salmon (1981), op. cit., p.202.
127   Tom Garvin and Anthony Parker (1972), 'Party Loyalty and Irish Voters: The EEC Referendum as a Case-Study', *Economic and Social Review*, 4(1), 35–9. Cited in Salmon (1981), op. cit., p.202.
128   Moreover, in an open letter to the *Irish Times* on 19 September 1970, a group of anti-Marketeers maintained that 'we have followed a policy of military neutrality since the foundation of our state, which is quite as legitimate and important for us as is the similar long-established policy for the people of Sweden and Switzerland'. Patrick Keatinge (1972), 'Odd Man Out? Irish Neutrality and European Security', *International Affairs*, 48(3), 440.
129   Ibid., 441.
130   Conor Cruise O'Brien (1972), *States of Ireland*, London: Hutchinson, p.292.
131   Keatinge (1972), op. cit., 438.
132   Salmon (1982), op. cit., 215.
133   Salmon (1981), op. cit., p.205.

134   Ibid.

135   Ibid., p.210.

136   Brendan O'Leary (1987), 'Towards Europeanisation and Realignment?: The Irish General Election, February 1987', *West European Politics*, 10(3), 461.

137   Dermot McAleese and Alan Matthews (1987), 'The Single European Act and Ireland: Implications for a Small Member State', *Journal of Common Market Studies*, 26(1), 40.

138   Ibid., 46–7.

139   For example, during the parliamentary debate in 1962, 5000 anti-Market protestors demonstrated in front of the *Storting* and nearly twice that number gathered for a rally in City Hall Square. Miljan (1977), op. cit., p.205.

140   Indeed, as the chief British WFTA negotiator Reginald Maudling observed, the question of the tariff on Norwegian fish fingers had been both a vexed and vital one in the initial Stockholm negotiations leading to EFTA. Reginald Maudling (1978), *Memoirs*, London: Sidgwick & Jackson, p.75.

141   Miljan (1977), op. cit., pp.218–19.

142   Ibid., pp.222–3.

143   Hilary Allen (1979), *Norway and Europe in the 1970s*, Oslo–Bergen–Tromsø: Universitetsforlaget, p.150.

144   Ibid., p.166.

145   Ibid., p.156.

146   Ibid., p.134.

147   Fanning (1972), op. cit., 207.

148   Alastair H. Thomas (1973), *Parliamentary Parties in Denmark 1945–1972*, University of Strathclyde Occasional Papers 13, p.80.

149   Miljan (1977), op. cit., p.227.

150   Sten Sparre Nilson (1978), 'Scandinavia', in D. Butler and A. Ranney (eds), *Referendums*, Washington, DC: American Enterprise Institute, p.185.

151   Ibid., p.189.

152   Miljan (1977), op. cit., p.227.

153   Ibid., pp.206–8, 210.

154   Leslie (1975), op. cit., 71–3.

155   Allen (1979), op. cit., pp.162–3.

156   Ibid., pp.146–7.

157   Miljan (1977), op. cit., p.227.

158   Allen (1979), op. cit., p.139.

159   Ibid., p.141.

160   Ibid., pp.169–70.

161   Ibid., p.175.

162   Ibid., p.181.

163   Monnet (1978), op. cit., p.512.

164   Barbara Castle (1980), *The Castle Diaries 1974–76*, London: Weidenfeld & Nicolson, p.141.

165   Jay (1980), op. cit., p.488. Also Stephen L. Bristow (1975), 'Partisanship, Participation and Legitimacy in Britain's EEC Referendum', *Journal of Common Market Studies*, 14, 298.

166   Jay (1980), op. cit., p.485.

167   A.P. Brier and A.P. Hill (1977), 'The Estimation of Constituency and Party Voting in the British Referendum of June 1975', *Political Studies*, 25 (1), 93–102.

168   Jay (1980), op. cit., p.487.

7 The Road to the Maastricht Summit 1991. The European Community becomes the Major West European Power Base

The Union shall promote economic and social progress which is balanced and sustainable ... assert its identity on the international scene ... and strengthen the protection of the rights and interests of the nationals of its member-states.

Treaty of European Union, signed in Maastricht on 7 February 1992

In December 1991, the Heads of State of the 'Twelve' convened in the Dutch border town of Maastricht and countenanced a Treaty on European Union which claimed to mark a new stage in the process of creating an 'ever-closer union' among the peoples of Europe and one in which decisions would be taken 'as closely as possible' to the citizen. The European Community (which officially replaced the 'European Economic Community') made provision for the establishment of economic and monetary union and, ultimately, a single currency; a common foreign and security policy and, ultimately, a common defence policy; common citizenship, as well as close cooperation on justice and home affairs. Two months earlier, in the Byelorussian (Bielarus) capital of Minsk, Heads of State of eight (subsequently eleven) of the former republics of the USSR met to create a Commonwealth of Independent States (CIS) to replace the defunct Union of Soviet Socialist Republics – a victim of the centrifugal forces released by the abortive anti-Gorbachev coup in August. As one 'Union' (among the peoples of the European Community) came into existence, another (based on the Soviet empire) ceased to exist.

It is on this sharp contrast of consolidated integration in Western Europe and dramatic disintegration in Eastern Europe that Chapters 7 and 8 concentrate. The present chapter contains sections on the enlargement of the Community in the 1980s to include the 'new democracies' of Greece, Spain and Portugal; the progress of integration within the EC from the Hague summit in 1969 to Maastricht in 1991, and the subsequent referenda on the ratification of the Treaty of European Union in Denmark, Ireland and France; and the application of the 'EFTA neutrals' for EC membership.

The 'Nine' becomes the 'Twelve'

The same month, June 1975, as the overwhelming majority of voters confirmed Britain's continuing Common Market membership, the Karamanlis government in Greece lodged an application to join the community. The Greek initiative was followed by similar applications from Portugal and Spain in March and July 1977, respectively. In each of these cases the motivation was primarily political: having recently emerged from the shadow of authoritarian regimes, Spain, Portugal and Greece craved international recognition and viewed accession to the EC as a springboard to rehabilitation within the international fraternity. All three, in short, desired to undertake a prominent part on the European stage and to shed the role of pariah. For Spain, for example, entry into the EC, as Alfred Tovias has written, 'could be regarded as part of a general activation of her foreign policy in all directions'.[1] Hence between 1976 and 1979, Spain entered the Council of Europe, re-established diplomatic relations with the Soviet Union, participated in the Non-Aligned summit in Havana, became a member of the UN Security Council, successfully bid to stage the third round of the CSCE (set for 1980), achieved observer status at both the Organization of American States and the Andean Pact, and became a member of the Inter-American Development Bank.

Importantly, Community membership was also viewed by the Mediterranean states as a guarantee for the preservation of their new democratic institutions during the transition to pluralist politics. Peter Holmes has remarked that, at the time she embarked on negotiations, Spain was probably not expecting very much in economic terms from membership, but was fully convinced that involvement in the Community constituted an integral part of her democratic evolution.[2] It was recalled that, when in February 1962 Fernando Maria Castilla y Maíz, the Spanish foreign minister, had submitted a petition to the Council of Ministers requesting an association agreement, it was rejected by reference to the premises of the Birkelbach report that Spain was not a pluralist democracy.[3] Spain's approach to the 'Six' in 1962 should be viewed against the backdrop of the Basque separatist organization ETA's engagement in an armed struggle against the Spanish state which led to the declaration of a state of emergency and a number of much-publicized show trials serving to highlight the anti-democratic character of the Franco regime. Matters culminated in an exodus of ambassadors from Spain in 1975 following the execution of five terrorists; from the ensuing international storm of protest, it was clear that Spain would remain isolated as long as authoritarianism held sway.[4]

The same was broadly true in Portugal where Antonio de Oliveira Salazar's *Estado Novo* between 1930 and 1968 was explicitly anti-modern and anti-democratic. Moreover, whilst Marcello Caetano's appointment as prime minister in 1968 brought the promise of change, little was achieved before 25 April 1974, when the *Estado Novo* fell at the hands of a military coup which enjoyed the enthusiastic backing of the mass of the people. Notably instrumental in the overthrow of authoritarianism were the middle ranks of the officer corps which recognized that the guerrilla wars raging in Portuguese Africa simply could not be won.[5]

Similarly, post-war Greek politics until Karamanlis could at best be described as a system of 'guided democracy' or 'restricted parliamentarism' in which the function of elections was restricted to legitimizing the anti-communist right.[6] The left was banned during the 1946–9 civil war, a proscription which remained until the re-emergence of Constantine Karamanlis and the advent of pluralism in 1974. Karamanlis' New Democracy party won 54.4 per cent of the vote and a crushing parliamentary majority of over two-thirds of all seats on 17 November 1974 – based on the slogan 'Karamanlis or the tanks' – a failed military coup in February 1975 giving him the opportunity to move decisively against those sympathetic to the previous regime.[7]

All in all, except for the extremely unstable Portuguese First Republic between 1910 and 1926 and the short-lived and highly polarized Spanish Second Republic from 1931 to 1936, there was little or no democratic tradition on which to build in the Mediterranean states; this meant that in a real sense their EC applications symbolized a commitment successfully to make the shift to pluralist politics. Seeking membership, in sum, represented a statement of democratic intent.

However, in view of the absence of pluralist roots in the region, a successful outcome of the democratization process could not be assumed, particularly since it was being attempted at a time of deep international recession. The post-1973 oil price rises had a devastating impact in Greece, Spain and Portugal as they were the most energy-dependent countries in the OECD.[8] In the Portuguese case, economic destabilization (exacerbated by the need to repatriate hundreds of thousands of people from the lost colonies) led to political destabilization and an attempted leftist coup at the end of 1975. Without prompt Western intervention to fortify the economy, right-wing dictatorship might well have been replaced by left-wing authoritarianism in Portugal and democracy snuffed out at birth. In October 1975, the 'Nine', backed by the US, decided to grant extraordinary financial aid worth nearly 200 million dollars from the European Investment Bank and to open immediate discussions on the improvement of the 1972 Portuguese-EC industrial free-trade agreement. In June 1977, 14 states, acting under the auspices of the IMF, provided Portugal with a further 750 million dollars over an 18-month period.

The Community's action to sustain the Portuguese economy and, by extension, the country's nascent democracy – which was closely followed by formal applications from Portugal and Spain for EC membership – occurred at a time when the 'Nine' were faced with seemingly intractable problems. The Tindemans Report on European (Political) Union had been quietly shelved and the momentum of integration had markedly slowed. The first decade of the Community had been characterized by high growth rates, virtually full employment, low inflation rates and payments surpluses, but the picture had dramatically altered by the time the Mediterranean states applied to join. Behind the formal expressions of welcome, the EC had two major sources of concern about an expansion of the Community. First, all three applicants were relatively poor and resources from the richer members would be needed to promote their economic development.[9] Second, all three Mediterranean states marketed agricultural products – wine, citrus fruit and olive oil – which would compete with French and Italian goods.[10] Equally, a rejection of the three applications was considered out of the question on grounds of the damage it might cause the Community's image and, more importantly, the embryonic democracies themselves. Admittedly, all three were perceived in Community terms as developing countries, heavily reliant on relatively backward agricultural sectors and burdened with acute regional problems. But all three had forged agreements with the Community during the long years of authoritarianism and now sought to expand links rather than create entirely new ones.

Thus Greece gained association with the EC through the Athens Agreement in 1961, although the harmonization of agricultural policies stipulated by the agreement was never really achieved. Spain signed a preferential agreement with the 'Six' in 1970 which resulted in a 25 per cent reduction in Spanish tariffs and a 60 per cent reduction on most Spanish industrial exports to the Community. EC proposals for an industrial free-trade arrangement fell on deaf ears in Madrid, however, both during the twilight years of the Franco regime and thereafter. Portugal, in contrast, signed an industrial free-trade agreement with the Community, along with the other EFTA states in 1972, and by July 1977 Portuguese industrial exports, apart from a few 'sensitive' products, enjoyed free access to the Community. Commenting on the Greek, Spanish and Portuguese positions, Loukas Tsoukalis observed that: 'Their geographical situation and economic model – which could be drastically changed only at a very high cost – as well as their previous association with the Community, left the three countries with no option but to apply for membership.'[11] Nonetheless, there were important differences in the political and economic situations in the Mediterranean states at the time they sought EC membership. In Portugal, for example, ten articles in the April 1976 constitution set out the way the country would move democratically towards a socialist economy. The extent of cross-party support for Community membership also varied. A brief note on each is thus in order.

The Accession of Greece

In the case of Greece, which became the tenth Community member on 1 January 1981 – three years before the date envisaged by the 1961 Association agreement – it was probably felt in high-level EC circles that, with a population of only nine million, membership was not likely to impose an unduly onerous burden even if, as the Commission insisted, there were potentially serious agricultural and regional problems. Moreover, tension in the eastern Mediterranean, in the form of Greek relations with Turkey (Turkey occupied Northern Cyprus and an 'independent' Turkish–Cypriot state was declared in 1983) as well as the uncertainty in Yugoslavia after Tito's death in 1980, created consternation in Western capitals and provided valuable leverage for the Greeks in their accession negotiations.[12] In truth, though, early membership also owed much to the personal reputation of the prime minister (and, after May 1980, president) Karamanlis who in 1974 replaced the Junta of Colonels that had seized power on 21 April 1967 and who was active in lobbying support for Greek entry in the corridors of power in Brussels.

For many Greeks, the Community represented the only alternative to continued dependence on America and a White House which had bolstered the Colonel's regime and also maintained close links with Turkey after the Turkish invasion of Cyprus. For others, membership denoted the menacing prospect of a large influx of foreign investment (guaranteed by the constitution) seeking to exploit the relatively low wage levels and the various incentives designed to attract industry away from the Greater Athens area (where more than 45 per cent of industrial workers were based). Even among pro-Marketeers, there was concern about the extent of the structural adaptation that would be enforced by membership. In the debate on ratification of the Treaty of Accession, Karamanlis acknowledged that considerable effort would be necessary to modernize Greek industry, overhaul a relatively inefficient agricultural sector and transform public and private administration (where corruption was endemic).[13] The problem was that, whilst the economy developed rapidly in the 1950s, it slowed markedly during the Junta years, which witnessed rising unemployment, high inflation, soaring defence expenditure and a lack of investment. What investment there was, moreover, tended to be directed towards property – rather than being more productively channelled – while a fundamental weakness of the economy lay in the fact that much of industry comprised small- and medium-sized enterprises (SMEs) which achieved relatively low productivity and yet lacked sufficient capital for expansion.

As in Portugal, there were deep divisions between the main Greek parties over the Common Market. In contrast to the governing New Democracy, the Socialist Party (PASOK) under Andreas Papandreou (which gained 25 per cent of the vote in 1977) was opposed both to the EC and to NATO which Greece joined in 1952. PASOK and the Communists boycotted the parliamentary vote on the ratification of the Treaty of Accession in June 1979. PASOK's idiosyncratic variant of socialism combined Marxism with cultural nationalism and an espousal of pan-Hellenic tradition in a synthesis which rejected multinational capitalism and supranational integration in favour of Greek democracy and the virtues of the national community. Although when PASOK won an expected victory at the polls in October 1981, the new government demanded a renegotiation of Greece's terms of entry, Papandreou never pushed his threat of a referendum on continuing membership of the Community. Yet the prime minister's hawkish stance doubtless contributed to a package of measures from Brussels in 1983 which sought to accommodate the particular economic and social problems faced by Greece and to facilitate its integration into the European Community. Greece in turn made the Integrated Mediterranean programmes set out by the European Council in March 1985 a *sine qua non* of Spanish and Portuguese entry.[14]

The Accession of Portugal

For Portugal, as for Spain, establishing stronger links with the EC probably assumed no more than second-rate importance in the first two post-Caetano years.[15] However, by the end of 1975 the Socialist Party, which until the previous year had been anti-Community, began to view Portuguese membership as a way of preventing a second Communist coup attempt, being confirmed in this reappraisal of matters by its fraternal parties in Britain and West Germany. Economically, in short, Portugal might not be ready for membership but, politically, membership appeared crucial in stabilizing the domestic situation.[16]

Despite difficulties in maintaining a durable coalition, a measure of enhanced stability was achieved in summer 1976 when General Ramalho Eanes was elected president. Eanes, who had played a crucial role in suppressing the attempted left-wing military coup in late 1975, was the candidate of the three main political parties – although not, of course, the Communists – and gained 62 per cent of the popular vote. At the time of Eanes' accession to office and the subsequent Portuguese application to join the Community, three background factors warrant emphasis. First, the Portuguese economy was so backward that, unlike Spain or even Greece, it did not pose a threat to the Community, which in turn was generally supportive towards the request for membership. Second, under the auspices of the European Investment Bank and the IMF, the 'Nine' had already invested in the Portuguese economy with a view to preventing a democratic collapse and therefore had an obvious vested interest in its future consolidation. Third, the Portuguese application inevitably became embroiled with that of Spain – not least as a result of Greece's insistence on the need for an integrated Mediterranean strategy – and was, accordingly, slowed down.

When the severe impact of the second oil crisis of 1979 again exposed the highly peripheral and vulnerable nature of the Portuguese economy, the case for enhanced protection under the Community umbrella appeared to be reinforced. In addition to the increased incidence of unemployment among Portuguese guestworkers across Western Europe, EC protectionism against labour-intensive products hit Portugal's textile sector extremely hard, whilst its balance of payments problems were aggravated by a lack of confidence on the part of foreign investors. Foreign investment, moreover, was highly unlikely to be attracted so long as Portugal remained constitutionally committed to building a socialist economy.[17] Consequently, a primary aim of the pro-Market parties, the Democratic Alliance and Socialists – which at the 1980 parliamentary election received a combined 75 per cent of the popular vote – was to revise the 1976 form of government in the interests of private enterprise. After all, key sectors such as armaments, oil refining, iron and steel, base petrochemicals, fertilizers, cement and banking and insurance all fell within the preserve of the state. Community membership, it was hoped, would reverse matters by linking Portugal to the EC's free-market model, as well as transforming Portugal – its administration, tax laws, social welfare, etc. – into a modern late 20th-century society.

The anti-Marketeers had two principal constituencies. On the one hand, the Communists, who dominated the trade union movement and gained 16 per cent of the vote in 1980, canvassed closer links with the Soviet Union and COMECON. On the other hand, the left-wing military, particularly within the Revolutionary Council (abolished by the constitutional revision of October 1982) tended to favour a Third Word, pro-African orientation. However, during the protracted negotiations in Brussels, one factor in particular strengthened the pro-Marketeers' hand. In 1983 Mário Soares and the Socialists were returned to office and strongly promoted EC membership as a means of extricating Portugal from its deep-rooted financial problems. Indeed, Soares implemented a severe austerity programme designed to reduce inflation and trim the economy in readiness for entry into the Community.

The Accession of Spain

Unlike Portugal, there was broad cross-party consensus in Spain in favour of EC membership and recognition that no viable economic alternative existed to full integration into the West European mainstream. Hence when on 28 July 1977, only six weeks after being elected to office, the centrist UCD under Adolfo Suarez submitted an application to join the EC – formal negotiations began on 5 February 1979 – it was backed by the Socialists (PSOE) under Felipe González and, significantly too, by the Communists. The two left-wing parties, to be fair, ultimately wanted to alter the capitalist character of the Community, the PSOE declaring that it would work for a 'democratic, socialist non-imperialist Europe'.[18] But this was nothing like the root-and-branch anti-Market stance of the Greek PASOK. The point stands that, alone among the new Mediterranean democracies, Spain's application to join the Community was supported by all the major political parties.

The Spanish application could be viewed as the logical culmination of an 'economic Europeanization of Spain' which began in the 1950s, predicated on a recognition that autarky had not succeeded in advancing the nation's industrial development.[19] Although West European trade was initially small in scale – in 1959 exports accounted for only 4 per cent of GNP – 'Europe' was considered an important market for Spain, absorbing about one-quarter of her total exports. Indeed, an approach to Brussels in 1962 for an association agreement, although rebuffed on political grounds, reflected the heightened priority attached in Madrid to encouraging commercial links with Western Europe. During this period of economic liberalization, however, Spain did succeed in becoming a member of the IMF, the International Bank for Reconstruction and Development (World Bank) and the OEEC, whilst the 1959 Stabilization Plan, presented by the new technocratic administration, facilitated an influx of foreign multinational capital.[20] For more than a decade after the rejection of Spanish overtures for an association agreement, the persistence of authoritarianism proved the ultimate stumbling-block to closer ties with the Community; indeed the execution of Basque terrorists in September 1975 during 'the last spasm of Francoism' so outraged the international community that it prompted the European Commission to call for a suspension of trade with Spain.[21] It was not until after Franco's death on 20 November 1975, in fact, that integration with the EC became a realistic possibility.

The Spanish application for Community membership which, incidentally, substantially pre-dated the popular referendum of December 1978 ratifying the new constitution, was supported not only by all the major political parties, but also by the majority of those engaged in industry and agriculture. In 1979 agriculture accounted for a sizeable 19 per cent of the economically active population and approximately 10 per cent of GNP, and farmers were understandably enticed by the potential benefits of the CAP. Spain also had a fishing fleet which was almost equal in size to that of the entire Community and relished the prospect of increased markets. Only in Galicia, the poorest region – with income levels barely half the national agricultural average – which was heavily dependent on very small beef and dairy farms, was there hesitancy. Spanish milk prices were above CAP levels and Galicia, especially, feared the consequences if they fell.[22] Whilst there was strong support among corporate-sector elites for Spanish membership, the general public, although largely amenable, was predominantly ignorant and indifferent to the Common Market. In a poll commissioned by the government in autumn 1979, 67 per cent of respondents favoured EC accession, compared with only 7 per cent who were against, although only 10 per cent could identify existing member-states and 30 per cent admitted that they knew nothing about the whole issue.[23]

The only Mediterranean application to encounter significant opposition within the EC was Spain's bid for membership, largely because of fears about the effects of competition from Spanish fish, fruit and vegetables. Whereas Britain and Denmark favoured 'widening' the Community to incorporate Spain and Portugal, Italy and particularly France placed tactical weight on the importance of 'deepening', and its corollary, the need first to resolve the deadlock regarding Britain's budgetary contribution. Especially in southern France, there was apprehension about the implications of Spanish agricultural competition, anxiety fed by Gaullists under Jacques Chirac and Communists under Georges Marchais. Indeed, in June 1980, president Giscard d'Estaing called for a temporary embargo on the whole process of EC enlargement. The problem was that, since Spanish prices were below EC levels for many fruit and vegetable products, free competition was thought likely to reduce the earnings of French and Italian producers.[24] There was also a more general concern across the Community about a substantial expansion of Spanish wine and olive oil production.

Consideration of the Spanish application proved extremely protracted and bred intermittent frustration and desperation in Madrid. Formal negotiations did not begin in earnest until autumn 1979; ironically, this was about a year after Spain had reached a free-trade agreement with EFTA (the first the latter had entered into with a non-member state). The main bone of contention concerned the period of adaptation for Spanish industrial and agricultural produce. Madrid sought a relatively short transitional period for her largely competitive agriculture and a much longer one for her more vulnerable industrial sectors.[25] French and Italian opposition slowed the pace of progress to the point where, at the end of 1983, Socialist prime minister González communicated with each government leader in the Community, asking where he or she stood on the question of Spanish membership.[26] Although the election of François Mitterrand as the first Socialist president of the French Fifth Republic in 1981 appeared to inject some momentum into the negotiations on Spanish entry, it was not until June 1983 that the European Community, in its deliberations on the future allocation of budget contributions, assumed both Spanish and Portuguese membership.[27] By then, Spanish entry had become bound up with her continuing membership of NATO.

On 30 May 1982 Spain became the 16th member of the Atlantic Alliance, a decision taken by the UCD cabinet of Calvo Sotelo in the face of opposition from the Socialist Party and a majority of the public. In September 1981, an opinion poll had revealed that 43 per cent of those questioned were against Spain joining NATO and only 13 per cent in favour. Two years later, however, the González government reversed its position and came out in favour of remaining in the alliance. It may be assumed that in practice the EC leaders made continuing Spanish membership of NATO a precondition of her admission into the Community. At the Dublin meeting of EC foreign ministers in September 1984, called expressly to discuss negotiations with Spain, there was certainly recognition of the need to act decisively to assist González in his task of convincing his party to support continuing NATO membership. It was accordingly agreed to present a comprehensive package that would provide for definite Spanish entry into the Community. Spain and Portugal finally signed an EC accession treaty on 12 June 1985.

By the time all the Mediterranean systems had become EC members in 1986, pluralist democracy in the region appeared more entrenched. True, the shock waves generated by the attempted military coup in Spain in February 1981 reverberated across the Community and emphasized the need for a sympathetic response in Brussels to the teething troubles of a regime which, it seemed, was struggling to make the transition to democracy. However, shortly thereafter, there was evidence in all three 'new democracies' of an alternation in power – usually a reliable indicator of the legitimacy of new regimes – with the advent (or return) to office of the Socialists in Greece in 1981, Spain in 1982 and Portugal in 1983. Portugal, moreover, became less 'semi-presidential' after the 1982 constitutional revision, the Communist parties in the region were in decline, and the anti-system PASOK moderated its radical nationalist stance once in office. Perhaps, however, it might not be regarded as entirely in keeping with the spirit of representative government that the decisions of the Mediterranean systems to accede to the EC were not ultimately backed by majorities of the citizenry in popular referenda. This had been the practice (outside Britain) at the time of the previous enlargement of the Community in 1972 and will also be the case when negotiations on the entry of the 'EFTA neutrals' are completed in the mid-1990s. Such a process might well have served to combat some of the widespread ignorance about the Community among many voters.

The entry of Spain, Portugal and Greece into the EC permitted the incorporation of countries which – unlike the Danubian, Adriatic and Baltic initiatives discussed elsewhere in this volume – had never aspired to local (regional-specific) forms of integration. The increased size of the Community, however, tended to superimpose a North–South divide on the tensions existing between those more 'reluctant Europeans' in Britain and Denmark and the founder-members in the Six. Admittedly, during the year the Mediterranean states formally joined, EC leaders made plans for the creation of a single internal market by 1 January 1993. Yet in turning to consider the progress of integration within the Community and the road to the Maastricht summit in December 1991, Bertrand Russell's description of the universe as 'all spots and jumps' comes readily to mind.

The Road to Maastricht and Beyond

In September 1991, the President of the European Commission, Jacques Delors, calculated that of the 34 years the Community had been in existence, 'ten had been dynamic, five had been years of crisis and the other nineteen had been years of stagnation'.[28] Delors did not elaborate further or specify which years belonged to which categories, although it was clear from his remarks that progress towards 'the ever closer union among the European peoples' envisaged by the 1957 Rome Treaty had been, at best, fitful. The momentum towards Community integration, in short, has been uneven, with periods of acceleration followed by times when the motor of change has stalled or, indeed, suffered mechanical difficulties. (For milestones of European political and economic cooperation, see Tables 7.1 and 7.2, respectively.)

The dynamic years comprised at least two distinct periods. First, there was the six-year phase following the retirement of de Gaulle in 1969. This embraced the Hague Summit in December 1969 at which priority was given to advancing political union; the plans set out in the Davignon Report in 1970 to coordinate foreign policy (albeit outside the Community framework) in a conference of foreign ministers; the enlargement of the Community with the accession in 1973 of Britain, Denmark and Ireland; the creation in 1974 of the European Council, which promptly made plans for the direct election of the European Parliament; and the 1975 Tindemans Report on European Union. In the economic sphere, the 1970 Werner Report presented the case for the harmonization of economic, fiscal and budgetary policy, while in 1975 a Regional Development Fund was set up.

Although 1977 witnessed the establishment of the European Monetary System (EMS) – which provided for a European Currency Unit (ECU) and an exchange rate mechanism – the second period of dynamic development in the evolution of the Community coincided with the impending accession of Portugal and Spain in 1986. The Delors Commission's White Paper, 'Completing the Internal Market', in June 1985 was followed in 1986 by the Single European Act which made provision for the creation of a genuine internal market by the end of 1992. 1985 also saw the adoption of an Integrated Mediterranean Programme designed over a seven-year period to 1991 to facilitate the integration of the southern European states. 1992, in fact, came to symbolize all that was dynamic and forward-looking in the Community's endeavours and was regarded as constituting a crucial landmark in the progress towards economic and political union.

The crisis years in the EC's history have also encompassed two distinct periods. The first was a four-year interlude beginning with de Gaulle's unilateral veto of British membership in January 1963. This came in the same month as the Franco-German Treaty of Friendship rattled the confidence of the smaller Community states. The crisis in EC relations deepened when, in June 1965, de Gaulle led a seven-month boycott of the Council of Ministers – the so-called 'empty chair' era – and ended only when the dust finally settled on the General's second veto of British accession in November 1967. The tortuous events of summer 1965 were largely a response to the tactics of the 'Five' in seeking to link plans to increase the powers of the European Parliament, vest the Community with its own budget and introduce majority voting in the Council of Ministers (all of which France opposed) with measures completing the CAP which were firmly in French interests. De Gaulle (who was convinced that French industry was not ready for unprotected competition) inveighed against the Commission and supranationalism in roughly equal measure and largely got his way in the so-called Luxembourg Compromise of 1966.[29] The right of veto in the Council of Ministers was tacitly recognized in cases where member-states considered their vital national interests to be at stake.

There was a further three-year period of tension, leading to a short-lived trauma in EC relations between 1979 and 1982. These years spanned the arrival of Margaret Thatcher as British prime minister in May 1979, the defeat of Valéry Giscard d'Estaing by François Mitterrand in the French presidential election of May 1981 and the Argentinian invasion of the Falklands in 1982. Thatcher's fundamental objection, forcefully and frequently expressed in Brussels, was to the size of Britain's contributions to the EC budget and, by extension, the disproportionate amount of the Community budget devoted to funding a CAP from which Britain benefited relatively little.[30] For the original Six there was a strong attachment to the CAP for, in spite of encouraging massive overproduction by guaranteeing prices for farm products, it remained the only major testament to Community policy. From a British standpoint, however, farmers constituted fewer than 10 per cent of the EC workforce and provided less than 5 per cent of goods and services, yet the CAP accounted for almost 60 per cent of the EC's budget. Indeed, by the time of Thatcher's defeat as Conservative leader in 1990, the Consumers' Association estimated that the average UK family of four paid £14 per week to support Community farmers. In addition to the critique of the CAP, there was strong British resistance to plans to increase the proportion of VAT revenue contributed by member-states to the EC budget to stave off the insolvency that stalked the Community in the late 1970s and 1980s. Matters came to a head in May 1982: when Britain vetoed a proposal on higher target prices for food, the Nine proceeded to ignore the 1966 Luxembourg Compromise and refused to accept the veto.[31] Relations improved noticeably the same year, however, when there was initial Community solidarity in supporting Britain after the Argentinian invasion of the Falklands.

In Delors' submission, the vast majority – that is, virtually two decades – of the Community's history have comprised years of stagnation. Certainly, the two years immediately prior to the Hague Summit in 1969, the deep economic recession in the second half of the 1970s and, indeed, the second half of the 1980s (until the 1989 autumn revolutions in Eastern Europe) would appear to fit this description. Several factors contributed to the phenomenon of *immobilisme*.

First, there was the intermittent fear on the part of the smaller member-states that their interests would be jeopardized by the emer-

Table 7.1   European Political Cooperation 1969–93: The Major Milestones

---

1969   Hague Summit of Six. Foreign ministers instructed 'to study the best way of achieving progress in the matter of political unification within the context of enlargement'.

1970   Luxembourg Report by Etienne Davignon. Foreign ministers to meet at least twice yearly in the Conference of Foreign Ministers – namely, European Political Cooperation (EPC) – which was wholly outside the Community framework.
Official start of Strategic Arms Limitation (SALT) talks.

1974   Creation of the European Council largely at the instigation of the French President, Giscard d'Estaing. Heads of national governments to meet three times annually (amended in 1986 to twice).

1975   EC separately represented at the Conference on Security and Cooperation in Europe (CSCE) in Helsinki.
Tindemans Report to European Council on European Union.

1979   First direct elections to the European Parliament.

1980   Venice Declaration. The 'Nine' sought, independently of the US, to offer fresh impetus to the Arab–Israeli peace process.

1981   London Report on Foreign Ministers. Artificiality of the distinction between the Foreign Ministers' Conferences and Community business recognized and Commission gradually involved in all EPC business.

1982   Initial solidarity among the Ten in support of Britain after the Argentinian invasion of the Falklands. EC embargo on Argentinian goods.

1983   At the initiative of Altiero Spinelli, the European Parliament drew up its own Draft Treaty for European Union.

1985   Single European Act. Very limited on political front; modest increase in the scope of the Council.

1989   Delors' speech at Bruges: the EC must respond to the 'acceleration of history'.

1991   European Council at Maastricht. European Political Union proposals included common Europe citizenship, but no reference to federation.

1992   (2 June) In a referendum, Danish voters refused by a narrow majority to ratify the Maastricht Treaty.

1992   (18 June) Irish voters gave a clear 'yes' in a Maastricht referendum.

1992   (20 September) The French gave *'un petit oui'* to Maastricht in a referendum called by President Mitterrand.

1992   (6 December) Swiss voters narrowly rejected European Economic Area (EEA) membership in a referendum.

1992   (11–13 December) European Council at Edinburgh.
John Major achieved 'Rubik's cube deal' including opt-outs for Denmark on a single currency and common defence, clearing the way for a second Danish referendum on European Union.

1993   (1 February) Negotiations began on the admission of new EFTA members.

1993   (18 May) Second Danish Referendum on Maastricht.

Table 7.2   European Economic Cooperation 1968–92: The Major Milestones

1968	Internal customs duties abolished and a common external tariff imposed. Completion of a Common Agricultural Policy (CAP).
1970	Werner Report argued for the harmonization of economic, fiscal and budgetary policy. Agreement reached that the EC should be financed out of its 'own resources' which for an interim period (until 1975) would derive mainly from tariffs on food imports into the Community.
1975	Creation of EC Regional Development Fund. Tindemans Report suggested a 'two-speed Europe' in which the rate of economic and financial integration could vary from one member-state to another.
1979	Following a Franco-German initiative, the creation of a European Monetary System (EMS). Provision for a European Currency Unit (ECU) and an exchange rate mechanism. Britain did not join.
1981	Genscher–Colombo Plan for an increase in Community budget.
1983	Common Fisheries Policy completed.
1985	Adoption of the Integrated Mediterranean Programmes designed over a seven-year period to facilitate the integration into the EC of Greece, Spain and Portugal.
1986	Single European Act – the achievement of a genuine internal market by 1 January 1993.
1987	Turkey applied to join the EC.
1989	Austria applied to join the EC.
1991	Maastricht summit set timetable for Economic and Monetary Union (EMU), including European Central Bank and common currency by 1 January 1999.
1992	(2 May) European Economic Area (EEA) agreement permitted the free movement of capital, goods, labour and services between EC and EFTA countries – an internal market of 380 million persons.
1992	(September) UK withdrew from the Exchange Rate Mechanism.
1992	(December) European Council meeting in Edinburgh. The main economic elements in the 'Rubik's Cube deal' (1) A budget deal to the year 2000 involving phased increases to 1.27% GDP by 1999. (2) An economic recovery package stimulating growth through funding infrastructural development. (3) A doubling in the size of the fund for the so-called 'cohesion countries' – Spain, Portugal, Ireland and Greece – to help them prepare for a single European currency.

gence of a large-state power axis. In assuaging these anxieties, the institution of a rotational presidency of the European Council was important, since it afforded each member-state, in turn, the opportunity to set the Community agenda.

Second, there were the problems of accommodation facing fresh Community entrants. New member-states, unaccustomed to the EC's arcane ways, inevitably took time to 'settle in'. Moreover, the accession of the three Mediterranean states raised the wider question of the regional redistribution of Community funds from the prosperous North to the poorer South.

Third, those member-states experiencing relatively high levels of government instability and a succession of prime ministers inevitably suffered from a lack of continuity of leadership in the European Council; thus any new incumbent's contribution was likely to be constrained by the need first to 'learn the ropes' of summit practice. Personality conflicts and other interpersonal animosities among heads of state could also stifle progress. For example, Britain's 'Iron Lady' clearly resented the domination of Community business by the long-serving French and German leaders, Giscard and Helmut Schmidt, together with their somewhat patronizing manner and apparent tendency to view the Community as their own exclusive club.

Finally, conflicts of national interest fuelled a tendency to defer decisions and to operate on the basis of a type of consensualism of the lowest common denominator. Instrumental or utilitarian considerations have therefore been uppermost. As Thatcher tersely put it in 1981: 'There is no such thing as a separate Community interest; the Community interest is compounded of the national interests of the ten member-states.'[32]

Indeed, the notable economic progress made by the Six during the first decade of the EEC's existence was facilitated in large part by the fact that major Community developments served the interests of both its core members, France and Germany. By 1968, the EC had achieved the abolition of internal customs duties and the application of a common external tariff. More particularly, a Common Agricultural Policy was achieved in parallel, based on common prices and preferential treatment for the products of Community farmers, backed by duties on imports and financial support for exports. Crucially, this was valuable to both Paris and Bonn: having lost her breadbasket in central and eastern Europe, the Federal Republic was more than willing to offer France the historic deal over the CAP – high guaranteed farm prices for French farmers in return for open French markets for European manufactured goods.

Yet when the Hague summit in 1969 spoke of the 'completion, deepening and enlargement' of the Community,[33] it was plain that a start had yet to be made on the three basic stages leading to economic union – the achievement of a single market, a single currency and, ultimately, a single economy. A customs union should thus not in any way be confused with economic union. Admittedly, in June 1985 the Delors Commission presented a White Paper to the Council of Ministers setting out the prerequisites necessary for realizing a genuine internal market. It listed about 300 measures that would need to be taken in order to remove remaining internal barriers to the free movement of goods, persons, capital and services; most of these were enshrined in the Single European Act of 1986.[34] The questions of a single currency and a timetable for economic union, however, were deferred and taken up in earnest only at the European Council meeting in Maastricht in December 1991.

On 3 September 1973, Monnet had written to Brandt: 'I think that the Community institutions, as a whole, talk but do not act ... and we risk letting ourselves drift into taking no decision.'[35] Accordingly, he campaigned behind the scenes for regular meetings of Heads of State in what he described as a 'European Provisional Government'. Ironically, when Monnet's goal was attained in 1974 in the form of the European Council, it enhanced the inter-governmental character of the Community rather than representing a significant step en route to political integration. Earlier, Monnet had insisted that the concepts of federation and confederation lacked precision and were poorly understood, and that what the Community was creating was *sui generis*.[36] Nonetheless, it seems reasonable to conceive of political integration in three stages: the generation of common policies, the creation of common citizenship and the completion of a single polity or single institutional framework. Common policies had been developed, especially in the fields of agriculture, energy and the environment, as had notable social and regional policy initiatives (although, significantly, not in the area of defence and security). The regular meetings of EC foreign ministers set up in 1971 operated for a decade outside the formal framework of the Community. Proposals for common citizenship emerged only at Maastricht in 1991 and the ensuing treaty made no reference at all to federalism. Thus, if anything, political union has proved even more of a mirage than economic union. Political cooperation, if not political integration, has advanced significantly within the Community, however, and from its creation the European Council has become the major agenda-setting forum.

That particular interest focused on the Maastricht European Council meeting in December 1991 was the product of several factors. First, the end of the Cold War refashioned the geopolitical landscape of the continent, allowing Sweden in summer 1991 to follow Austria as the second 'EFTA neutral' to apply for full Community membership. This, in turn, contributed to a lively debate about the relative merits of 'widening' against 'deepening' the Community. Whilst in

'Euro-sceptical' circles, especially in Britain, there was a strong preference for extending the membership of the Community (i.e. 'widening') rather than increasing its central powers (applications from the
former COMECON states were welcomed in principle), French President Mitterrand and German Chancellor Helmut Kohl, in contrast,
were vociferous advocates of federalism (i.e. 'deepening').

Second, the collapse of the Soviet Union, the EC's recognition of
the Baltic 'successor states' and its attempt (albeit unsuccessful) to
mediate in the escalating Yugoslav conflict vested the Community
with enhanced moral authority and emphasized its role as the major
politico-economic power base in the New Europe. The leaders of the
'Twelve' were aware, during the build-up to Maastricht, that the
decisions they took at the European Council would be weighed across
the continent and this attached increased importance to a successful
outcome.

Finally, on the eve of 1992 – set by the Single European Act for the
completion of an unrestricted internal market – there was concern in
many quarters to maintain and, indeed, to quicken the momentum of
integration. Thus both Italy and Holland produced radical drafts for
federal political union when they followed each other in holding the
presidency of the European Council in the 12 months leading to
Maastricht. The Italian case for political integration, which was presented in November 1990, was based largely on the need for a higher
EC profile in international affairs.[37] This, it was argued, was necessary in order more effectively to defend the Community's collective
interests and contribute to building an international order based on
justice and a greater respect for human rights. Although there was no
explicit reference to federalism or federation, a common foreign and
security policy was counselled, directed at the consolidation of democracy, the peaceful settlement of disputes, arms reductions, the
expansion of international trade and support for international organizations like the UN and CSCE. The Italian document also canvassed European citizenship (which would gradually supplement,
but not replace, national citizenship) and an increase in the legislative
powers of the European Parliament.

The same month as the publication of the Italian draft, Jean-Pierre
Cot, the chair of the Socialist group in the European Parliament,
outlined several ways in which democratic control in the Community
could be strengthened; indeed, his proposals became a not unimpor-
tant component of the pre-Maastricht agenda.[38] Cot held that democratic accountability could be increased (1) by giving the European
Parliament the right of co-decision with the Council of Ministers on
EC legislation; (2) by improving collaboration between the European
Parliament and national assemblies, which in turn should ponder

ways of improving the scrutiny of their ministers' actions; and (3) by making meetings of the Council of Ministers open to the public.

In Britain, in particular, the prospect of a federal political union triggered a revival of nationalism or, at least, tactical nationalist rhetoric. This was primarily expressed as a concern for the protection of national sovereignty, especially in relation to the pursuit of independent foreign, security and defence policies. Declaring in his valedictory Social Democratic Party broadcast in September 1991 that 'a United States of Europe is neither historically desirable nor politically wise', David Owen warned of the possible need to organize a cross-party 'Little Englander' front, asserting that to accept a single European currency, common European foreign policy and European defence community would mean that Britain was no longer an independent nation. It was countered that this type of statement, for all its patriotic resonance, chose to ignore the extent to which the political and economic sovereignty of the House of Commons had already been compromised by membership of international organizations. No unilateral British defence initiative, it was pointed out, could be enacted without reference to NATO; Britain's stake in the Uruguay Round of the GATT free-trade talks was held entirely by the EC; and as a member (then) of the Exchange Rate Mechanism (ERM) – the first stage in European Monetary Union – the Chancellor of the Exchequer's freedom to adjust interest rates was severely constrained. The populist anti-federalism of the likes of the Bruges Group, it was concluded, was premised on a narrow and outdated view of sovereignty. As former foreign secretary, Geoffrey Howe, noted in the House of Commons: 'There is great confusion in regarding sovereignty as in some way akin to virginity – now you have it, now you don't'!

After extended deliberations, the European Council meeting at Maastricht in December 1991 approved a broad package of proposals covering two main areas – European Political Cooperation and Economic and Monetary Union. Progress in the field of political integration was relatively modest and constituted in the main an exposition of the concept of European citizenship.

Citizens of member-states were to be entitled to European citizenship, enabling them to participate and stand as candidates in municipal elections in the member-state in which they were resident. This right was to be exercised subject to detailed arrangements to be adopted before 31 December 1994. In addition, every citizen of the proposed European Union residing in a member-state of which he was not a national was to be entitled to vote or stand as a candidate in elections to the European Parliament in that state (subject to detailed arrangements by 31 December 1993). Furthermore, EC citizens would be permitted, when abroad, to have recourse to any Embassy of a member-state and have the right to ask for protection.[39]

A number of modest reforms of Community institutions (outlined in basic form in Table 7.3) were also proposed. In particular, the Council and Commission were to be assisted by two new bodies – an Economic and Social Committee and a Committee of the Regions – acting in an advisory capacity. The European Parliament (whose consultative role was not otherwise enhanced) was empowered to appoint an Ombudsman to receive complaints from citizens regarding maladministration in the activities of all Community institutions except the Court of Justice.[40]

Significantly, arrangements for a common foreign and security policy did not form part of the provisions of the original treaty establishing the European Community. Their objective, in the Maastricht treaty

Table 7.3   The Political System of the European Community

THE EUROPEAN COUNCIL (created in 1974)

Twice yearly meetings of Heads of Government to discuss general and foreign policy. Proposes policy to the Council of Ministers. Supreme agenda-setting and decision-making forum in the Community.

COMMISSION $\rightarrow$	COUNCIL OF MINISTERS $\rightarrow$	EUROPEAN PARLIAMENT
President. 17 commissioners. Proposes new laws and implements policies agreed by the Council of Ministers after consultation with parliament. Administers EC funds and subsidies.	12-strong law-making body. Usually operates by majority vote. Decides most issues.	518 directly-elected MEPs: 81 each from UK, Germany, France and Italy.* Scrutinizes Commission proposals for legislation; votes on amendments. In theory, can sack Commissioners and reject the budget. In practice, only a consultative body.

COURT OF JUSTICE

13 judges appointed by member-states.
Can quash any Commission measure and interpret Community law.
Individuals as well as member-states can bring cases to the court.
Court's decisions binding in member countries.
Increasing power and influence.

*It was agreed at the Edinburgh Summit in December 1992 that Germany would receive 18 new members of the European Parliament and most other member-states would also get small increases (Britain, for example, was allocated 6 extra MEPs). This decision has yet to be implemented.

however, was the important one of enabling the EC to develop a single voice capable of asserting its identity and authority on the international stage. The European Union and its member-states, it was declared, should define and implement a common foreign and security policy, including the eventual framing of a common defence policy which might in time lead to a common defence. The 9-member Western European Union (WEU), which was envisaged as playing an integral role in the future, was requested to work out the detail and implement those decisions and actions of the Community which had defence implications. The Council would then, in conjunction with the institutions of the WEU, adopt the necessary practical arrangements. In addition, a Political Committee was to be created to monitor the international situation in areas covered by common foreign and security policy.[41]

Considerably more far-reaching proposals were set out in the realm of economic integration than in the political sphere. In the achievement of economic union, great emphasis in the Maastricht Treaty was placed both on the principle of an open market economy with free competition and on the importance of the sustained convergence of the economic performances of member-states. Member-states were entreated to avoid excessive government deficits, and the Commission was empowered to monitor the development of the budgetary situation and the stock of government debt in members-states with a view to identifying gross errors. A complex set of evaluative criteria were to be employed in assessing economic performance, notably whether the ratio of the projected or actual government deficit to GDP exceeded a specified reference value. A protocol to the treaty enumerated an excessive deficit procedure. In essence, the Commission was authorized to report when an excessive deficit existed and could, as a last resort, employ one of three sanctions against the offending member-state: it could ask the European Investment Bank to reconsider its lending policy towards it; require the transgressor to make a non-interest-bearing deposit of an appropriate size with the Community until the excessive deficit had been corrected; or, ultimately, impose fines.[42]

Monetary union, which was to be completed in three stages, would focus on three institutions – a European System of Central Banks (ESCB), a European Central Bank (ECB) and a European Investment Bank. The principal objective of the ESCB (comprising the ECB and national central banks) was the maintenance of price stability. Its remit included responsibility for defining and implementing the monetary policy of the Community, conducting foreign exchange operations, holding and managing the official foreign reserves of member-states, and promoting the smooth operation of payments systems. At the apex of the ESCB network, the ECB would have exclusive rights to authorize the issue of banknotes within the Community. The European Investment Bank, in turn, would grant loans to facilitate the funding of projects – *inter alia* for advancing less-developed regions – which were of such a size or character that they could not adequately be funded at the national level.[43]

The initial stage in monetary union, lasting to the end of 1993, was to be a basic fitness exercise, getting member economies into shape for things to come, during which governments were to be urged to demonstrate strict budgetary discipline. Over the course of the second stage, member-states were exhorted to endeavour to avoid government deficits, adopt programmes intended to ensure the lasting convergence necessary for the achievement of economic and monetary union – particularly with regard to price stability and sound public finances – and start the process leading to the independence of the central bank. A European Monetary Institute (EMI) would monitor progress at this second stage, as well as strengthen cooperation between the national central banks and coordinate the monetary policies of member-states. It would also supervise the use and development of the ECU and the smooth functioning of the ECU clearing system. By 31 December 1996, at the latest, the EMI was to prescribe the regulatory and organizational framework necessary for the ESCB to perform its tasks at the third stage of monetary union (the EMI was in fact to be dissolved on the establishment of the ECB).[44]

The third stage would involve the irrevocable fixing of exchange rates, leading to the introduction of a single currency (the ECU). By then, member-states would be expected to have achieved a significant degree of sustainable convergence as measured by four indicators: (1) a high degree of price stability in relation to the inflation rates in the three member-states performing best in terms of price stability; (2) the absence of an excessive budget deficit; (3) a position within the normal fluctuation margins provided for by the exchange-rate mechanism of the EMS; and (4) the achievement of long-term (stable) interest-rate levels. Other contextual factors taken into account would be the development of the ECU, the situation of the balance of payments on current account, and an examination of the development of unit labour costs and other price indices. By 31 December 1996, at the latest, the European Council was to determine whether a majority of states had fulfilled the necessary conditions for the adoption of a single currency. If a date for the start of the third stage had not been set by the end of 1997, it would start in any case on 1 January 1999.[45] However, in a separate protocol it was recognized that the UK should not be obliged to move to the third stage of EMU without a separate decision of government and parliament.[46]

Finally, two new funding bodies created by the treaty on European Union warrant mention. One was the European Social Fund designed to facilitate the employment of workers in the single market and to increase their geographical and occupational mobility within the Community. It would place particular emphasis on re-skilling. The other was a Cohesion Fund set up to provide a financial contribution to projects in the fields of the environment and trans-European networks (especially in the area of transport infrastructure).[47]

The Maastricht Treaty was by its nature a compromise, which on the matter of political union saw France and Germany conceding virtually all Britain's demands. The dreaded 'F-word' (federalism), much discussed in the press beforehand, was deleted by officials prior to the Maastricht summit; this was essential in order to allow John Major's Conservative government, faced with a general election within six months, to sell the package to voters, Britain also resisted giving the European Parliament genuine equality of law-making power with the Council of Ministers. London also demanded and gained an opt-out clause on the Social Charter.[48] Indeed, faced with British intransigence on political union and her insistence that the treaty should not involve a loss of so-called 'sovereignty', the French and German governments fell back on monetary union as a way of promoting European integration.

The Maastricht programme for economic integration, which set out a timetable for monetary union, bore witness to the indigenous spirit of utilitarianism in approaches to Community decision-making. Thus disquiet over the workings of the Exchange Rate Mechanism (ERM) and the suspicion that the *Bundesbank* put German monetary conditions before those of the Community led French politicians, albeit with an eye to national advantage, to canvass monetary union. A European Central Bank would replace the *Bundesbank* and in this way, it was implied, France and her allies, rather than Germany, could manage European monetary policy. For all the trumpeting both before and after the event, the Maastricht Treaty left several loose ends untied and, like similar summits before it, constituted a case-study in consensualism of the lowest common denominator. In view of Britain's generally recalcitrant stance on integration, there was both irony and validity in the British foreign secretary Douglas Hurd's remark in the House of Commons that Maastricht left open the following crucial question: 'How does the Community exercise its authority; how and when should decisions be taken?'

Critics of the European Political Union formulated at Maastricht concentrated on what they saw as the chronic weakness of the democratic, federal elements in the treaty – something which, it was suggested, posed a serious risk to the popular legitimacy of EC institutions.[49] The principle of 'subsidiarity' integral to federal systems – denoting a commitment to devolve decision-making as closely as possible to the citizens – had been used shamefully by Britain as a tactic to justify retaining power in national capitals. This, coupled with a refusal to strengthen the European Parliament (the creation of an Ombudsman excepted), meant there was insufficient democratic control of the Community institutions in Brussels. This 'democratic deficit' had urgently to be made good, critics contended.

Critics of the Economic and Monetary Union worked out at Maastricht – and in particular the timetable for the completion of monetary union by 1 January 1999 – concentrated on what they regarded as the economic straitjacket imposed on member-states and argued for a more flexible ERM which would allow for a modicum of national autonomy over monetary and fiscal policy. The notion that parities should be irrevocably bound together was attacked as absurd in view of the contrasting levels of productivity and the range of national economic institutions inside the ERM. To compound the folly, it was insisted, the obligation to meet a strict set of convergence criteria – limits on budget deficits, inflation targets, etc. – simply could not be attained by many of the poorer states. What was necessary, according to the hawks, was for governments to have the freedom to launch national policies of wealth creation, employment reduction and welfare improvement.[50]

Ratifying Maastricht

In April 1992, the European Parliament, by a vote of 226 to 62 (with 31 abstentions), approved a resolution calling on the 12 national parliaments to ratify the Maastricht Treaty on European Union (there was in truth little enthusiasm for this, given that the European Parliament itself did not gain any extra powers). In only two member-states, Denmark and Ireland, was a popular referendum also required although, following the unexpected rejection of Maastricht by the Danish voters in June 1992, President Mitterrand also saw fit to put his position on the line by calling a referendum (ultimately fixed for September) on the question of ratification. In her debut speech in the House of Lords in July 1992, moreover, Baroness (formerly Margaret) Thatcher of Kesteven pressed for a referendum in Britain, arguing that, since all three main parties supported Maastricht, the electorate lacked a channel for expressing its views. She added: 'Scepticism, justifiable scepticism, is on the increase and people feel their governments have gone ahead too fast so that now the gap between government and the people is too wide.'[51] Not surprisingly, these sentiments were not acknowledged by John Major who rejected demands for a referendum.

The result of the Danish referendum of 2 June 1992 on ratifying the Maastricht Treaty placed a large spoke in the wheels of European integration and left it (in the short term at least) in decided disrepair. Reminiscent of the situation in Norway in September 1972, almost five-sixths of Danish parliamentarians were in favour: 130 of the 179 *Folketing* members backed the third reading of the Treaty bill, with opposition coming only from the Progress Party, the Socialist People's Party and one member of the Christian group. However, 50.7 per cent of voters rejected Maastricht.[52] As in the 1976 referendum on the Single European Act, the opposition-based Social Democrats were divided, less than 60 per cent of their voters backing Maastricht. Unlike 1976, there were also significant defections among supporters of Schlüter's centre-right coalition (particularly Christians)[53] which officially canvassed ratification. It was an extremely close result – only about 46 000 voters separated the two sides – but one which seemed to surprise many outside observers, despite the fact that opinion polls in early May had given the rejectionists a 3 per cent lead.[54] For weeks beforehand, moreover, surveys had indicated one-third of voters in favour of Maastricht, one-third against and one-third undecided.

Two factors appear to have tilted the scales narrowly against Maastricht. First, the Social Democrats were engaged in an internal power struggle when the referendum was announced – only when Poul Nyrup Rasmussen was elected as their new chair following an extraordinary party conference could the Social Democrats turn their sights to the campaign – and, in any event, their voters remained badly divided on the issue, as they had been for two decades.[55] Second, a series of scandals (arising, among other things, from charges levelled against the former Minister of Justice, Erik Ninn-Hansen, regarding the deportation of Tamil refugees) served to discredit the government and, in particular, to increase the distance between politicians and the people. This contributed to a diffuse protest against Maastricht which, in addition, variously embraced anxieties concerning future defence arrangements, objections to the standardizing of immigration policy and, not least, opposition to the idea of European citizenship.[56] The result, incidentally, breathed new life into the 'People's Movement Against the EC' which during the campaign had tended to view Denmark as a continuing part of the Community and its task, therefore, to make the best of a bad situation. One of the Movement's members of the European Parliament even announced on polling day that she would found a new party, acknowledging Denmark's membership of the EC but committed to opposing Union.[57]

The Danish referendum was quickly followed on 18 June 1992 by the Maastricht referendum in the Irish Republic. The governing Fianna Fail under Albert Reynolds – indeed all four main parties – favoured Maastricht and issued a joint appeal to voters in which prominence was given to the economic benefits accruing from Community membership. The cabinet even claimed that a 'yes' vote would enable Ireland to receive a six billion punt package, although this sum was not ultimately sanctioned in Brussels. The opposition to Maastricht – the only significant anti-treaty party being the Democratic Left – invited Danish speakers to address their rallies and counselled voters not to be 'mass tricked' into forfeiting the nation's sovereignty or compromising its neutrality. Irish neutrality in fact re-emerged as a popular issue during the campaign, 55 per cent of survey respondents indicating support for it; this prompted the government, seeking to defuse matters, to undertake to hold a referendum on neutrality in 1996. There was apprehension, too, about possible conscription into a European army.

Deeply intertwined with the questions of economic and political union was the issue of abortion. This was because the Irish protocol to the Maastricht Treaty, protecting the clause in the Irish constitution on abortion, alienated both pro- and anti-abortion groups. There were widespread fears among women that its acceptance would entail a reduction in their right to travel abroad for an abortion, anxieties which persuaded the government to promise a further referendum on abortion in November 1992. The anti-abortion group, the Society for the Protection of Unborn Children, was particularly active and it was in conservative rural areas, where Catholic observance has remained high, that the pro-life lobby had its greatest impact.[58]

An opinion poll in the *Irish Times* on the eve of the referendum revealed that 49 per cent of voters favoured ratifying Maastricht, 28 per cent were against and 23 per cent were undecided. It was clear that, in the final stages of the campaign, there had been a surge of support for the treaty in Dublin, where 54 per cent supported it, but a decline in backing in the north and west, where only 45 per cent approved. Although the electoral climate seemed set fair, the Danish result was a timely reminder that nothing could be taken for granted and, despite their outward show of confidence, many Irish political leaders were privately holding their breath. In the event, an overwhelming majority of Irish voters backed the Maastricht Treaty: 69 per cent favoured its ratification compared with 31 per cent who were against. Turn-out was 57 per cent. In only four of the 41 constituencies did the negative vote exceed 40 per cent, whilst the strongest support derived from the three western constituencies and the middle-class areas of Dublin.[59]

Notwithstanding the favourable outcome in Ireland, the mood across the EC capitals remained relatively muted, with tacit recognition of the setback represented by the Danish result. In Denmark itself, the leader of the anti-Maastricht Socialist People's Party, Holger Nielsen, insisted that the other EC countries should respect the democratic decision of the Danish voters and renegotiate part of the treaty. He reiterated demands for stronger environmental and social policies and for more powers for the European Parliament. The initial response of the 'Eleven', however, was to rule out renegotiation. Immediately after the Danish result, Mitterrand and Kohl drew up a joint declaration expressing their determination to ensure that the Maastricht Treaty was enforced by the end of the year. Mitterand also staked his presidency on ratification by announcing a French referendum on Maastricht. An opinion poll in *Le Parisien* shortly after his decision showed 69 per cent in favour of ratification and 31 per cent against although, interestingly, only 58 per cent said they would vote. Following the necessary parliamentary steps, the referendum was fixed for 20 September 1992.

In the event, despite overwhelming parliamentary support, the French referendum produced only *'un petit oui'* in favour of ratifying Maastricht: 51:05 per cent voted 'yes' compared with 48.95 per cent who came out against. The turn-out, at nearly 70 per cent, was significantly higher than had been suggested by the opinion polls. Predictably, the result was dismissed as a 'Pyrrhic victory' by the National Front leader, Jean-Marie Le Pen, who emphasized that only one out of every three eligible voters had supported Maastricht.

The few thousand 'yes' votes that made the difference came from the industrialized areas of the Île de France (where 55.5 per cent voted in favour) and particularly from Paris (where average support was 62.5 per cent). Poll analysis indicated that it was the late intervention on the 'yes' side of Jacques Chirac, Gaullist RPR leader and mayor of Paris, that had such a telling effect in the capital and saved Mitterrand from defeat. In contrast, rural areas were almost solidly against the treaty (the highest negative figure was recorded in Picardy, with 57.5 per cent opposed to Maastricht), and voting patterns often crossed party lines, reflecting local conditions of high unemployment and rural decline. In general, the wealthier, educated, urban middle class was most likely to favour ratification.

Mitterrand's rationale in calling the referendum was almost exclusively tactical in that he calculated that he could divide the opposition and bolster his own Socialist Party ahead of the general election in March 1993. The Gaullists did indeed split: the anti-Maastricht lobby was capably orchestrated by Charles Pasqua and Philippe Séguin and Le Pen's FN was, of course, against. Approximately two-thirds of Giscard d'Estaing's Union for French Democracy (UDF), however, voted in favour of consolidated European integration.

As for Mitterrand, his personal authority appeared seriously weakened by the narrowness of the margin of victory. Several Socialist leaders, including former prime minister Michel Rocard and party secretary Laurent Fabius, even insisted that France would have to revise the aims of Maastricht to take account of the unexpected recalcitrance from within the ranks of their own party. An estimated 21 per cent of Socialists had failed to follow the president. Indeed, it appears that the narrow French majority for ratifying the Maastricht Treaty was achieved despite, rather than because of, Mitterrand.

Meanwhile, parliamentary approval of the Maastricht Treaty even came into question in Germany, despite Kohl's strongly supportive stance. There were two main lines of dissent: critics of economic and monetary union and opposition from the regions *(länder)* which were demanding a fair application of the subsidiarity principle. In the regional context, the 16 state governments threatened to veto the Maastricht Treaty in the *Bundesrat* (upper regional assembly) unless they gained representation in the Council of Ministers not only in respect of traditional areas of regional competence, such as education and culture, but also in taxation, defence and foreign policy – all three federal preserves.[60] In the economic context, a manifesto in June 1992 from 60 leading economists, including Karl Schiller, a former economics and finance minister, denounced EMU claiming, among other things, that the so-called convergence criteria were too weak and could be further diluted by setting the last deadline for a common currency at 1 January 1999. At the same time, popular attitudes to EMU were confused and negative: in summer 1992, 72 per cent of Germans wanted to retain the Deutschmark, only 22 per cent were willing to accept a common European currency and 70 per cent wanted to retain full sovereignty.

Significantly, although the German *Bundestag* ratified the Maastricht Treaty in December 1992 by a large majority, it nevertheless asserted that any proposal involving the transfer of sovereignty would require a two-thirds majority and that the *länder* should be consulted on issues affecting them. It also stipulated that, in line with the British, there must be a full vote before Germany participated in economic and monetary union.

Crucially, as Delors stated immediately afterwards, the Danish 'no' vote might well have repercussions for the prospects of the enlargement of the Community, in particular, for the group of 'EFTA neutrals' that had applied to join.[61] True, only a month before Maastricht, on 2 May 1992, they had numbered among the total of 19 states which had underwritten an EEA agreement creating a European Economic Area of 380 million persons. Protracted negotiations lasting over three years ultimately realized this major step towards West European integration by facilitating the free movement of capital, goods, labour and services between EC and EFTA countries. But the EFTA states were not permitted any voice in the decision-making bodies of the Community and it was, above all, a concern to influence policy from within which dictated the neutrals' formal applications to join.

The Integration of the 'EFTA Neutrals'

For over four decades, the cartography of West European economic integration followed the contours of the major security policy systems that emerged in the wake of the Cold War. In other words, the small 'peripheral' states that were not aligned to the principal regional defence bloc, NATO, found access to the expanding Common Market complicated both by their position of neutrality and by the likelihood of an adverse Soviet reaction to links with the EC. The end of the Cold War, however, fundamentally altered the geopolitical and security landscape of the European continent and, as a by-product, enabled the 'EFTA neutrals' of Austria, Sweden, Switzerland and Finland to seek full membership of the EC. It is worth examining each case briefly in turn since there were important differences in their perspectives on and scope for wider economic integration.

Austria

Acceptance in 1955 of an international obligation to remain neutral facilitated the re-establishment of full Austrian independence and the maintenance of her territorial integrity, although the dictates of permanent neutrality imposed obvious limitations on Austria's subsequent approaches to European integration. These potential economic costs were of lesser importance at the time, since neutrality possessed the supreme functional logic of permitting the rehabilitation of Austria as an autonomous state; indeed, it provided its basic *modus vivendi*. Austria re-emerged as a sovereign entity within a decade of the defeat of the Axis powers. She had been the only country under partial Soviet occupation to participate from the outset in the Marshall Plan and the OEEC; moreover, her Western orientation was confirmed shortly after regaining independence by the achievement of observer status in the Council of Europe and full membership in 1956.[62] In the immediate post-war years, however, the primary challenge was one of wresting control of Austria from the Allied Control Council and the occupation forces. Indeed, the presence of Soviet troops in a zone in eastern Austria meant that the successful management of her *Ostpolitik* would provide the key to her future independence.

The overriding rationale of the distinctive Grand Coalition between the Austrian Socialist Party (SPÖ) and the Austrian People's Party (ÖVP) – significantly this initially included the Communist Party – that dominated Austrian politics between 1945 and 1966 was thus to deny the occupying powers grounds for interfering in Austria's internal affairs. Austria accordingly acquired a reputation as a showcase of consensus politics. Yet, during the vicissitudes of the Cold War, the risk of the partition of territory on her eastern flank loomed as a real threat. When, against the background of the new East–West under-standing which spawned the Geneva summit of July 1955, the Soviet Union ultimately came to the negotiating table, it demanded that a broad Austrian commitment to neutrality be incorporated into the State Treaty. Austria resisted this, however, and, in the so-called Mos-cow memorandum of 15 April 1955, accepted the requirement of neutrality only outside the State Treaty. At Soviet insistence, though, Article 4 of the State Treaty (15 May 1955) expressly prohibited either direct or indirect political or economic union between Austria and Germany. In October 1955, the Austrian parliament legislated so as to incorporate permanent neutrality into the constitution.

Economic integration possessed as powerful a logic for the fully independent Austria as neutrality had commanded in re-establishing her sovereignty. Indeed, a dominant theme in the early European integration debate in the second half of the 1950s was the need to avoid a repetition of the inter-war experience when, following the collapse of the Hapsburg Empire, Austria was effectively ostracized and her exports foreclosed by the successor states' policy of promot-ing their own industries behind high tariff walls. As Mark Schulz has emphasized, this historical experience undoubtedly contributed to explaining why business, agriculture and labour interests were unanimous in believing that Austria needed urgently to achieve an agreement with the Community.[63] Evidently, the Austrian govern-ment contemplated possible accession to the European Coal and Steel Community in1956, although this was no longer seriously entertained once the Common Market had been created.[64] Instead, Austria sub-mitted a formal application for association with the EEC in December 1961. When de Gaulle vetoed Britain's application in January 1963, negotiations between Austria and the Six had not even begun, but Austria still chose to pursue a unilateralist strategy – the so-called Independent Approach, *Alleingang*, of 1963–7 – aimed at securing a separate association agreement. Significantly, the government repeat-edly held that solidarity with EFTA could not be allowed to take precedence over Austria's economic interests, in furtherance of which progress was made on a range of issues, including tariff reductions and Austrian adoption of the EEC's Common External Tariff. How-ever, in June 1967, the Independent Approach negotiations ultimately foundered on the rock of an Italian veto, ostensibly used in protest against terrorist activity in South Tyrol. The European Parliament's Birkelbach Report was in any event unsympathetic towards preferen-tial association agreements, noting that entry into association with the Community did not mean that a state got 'an opportunity to pick the raisins out of the cake'.[65] It favoured agreement only with those states intending to apply for full membership but needing a transi-tional period in which to adapt their economies. Finally, it is worth noting that the Soviet Union had orchestrated a campaign against Austria's association plan.

In an interesting analysis of the domestic political scene during the years of the Independent Approach, Katzenstein has emphasized the sharp contrast between widespread popular indifference towards European integration – the issue was generally viewed positively, but not regarded as particularly salient – and the intense elite conflict on the question.[66] He argues that European integration was the single subject to mark a significant ideological divergence between the ÖVP and SPÖ. The Socialists preferred Austrian membership of the 'red' EFTA to the 'black' EEC, and between 1963 and 1967 they sought to slow down Austria's drive towards the Community. The ÖVP, in contrast, was consistently more pro-Market because it perceived possible domestic gains in a supportive stance on European integration. The business wing of the ÖVP in particular hoped, by stimulating the inflow of foreign capital, to break the Socialists' control of Austria's nationalized industries, which together constituted nearly three-quarters of the national industrial capacity.

In order to protect Austrian neutrality, special provisions were written into the industrial free-trade agreement with the EC on 22 July 1972 – there were parallel agreements with Sweden, Portugal, Switzerland and Iceland – governing *inter alia* armaments, and it was accepted that the arrangement could be suspended in the event of international tension or conflict. The principal commercial provisions of the free-trade treaties included the removal of quotas and tariffs on most manufactured goods (to be completed by January 1977); a slower phase-in for 'sensitive products' like metal and paper goods which the Community was determined to protect through more gradual tariff reductions; and the lodging of a similar extended timetable of tariff reductions on a small number of products based on agricultural commodities. Agriculture itself was exempted from the agreements at the Community's insistence. From 1972 to the mid-1980s, no fundamental change in Austria's relationship with the EC was on the political agenda. However, the ratification of the Single European Act in 1986 marked a renewed phase of dynamic development in the life of the Community: indeed, it was the implications for non-member states of its intention to complete a single internal market by 1 January 1993 which rekindled the 'European Integration' debate in Austria.

There is a *prima facie* case for arguing that Austria's decision to apply for full EC membership – formally submitted in July 1989 – was taken in almost unseemly haste by the so-called 'new Grand Coalition' of SPö and ÖVP shortly after the 1986 general election. Certainly, a possible application to join the Community had not featured, indeed had possibly even been suppressed, during the foregoing election campaign. Although, in the build-up to the formal announcement to apply, the Greens emerged as the only outright anti-EC party – the Freedom Party (FPÖ) was supportive, albeit in the somewhat opportunistic and populist manner of its leader Jörg Haider – it was noticeable how, in contrast to the Independent Approach years of the mid-1960s, SPÖ's support for accession increased, whereas the opposite trend was apparent in the ÖVP whose agricultural wing proved particularly recalcitrant.

An elite-level discussion about the possible implications of EC membership for Austria's obligation to permanent neutrality developed in 1988–9 when, against the background of Soviet *perestroika* and amicable East–West relations, a consensus quickly emerged about the legal and political compatibility of neutrality and integration. There were powerful domestic reasons for avoiding a public debate on neutrality, however, since opponents of further integration – the Greens, Communists and, indeed, a substantial element of the SPÖ left wing, together with vulnerable business interests – could clearly exploit the matter to their own advantage. Interestingly, moreover, the evidence from the opinion polls indicated that the sanctity of neutrality had become deeply internalized among the body of the citizenry. Although down from a high point of over 80 per cent during November 1990–January 1991, as many as two out of three respondents were not willing to sacrifice neutrality on the altar of European integration.

According to conventional legal wisdom, Austrian membership of the EC would involve a *Gesammtanderung* of the Federal Constitution which would require, in addition to two-thirds approval in both houses of parliament, majority support at a mandatory referendum. Yet opinion polls have shown that majority, although relatively secure, to be declining. In summer 1991, for example, 55 per cent of Austrians favoured membership, compared with 42 per cent who were against and 3 per cent undecided.[67] By March 1992, well before the popular Danish rejection of Maastricht, pro-Market support had dropped a little to 51 per cent, compared with a relatively stable 41 per cent opposed to membership (and a growing 8 per cent undecided), although in both the two governing parties there were clear majorities – nearly two-thirds in SPÖ – in favour of joining (see Table 7.4). In short, whilst in spring 1992 pro-Market support in Austria was surpassed only in Finland among the small neutral EFTA states (see Table 7.5), it cannot be assumed that an affirmative vote will ultimately materialize at an EC membership referendum. Opposition has principally emanated from Freedom Party supporters, the Greens, the older generation and, above all, the farmers, 65 per cent of whom are hostile to membership. As in Switzerland, Finland and Sweden, Austrian farmers are concerned about the implications of Community membership for their subsidies (which are in excess of the EC's),

Table 7.4   Support for EC Membership in Austria by Political Party in March 1992

	Per cent for	Per cent against	Per cent undecided
Socialist People's Party (SPÖ)	61	31	8
Catholic People's Party (ÖVP)	55	42	3
Freedom Party (FPÖ)	47	47	6
Greens	50	48	2
National average	51	41	8

Source: 'Durch sichtbare Einigkeit zum Beitritt in die E.G.', *Der Standard*, 9/10 May 1992, p.5.

Table 7.5   Support for EC Membership among the 'EFTA Neutrals' in March 1992**

	Per cent for	Per cent against
Finland	55*	21
Austria	51	41
Sweden	44	36
Switzerland	44	42

*Other data used in this study – presented later – put the extent of pro-Market support in Finland at 51 per cent, exactly on a par with Austria.
**Pro- and anti-Market opinion in the third Nordic EFTA state, Norway, was tied at 43 per cent each in March 1992.
Source: Fritz Plasser and Peter A. Ulram, 'EG – Meinungstrend in Österreich', Presseunterlage für das Privatissimum in der Reisnerstraße on 7 Ma 1992.

together with their capacity to compete with large-scale producers elsewhere in the 'Twelve'.

Finally, in the way the collapse of monopoly communism has fundamentally altered Austria's geopolitical position between the Two Europes, so too has it potentially strengthened her geo-economic location between East and West. Austria, in short, stands to profit enormously from the consolidation of market economies in the former COMECON countries with which she has longstanding links. Paradoxically, whilst the collapse of the Soviet Union facilitated closer

Austrian integration with the European Community, it also created opportunities which reduce the pressing need for closer integration with Western Europe.[68]

Sweden

A longstanding adherence to neutrality, dating back to 1814, proved the ostensible stumbling-block to a Swedish application for full Common Market membership in 1961, although after Britain's application to join, a broad cross-party consensus (embracing all but the radical left) emerged on the need for some form of strengthened linkage with the Community. Thus at the Riksdag's EC debate on 25 October 1961 the Social Democrats and Centre (whose agricultural wing was concerned to protect farm subsidies) favoured (only) an association agreement; the Conservatives and Liberals, backed by the industrial and business lobbies, sought full membership, albeit with escape clauses for Swedish neutrality – a stance reiterated in 1967; while the Communists alone remained opposed to any arrangement with the EEC. In any event, following a tripartite governmental meeting in Vienna in October 1961, Sweden applied for associate Community membership along with Austria and Switzerland. Though ultimately thwarted by de Gaulle's veto of Britain's application in January 1963, the fitful EC debate in Sweden continued to focus on the question of how to become a full member without having to meet the obligations of full membership.[69] In 1967, at the time of the second UK application, the Swedish government, apparently persuaded by the tactical line peddled by business and the political right that de Gaulle's bombastic approach had substantially set back the cause of political union within the Six, decided to seek negotiations with the Community 'with the aim of ensuring that Sweden will participate in the enlarging of the EEC in a manner consistent with her policy of neutrality'. The government in effect left the form of membership open to negotiation. This proved academic, however, when de Gaulle again intervened to torpedo British membership.

By the early 1970s, two developments contributed to the need for a careful reappraisal of Sweden's position towards the Common Market. First, the militarily and politically sensitive sectors of her economy – engineering and electronics – had become (and needed to remain) overwhelmingly integrated into the economies of the EEC states. Second, the Community stood on the threshold of expanding to include the UK which was a significant trading partner of Sweden.[70] Yet on 18 March 1971 the Swedish government announced that participation in the type of foreign policy cooperation envisaged by the Davignon Report was not consistent with the resolute pursuit of neutrality.[71] Admittedly, James Waite has argued that the 1972 industrial free-trade agreement, signed in tandem with the other EFTA countries, differed little in its essentials from the full membership denounced in 1971; it was, he asserted, the same general concept in a new shroud.[72] But this appears to miss the vital point. *De facto* integration was, indeed, intensified, a process essential to maintain a domestic economy strong and sophisticated enough to serve the requirements of armed neutrality. But *de jure* integration – formal, legal affiliation with an organization committed to long-term political and economic union – was studiously avoided. Indeed, until the achievement of the Single European Act in 1986 marked a decisive further step along the road to deeper Community integration, Sweden remained content with the status quo of an industrial free-trade agreement; the EEC question did not form part of the domestic political agenda.

In fact the EEC was still not an issue at the 1988 general election. The Conservatives (*Moderaterna*) were the only party to canvass membership, one of their posters boldly insisting that 'Sweden Needs Europe More than Europe Needs Sweden'. But compared with taxation reform and privatization, 'Europe' was not a major campaign theme of the Conservatives.[73] In any event, prime minister Ingvar Carlsson declared on polling night that his re-elected (minority) Social Democratic government would not consider EEC membership before the completion of the single internal market in 1992 at the earliest. The Left-Communist leader, Lars Werner, retorted that any move towards Brussels would be blocked by a new alignment of environmentally-friendly parties – the Communists and the Greens (as in Austria) and the Centre Party (representing farmers and small businesses). Not surprisingly, when the picture radically changed and in November 1990 four-party agreement was reached in the Riksdag between the Social Democrats, Conservatives, Liberals and Centre on a formal application for EC membership, the Greens accused the Centre of sacrificing its anti-Market stance in order not to risk exclusion from a future three-party non-socialist coalition. On 12 December 1990 the Riksdag decided, with dissent only from the Left-Communists (now renamed simply Leftist Party)[74] and the Greens, that Sweden should seek EC membership whilst *preserving her neutrality*, though the Liberals were willing to abandon neutrality altogether.[75] On 1 July 1991, Sweden formally applied to join. Sweden, it was stated, would play her full part in moving towards political union but would not involve herself in Community-specific defence arrangements (such as a revamped Western European Union). Incidentally, the Carlsson cabinet's sudden shift in favour of full EC membership constituted a unilateral breaking of ranks with the other Nordic EFTA states during the European Economic Area negotiations and left the Finns in particular surprised, embarrassed and not a little vexed.

Three factors combined to sway the Swedish government in favour of full EC membership. First, the emergence of the New Europe, symbolized by the breach of the Berlin Wall on 9 November 1989, materially altered the old Cold War security configuration on the continent and, by extension, the context of Swedish neutrality. Thus Sweden's application, in contrast to Austria's, post-dated the 1989 revolutions in the East European communist states which in turn both facilitated and, equally importantly, enabled the government to rationalize its changed stance. The rhetorical emphasis, in short, was placed on changes in the external environment of security policy. For example, when Carlsson opened the Social Democrats' Party Congress on 15 September 1990 he observed that, in a Europe in which the East–West divide had lost much of its significance, the traditional obstacle of neutrality in considering Swedish membership of the EC had also lost its moral force.[76]

Second, whilst the official Swedish position had earlier been that possible EC membership could not be contemplated before the joint EC–EFTA talks on a European Economic Area agreement had been completed, the very slow progress in these talks, and a recognition that even a successful *dénouement* would not enable her to exercise influence on EC decisions – which would remain a closed door – prompted Sweden to exploit the changed security climate in Europe to break ranks. Plainly, the EEA negotiations would not pass Sweden the holy grail she had long sought – the full benefits of EC membership without the full costs.

Finally, the conversion of the peak labour federation, LO, with its close ties to the governing Social Democrats, meant that both the leading sectoral organizations in Sweden – the employees and labour – favoured EC membership at a time when their cooperation was supremely important if the cabinet was to achieve the stabilization measures necessary to reverse the lurch towards recession. LO became convinced that the celebrated Swedish welfare model would be endangered if the nation's export industries did not possess adequate foreign outlets for their products. It was also viewed as essential that the West should act in consort at the European level in order to exert effective influence over the increasing internationalization of the economy. The employers' organization, SAF, and influential business voices, moreover, had for some time criticized the potential economic costs of neutrality and favoured EC membership. For instance, Volvo director Pehr Gyllenhammar wrote in the independent daily *Dagens Nyheter* over the summer of 1990 that Sweden's failure openly to condemn the Iraqi regime testified to the way neutrality had outlived its usefulness and concluded that, once it was abandoned, Sweden could take the welcome step of participating in the surge towards European union.[77]

Six months after the formal submission of a Swedish application for full EC membership, the outcome of the popular referendum on accession – likely to be held in 1994 – looked a foregone conclusion. In a study commissioned by the newspaper *Göteborgs-Posten* and published in December 1991, twice as many citizens favoured membership as opposed it.[78] The survey research, moreover, revealed two contrasting voter stereotypes on the EC question. The typical 'pro-Marketeer' emerged as a male aged 50–64 years who owned his own business, lived in a larger town and voted Liberal. The typical 'anti-Marketeer' was an older woman, employed in the public sector, resident in a small northerly town and a supporter of the Leftist Party. During the first half of 1992, however, popular opposition to membership rose sharply and, by May, a clear majority of respondents opposed membership (see Table 7.6). Part of the heightened negativity related to the general work situation and fears of a further rise in unemployment as a corollary of the government's concern to get the economy lean and 'Euro-fit'. But there were other relevant factors as well.

Table 7.6   The Growth in Popular Opposition to Swedish Membership of the EC, 1991–2

	Per cent in favour	Per cent against	Don't know
December 1991	48	24	27
March 1992	44	36	20
May 1992	35	40	26

Sources: 'Många osäkra i EG frågan', *Nordisk Kontakt*, 12/1991, 92–3; 'Risk för partisplittring efter växande EG – motstånd', *Nordisk Kontakt*, 3/92, 82–3; 'Ruotsalaiset vastustavat EY-jäsenyyttä', *Kristityn Vastuu*, 14 May 1992.

Having suffered a bad election defeat in September 1991 and shifted to opposition, the Social Democrats adjusted their strategy so as to reflect growing misgivings in their ranks about full EC membership. Opinion polls indicated that 47 per cent of party supporters opposed joining whereas only 33 per cent were in favour. Indeed, on 19 March 1992, the SDP announced that it would not canvass an unqualified 'yes' but, instead, intended to illuminate both sides of the argument in what it called an 'educational campaign'. The Centre Party, although a governing party, had long been internally divided on the EC question and, faced with the real risk of party fragmentation, no longer felt able to paper over the cracks. Announcing a 'neutral line' on the EC on 27 March 1992, the Centre leader Olof Johansson noted that, simply because the party had backed the Swedish application to join, this did not mean it would necessarily say 'yes' to the terms of membership. In the same month, surveys showed that 58 per cent of Centre supporters opposed full membership and only 19 per cent favoured it. Finally, the formation in January 1992 by Social Democratic and Centre Party journalists of 'The Alternative to the EC' and increased support for the 'No to the EC' group both focused and mobilized anti-Market sentiment. As in Austria, the outcome of the Swedish EC referendum looks anything but a foregone conclusion.

Switzerland

It is legitimate in the Swiss case, according to Daniel Frei, to interpret neutrality in terms of isolationist nationalism, since he claims that it is impossible to find any compelling reason for Switzerland's deliberately maintaining a neutral stance.[79] 'Whoever talks about the "British whale" and the "Russian bear",' Frei notes, 'should not forget the "Swiss hedgehog"; it constitutes a far better symbol of Swiss politics than the "yodelling cheesemakers" or the "gnomes of Zurich".'[80] True, certain historical experiences created a tendency to transform neutrality into an ideology, not least the traumatic war years of 1940–45 when Switzerland was surrounded by (and in the Allied view bent some way towards) the hostile Axis powers.[81] But, it is argued, there have been no overwhelming geopolitical (strategic-security) grounds for her neutrality. Yet Switzerland has remained strictly outside international formations: she is not a member of the UN and only joined the Council of Europe in 1962 when it was clear that the organization lacked real political muscle.

Instrumental economic considerations, however, have fashioned international affiliations widely assumed to be consonant with and not to compromise Swiss neutrality; these included membership of the OEEC in 1948, for example. It was the need to protect her fundamental economic interests which cast Switzerland in the role of active founder-member of EFTA – having supported the Maudling talks and the abortive WFTA plan – and it was her extensive commercial ties with the Common Market which dictated the need for an EEC association agreement in 1972 along with the other EFTA states. At that time 48 per cent of Swiss exports went to the Community, while the EEC provided 69 per cent of Swiss imports. At the Swiss referendum in December 1972 to ratify the EEC association agreement, 72.5 per cent of voters (on a 52.9 per cent turn-out) approved the agreement while only three main political parties opposed it: the Communists, the Swiss Republican Movement and the National Action Party

Against Undue Foreign Influence on Folk and Homeland. The primary reasons cited for rejecting the agreement – and they did not vary much with the age of voters – were a concern to stem the influx of foreign labour, to protect Swiss agriculture and to preserve neutrality. On this last point, the Federal Council (cabinet) described the 1972 agreement, somewhat opaquely, as 'an intermediary solution between accession and isolation',[82] by which it presumably meant that Switzerland would gain most of the economic benefits of EEC membership with none of the political costs.

It was noted earlier that, for most of the two decades after the Second World War, Austrian attitudes towards European integration were both extremely stable and broadly positive, although the issue was not regarded as one of great immediacy or importance. In Switzerland, however, propositions about the extent of the internalization of a neutralist culture and the saliency of the European integration issue cannot be subjected to empirical investigation because the first opinion poll on the matter was not conducted until November 1986. Interestingly, there were then almost as many Swiss respondents who favoured European unification as in two former EFTA members of the Community (the UK and Ireland) and a much higher proportion than in a third (Denmark): 61.5 per cent in Switzerland supported the creation of a European confederation, compared with 69 per cent in the UK, 66 per cent in Ireland and only 45 per cent in Denmark. Perhaps more significantly, 42.8 per cent also answered in the affirmative to the question: 'Is a possible accession in the future desirable?' while 42.5 per cent of those interviewed replied negatively.[83]

On the face of it, then, neutralist attitudes appeared to lack the deep roots commonly supposed, although an opinion poll is not, of course, a referendum. Indeed, there was a powerful reaffirmation of isolationism when, at a referendum on 16 March 1986, 75.7 per cent of voters rejected UN membership. The rebuff this represented for the political elite was so enormous that it triggered a debate in the media about the growing risks of isolation and the need to foster closer relations with the European Community. To be sure, a growing number of technical cooperation agreements had been signed in the fields of industry and research in the wake of the April 1984 EFTA–EC Luxembourg Accord. Thus it was no surprise when Switzerland joined her EFTA partners in promoting the European economic space notion or when she ultimately signed a European Economic Area (EEA) agreement between EC and EFTA states on 2 May 1992.

The announcement on 18 May 1992 of an imminent application to join the EC was nonetheless surprising, even though it came very shortly after a referendum at which 56 per cent of voters favoured Swiss membership of the International Monetary Fund (IMF) and the World Bank.[84] It was also highly ironic in an historical perspective that the risk of isolationism was given as the primary reason for the timing of the EEC application. Advocates of EEC membership, led by foreign minister René Felber, held that unless Switzerland applied to join, the country would risk isolation if the EEA treaty did not gain popular approval at the referendum scheduled for December 1992.

By the same token, it cannot tacitly be assumed that Swiss voters will abandon neutrality and isolationism in favour of full EC membership. First, there are relatively exacting constitutional requirements to be met. Since 1977, if a treaty has involved adhering to a supranational community, a referendum is compulsory, requiring a double majority of voters and cantons (there are 26 cantons and half-cantons).[85]

Second, there is bound to be opposition from the Swiss Farmers' Union since Swiss agriculture is one of the most protected in Europe and such protection is viewed as a means to its survival. Finally, a potentially very high democratic deficit could be incurred if Switzerland joins. This is because the nation's unique reliance on the mechanisms of direct democracy is such that any transfer of sovereignty would denote an equivalent loss of power for citizens less able to influence legislation in the transferred areas through their traditional instruments of the referendum and popular initiative. From a Brussels perspective, of course, the integration of the highly decentralized Swiss confederation as a full Community member would represent a considerable 'subsidiarity bonus' which could be deployed against those in Britain and elsewhere who have tended to view federal political union as synonymous with increased centralization.

In fact, there was solid evidence to justify Felber's strategy of seeking full EC membership as a safeguard against possible isolation when, at the EEA referendum on 6 December 1992, 50.3 per cent of Swiss voters rejected membership of the European Economic Area. Citizens cast ballots at both the national and cantonal level and, at the latter, the ethnic contours of 'European' opinion were plainly apparent. In contrast to an average of over 75 per cent in the six French-speaking cantons favouring the EEA, the German- and Italian-speaking cantons produced a clear negative majority. The anti-membership lobby was a disparate grouping, embracing a patriotic older generation of conservatives led by Christian Blocher, and a younger cohort of ecologists. The conservatives stressed that the EEA's obligation to adopt the EC's single market arrangements for the free movement of capital, labour, goods and services would entail Switzerland being overrun by (job-poaching) foreigners who already comprised 18 per cent of the population. The Greens, for their part, exploited popular fears that 'sacred' Alpine land would be snapped up by outsiders. Although the negative Swiss vote looked likely merely to postpone for a few months the implementation of the EEA, it served, more significantly, to delay consideration of Switzerland's application for full Community membership which, unlike the cases of Austria, Sweden and Finland, was not set at 1 January 1993. Incidentally, exactly a week after the Swiss vote, a referendum in the miniscule EFTA state of Liechtenstein approved the same EEA treaty.

Finland

When on 18 March 1992, 133 of the 200 *Eduskunta* members voted in favour of applying to join the 'Twelve', Finland became the third 'EFTA neutral' since 1989 and the first successor state of the 1917–23 period to seek full EC membership. If Swedish neutrality was based on history and tradition and the Swiss on a strong predilection for nationalist isolationism, the limits of Finnish neutrality (as in the case of Austria's permanent neutrality) were defined by Cold War politics and Soviet security policy, especially the Kremlin's almost obsessional concern about a possible resurgence of German militarism. The 1948 Treaty of Friendship, Cooperation and Mutual Assistance (FCMA) asserted that 'in the event of Finland, or the Soviet Union through Finland, becoming the object of an armed attack by Germany, or any other state allied with the latter, Finland will ... fight to repel the attack'. Unlike Austria, however, Finnish neutrality did not rest on legal specification – the preamble to the FCMA treaty alluded only generally to 'Finland's desire to remain outside the conflicting interests of the great powers' – but simply on a unilateral proclamation of intent by the Finns backed by skilful diplomacy. For the Finns, neutrality became very much the art of the possible, the credibility of the policy resting in large part on its recognition by the Kremlin.[86]

Two crises in Finno-Soviet relations – the 'Night Frost' of 1958–9 and the 'Note Crisis' of 1961–2 (the latter mirroring wider strains in superpower relations over Berlin) pointed up the limits of Finland's neutrality and the way she, and probably the West in general, underestimated Soviet concern about a revival of German strength within NATO. Old Nazi ghosts still haunted the Kremlin and the spectre of renewed German imperialism stalked every Finnish economic move westwards: associate membership of EFTA was achieved with much difficulty in 1961, but Nordek was simply not risked.

The audacious way in which Finland sought to exorcise the past and create room for manoeuvre was to cast itself (with Soviet acquiescence, even encouragement) in the role of 'honest broker', seeking to reduce tensions between the superpowers. Following a Finnish initiative, the Strategic Arms Limitation Talks (SALT) began in Helsinki in 1970, the Soviets and Americans having spent the previous year there negotiating whether to negotiate. Then, alternating between Helsinki and Vienna, the SALT rounds culminated in the staging of a Conference on Security and Cooperation in Europe in the Finnish capital in 1975. For the host nation this phase of bold international diplomacy had three main purposes. First, it was designed further to consolidate relations of trust with the Kremlin, whilst projecting an image of active neutrality on the world stage. Second, it was hoped to establish the machinery for regular superpower consultation with the long-term goal of defusing old Cold War antagonisms and reducing the significance of the East–West divide in Europe. Third and no less importantly, it was hoped, through the achievement of both the aforementioned aims, to create the leverage with which to facilitate the extension of Finland's trade links with Western Europe.

Concern to anticipate Soviet reaction, then, was the primary trait of Finnish post-war foreign and commercial policy-making (indeed, even domestic coalition-building).[87] Relations of mutual trust between the respective heads of state and the development of a type of *saunapolitik* were essential to the successful management of Finno-Soviet affairs. In the case of initiatives to strengthen Finland's economic links with Western Europe, personal assurances from the long-serving president, Urho Kekkonen, of the *status quo ante* of amicable Soviet relations were, it seems, a precondition of a successful outcome. Although cast as something of a 'belated European', Finland was able to join the Nordic Council in 1956, gain an association agreement with EFTA in 1961, an industrial free-trade agreement with the EC in 1974 and become an OEEC member in 1968.

The disintegration of the Soviet Union over autumn 1991, the termination of the FCMA treaty (this cornerstone of post-war Finnish foreign policy had become a millstone) and, more widely, the demise of the overarching imperative of seeking to survive as a Western pluralist democracy whilst sharing a 1000–kilometre frontier with the USSR all contributed to a fundamental change in Finland's geopolitical position. Conditions of greater latitude and licence were created in relation to *Westpolitik*. Equally, the collapse of Finno-Soviet trade – based since 1948 on five-year barter agreements, which had buoyed Finland against the worst effects of recession in Western Europe in the 1970s – meant a radical change in Finland's geo-economic position and highlighted the need to strengthen her export competitiveness in Western markets (in the early 1980s, Soviet trade accounted for about 20 per cent of total Finnish trade but, by 1991, less than 5 per cent of Finland's total exports). EC membership, though, was not an issue at the March 1991 general election. The Conservatives were known to be in favour, but there was a conspiracy of silence on the Community issue among party leaders who insisted tactically that, since the EEA negotiations were still in progress, these should be brought to a successful conclusion before other measures were considered.

By the time the four-party non-socialist coalition decided to apply in February 1992, it was widely assumed in elite circles that there was no real alternative to EC membership, and something of a virtue was made of climbing onto the bandwagon of 'EFTA neutrals' rolling towards Brussels. Negotiating strength, it was implied, lay in numbers. As in Sweden, however, popular opposition to membership had grown. According to a *Helsingin Sanomat* poll in January 1992, support had dropped from 65 per cent in summer 1991 to 51 per cent.[88] Ironically, the strongest grassroots opposition emanated from the ranks of the leading government party, the Centre (formerly Agrarians), in which 54 per cent of supporters were against Community membership, whilst only 16 per cent of farmers were in favour. Yet remarkably, in coalition with the strongly pro-Market Conservatives (82 per cent of whose supporters were in favour; see Table 7.7), the Centre leaders contrived to win the party round to a formal application for membership (the anti-EC Christian League was able to remain in the governing coalition). The Alternative to the Common Market movement, *'Vaihtoehto EY: lle'*, will nonetheless seek to exploit the rising tide of opposition before the promised referendum on Finnish accession, likely to be held in 1994.

Table 7.7   Support for Finnish Membership of the EC by Party (January 1992)

	Per cent in favour	Per cent against	Don't know
Centre	33	54	13
Social Democrats	56	36	8
Conservatives	82	12	6
Leftists	34	48	17
Greens	65	29	7

Source: 'Keskustan väki penseä EY: lle', *Helsingin Sanomat*, 4 February 1992, p.7.

The applications of the 'EFTA neutrals' (Austria, Sweden, Switzerland and Finland) for full Community membership between 1989 and 1992 demonstrated that neutrality had lost much of its substance, if not necessarily its symbolic importance, in the post-Cold War New Europe. Neutrality no longer appears a real impediment to European integration, although Sweden and Finland, in particular, have made a point of eschewing future involvement in any EC-based defence arrangements. The EFTA applications, moreover, have generally been welcomed, since it is recognized that, as developed economies, they will not constitute a burden on the Community budget. Equally, the growth in popular opposition to Community membership – by October 1992 there was no longer a majority of Finns in favour of accession – and concerns to protect national sovereignty have led to the expectation in some EC circles that the EFTA newcomers will join forces with Britain and Denmark in an anti-federalist lobby against the more ardent proponents of increased political integration. Certainly the accession of the EFTA neutrals will doubtless expedite – or at least assist those canvassing – the comprehensive reform of the Community institutions necessary to accommodate an increased membership. In all the applicant states, extensive concern has been voiced about the likelihood of their inadequate representation on the EC's decision-making bodies, as well as the paramount need for steps to reduce the so-called 'democratic deficit'.

A postscript on the 'widening' of the Community is in order since, in April 1987, Turkey also applied to join the EC. Developments from the Balkans, through the Black Sea area and the Caucasus to the central Asian (Muslim) republics of the Commonwealth of Independent States (comprising 11 of the 15 former Soviet republics) have facilitated Turkey's emergence as a regional power of some significance. The Turks, indeed, have taken the initiative in the formation of a Black Sea Cooperation Council which seeks to incorporate not only her ancient rival Greece, but also the warring Caucasian states of Armenia and Azerbaijan. Two main obstacles nonetheless have stood in the path of Turkish accession to the EC. One is Cyprus. In Nicosia the Istanbul government is blamed for encouraging the intransigence of the local Turkish Cypriot leadership and undermining the UN's mediation role. The other is the conflict with the Kurdish separatists in eastern Turkey and across the border in Iraq. It is this military repression which has most jeopardized an accommodation with Brussels. If Turkey were to grant the Kurds full democratic and national rights, this could well open the door to a full customs union between the EC and Turkey, the granting of full rights to Turkish migrant workers in the EC and possible membership of the Community by the end of the century.[89]

Conclusions

Over twelve months after the summit, the Maastricht Treaty had still not been ratified in all twelve Community countries. However, at the beginning of 1993, with most of the provisions of the single internal market in place, European Union, which after the June 1992 Danish referendum had faced the serious risk of derailment, appeared back on track. There seemed in fact the distinct possibility that the Maastricht Treaty would come into force on 1 July 1993.

Having achieved opt-outs on the single currency and common defence at the Edinburgh European Council in December 1992 – a summit which, according to John Major, 'delivered a message of hope for growth and openness in Europe' – the Danish government was committed in short order to putting legislation embodying the exemptions to the Maastricht Treaty before the *Folketing*. Since the previously anti-EC Socialist People's Party came out in favour of the 'Rubik's cube deal' worked out at Edinburgh – and only the Progress Party, among the *Folketing* groups, remained opposed – there was a reasonable prospect of a 'yes' vote in a fresh referendum set for 18 May 1993. Nothing, however, could be taken for granted. An opinion poll, published in the national daily *Berlingske Tidende* in mid-December 1992, whilst showing 54 per cent in favour, also indicated that 22 per cent of citizens were still undecided. There remained uncertainty and ambiguity, moreover, regarding the timing of British ratification of Maastricht, with Major apparently linking British approval to a successful outcome of the second Danish referendum. Continuing 'Euro-sceptical' opposition within the governing Conservative Party win hardly facilitate the prime minister's task.

Aside from the resolution of the 'Danish Question', there were other tangible results of the Edinburgh summit which gave grounds for cautious optimism about the future of West European integration. Against the backcloth of mounting recession and rising unemployment, there was agreement on an economic recovery package stimulating growth through financing infrastructural development; a deal was done doubling the fund for the so-called 'cohesion countries' – Spain, Portugal, Ireland and Greece – to assist their preparations for a single European currency; and there was a commitment from 1 January 1993 to begin negotiations with the 'EFTA-neutrals', Austria, Sweden and Finland, on entry. Discussions with Norway (after the Labour Party voted in favour, Norway re-applied on 24 November 1992) look set for late 1993 or early 1994. If there are positive outcomes in the proposed referenda on accession – this cannot be assumed – all the EFTA applicants, except Switzerland, could be full EC members by 1995.

By the new century, the EC association agreements with Poland, Hungary and the linked sovereign states of the Czech Republic of Bohemia and Moravia and Slovakia could also have been converted into full membership. The future of the rest of central and eastern Europe, however, remains problematical – riven as it was by the centrifugal forces of nationalism and counter-nationalism in the wake of the failed anti-Gorbachev coup of 19–21 August 1991. But links with the EC are likely to be sought; in June 1992, for example, the newly-independent Slovenia asked to join the Community and the Baltic republics may soon follow suit. Indeed, it is to the challenges facing post-communist Eastern Europe and EC attitudes to them that we now must turn.

Notes

1　Alfred Tovias (1984), 'The International Context of Democratic Transition', *West European Politics*, **7**(2), 163.
2　Peter Holmes (1983), 'Spain and the EEC', in D.S. Bell (ed.), *Democratic Politics in Spain*, London: Pinter, pp.165–79.
3　Benny Pollack, with Graham Hunter (1988), *The Paradox of Spanish Foreign Policy*, London; Pinter, pp.135–9.
4　Ibid., p.137.
5　Thomas C. Bruneau (1984), 'Continuity and Change in Portuguese Politics: Ten Years after the Revolution of 25 April 1974', in Geoffrey Pridham (ed.), *The New Mediterranean Democracies: Regime Transition in Spain, Greece and Portugal*, London: Cass, p.73.
6　Christos Lyrintzis (1988), 'Greece: Recent History and Politics', in *Western Europe 1989: A Political and Economic Survey*, London: Europa, pp.235–9.
7　P. Nikiforos Diamandouros (1984), 'Transition to, and Consolidation of Democratic Politics in Greece, 1974–1983: A Tentative Assessment', *West European Politics*, **7**(2), 50–71, especially 59.
8　Tovias (1984), op. cit., 160.
9　Ibid., 161.
10　Roy Price (1989), 'Working Towards Integration in a Divided Continent', in *Western Europe 1989*, op. cit., p.4.
11　Loukas Tsoukalis (1978), 'A Community of Twelve in Search of an Identity', *International Affairs*, **54**(3), 438.
12　Geoffrey Edwards (1981), 'The Future Challenge: New and Potential Members', in Carol and Kenneth J. Twitchett (eds), *Building Europe: Britain's Partners in the EEC*, London: Europa, p.229.
13　Ibid., p.231.
14　Derek W. Urwin (1992), *The Community of Europe: A History of European Integration since 1945*, London and New York: Longman, pp.207–8.
15　Tovias (1984), op. cit., 161.
16　Ibid., p.162.
17　Tom Gallagher, 'Recent History and Politics of Portugal', in *Western Europe 1989*, op. cit., 393.
18　Pollack and Hunter (1988), op. cit., p.138.
19　Ibid., pp.132–4.
20　Loukas Tsoukalis (1977), 'The EEC and the Mediterranean: Is "Global" Policy a Misnomer?', *International Affairs*, July, 422–38.
21　Paul Preston (1986), *The Triumph of Democracy in Spain*, London and New York: Methuen, p.74.
22　Holmes (1983), op. cit., p.173.
23　Edwards (1981), op. cit., p.226.
24　The CAP protected fruit and vegetables by import restrictions rather than internal market intervention, and this led the French and Italians to call for an extension of CAP mechanisms in this sector before Spanish accession so that stockpiles could be used to hold up prices. Holmes (1983), op. cit., pp.172–3.
25　Pollack and Hunter (1988), op. cit., p.139.
26　Urwin (1992), op. cit., p.210.
27　Pollack and Hunter (1988), op. cit., p.139.

28   Jacques Delors, 'Ties make for Peace', *The Guardian*, 13 September 1991.
29   Commenting on the Luxembourg Compromise, Peter Calvocoressi has noted that it sanctioned an impasse. 'It bowed to French intransigence by accepting a recipe for stagnation, but provided in consequence an embarrassing accumulation of unresolved issues.' Peter Calvocoressi (1991), *Resilient Europe 1870–2000*, London and New York: Longman, pp.236–7.
30   Urwin (1992), op. cit., pp.201–2.
31   Ibid., pp.202–3.
32   Derek W. Urwin (1989), *Western Europe since 1945*, Fourth Edition, London: Longman, p.369.
33   Geoffrey Edwards, 'International Relations and Defence in Western Europe', in *Western Europe 1989*, op. cit., p.62.
34   Urwin (1992), pp.236–7.
35   J. Monnet (1978), *Memoirs*, London: Collins, p.505.
36   Ibid., p.523.
37   'Vision of a Europe marching in Step', *The Guardian*, 22 November 1990.
38   'Democracy Before the Assizes', *The Guardian*, 23 November 1990.
39   Council of the European Communities and Commission of the European Communities (1992), *Treaty on European Union*, Luxembourg: Official Publications Office, pp.15–16.
40   Ibid., p.63.
41   Ibid., pp.123–9, 242–6.
42   Ibid., pp.28–9.
43   Ibid., pp.29–31.
44   Ibid., pp.36–9.
45   During the third stage of monetary union, an Economic and Financial Committee was envisaged, to keep under review the economic and financial situation of the member-states and of the Community and to examine, at least once annually, the situation regarding the movement of capital and the freedom of payments. *Treaty on European Union*, pp.43–4.
46   Ibid., pp.191–3.
47   Ibid., pp.46, 51.
48   Ibid., p.197. The Social Charter of 1989 sought to promote employment, improved living and working conditions, proper social protection, dialogue between management and labour, and the development of human resources with a view to achieving high employment and the combating of exclusion.
49   John Palmer, 'United we prosper', *The Guardian*, 3 July 1992, p.21.
50   Will Hutton, 'Maastricht's mistakes', *The Guardian*, 10 February 1992, p.11.
51   'EC out of touch – Thatcher', *The Guardian*, 3 July 1992, p.6.
52   'EC chaos after "No" vote', *The Guardian*, 3 June 1992, p.1.
53   'Danska Kr F-basen röstar nej i juni', *Kristet Ansvar*, 14 May 1992, p.16.
54   'Dane In, Dane Out Debate', *The Guardian*, 15 May 1992, p.25.
55   'Danebrog og det blå stjerneflag', *Nordisk Kontakt*, 5/1992, 23.
56   'In Defence of the Realm', *The Independent on Sunday*, 7 June 1992, p.19.
57   'Mistillidsvotum i Danmark – mange årsager til nederlaget', *Nordisk Kontakt*, 5/1992, 21.
58   Joe Joyce, 'Why Irish ayes are smiling', *The Guardian*, 18 June 1992, p.21.
59   'Irish give kiss of life to EC union', *The Guardian*, 20 June 1992, p.1.
60   'German threat to Maastricht', *The Guardian*, 12 June 1992, p.1.
61   'The EC puts brave face on snub', *The Guardian*, 4 June 1992, p.1.
62   Manfred Scheich (1973), 'The European Neutrals After Enlargement of the Communities – The Austrian Perspective', *Journal of Common Market Studies*, **12**, 235–47.
63   D. Mark Schultz (1992), 'Austria in the International Arena: Neutrality, Euro-

pean Integration and Consociationalism', in K.R. Luther and W.C. Müller (eds), *Politics in Austria: Still a Case of Consociationalism?*, London: Frank Cass, p.177.

64   Peter J. Katzenstein (1975), 'Trends and Oscillations in Austrian Integration Policy Since 1955: Alternative Explanations', *Journal of Common Market Studies*, **14**, 173.
65   Schultz (1992), op. cit., p.180.
66   Katzenstein (1975), op. cit., 181–4.
67   I am grateful to Dr Richard Luther of the Centre for European Studies at the University of Central Lancashire for the opinion poll data.
68   Schultz (1992), op. cit., p.196.
69   Toivo Miljan (1977), *The Reluctant Europeans: The Attitudes of the Nordic Countries towards European Integration*, London: Hirst, p.240.
70   Ibid., p.238.
71   Ibid., p.255.
72   James L. Waite (1973), 'The Swedish Paradox: EEC and Neutrality', *Journal of Common Market Studies*, **12**, 328.
73   David Arter (1988), 'A Tale of Two Carlssons: The Swedish General Election of 1988', *Parliamentary Affairs*, **42** (1), 84–101.
74   David Arter (1991b), 'The Swedish Leftist Party: '"Eco-Communism" or Communist Echo?', **44**(1), 60–79.
75   'Sverige bädder för EG-ansökan i slutet av juni', *Nordisk Kontakt*, 5/1991, 82–3.
76   'Sverige överväger medlemskap i EG', *Nordisk Kontakt*, 13/1990, 63.
77   'Slopa neutraliteten', *Nordisk Kontakt*, 10/11, 1990, 73.
78   'Många osäkra i EG-Frågen', *Nordisk Kontakt*, 12/1991, 92–3.
79   Daniel Frei (1973–4), 'Switzerland and the EEC: Facts and Trends', *Journal of Common Market Studies*, **12**, 248–64.
80   Ibid., 260.
81   Clive H. Church, 'Switzerland: Recent History and Politics', in *Western Europe 1989*, op. cit., pp.446–67.
82   François Saint-Ouen (1988), 'Facing European Integration: The Case of Switzerland', *Journal of Common Market Studies*, **26**(3), 281.
83   Ibid., 277.
84   John Palmer, 'Swiss to break with neutrality policy and apply to join EC', *The Guardian*, 19 May 1992, p.8.
85   Jean-François Aubert (1978), 'Switzerland', in A. Ranney and D. Butler (eds), *Referendums*, Washington DC: American Enterprise Institute, p.41.
86   The term 'neutrality' was first used officially in a joint communiqué on a Soviet visit to Finland in 1957. On the 12th anniversary of the FCMA in 1960, *Pravda* described the treaty as 'an international juridical document which confirms Finnish neutrality'. The official Soviet view was more equivocal and generally less expansive, however, and in the late 1960s – as we noted in the context of the Nordek discussion – there was a marked Soviet reluctance to refer to Finnish neutrality. See Roy Allison (1985), *Finland's Relations with the Soviet Union, 1944–84*, London: Macmillan, pp.95–8.
87   Arter (1987), *Politics and Policy-Making in Finland*, Wheatsheaf: Brighton, pp.186–93.
88   'Keskustan väki penseä EY:lle', *Helsingin Sanomat*, 4 February 1992, p.7. 38 per cent were against and 12 per cent 'don't knows'.
89   Pam O'Toole, 'Turkey Driven to Diplomacy', *The Guardian*, 16 December 1992, p.9.

8   The Road to Minsk 1991. Accelerated Disintegration in Eastern Europe

> The political order in one or another country changed in the past and may change in the future. This change is the exclusive affair and choice of the people of that country. Any interference in domestic affairs and any attempt to restrict the sovereignty of states, both friends and allies or any others, is inadmissible.
>
> Mikhail Gorbachev, Speech at the Council of Europe, July 1989

The overthrow of communism in the satellite states over the second part of 1989, followed two years later by the collapse of the multi-ethnic communist federations of Yugoslavia and the Soviet Union itself, represented the unexpected but wholesale fragmentation of the post-Second World War order in Eastern Europe. The centrifugal forces released by events, moreover, led a bewildering array of 'nations' to declare, demand or at least desire the right to statehood. Nationalism was once again running amuck in central and eastern Europe, and it was by no means certain that the Western political leaders were better equipped to evaluate the merits of the multifarious claims to independence than their illustrious predecessors had been at Versailles in 1919.

This chapter analyses the dramatic sequence of events which began with the emergence of Mikhail Gorbachev as Soviet leader in 1985, gained irreversible momentum during the autumn revolutions of 1989 with the breaching of the Berlin Wall (the symbol of the Cold War) on 9 November, and culminated after the abortive hardline coup in Moscow in August 1991 in the break-up of the Soviet Union. This federation was partially replaced by the creation in Minsk in October 1991 of a Commonwealth of Independent States (CIS). The chapter is in four sections. First, there is a discussion of Gorbachev and his attempt to 'liberalize' communism in the Soviet Union; then some of the problems of evaluating nationalist claims in Eastern Europe are identified; next, the challenges of national integration in the post-communist successor states are considered; and finally, the economic challenges facing the region are discussed. Whilst the 12 Community leaders were preparing for the Maastricht summit and the road towards consolidated West European integration that appeared to lie ahead, the leaders of the eight former Soviet republics that simultaneously met at Minsk were confronted with a seemingly accelerating process of disintegration which meant that necessity became in large part the mother of some form of association.

Gorbachev and Reformist Communism

Any history of the spiral of events (see Table 8.1) that led to the disintegration of the Soviet empire in Eastern Europe and culminated in the collapse of the Soviet Union itself must weigh the central role played by Mikhail Gorbachev, who became First Secretary of the Soviet Communist Party in March 1985 at the age of 54. Within two days of his appointment he coined the term *perestroika* – a restructuring of production – and set the stage for a series of achievements that broke the old mould of state–society relations. Limitations of space prevent all but the briefest review of Gorbachev's record. A number of key points nonetheless warrant emphasis.

First, there was little realistic alternative to the decentralization Gorbachev instituted in the economic sphere, since in February 1986 the whole Soviet economy was threatened by the collapse of international oil prices and a production system hamstrung by over-centralized planning and engrained dogma. Initially, Gorbachev hoped to effect purely economic reforms and strove to use the benefits of technology to accelerate Soviet development. The slogan was *uskoreniye* (acceleration). Factory managers were to be given more discretion in determining productmixes – instead of being dictated to by the central plan – and investment was to be directed towards high-level engineering and automation. Factories incurring regular losses were also to be allowed to go bankrupt. It was only when these relatively minor economic reforms failed that there was a need for *perestroika* within the political system. Though almost certainly not predetermined, it is for these political reforms that Gorbachev will be most remembered and these which indirectly led to the disavowal of a single-party system and, ultimately, to the break-up of the Soviet Union itself.

Thus the use of KGB-administered fear as the dominant mode of societal management was abandoned – fear, indeed, largely evaporated among citizens – and the Soviet Union became a mobilized polity in which society could bring influence to bear on the state. There was powerful evidence of this in the way, in spring 1990, 200 000 persons marched on the Kremlin successfully to call for an end to the Communist Party's monopoly of power. Article six of the constitution was dropped; the Communist Party was subsequently removed from government and a new presidential system introduced in which a presidential council replaced the politburo. Significantly for later events, although Gorbachev became the first president in 1990, he was not popularly elected to the office.

As a corollary of the jettisoning of custodial management techniques, political prisoners were freed (in February 1986, Anotoly Shcharansky was liberated after eight years in gaol, followed in December the same year by the release of Andrei Sakharov) and liberal rights tolerated. A free press was instigated, wider opportunities for travel and emigration, especially for Soviet Jews, introduced and official religious oppression halted. In December 1989, private talks with Pope John II led to the establishment of diplomatic relations with the Vatican.

Next, the structures of representative democracy were built and a functioning system of parliaments at the central, republican and local levels created. In the majority of these, moreover, the Communist Party found itself with only a minority voice. Crucially, in June 1988, the Communist Party acquiesced in a system of contested elections to a Soviet parliament. Whilst one-third of the seats were reserved for various organizations, including the Communist Party, two-thirds were freely contested. This stimulated pluralist activity of all sorts and, in the Baltics and Caucasia, Popular Front Movements developed. These were 'coalitions of reformist and populist forces, including communists outside and within the governing republican establishments'.[1] Thus the Estonian and Latvian Popular Fronts were officially founded on 2 and 9 October 1988, respectively, whilst *Sajudis* in Lithuania was launched on 23–4 October the same year.

Parliamentary structures in turn created channels for the articulation of long-suppressed nationalisms ('counter-ideologies', of course, in the Marxist schema) in the republics and enforced a degree of political decentralization that would have been inconceivable in 1990, let alone when Gorbachev came to power five years earlier. Indeed, the Union Treaty which was due for signature on 20 August 1991 – and sparked the hardline coup against Gorbachev – would have created a confederal Union of Soviet Sovereign Republics and vested those republics with considerable powers of taxation.

Rightly, Gorbachev was acknowledged in the West for significantly contributing to ending the Cold War and improving relations with the US – witness the Soviet withdrawal from Afghanistan in July 1986

Table 8.1 The Main Events in Central and Eastern Europe, December 1988 to December 1992

Date	Event
December 1988	In a landmark speech to the UN General Assembly, Gorbachev announced the withdrawal of 240 000 troops from Eastern Europe.
11 February 1989	Reforming Communist government in Hungary became the first in the Warsaw Pact to drop the constitutionally enshrined 'leading role' and approved the creation of independent parties.
26 March 1989	Elections to Supreme Soviet. New radical elements elected.
7 April 1989	Polish government agreed to legalize Solidarity.
July 1989	In a watershed speech in the Council of Europe, Gorbachev abandoned the Brezhnev doctrine of concerted armed intervention in favour of a laissez-faire approach to developments in the COMECON states (the so-called 'Sinatra doctrine').
24 August 1989	Tadeusz Mazowiecki in Poland became the first non-communist prime minister in the Warsaw Pact.
10 September 1989	Hungarian border with Austria opened to East Germans wishing to leave.
18 October 1989	No support for Honecker on 40th anniversary of East German state; President resigned.
9 November 1989	Breach of Berlin Wall. East Berliners allowed freely through to West for the first time since 1961.
10 November 1989	Todor Zhivkov toppled in Bulgaria by reformist Communists.
24 November 1989	Culmination of Czech 'Velvet Revolution'. Dubcek returned to Prague. Politburo and government resigned.
November 1989	Council of Europe accorded Poland, Hungary, the USSR and Yugoslavia 'special guest status'.
25 December 1989	Execution of Ceauşescus in Romania.
29 December 1989	Vaclav Havel elected President of Czechoslovakia.
13 January 1990	Ethnic disturbances in Soviet republic of Azerbaijan.
7 February 1990	Soviet Communist Party renounced its 'leading role'.
11 March 1990	Lithuanian parliament declared independence from Soviet Union.
18 March 1990	First free elections in East Germany since 1932. Christian Democrats and their allies gained 48 per cent of the vote.
8 April 1990	Communists won only 20 per cent in Slovenian elections.
4 May 1990	Latvian parliament voted for independence, albeit with an indeterminate transitional period.
3 October 1990	Reunification of the two Germanies.
November 1990	Czechoslovakia and Bulgaria granted 'special guest status' in Council of Europe.
13 January 1991	Fourteen killed in clashes with Soviet troops in Vilnius (Lithuania).
9–10 February 1991	In a referendum in Lithuania, 90.5 per cent favoured an 'independent and democratic republic'.
26 February 1991	Warsaw Pact formally disbanded.
1 March 1991	Leaders of the Serbian minority in Croatia stated that they wished to remain part of Yugoslavia.
3 March 1991	Referenda in Estonia and Latvia produced pro-independence majorities.
17 March 1991	Gorbachev's referendum on the preservation of the Soviet Union.

31 March 1991	Referendum on independence in Georgia.
25 June 1991	Slovenia and Croatia declared their independence.
19 August 1991	Anti-Gorbachev coup in Moscow. Collapsed in the face of resistance of Boris Yeltsin, President of the Russian Federation, and troops loyal to him.
22 August 1991	European Community recognized the independence of the Baltic states.
October 1991	Eight (subsequently eleven) of the former Soviet republics met in Minsk to form a Commonwealth of Independent States.
November 1991	Macedonia declared independence. EC recognition blocked by Greece.
December 1991	The EC, at the behest of Germany, undertook to recognize any republic that sought independence provided it respected human and minority rights, accepted existing borders and cooperated with the EC and UN.
16 December 1991	Poland, Czechoslovakia and Hungary (the Visegrad Triangle) signed a treaty of association with the EC.
December 1991	Gorbachev resigned.
15 January 1992	EC recognized Slovenia and Croatia.
10 February 1992	Airlift of American food to Russia began against the background of radical rightist demonstrations against Yeltsin's economic reform programme.
1 March 1992	Bosnia-Herzogovina voted for independence.
7 April 1992	Bosnia recognized by the EC.
June 1992	Lithuanian referendum. An overwhelming majority voted for the withdrawal of former Soviet troops by the end of 1992.
25 June 1992	Slovenia asked to join the EC.
27 June 1992	In a referendum, 93 per cent of Estonian voters favoured the new constitution.
July 1992	Havel resigned; Czech provinces and Slovakia agreed on a separation.
20 July 1992	Latvia abandoned the Russian rouble in preparation for its own currency, the 'lat'.
July 1992	Yeltsin at the CSCE meeting in Helsinki undertook to withdraw former Soviet troops from the Baltics within two years.
August 1992	Calls for military intervention in the Yugoslav civil war from, among others, Margaret Thatcher.
October 1992	Lennart Meri, leader of *Isamaa*, elected President of Estonia.
October 1992	Sajudis, the nationalist movement, and its leader V. Landsbergis defeated at the polls by the former communist Democratic Labour Party.
November 1992	First non-communist government in Bulgaria under Filip Dymitrov resigned after a no-confidence vote.
November 1992	The National Salvation Front of communists and nationalists stated that it would defy President Yeltsin's ban.
December 1992	Presidential and parliamentary elections in Slovenia. On a turn-out of 76 per cent, Liberal Democrats, led by the prime minister, Janez Drnovsek, won 24 per cent of the vote to become the largest party in the 90-member national assembly. Slovenia expected to be admitted to the Council of Europe in 1993.

– although his championing of arms reductions also possessed a functional economic logic in permitting cuts in the huge proportion of Soviet spending devoted to defence. He also facilitated the liberation of Eastern Europe from state communism. Faced with demands from conservatives like Gromyko and Ligachev for action (as in Hungary 1956 and Czechoslovakia 1968) to suppress liberal developments, Gorbachev stood firm on a policy of non-intervention. Notably, the same week in early June 1989 as the Chinese leadership sent troops into Tiennamen Square to break up students demonstrating for reforms, Moscow declined to intervene in Warsaw after the Polish Communists agreed to share power with Solidarity. The policy observed was what Gennady Gerasimov referred to as the 'Sinatra doctrine' – the essence of which was presented in a speech by Gorbachev at the Council of Europe in July 1989 – namely, that the East European 'satellites' could 'do it their way'.[2] The autumn revolutions of 1989, culminating in the collapse of the Berlin Wall on 9 November, bore overwhelming testimony to the fruits of the Sinatra doctrine; when the Romanian dictator Ceauşescu was summarily executed on Christmas Day, the gale of political change in Eastern Europe had blown communism away.

The Sinatra doctrine was not subsequently applied to the demands of the Soviet republics for independence, however. Mindful of the need to appease the conservatives and preserve his own power base, Gorbachev condoned – though he probably did not personally authorize – the military intervention which led to a bloodbath in the Lithuanian capital, Vilnius, on 14 January 1991. In addition to the problems caused by the rising tide of nationalism in the republics, the drift towards political disintegration was accelerated by the chaotic state of the economy: output was plummeting and the budget deficit ballooning, foreign trade was in ruins and price rises were approaching a hyperinflation level.

In his last significant act as Soviet leader, Gorbachev attended the G7 Summit of advanced industrial nations in London in July 1991, seeking to trade his personal stature in the West for an aid programme to fortify the enfeebled Soviet economy. Prior to his arrival, Vladimir Shcherbakov, the first deputy prime minister, indicated that the Soviet Union was looking for a 6–7 billion pound exchange stabilization fund to cushion the balance of payments crisis which the introduction of a convertible rouble would entail.[3] In the event, whilst the G7 leaders recognized both the need to integrate the Soviet Union into the Western economy and the importance of attracting private business investment into those sectors of the Soviet economy with reasonable export potential, Gorbachev left without his loan and only the loose promise of associate membership of the IMF. Indeed, the British prime minister John Major's five-point plan for greater global economic and political cooperation, which served as the G7 agenda, contained only two very roundly-worded commitments of relevance to Gorbachev: the need to help eastern and central Europe as well as the Soviet Union, and the need to lift trade barriers with the former COMECON bloc.[4] In all this it was clear that the Western leaders were concerned to ensure that they gained value for any money poured into the Soviet Union; in other words, that there was firm evidence that any financial aid would be a sound investment in assisting in the shift to a market economy. Until then, wallets would not be opened.

Having returned largely empty-handed from London, Gorbachev had few cards left to play. His popularity in the West stood in sharp contrast to a growing body of disgruntled Soviet citizens – those standing in the interminable bread queues – and to heightened concern among hardliners about the impending collapse of the old Kremlin-dominated union. Although the coup – Gorbachev was placed under house arrest while on holiday in the Crimea – failed, events moved quickly and Gorbachev, who lacked elected authority, was soon outmanoeuvred by Boris Yeltsin, the elected leader of the Russian republic. Broadly contemporaneous with the events leading to the collapse of the Soviet Union, a second communist federation began to crumble in June 1991, when civil war broke out in Yugoslavia. The secessionist republics of Slovenia and Croatia were being held in check by Serbian leader Slobodan Milosevic and the federal army he controlled. The most pressing feature of the imbroglio in Eastern Europe which faced EC leaders over the autumn of 1991 was thus a series of demands for recognition from the successor states of 1919–23 (the Baltic republics) and from the secessionist states of the moribund Soviet and Yugoslavian federations (to begin with, Slovenia, Croatia, Ukraine and Georgia). This, of course, raised the complex historical issue of evaluating nationalist claims. Whilst not all the putative nations of Eastern Europe were (as yet) demanding a state, this neither obviated nor vitiated the question: on what basis were the claims of those nations who did aspire to statehood to be evaluated?

Evaluating Nationalist Claims in Eastern Europe

Certainly if language was used as the criterion of nationality (in other words, the existence of an indigenous tongue spoken by the vast majority of the population at the time of the claim to statehood), many of the pretender states of central and eastern Europe would have failed the test. Ukraine was a case in point. Despite the activities of the People's Movement for the Reconstruction of the Ukraine, formed in September 1989 and led by the poet Ivan Drach, together with the work of the Ukrainian Language Society, about half the 52 million citizens spoke no Ukrainian, or alternatively spoke it very poorly. Over three centuries of 'Russification' – in 1876, for example, Czar Alexander I ordered schooling to be conducted solely in Russian – had taken an inevitable toll and books in Ukrainian constituted only about 20 per cent of all published volumes. As Ryszard Kapuścínski observed: 'The average Ukrainian is not even familiar with the names of the greatest Ukrainian writers of the twentieth century, Mikola Khvileva and Vladimir Vinnitchenko.'[5] To be fair, there was significant regional variation in the incidence of spoken Ukrainian which was higher in the west, in former Austrian and Polish Galicia, than in the larger, more Russianized eastern Ukraine. But when on 24 August 1991 the Highest Council of the Ukraine, meeting in Kiev, proclaimed 'the creation of an independent Ukrainian state', it could not convincingly be legitimized by reference to linguistic nationalism.

The same was true in Bielarus, which had formerly been a province of Lithuania, Poland and Russia, since the indigenous language survived only in the form of a minority rural dialect. Indeed, Bielarus was a case of a successor state which achieved statehood and only then set out to create a sense of nationality through promoting the native language in the schools. Bielarus was made compulsory for all children over the age of six and also became the official state language. Yet as a young university graduate noted: 'They are printing all these Bielarussian books that no one ever reads. They just end up in the libraries. I have always spoken Russian and see myself as a Russian'.

On somewhat safer ground, no doubt, were claims to statehood based on evidence of a mass national consciousness – a sense of national identity. In Estonia, for example, such factors as the illegal abortion of statehood in 1940, the stringent programme of Russification and the window on Western Europe provided by Finnish television – which enabled citizens to compare their lot with that of their Finno-Ugric relatives across the Baltic – combined to fuel an apparently strong popular sense of national awareness. When asked the question, 'How would you wish to see Estonia in the year 2000?', a survey of 1309 citizens in January 1990 revealed that 60 per cent wanted an 'independent Estonian republic' and 26 per cent a 'sovereign Russian republic' (a somewhat ambiguous term given currency by Vaino Väljas, the reform-minded Communist leader).[6] However, the evidence would also seem to support the view that 'national consciousness' develops unevenly among social (or, in this case, ethnic) groups.[7] Whereas 87 per cent of Estonians favoured full independence, only 16 per cent of the ethnic minority groups (Russians, Byelorussians and Ukrainians) did so, 57 per cent of them preferring the option of 'the sovereign Russian republic'.

Furthermore, if the evidence of mass nationalist action – such as human chains linking the Baltic states and the major Ukrainian cities and civic demonstrations – appeared to confirm the results of the Estonian questionnaire on independence, a high level of popular mobilization could not be regarded *ipso facto* as objective evidence of national consciousness. It was evident, for instance, that, with the ruling party facing a crisis of legitimacy, Communist leaders like the Estonian Väljas sought to befriend nationalist and, indeed, environmentalist causes as a way of sustaining the party's monopoly of power in the face of centrifugal forces promoting political pluralism.

Yet faced with the resurgence of nationalist claims across postcommunist Eastern Europe, the 'peacemakers' of the New Europe – judging at least by the statements of Western leaders severally and the EC collectively – appeared to view the rival demands for statehood largely in terms of what was politically expedient – that is, in the interests of the West. In August 1991, after the failure of a first EC peacekeeping mission, Danish foreign minister Uffe Ellemann-Jensen's threat to recognize secessionist Slovenia and Croatia was clearly intended as a sanction against what was presented as a militant, neocommunist Serbia and the federal army it controlled. Confirmation of this came at the end of October when the EC gave Serbia until 5 November either to agree to its plan for an association of sovereign Yugoslav republics or to face economic sanctions and the possible recognition of Croatia and Slovenia.

By then, it seemed that Margaret Thatcher was agitating for British recognition of Croatia and had pressed her case in discussions with Douglas Hurd, the foreign secretary. Thatcher was reported to have been impressed with the 'democratic free-market stance' of the Croatian leader, Franjo Tudjman – in contrast to Milosevic's hardline communism – and his strenuous efforts (shades of Masaryk) to align his Democratic Union with the British Conservative Party and the German Christian Democratic Union; in other words, to curry Western favour.[8] It was apparent Western bias towards the secessionist republics which concerned a Serbian reporter for Yugoslav television: 'Serbia fought on the Allied side in both wars; Croatia on the German side', he declared (not a little tendentiously). 'The Croats were defeated in the First World War, we were victorious. We did not take over. A beaten nation, they opted for union with us.'[9]

Ultimately in December 1991, at the behest of the Germans, the EC adopted the minimalist line – and one unrelated to the inherent merits of the claims to nation-statehood – of undertaking to recognize any republic that sought independence, provided it respected human rights and minority rights, accepted existing borders and cooperated with the Community and UN. Despite the obvious political expediency informing such an approach, the Twelve remained divided over the recognition of Croatia and Bosnia, whilst refraining from recognizing Macedonia out of respect for Greek objections. If the hasty German-led EC moves to recognize Croatia over the autumn of 1991 (it was formally recognized in January 1992) signalled a further intensification in the escalating civil war in the former Yugoslavia, the precipitate recognition of Bosnia on 7 April 1992 amounted to the recognition of a state riven by a three-way conflict between Serbs, Croats and Muslims. A catalogue of atrocities associated with 'ethnic cleansing' led to the subsequent deployment of a (largely ineffectual) UN peace-keeping force. Bosnian statehood in short was recognized, despite the fact that a Bosnian nation conspicuously failed to exist. In the case of the former Yugoslav republic of Macedonia, which declared its independence in November 1991, Greece successfully blocked recognition of the new state under its name 'Macedonia-Skopje', arguing that it would trigger expansionist claims on Greek territory and revive old Balkan enmities. At the June 1992 European Council meeting, the Community leaders formally committed themselves to withhold diplomatic recognition from Macedonia until it changed its name. The Edinburgh summit in December 1992 did nothing to resolve the impasse on Macedonia.

The Challenge of National Integration in the Successor States

Aside from the question of recognition by the EC, the successor states of post-communist Eastern Europe (both those with a history of independence and those without) faced the challenge of integrating their national minorities. During the long years of state communism, ethnic nationalism had constituted a counter-ideology which was sacrificed on the altar of democratic centralism – control from Moscow and/or the ruling Marxist–Leninist party in the capitals of the satellite states. National minorities were forcibly integrated into the state by a combination of reductionism (marginalizing their language and culture) and repression. Only in Yugoslavia was there a recognition of ethnic diversity – a situation of 'nothing but nationalities' – the subsequent conflagration demonstrating, however, that ethnic conflict had been contained rather than resolved.

In general, old strains between the 'winning' and 'losing' nations of 1919 were perpetuated under communism. In Czechoslovakia, for example, there was confirmation of the earlier power relationship between dominant Czech and subject Slovaks; it was significant that a primary objective in introducing a federal constitution in the aftermath of the Soviet invasion on 21 August 1968 was to redress the balance in favour of the Slovaks. Nonetheless, the peaceful Velvet Revolution of November 1989 opened the way to a revival of Slovak separatism and threatened the basis of the state that had been so skilfully created by Masaryk and Beneš and, ironically, that Jan Palak had sacrificially laid down his life for at the foot of the Wenceslas statue in January 1969. Indeed, the re-emergence of the inter-war successor states opened up ethnic wounds which, deriving from the initial period of state-building, had festered under the long decades of communism.

In Czechoslovakia, the Slovak National Party, heirs of the Hlinka-led party of the inter-war republic, polled 11 per cent in elections to the House of the People (lower house) in June 1990 (admittedly, only one-third of the support gained by the Slovakia-based People Against Violence) and a higher 13.9 per cent in the ballot to the Slovak National Council. In Romania, the Hungarian Democratic Union of Romania (HDUR), the organ of the Transylvanian Magyars (the largest ethnic minority in Europe), managed an apparently modest 7.2 per cent in elections to the national Chamber of Deputies in May 1990, but still became the second largest party. In Covasna and Harghita, the two Magyar-dominated counties in Transylvania, moreover, HDUR polled 77 and 85 per cent of the vote, respectively. Support for ethnic nationalist parties, of course, is not *ipso facto* synonymous with separatism; on the contrary, these parties may serve as important vehicles in integrating national minorities. Rather, it may be the absence of ethnic parties – as a consequence of repressive conditions – which may pose the threat. In Bulgaria, where the Turkish Muslim minority numbers 10 per cent of the total population, parties based on religious allegiance or ethnic identity were proscribed in connection with the legislative election of June 1990. *Ilinden*, which advocated the cession of south-west Bulgaria to Yugoslavia, was in fact banned.

In the Baltic states, the principal obstacle to national integration has stemmed from the imperialist attitudes of the political class representing the indigenous majority towards the ethnic minorities of the former Imperial power (Russians, Byelorussians and Ukrainians). There has been the same pressure to invert earlier power relationships and demote old elites as followed the original achievement of independence in 1919. Hardline nationalists held that citizenship should be conferred only on those who lived in the Baltic republics before 1940, along with their descendants, and that citizenship alone should bestow property rights and the right to employment in the public sector. Significantly, on 27 June 1992 when 93 per cent of Estonian voters approved a new constitution, most Russians, lacking citizenship, were not enfranchised. [10] It was the same story at the first post-communist general election in September 1992. When the new parliament, *Riigikogu*, nominated the former foreign secretary, Lennart Meri, as head of state, he was less than equivocal on the question of the repatriation of the Russian minority. Initially at least (his stance subsequently appeared to become more moderate), Meri canvassed Western aid in resettling at least half the ethnic Russians in the de-populated and heavily forested regions between Moscow and St Petersburg. He remained evasive, however, on whether pressure should be exerted on those refusing to go.[11]

Such a xenophobic stance may be regarded as a logical extension of the strident line of ethnic exclusivity used to good effect in mobilizing native Estonians in the fight to regain *Iseivuus* (independence). Thus the Estonian Congress – launched on Independence Day (24 February 1989) at the initiative of Trivimi Velliste – sought to register all those who had been Estonian citizens at the time of the illegal 'occupation' on 17 June 1940 and their offspring. Its aim was twofold. First, it purported to act as a channel to express the will of the Estonian nation, in contradistinction to the spurious claims of the Supreme Soviet (monopolized by the Communist Party which put up official candidates) to represent the will of the people. Second, the Congress sought to create a legal state authority – that is, to reconstitute the independent Estonian state (compare the legal continuity which still existed at the international level). In short, the twin functions of the Estonian Congress were to represent the indigenous nation and to repossess the state. According to Sirje Endre, the act of registering as an Estonian could also generate an aesthetic quality: 'When a person signs and reflects upon the fact that he is truly a citizen of the legal Republic of Estonia, he becomes consciously aware of all his past, his progenitors, his ancient land, his five thousand years spent here on the Baltic Coast … and this might become an essential mental turning point, elevating our degraded people again into proud citizens.'[12]

The National Congress idea was subsequently adopted in Georgia in its bid for secession from the Soviet Union, whilst in Kiev in spring 1990 inhabitants were encouraged to enrol as citizens of a proposed Ukrainian National Republic. Moreover, even after Latvia regained independence, a Citizens' Committee continued to compile a register of former citizens. In Lithuania, in contrast, citizenship was quickly granted to all permanent residents. The peacemakers of 1919–23 envisaged legal guarantees for ethnic minorities in the new states they had recognized. Although these safeguards were often flouted – in Lithuania for example – it is important to recall that liberal arrangements were intended. Seven decades later, despite its initial enthusiasm to receive the Baltic states, the Council of Europe initially deferred membership pending an examination of their constitutional provisions for minorities. The risk remains that the problems of integrating national minorities which beset the inter-war successor states will be reinforced in the post-communist successor states.

The Economic Challenges Facing the Post-Communist States

A second important challenge facing the post-communist states, and one crucial to their collective stability, lies in the realm of regional economic integration. There are four vital links in the chain. First, there is an urgent need to reintegrate the economies of the former Soviet Union; second, trade between the central European states needs to be stimulated; third, a market-based COMECON network, with commercial flows between Russia and central Europe, is essential; and, finally, agreements between the EC and the eastern European states severally or en bloc might be promoted in the medium term at least. Before considering these points in turn, a brief note on COMECON is in order since its demise resulted in considerable disruption to intra-regional trade.

The Role of COMECON

After the strident economic nationalism of the inter-war period, a resurgence of Russian imperialism, in the guise of the 'liberating' Red Army, facilitated a degree of economic integration among the successor states of Eastern Europe after the Second World War. This occurred within the Committee for Mutual Economic Assistance (COMECON), formed in 1949, which represented an explicit response both to Marshall Aid and to incipient projects for West European unity.

Initially, COMECON cooperation involved only the exchange of goods, but by 1954 the member-states of Bulgaria, Hungary, Romania, Czechoslovakia and the Soviet Union had made a hesitant start in coordinating their economic plans in the field of production.[13] COMECON, however, was never more than a trade bloc dominated by the Soviet Union and was emphatically not a Communist Common Market. Although the concept of 'socialist economic integration' became acceptable by 1969, it was at no point legally defined, involved merely a *rapprochement* between the various national economies, and was to be achieved primarily through the medium of the national communist parties rather than by creating supranational institutions (to which Romania, in particular, was averse). COMECON, in short, remained simply a consultative and advisory body in which member-states jealously safeguarded their national sovereignty. Indeed, it was founded, as W.E. Butler has noted, 'on an Englishman's dream' – that is, the preservation of state sovereignty whilst simultaneously pursuing a more rational internalization of productive forces.[14]

For a quarter of a century, COMECON refused to recognize the EEC on political grounds and even when on 20 March 1972 Brezhnev, in a major speech to the trade unions, expressed the willingness of the Soviet Union (and by extension its satellites) to negotiate with the Community, it was with the strict caveat that existing COMECON relationships should not be disturbed. At that time, the EC's share of world trade was no less than quadruple that of COMECON. After a period of atrophy, however, efforts were made to revamp COMECON not least because, in the wake of the Yom Kippur oil crisis and Western recession, this would serve to enhance the Soviet's bargaining capacity in European affairs. The 16 May 1973 agreement between COMECON and Finland (the latter had recently negotiated an industrial free-trade agreement with Brussels) was viewed by both parties as a blueprint for a treaty between the EEC and COMECON, creating cautious optimism regarding a growing rapport between the two Europes.

Although COMECON was characterized by a generally low trade intensity on the part of member-states, the more trade-dependent countries increasingly sought outlets in the West. By 1968, for example, an annual average of 24 per cent of Hungarian and 25 per cent of Polish exports went to Western Europe. Furthermore, informal deals between the EEC and Hungary, Bulgaria, Poland and Romania were struck – in each case involving agricultural goods like pork, dairy products, eggs and poultry – before the Brezhnev speech. The first EC–Polish agreement on eggs dated back to April 1965. The need for a pragmatic, non-ideological search for markets was well captured by the Hungarian prime minister in 1968: 'The Common Market is a fact and we, who are always realists, have to acknowledge its existence.' He added that 'if our commercial relations required us to call on some of the Brussels offices ...we would not consider this step as a renunciation of our principles'.[15]

In fact, a commitment to an EEC-COMECON dialogue did not form part of Soviet foreign policy until 1974.[16] The official EEC-COMECON meeting in Moscow in February 1975 – the year of the first European Security Conference – moreover, achieved little of significance. The EEC sought to target individual East European states, whereas the USSR and its satellites insisted that all approaches must be channelled through COMECON. Trade between the two blocs continued to increase nonetheless. For the COMECON states, commercial links with the EC were viewed as a means of acquiring hard currency, attracting credit facilities and purchasing modern technology and equipment.

The recession affecting Western industry in the late 1970s, however, heightened a mood of protectionism among affected sectoral interests within the Community; thus the export of Soviet and East European manufactured goods to the West dropped significantly for three consecutive years between 1980 and 1982. Moreover, even though access to the Community market and socialist state indebtedness were plainly interlinked, the development of an EC export credit policy was precluded by the fact that export credit was jealously guarded by national governments, who in turn were influenced by powerful domestic export lobbies. The declaration of martial law in Poland in December 1981 led the Community to split from the US economic sanctions policy against Poland and the Soviet Union; member-states found it expedient to use the Community framework to articulate a pragmatic line (minimal trade restrictions) which maintained an implicit distinction between commercial and security considerations.[17] Gradual West European economic recovery, the lifting of martial law in Poland in July 1983 and, ultimately, the advent to power of Gorbachev in the Soviet Union all facilitated and expedited the search for a framework agreement between the EC and COMECON which, it was hoped, would presage bilateral agreements between the Community and individual COMECON states. Finally, in May 1988, the EC foreign ministers underwrote a mutual recognition agreement which opened the way for the establishment of full diplomatic relations between the Community and individual COMECON countries.

Although COMECON was not anchored in the West European model of economic integration – there was, for example, no common labour market – the extent of the intra-regional trade flows it generated and the *de facto* coordination of the member economies it achieved should not be underestimated. By 1989, three-fifths of COMECON trade was conducted between the member-republics of the Soviet Union and her East European satellites; this represented a level of internal trade as high as that between EC member-states. Industries such as buses, trucks and shipbuilding depended on the Soviet market for as much as three-quarters of their sales.

The autumn revolutions of 1989 and the progressive deterioration in the Soviet economy radically changed matters. Certainly the scale of the Soviet economic malaise fuelled conservative opposition to Gorbachev and his brand of 'liberal communism'. World Bank estimates put real inflation in the half year preceding the coup at 140 per cent and calculated that output was down 20 per cent and oil production by 15 per cent. Indeed, it was with a view to attracting extra hard-currency earnings that the Soviet Union shifted the base of COMECON trade to hard-currency transactions from 1 January 1991, with the result that intra-regional trade dropped dramatically.

Economic Disintegration and the CIS

After the abortive anti-Gorbachev coup in autumn 1991, the paramount need was to reintegrate the republics of the former Soviet Union against the backdrop of the EC's recognition of the independence of the Baltic states, unilateral declarations of independence or sovereignty elsewhere (Ukraine, Armenia and Georgia), and mounting nationalist pressures for sovereign economies and separate currencies. In large part, this escalating polarization constituted a logical response both to the longstanding domination of Moscow and its corollary, the creation of all-union conglomerates manned by imported Russian labour which were designed to undermine a sense of economic sovereignty and/or nationality in the republics.[18] It was also, of course, a more general protest against the endemic mismanagement of democratic centralism – the inability of communism to deliver prosperity or even basic foodstuffs.

It was ironic that the Stanislav Shatalin Plan for an 'Economic Union of Sovereign Republics', which was rejected by Gorbachev in autumn 1990 because it was too radical and risked alienating the conservatives, was viewed a year later as too conservative by the republics. The Shatalin Plan was a prescient document in many ways which recognized as its point of departure the need to devolve substantial powers to the republics, whilst accepting too the principles of voluntary membership of the economic union and of the entrepreneur and enterprise being the sheet-anchor of the productive process. Indeed, the Shatalin Plan spoke (fancifully) of selling 46 000 industrial enterprises and 76 000 trading firms within a period of 500 days![19] According to Shatalin, moreover, the republics had the exclusive right to own, use and dispose of the national wealth on their territories, including land, minerals and offshore resources. In general, the plan envisaged a degree of harmonization broadly comparable to that involved in the transition to the EC's single internal market on 1 January 1993: customs barriers were to be abolished and there was to be free movement of goods, capital and labour.

After the failed coup of 19–20 August 1991, the primary stumbling-blocks to the acceptance of a Shatalin-style confederal formula were, first, defence and security, both of which were vested in the centre and, second, the plan's implicit commitment to a common currency.[20] True, under acute pressure to stave off wholesale economic collapse and with an obvious view to attracting urgent Western aid and investment, an economic cooperation treaty, devolving powers in much the manner of Shatalin, was signed and a union of sovereign Soviet republics – later called the Commonwealth of Independent States (CIS) – accordingly set up on 18 October 1991.[21] Agreement was reached on a single monetary and banking system, joint tariff control and coordinated energy, transport and communications policies. Significantly, though, the strength of nationalist sentiment in the republics prevented the Ukraine, Georgia, Moldavia (subsequently Moldova) and Azerbaijan from signing, whilst the three fully independent Baltic states took no part in the negotiations. Initially then, only eight (later 11) of the original 15 republics of the USSR were party to the economic union – testimony to the force of political and economic nationalism in the region.

Indeed, the fledgling CIS was riven by division – particularly ethnic rivalry – during the first year of its existence, and its future continues to look less than wholly secure. Thus there was conflict between ethnic Russian separatists (backed by the former Soviet army) in the breakaway Trans-Dnestria republic (set up in 1990) and the majority Romanian speakers in Moldova; conflict between Azeris and Armenians over the Nagorny Karabakh enclave, and between Georgia (not a CIS state) and the South Ossetia minority seeking union with the North Ossetians in Russia, as well as conflict within the Russian Federation itself. In March 1992 Tartarstan, 500 miles east of Moscow, voted for independence (though probably intending something less than statehood); there were also secessionists in Siberia and even calls for a Urals republic. Significantly, on 6 July 1992, the CIS presidents decided to create a joint peacekeeping force to deal with ethnic disputes, although its composition proved problematic from the outset. In addition to ethnic tensions, economic reform in the key Russia Federation floundered; in summer 1992, the IMF insisted on a reduction in inflation rates, cuts in the money supply and the dismantling of collective farms before extra loan funding could become available (Russia was not able to meet these conditions). Finally, there have been the problems encountered in a single rouble zone as a result of attempts by CIS members to set up their own currencies. The force of economic and political nationalism within the CIS has been reflected in the jealousies and suspicion characterizing relations between the heads of the 11 member-republics.[22] Consolidation and integration within the CIS are thus top priorities in the former COMECON region.

Yet the CIS' future looks bleak. More than 12 months after its inception it has failed to take on any really substantive form and involves, according to Jacek Rostowski, 'little more than a series of summit meetings'.[23] Few experts expect it to survive more than another two years at most. Even if it does, it will then most probably comprise only a rump grouping of Russia, Bielarus, Armenia and perhaps Kazakhstan. The situation in which the banking system deploys roubles whilst cash exchanges are in the new native currencies is proving particularly problematical. Meanwhile, the economic situation in the Russian Federation has deteriorated progressively and the risk of an extremist backlash looms ever nearer. Average wages in St Petersburg had slumped to the equivalent of £7 per month by the end of 1992, whilst earlier in the autumn the self-styled National Salvation Front in Moscow stated that it would ignore President Yeltsin's proscription, something which clearly threatens the position of the Russian government.

Indeed, it is plain that, as long as the post-communist economies have to struggle to deliver improved living standards, democracy both in Russia and across Eastern Europe will be precariously poised. According to a survey in Hungary in 1992, only 6 per cent of respondents believed that conditions had improved since the collapse of communism, and no less than 73 per cent thought the whole democratic system was misconceived. In summer the same year, 50 per cent of Polish adults felt that democracy was useful only if it generated wealth, compared to only 18 per cent who perceived its benefits in terms of freedom and the protection of human rights.[24] In Russia, moreover, democracy is still widely viewed as an imported Western abstraction. According to a poll in the liberal St Petersburg newspaper *Chas Pik* in October 1992, only 36 per cent of people in the city believed that the government could solve the nation's problems – less than half the number of 12 months earlier.[25]

Commercial Links among Post-Communist States

At some distance from the disintegrating Soviet Union and nascent CIS, the recovery of full sovereignty by the central European 'successor states' – who were relieved of the threat of Kremlin intervention in their domestic affairs – has pointed to a crucial challenge: the need to avoid the type of policies which (in the case of opposition to the former Imperial capital, Vienna) had contributed to destroying plans for a federation of Danubian states. To avoid a re-enactment of the atomization characteristic of the inter-war politics of the region, it was necessary to reforge the commercial links afforded the central European states, firstly by common membership of the Hapsburg Empire and then, via COMECON, of the Soviet Empire. A modest start was made with the formation of the Visegrad Triangle, a cooperation agreement launched in 1990 between Poland, Hungary and Czechoslovakia, which was designed to orchestrate their 'return to Europe'. In 1992 Ukraine sought membership of the Triangle.

A further economic challenge facing the post-communist states was the urgent need to restore patterns of trade between the central European states and the Soviet Union and, more particularly, the need to replace the 'socialist economic integration' of COMECON with market-based arrangements following the West European model. A plan outlined by the Czech foreign minister, Jiri Dienstbier, shortly before the anti-Gorbachev coup and subsequent collapse of the USSR struck at the heart of the problem. According to the Dienstbier plan, Western credits in the form of hard currency would be advanced to the Soviet Union with the aim of permitting it to purchase food and consumer goods from central Europe. It warrants emphasis that six decades of collectivist agriculture had transformed the Soviet Union from a net exporter of grain to the world's largest importer. In the late 1980s, the Kremlin spent £4.4 billion buying grain from the West and in the process used up a large proportion of its hard-currency earnings from oil exports. The sale of grain and consumer items to the Soviet Union, Dienstbier contended, would enable central Europe to earn hard currency for their exports. The Soviet Union would repay in roubles (soft currency); these soft currency payments could then be reinvested in the modernization of the Soviet infrastructure – transport, electricity generators, water supply and distribution, and so on.[26]

Dienstbier lost office following the Czech general election of June 1992, his plan, in any event, having been overtaken by the collapse of the Soviet Union. Its essentials nonetheless retained their validity insofar as the onus was placed on the West to assume an active role in stimulating trade flows between the former Soviet Union and her COMECON partners. One way round would have been to apply the Dienstbier blueprint with the Russian Federation under Yeltsin as the primary recipient of Western credits. The Russian republic was, after all, clearly the dominant partner in the USSR, in 1990 contributing 60 per cent of total output, 63 per cent of energy production and 65 per cent of steel output, as well as selling goods to the other republics at rates considerably lower than world market prices. The lynchpin role of Russia in the former Soviet Union can be gained by the fact that no less than 65 per cent of Estonian trade in 1990 was with the Russian Federation, a statistic which highlighted the potential commercial costs of independence for the small Baltic states unless the acquisition of sovereignty could be accompanied by a measure of economic reintegration. The West, however, did not adopt a systematic Dienstbier-style approach to the need to promote intra-regional trade in Eastern Europe. As far as the Russian Federation was concerned, Yeltsin left the G7 summit in Germany in July 1992 with as little in real terms as Gorbachev had received the previous year.[27]

Finally, several of the former COMECON states, rather than looking towards Moscow, have set their sights on Brussels and sought to promote increased West European trade outlets by forging links with the expanding EC.[28] On 16 December 1991 Warsaw, Prague and Budapest, the Visegrad Triangle, signed a treaty of association with the Community. However, they were confronted by a strong vein of utilitarianism among the Twelve, who were unwilling to sacrifice national economic interests to achieve an accommodation. Hence over summer 1991 Poland's association talks almost foundered on the rock of the Community's refusal to jeopardize the CAP and open its markets to Poland's surplus agricultural produce. Clearly full membership will not be achieved unless and until the EC is convinced that, having proved themselves as successful market economies, the East European newcomers will not constitute a financial burden to existing members.

Perhaps, as in the case of the Mediterranean states, the recent overtures to Brussels from Ukraine, the Baltic states and Slovenia – as well as the aforementioned approaches from Poland, Czechoslovakia and Hungary – have also possessed a powerful geopolitical logic in that they have symbolized a desire to place post-communist systems firmly in the camp of Western pluralist democracies. In materially assisting the democratization process in the former COMECON bloc by developing personal contacts with West European parliamentarians and their party networks, it is the bridge-building role of the Council of Europe rather than ties with the European Community that needs emphasis.[29] Hungary became a full member in 1990, Czechoslovakia and Poland in 1991. In that same year the Council of Europe boasted 25 member-states, while five others enjoyed so-called 'special guest status', enabling them to participate in the deliberations but not the decisions of the parliamentary assembly. In the two-year period 1989 to 1991, the Council of Europe was transformed from a West European to a pan-European organ based on a commitment to democracy and respect for human rights. Over the same period and in tandem with the Council of Europe, the Conference on Security and Cooperation in Europe (CSCE) expanded from 35 to 51 members bringing, in addition, the new states of Eastern Europe, the US and Canada into the consultative process.[30]

Could the existence of organizations such as the Council of Europe and CSCE, already embracing the vast majority of continental states, be a precursor to the *de facto* emergence of a United States of Europe? Could such a political and economic union of continental states ever take *de jure* form and, if so, what form? Will the 21st century witness progress towards a single-campus Europe – based on the EC – or a multi-site arrangement comprising diverse and mutually overlapping organs, each with a specialist role? Can there, indeed, ever be a United States of Europe with the United States (of America) in Europe? At a press conference on 23 July 1964 President de Gaulle remarked: 'We have seen a number of otherwise strong and sincere minds advocate for Europe not an independent policy, which indeed they do not conceive of, but an organization incapable of one, dependent ... in the domain of defence and economy upon the Atlantic ... and consequently subordinated to what the United States calls its leadership.'[31] Seventeen years later, in the British House of Lords, Lord Tonypandy declared in contrast: 'I would rather that Britain were the 51st state of the United States than a twentieth part of Europe.' Have fundamental attitudes changed and has 'Atlanticism' been replaced by a genuine 'Europeanism'? In the concluding chapter of the present volume we shall consider these questions – looking to the future but with one eye firmly fixed on the lessons of the past.

Notes

1 John Hiden and Patrick Salmon (1991), *The Baltic Nations and Europe: Estonia, Latvia and Lithuania in the Twentieth Century*, London and New York: Longman, pp.149–150, 152.
2 'Putsch sends shivers through the West', *The Guardian*, 20 August 1991, p.18.
3 'Chaos Warning over Soviet Aid', *The Guardian*, 16 July 1991.
4 'G7 rift on curbing arms sales', *The Guardian*, 16 July 1991.
5 Ryszard Kapuścínski, 'A Period of Transition', *The Independent on Sunday*, 27 October 1991, pp.10–13.
6 'Viron asukkaat ovat hyvin erimielisiä maan tulevasta asemasta', *Helsingin Sanomat*, 25 March 1990.
7 The experience of the Czarist Russian province of Estonia is instructive. If the choral festivals which began in Tartu in 1869 brought the *maarahvas* (rural folk) together to sing in their own language – the Estonians were said at the time to be singing their way to freedom – von Rauch notes that, on the eve of the First World War, the Estonian (and, indeed, Latvian) masses were only interested in local affairs and the question of independence simply did not arise. See G. von Rauch (1974), *The Baltic States. Estonia, Latvia, Lithuania*, London: Hurst, p.8.
8 'Thatcher fighting for Croatia', *The Independent on Sunday*, 27 October 1991, p.1.
9 Phil Davison, 'Angry Serbs ask why the West backs Croats', *The Independent on Sunday*, 13 October 1991. See also Jessica Douglas-Home, 'The British role that left Yugoslavia in the lurch', *The Guardian*, 9 November 1991, p.27.
10 A two-year residence qualification was necessary before an application for citizenship could be lodged, and then a written and oral test in Estonian had to be passed. John Rettie, 'Estonia denies violating rights of Russians', *The Guardian*, 1 July 1992, p.8.
11 'Champion of the nation's identity', *The Guardian*, 6 October 1992.
12 Cited from a debate broadcast on Estonian radio on 10 January 1990.
13 Alexander Uschakow (1979), 'COMECON: Inter-State Economic Co-operation in Eastern Europe', in J.E.S. Hayward and R.N. Berki (eds), *State and Society in Contemporary Europe*, Oxford: Martin Robertson, p.223.
14 W.E. Butler (1975), 'Legal Configurations of Integration in Eastern Europe', *International Affairs*, **51**(4), 519.
15 Peter Marsh (1975–6), 'The Integration Process in Eastern Europe 1969 to 1975', *Journal of Common Market Studies*, **14**, 319.
16 Ibid., 320.
17 Peter Marsh (1984), 'The European Community and East–West Economic Relations', *Journal of Common Market Studies*, **23** (1), 1–13.
18 Terry McNeill (1979), 'State and Nationality under Communism', in Hayward and Berki, op. cit., pp.118–40.
19 Orlando Figes, 'Finding the price of freedom', *The Guardian*, 15 October 1990.
20 'Separatist Ukraine to print its own money', *The Guardian*, 3 October 1991.
21 'Economic Pact signed in Moscow', *The Guardian*, 19 October 1991.
22 David Hearst, 'Cry for Mother Russia', *The Guardian*, 24 July 1992, p.23.
23 Conversation with Jacek Rostowski, Department of Social Sciences, School of Slavonic and East European Studies, University of London, 21 October 1992.
24 Jonathan Luxmoore and Jolanta Babiuch, 'Flying from freedom', *The Guardian*, 2 November 1992.

25   Andrew Higgins, 'Doomsday in St Petersburg', *The Independent on Sunday*, 1 November 1992.
26   On the need for economic integration in Eastern Europe, see two articles by Shirley Williams: 'Poor fare at the Kremlin', *The Guardian*, 18 September 1991; 'Eastern spectre to scare smug EC', *The Guardian*, 7 October 1991.
27   'Yeltsin's hands tied to G7', *The Guardian*, 9 July 1992, p.1.
28   Alfred Tovias (1991), 'EC–Eastern Europe: A Case-Study of Hungary', *Journal of Common Market Studies*, **29**(3), 291–317.
29   Anders Björck, 'Europarådet och det nya Europa', *Nordisk Kontakt*, 3/1991, 4–5.
30   'Yeltsin bows to pressure and pledges Baltic troop pullout', *The Guardian*, 10 July 1992, p.8.
31   François Mauriac (1966), *De Gaulle*, London: Bodley Head, p.184.

9   Towards a United States of Europe?

What a curse to the earth are small nations! Latvia, Lithuania, Poland, Finland, San Salvador, Luxembourg ... There are many more: there is an appalling number of disgusting little stretches of the globe claimed, occupied and infected by groupings of babbling little morons – babbling militant on the subjects (unendingly) of their exclusive cultures, their exclusive languages, their national souls, their unique achievements in throat-cutting in this and that abominable little squabble in the past. Mangy little curs yap above their minute hoardings of shrivelled bones, they cease from their yelpings at the passers-by only in such intervals as they devote to civil-war flea-hunts.

Lewis Grassic Gibbon (1931), *A Scots Quair*

Ironically, the exception to the 'babbling little morons' of the interwar period, it appears, was Grassic Gibbon's own nation, Scotland, since four years before he completed *A Scots Quair*, C.M. Grieve (alias Hugh MacDiarmid) in *Albyn or Scotland and the Future* bemoaned the fact that 'Scotland is unique among European nations in its failure to develop a nationalist sentiment strong enough to be a vital factor in its affairs'.[1] Today, however, Scotland has taken its place among the 'mangy little curs' (in Grassic Gibbon's parlance) yelping for the right to recognition as an independent (or far more autonomous) nation – one of the plethora of 'unrepresented nations' emerging across the continent in recent years. Indeed, it has been the resurgence of such nationalist claims which has vested the New Europe of post-1989 with the distinctly familiar look of the New Europe which followed the Great War and spawned problems similar to those confronting the celebrated peacemakers of Versailles in 1919. In reviewing in this final chapter the main challenges to European integration from both an historic and a contemporary perspective, it is perhaps prudent to bear in mind Hegel's cryptic rejoinder that: 'What experience and history teach is that people and governments have never learnt anything from history or acted from the principles deduced from it.'

Four challenges have formed a common denominator between the two New Europes studied in this book. When viewed from the standpoint of the present they are, first, the vociferous articulation of political nationalism and the attendant problems of evaluating and resolving nationalist claims; second, the renewed spectre of economic nationalism and its corollary, the urgent need to reintegrate the economies of the successor states of post-communist Europe; third, the renewed challenge of democratization and building Western-style democracy in an Eastern Europe where it failed to take root between the wars; and, finally, the paramount need to build bridges between the two Europes.

The Resurgence of Political Nationalism

'Nations,' noted Ernest Renan in a celebrated lecture at the Sorbonne in 1882, 'are not something eternal. They have begun, they will end. They will be replaced, in all probability, by a European confederation. But such is not the law of the century in which we live.'[2] Nor it appears the current century, over 100 years after Renan's prophecy. Indeed, the disintegration of the Soviet Empire in eastern Europe, the collapse of the Soviet Union itself and then the fragmentation of Yugoslavia have confronted the 'peacemakers' of Brussels and Washington with similar problems of evaluating nationalist claims to those faced by the renowned peacemakers of 1919–23.

For example, there could be little doubt about the sympathy many in the West felt towards the Estonian foreign minister, Lennart Meri, who, appearing on BBC television's *Newsnight* on the evening of the attempted Soviet coup on 19 August 1991, scarcely disguised his disappointment that the West had not done more earlier to support the Baltic republics. The game of superpower politics and the Western concern to 'appease' Gorbachev by not taking sides in his nationalities problems (Bush also rebuffed Ukrainian independence at this time), it was implied, had taken precedence over the formal recognition of the rightful claim of a nation to regain its statehood.

Meri's words possessed the same moral authority as is so often generated by leaders when the small nations they head stand at the crossroads of history. In many ways they recalled the pathos evoked by Jan Masaryk, son of the founding-father of the Czech First Republic who, arriving in New York as a refugee in 1939 following the sellout of Czechoslovakia to Hitler, faced the hounds of the American press. In an oblique reference to the Anglo-French policy of so-called 'appeasement', Masaryk declared: 'I have repeated lately that my little country has paid almost the supreme price in trying to preserve European democracy and I say to you that if it is for peace that my country has been butchered up in this unprecedented manner, I am glad of it; if it is not, may God have mercy on our souls.'

In the event, developments in Moscow turned out advantageously for Estonia, the speedy recognition of the Baltic states in the wake of the hardliners' failed coup doubtless salving the majority conscience in a West which had long regarded the Baltics as a special case.

But what, it might reasonably be inquired, made them so special and elevated their claims above the procession of nations issuing unilateral declarations of independence, stretching from Slovenia and Croatia to Ukraine and Georgia? As journalists struggled with history and historians (the pedagogues of nations) with journalism, there was more than a touch of *déjà vu* irony in the fact that Bosnia, the nation where on 28 June 1914 the Austrian Archduke Franz Ferdinand was assassinated – an episode which, of course, precipitated the First World War – also declared itself sovereign and independent (civil war was to ensue). Like the Baltics, moreover, several of these nationalist claims – in Ukraine (1918–19), Georgia (1918–21), Croatia (1941–4) and Slovakia (1939–44) – could be backed by periods of independence or quasi-independence in the course of the 20th century.

If EC and US recognition of the blue and yellow Ukrainian flag was only a matter of time, other nationalist demands were to be unfurled, leading in some circles to speculation about the possible emergence of a Europe of 1000 flags. All in all, then, the resurgence of nationalism as probably the preponderant political force in late 20th century Europe has attached renewed importance to the Woodrow Wilsonian principle of national self-determination. It was this principle which inspired Western radicals at the end of the Great War. For the younger generation of 1919, like Harold Nicolson, it was the new 'successor states' which excited them and which they believed to be the justification of the suffering and victory in war.

It is in no way to impugn the vision of a post-1919 generation of intellectuals, vesting the nationalist principle with unquestioned legitimacy, to note that the question put by Renan, '*Qu'est-ce qu'une nation?*' (What is a nation?), is as valid and relevant today as in 1882 when he asked: 'Why is Holland a nation whilst Hanover and the Grand Duchy of Parma are not?' By his famous question, Renan intended, of course: 'Why was Holland a nation-state, a sovereign and independent polity, whereas Hanover and Parma were not?' More than a century after Renan's death, the world remains full of Hanovers and Parmas, that is – Charles E. Foster's terms – 'nations without a state', ranging from the Palestinians and Kurds to the Macedonians, Corsicans, Bretons, Friesians and Basques. There are over 20 'unrepresented nations' housed, so to speak, in a Bureau of Unrepresented Nations in Brussels, all seeking at the very least a more independent voice in the decision-making fora of the European

Community and many, indeed, claiming to have been victims of internal colonialism.[3]

Clearly, not all putative nations demand a state – the Alsacians are a case in point – but this does not detract from the salience of the question: 'On what basis are the claims of those nations who do aspire to statehood to be evaluated?' In light of the escalating demands for territorial sovereignty, this is obviously no idle theoretical question. Yet as E.J. Hobsbawm has reminded us: 'There is no way of telling how to distinguish a nation from other entities *a priori* ...as we can tell how to recognise a bird or to distinguish a mouse from a lizard. Nation-watching would be simple if it could be like bird-watching.'[4] Given that it is not, the key issue for the political historian is not so much 'What is a nation?' as 'Why are some nations recognized as having legitimate rights to statehood while other apparently equally valid claims are ignored?'

In this context, the experience of 1919–23 is particularly illuminating, since it points to the way nationalist claims to statehood were resolved largely on the basis of political expediency. True, the Big Four in Paris were called upon to adjudicate between a bewildering array of rival demands. The Czechs, Slovaks and Croats all claimed the right to independence, although Sinn Fein derided these claims and spoke dismissively of the Slavic races as lacking the historic pedigree of the Irish. Perhaps the point was taken. However, as Woodrow Wilson subsequently admitted: 'It was not within the privilege of the conference of peace to act upon the right of self-determination of any peoples except those which had been included in the territories of the defeated empires.'[5] When an Irish delegation visited the president in the United States before his journey to Paris, seeking his promise to request the peace conference to make Ireland independent, his first reaction, according to the Hunter Miller diary, had been 'to tell them to go to hell'![6] A principle was being applied to defeated states, it seems, which the victors refused to apply themselves.

In any event, some nations gained independence in 1919–23, whereas others had nationality – in the form of citizenship – thrust upon them. The Slovaks were conjoined willy-nilly with the Czechs; the Magyar-speaking Transylvanians with the Romanians; and the Croats and Slovenes with the Serbs. The principle of national self-determination, enshrined in Wilson's Fourteen Points, was compromised from the outset by considerations of *realpolitik* – especially the need to reward the Associate powers; the successor states of the New Europe emerged as multi-ethnic polities in which many of the autonomy problems of the old empires were revived in microcosmic form.

Three remarks will suffice to round off this brief discussion placing the resurgence of nationalist claims in an historic perspective. First, it is doubtful if the New Europe of post-1989 can be united or, indeed, peaceful unless and until the demands generated by resurgent nationalism are contained and resolved. Second, faced with the resurgence of nationalist demands, it appears that the peacemakers of post-1989 continue to view rival claims largely in terms of what is in the Western interest or closest to the Western heart.

Yugoslavia is an excellent illustration of this. EC recognition of the secessionist Slovenia and Croatia appeared intended, first and foremost, as a sanction against what was presented as a militant, neocommunist Serbia and the federal army it controlled. Equally, there were those who were impressed (very questionably) with the 'democratic free-market stance' of the Croatian leader, Tudjman and his determined efforts to align his Croatian Democratic Union with what he claimed were fraternal right-wing parties within the EC. As the powerful Ukrainian lobby in Canada (like the Czech lobby in the US during the Great War) demonstrated, nationalism, like any successful product, profits from effective marketing.

Yet the sheer complexity of assessing rival nationalist claims was forcefully brought home by the comments of the former Conservative minister, Nicholas Ridley, interviewed on BBC television's *Heart of the Matter*. Asked whether Britain and the outside world had a moral obligation to intervene in the former Yugoslavia, Ridley remarked that: 'It is a civil war between Serbs, Croats and Muslims [at least the Bosnian chapter of it] and I don't know which side we should be on.'[7] Indeed, thirdly, in an imperfect world, given the inherent difficulty in evaluating competing claims – and bearing in mind the existence of manifold political constraints – the implementation of the type of minority safeguards envisaged by the peacemakers of 1919–23 seems absolutely crucial.

Certainly, the history of the inter-war period demonstrated that nations are not necessarily denationalized by the incorporation of their citizens into a foreign state; on the contrary, a type of counter-nationalism feeding off the disprivileged status of significant ethnic minorities can easily be generated. In the New Europe of post-1989, counter-nationalism constitutes a potentially destabilizing force, particularly in the former Soviet republics and especially when expressed with the vehemence of, say, the Hungarian rejection of the Trianon Treaty of 1919. Asked to accept a humiliating peace, the Magyars responded: *Nem, Nem, Soha* (No, No, Never!).

The Spectre of Economic Nationalism

'The luxury and danger of separate national policies in Eastern Europe belong to the first decades of this century, not the last,' noted foreign secretary Douglas Hurd at the Conservative Party conference in September 1991, and he was absolutely right. Indeed, whilst events in the last decade of this century have pointed to the continuing and radical force of nationalism, the irony is that the substantive content of nationalism, or at least national sovereignty, has been substantially diminished by the need to create economies of scale. This is no more so than in the case of small states.

The economic viability of small nations was, of course, questioned as early as the 19th century. In 1885 Friedrich List wrote in *The National System of Political Economy* that 'a small state can never bring to complete perfection within its territory the various branches of production' and advocated *inter alia* a *Mitteleuropa* comprising the *Deutscher Bund* states, Belgium, Holland, Denmark and Sweden and also reaching deep into the Balkans.[8] Earlier, in the *Dictionnaire Politique*, Garnier-Pagès held that it was ridiculous that Belgium and Portugal should be independent states, since they were patently too small, whilst the map of the future Europe compiled by the Italian nationalist Guiseppe Mazzini in 1857 comprised only 12 states and federations.[9] The term *kleinstaaterei* – used to describe a network of miniscule states such as the Holy Roman Empire or the 19th-century German Confederation – was deliberately derogatory, in the same way as 'Balkanization', a term originally coined to depict the fragmentation of the Ottoman Empire, has retained a strongly perjorative connotation. Yet the 'kleinstaaterei' of the 1990s, it seems, are intent on pursuing an economic version of the 'Sinatra doctrine' by doing it their way: Georgia opted out of the CIS and on 20 July 1992 Latvia abandoned the Russian rouble in preparation for the introduction of its own currency, the 'lat'. The lessons of the inter-war years, in short, still need to be learnt.

Indeed, the re-emergence as pluralist politico-economic systems of the successor states of 1919–23 and indeed, the recent formation of new successor states from the collapse of the Soviet and Yugoslav federations, has raised afresh the spectre of the rampant economic nationalism that characterized the inter-war period and underscored the urgent need for the reintegration of the economies of the post-communist states into the common economic space formed by the moribund communist bloc in Eastern Europe.

The notion of reintegration warrants emphasis since it is a clear imperative of history that successor states do not become economically isolated, but are conjoined to wider regional economic groupings. It is worth recalling here Edgar Anderson's doleful verdict on the inter-war experience: 'The individualism of the states which emerged after World War I,' he notes, 'was so great that they could not and would not form a federation, although their economic problems ... clearly pointed to just such a necessity. They preferred isolated existence, jealously guarding their complete freedom of action, quarrelling with their neighbours and refusing to sacrifice any portion of their sovereignty for the sake of common interests.'[10]

Anderson was referring in particular to the chimera of the Baltic League, although economic nationalism was deeply rooted across inter-war Europe. It contained three main elements. First, there was the subordination of the economy and its deployment in the realization of nationalist political goals. This meant the zealous protection of any newly-won independence and sovereignty and the related concern to avoid economic dependence on the former Imperial power. Accordingly, a fundamental premise of economic nationalism was the aim of self-sufficiency or autarky. For example, at its inception in 1926, one of the basic objectives of Fianna Fail's *coru* (constitution) was to make Ireland (still, of course, the Free State) economically self-sufficient, consonant indeed with its leader, Eamon De Valera's vision of 'a frugal Gaelic Ireland, gnawed at as little as possible by the worm of civilization, especially the British, and in which there were to be no rich and no poor, but many small farmers and small industries scattered over the country.'[11]

A second element in inter-war economic nationalism was the propensity (rhetorically at least) to seek to organize the economy around the economic heart of the nation, in most cases meaning the peasants. Economic nationalism, in short, was frequently a close bedfellow of agrarianism. Gathered round an old 'steam radio' in a small village café, the French peasants heard themselves extolled as part of Vichy's National Renovation and, understandably, were led to expect preferential treatment from the regime (although the reality was very different). Indeed, Pétainist propaganda promoted the peasant as the model for a revitalized French nation and, in his broadcasts, the octogenarian Marshal commended the 'heroic patience, spiritual equilibrium and economic endeavour' of the peasants.[12]

Third, the economic nationalism of the first half of the 20th century was characterized by an insular and introverted orientation which was essentially antithetical to regional integration. As Tom Gallagher has noted, it was not until 1960, after years of recession, that Fianna Fail 'finally lifted the "green curtain" in favour of greater economic links with the outside world' and, by extension, recognized the failure of its blueprint for autarky.[13] At this stage, moreover, a paradox, well grounded in the inter-war experience, suggests itself; namely, that whilst the tendency to economic nationalism is probably greatest in small newly-sovereign states – the Alpine state of Slovenia, for example, has approximately as many inhabitants as Birmingham – it is precisely in these small states that the cost of such a programme is likely to be highest.

It is crucial to recall here that the dismemberment of the Romanov and Hapsburg empires signalled the collapse of regional common markets – that is, single internal markets – boasting a notably higher level of economic cohesion than the EC even after 1 January 1993. Before 1918, the Baltic States and the Congress Kingdom of Poland had thus formed part of a single customs area stretching as far as Vladivostock, whilst the much-maligned Austro-Hungarian empire constituted an economic unit marked by internal free trade, a common currency and a common customs tariff and was self-supporting to a remarkable degree. One of the foremost challenges of the inter-war years, therefore, was to create in an acceptable form organizations which would have the economic advantages of the former empires, without their evident political and social shortcomings.

When the Slovak, Milan Hodža, outlined his first Danube Plan in 1936, designed to create 'one single great economic unit in Central Europe', he insisted perceptively that 'the freedom and security of small nations can only be guaranteed by their federation'. Yet regional schemes for the reintegration of the economies of the successor states foundered on the rock of strong nationalist prejudices against the former Imperial centres.

For example, the Austrian Social Democratic Party's proposal for a federation of Danubian states in 1918 met with vehement Czech opposition. Beneš, the foreign secretary, depicted the economic union of the Hapsburg empire as 'a system of exploitation' directed against his nation and made it clear that, having severed the umbilical cord, the new Czech republic had absolutely no intention of entering a federation instigated and possibly dominated by the old colonial power.

To avoid a re-enactment of the atomization characteristic of the inter-war politics of the region, it will be necessary to reforge the commercial links afforded the central European states firstly by common membership of the Hapsburg empire and then via COMECON of the Soviet empire. Otherwise, there remains a real risk of history repeating itself, with the collapse of the Soviet system in Eastern Europe and subsequently the Soviet Union itself releasing forces of economic disintegration as powerful as those that dominated the inter-war period.

Perhaps the Czech model offers a modest step forward. When the two halves of Czechoslovakia split on 1 January 1993, it was nonetheless agreed to coordinate foreign, defence and economic policy. The Czech prime minister, Vaclav Klaus, noted that there would be a customs union, a free-trade zone, and free movement of labour, money and capital.[14] This might well be a blueprint that could be developed at the regional level.

The Renewed Challenge of Democratization

The New Europe of post-1989, like the New Europe moulded after the First World War, involves the challenge of sustaining pluralist Western-style democracy in successor states which had little or no democratic tradition at their inception and have little or no democratic tradition today after decades of monopoly communism. In several of the provinces of the defeated empires, especially those previously subject to Hungarian and Czarist Russian rule – Slovakia, Croatia and the Congress Kingdom of Poland, for example – there was at best limited regional autonomy, with the development of modern political structures badly retarded. Grassroots activity was conducted either under duress from the authorities or completely underground.

Even in those peripheral parts of the Romanov empire where democratic rights had been reluctantly conceded as a consequence of Nicholas II's October Manifesto of 1905, these had been effectively withdrawn or negated by the time of the 1917 revolutions. Only in the former Austrian territories of the Bohemian provinces, Slovenia and Galicia, and in Russia's Baltic territories was there an embryonic democratic tradition that could be built upon after independence.

Independence brought universal suffrage, but the transition to democratic politics was not generally achieved. Indeed, with the exception of Finland and Czechoslovakia, where the teething troubles of new regimes – problems of coalition-building and cabinet instability – were successfully negotiated, the successor states quickly succumbed to authoritarianism. These were Hungary (1920), Lithuania (1926), Yugoslavia (1929), Poland and Romania (1930), Estonia and Latvia (1934) which, under the influence of Italian fascism, paid increasing lip-service to neo-corporatist solutions.

In 1942, Hugh Seton-Watson put the pertinent question: 'Is democracy possible in Eastern Europe?' and proceeded to suggest a number of conditions which he believed needed to be met in order to create suitable circumstances for a decisive 'democratic breakthrough'. In pride of place, however, was a comprehensive programme of socialization or what he termed 'education in citizenship'. 'The peoples may be behind us in some ways but ... they are not wild savages to be permanently cowed by lion-tamers, snake charmers and witch-doctors. They are Europeans who have shown their worth in more than one historical crisis,' he concluded.[15] Seton-Watson's view that the continuation of an unhealthy democratic condition in Eastern Europe constitutes a menace to the rest of the continent is as valid today as when it was written at the time of the Nazi assault on Stalingrad. Nor should it readily be assumed that the East European states will necessarily be more successful given a second bite at the democratic cherry.

Certainly it is necessary to be alert to simplistic and tendentious scenarios. For example, commenting on the collapse of the anti-Gorbachev coup in August 1991, American President George Bush told a press conference in the White House grounds that the hardliners had underestimated the power of the people; whilst the hero of the hour, Boris Yeltsin, the President of the Russian Federation, reporting from his 'White House' (the Russian Parliament building) in Moscow, presented the struggle against the coup as a struggle for democracy.

The Soviet Union was unquestionably a mobilized society in which the old *non cogito ergo sum* ('I don't think, therefore I am') fear, deriving from the Stalinist era, had largely evaporated. It was significant that in spring 1990, a march of no less than 200 000 citizens descended on the Kremlin successfully to demand an end to the communists' monopoly of power. Similarly, in East Germany and Czechoslovakia over October and November 1989, the old order was repudiated in mass demonstrations of 'people's power'. But street mobilization does not *ipso facto* denote popular commitment to democracy. Indeed, in terms of its political development, the former Soviet Union is not appreciably more modernized than the Czarist empire after the first Russian revolution of 1905 when Nicholas II's October Manifesto ushered in a period of *Duma* democracy to complement a patchy network of local *zemstvos* (councils).

In the transition to democracy, the role of political parties will be crucial in organizing and educating voters. Thus, whilst in many West European democracies party identification appears to be relatively in decline – membership has dropped and electoral abstentionism increased – it is imperative in the 'new' democracies of Eastern Europe that durable patterns of partisan allegiance are developed.

Ironically, in both the 'old' and 'new' democracies of contemporary Europe there exists a body of anti-party sentiment. In Western Europe 'anti-parties' – groups like the Greens – emphasizing their flexible, non-bureaucratic, movemental character have flourished, especially among younger volatile voters disaffected with the traditional parties and their time-worn 'isms'. If a number of anti-parties have emerged in the West, Eastern Europe in 1989–90 comprised nothing less than a bloc of anti-party systems – systems in which parties still tended to be tarred with the brush of *the* party, that is the official ruling Communist Party which, of course, enjoyed an absolute monopoly of power.

The strength of anti-party sentiment was implicitly recognized in the names of the pioneering popular movements for change: Solidarity (Poland); Civic Forum (Czech provinces); People Against Violence (Slovakia); Democratic Forum (Hungary); National Salvation Front (Romania); Union of Democratic Forces (Bulgaria); Popular Front (Estonia and Latvia); and Sajudis (Lithuania). Frictions within these organizations quickly became apparent; Solidarity, for example, split into a Democratic Union and a Citizens' Centre Alliance before the 1990 presidential election. There have, indeed, been tentative signs that some of the East European polities may be entering a stage of development closely associated with the early phase of democratic transition in which catch-all reformist movements give way to a proliferation of class-based, sectarian or ethnic parties based on specialist clienteles. The role of responsible party leadership is crucial at this stage. So, too, is the generation of cross-national links which can serve as a useful agency for comparing notes on problems, strategies and policies. For example, the first congress of Central and East European Christian Democratic parties – Christian parties were in existence across the region except in Latvia – was held in Budapest in March 1990.[16]

However, democratization in Eastern Europe remains, almost literally, at the mercy of market forces and cannot be viewed in isolation from the concurrent drive to market-based production. The simultaneous shift to a competitive polity and a competitive economy is, however, enormously ambitious, since in the bulk of the region there is no real tradition of either. Russia well illustrates the historic absence of a profit motive. Until the beginning of this century, the majority of Russian entrepreneurs were either foreigners or state officials belonging to the class of the nobility.[17] Among the peasantry – 80 per cent of the Russian population – there was no real tradition of individual property rights before the revolution and virtually no experience of private land ownership, except for the brief period of Stolypin's reforms between 1906 and 1911. During Stalin's terror in the 1920s, kulaks, semi-kulaks and 'friends' of kulaks and semi-kulaks were ruthlessly purged, and the anti-kulak (anti-small business) mentality which developed then has persisted.

Both in Russia and elsewhere, moreover, the sheer enormity of the task of privatization and dismantling the command economy should not be underestimated. Whereas Thatcher's much-vaunted programme in the UK involved privatizing only about 20 enterprises, Poland in the early 1990s sought to sell off 7300 state-owned concerns, while the Romanians grappled with over 40 000. Whilst state-funded socialization schemes – in the form of various education for enterprise initiatives – taken together with a range of tax incentives may be deployed to promote a conducive business climate, this latter will be of no avail if citizens do not have the resources to invest – that is, the capital to buy shares. The issue of state bonds etc. has to a degree met this problem, although a key challenge in 'the transition to capitalism' phase is plainly maintaining the popular legitimacy of the process of shifting to the market. There is an obvious danger that, if ordinary people feel excluded by a domestic mafia of former communist officials and money-changers, popular support for economic reform will decline and the new capitalist class will largely comprise the likes of old communist security officers.[18] In such circumstances, the stage of 'capitalist consolidation' would involve the containment of potentially menacing levels of popular alienation.

It may be, of course, that the twin processes of political and economic modernization will prove complementary and mutually reinforcing, that economic reform directed towards privatization and the market (if successful) will sustain democratization by creating new interest groups, a greater diversity of power resources and enhanced demands for the representation of economic clienteles in the decision-making process.[19] Equally, democracy must be associated with a measure of prosperity and social improvement, otherwise, it stands to become both a target and medium for forces disaffected with the transition to capitalism. A further problem is that capitalism has generated the expectation of higher living standards and rising consumer expectations, but not a psychological preparedness to face the fall-out of a free market – unemployment, bankruptcies, etc. After all, the word 'unemployed' used not to be found in the Soviet dictionary!

The challenge of the re-emergent pluralist systems, then, is to deliver the material goods when both the workings of democracy and the economic performance of the former COMECON systems are the object of intense Western scrutiny. The basic conundrum is this: a record of successful democratic politics is important to potential Western investment – political stability is often underestimated as a factor in the evaluation of commercial risk – but without such investment to facilitate and consolidate a transition to the market, democracy will be vulnerable to extremist challenges.

Bridging the Two Europes

The end of nearly half a century of capitalist–communist Cold War confrontation has ironically revealed the continued existence of the two Europes described by François Délaisy in his book *Les Deux Europes* in 1924. The two Europes, as in Délaisy's day, are divided by levels of economic development rather than political doctrine: they are the Europe of the rich and the Europe of the poor. The gulf in living standards is yawning. According to an Institute for International Economics study in autumn 1991, Eastern Europe will require no less than 420 billion dollars' worth of annual investment for the next decade in order to catch up with average incomes in the European Community.[20] In other words, poverty in Eastern Europe will last for at least another generation.

The scale of the investment needed to remedy matters can be gauged from the problems of the newly reunified Germany. Indeed, in many respects, the obstacles in the path of the economic integration of Eastern (formerly COMECON) Europe and Western ('Community'-based) Europe have been mirrored in the problems of integrating the eastern Democratic Republic with the western Federal Republic. The reunification of Germany has entailed the only direct merger of market and command economy systems, with the eastern partition becoming at once a member of the EC. In the year following the collapse of the Berlin Wall, £52.3 billion dollars were invested in the eastern *länder*, but even this did not prevent an exodus westwards, with the abandonment of factories, high unemployment and a lack of business start-ups. More generally in eastern Europe, there is the risk that economic privation will trigger challenges to the territorial status quo. As one commentator has warned: 'Nationalism [and counter-nationalism in particular] breeds in poverty as surely as mosquitoes breed in swamp water, and Central Europe today is a poor place.'[21]

The need for cooperation between the two Europes pervaded the thinking of Milan Hodža's first Danube Plan in 1936. Then, the Central European economy was totally becalmed by the stagnating effects of recession and lacked both Western outlets for its overpriced agricultural surpluses and, as a consequence, the purchasing power to buy consumer goods back from the industrialized nations of Western Europe. It was this vicious circle of non-integrated economic regions which Hodža hoped to square by orchestrating the Central European economies in a Danubian federation.

Impatient with several neighbouring states for dragging their heels (a product of the political and economic nationalism already discussed), Hodža also indicted the Western powers for an engrained parochialism in economic outlook. Western Europe did not realize, either after the war or in the 1930s, the importance of integrating the two Europes, he contended, and held that the main weakness of Versailles was the absence of any provision for Central European cooperation that would have served as a bulwark against aggressive German nationalism. In support of his case, Hodža cited Doreen Warriner's Fabian Research series volume entitled *Eastern Europe after Hitler* and her contention that 'what is really needed is a European Federation covering the East and at least two important industrialised [Western] states, if not all'.[22]

The need for Western initiatives to diminish the enormous 'technology gap' between the two Europes was also evident in Gerda Zellentin's imaginative (albeit stillborn) proposal in the early 1970s for the EC to create a 'Fund for European Development and Cooperation' administered by the Community, to which all participants in the nascent Conference on Security and Cooperation in Europe (CSCE) would subscribe capital. The aims were to promote direct investment in the underdeveloped regions of the continent and to encourage East–West trade by establishing a clearing scheme to ensure convertibility into every European currency.[23]

The risk of repeating the same type of insularity which Hodža attributed to previous West European leaders should not be underestimated. The Swedish economist Nils Lundgrén has argued in *Ekonomisk Debatt* that 'we shall perhaps see the Berlin Wall rebuilt, but this time by Western Europe, not Eastern Europe',[24] whilst former Chancellor Nigel Lawson, speaking in the House of Commons 'European Debate' on 21 November 1991, also emphasized the need to confront the challenges of the wider Europe. 'We are fiddling with Western Europe while Eastern Europe burns', he insisted.[25] Indeed, perhaps the supreme challenge of the last decade of this century did not find a place on the Maastricht summit agenda; namely, how to achieve a sufficient measure of practical *de facto* integration between the two Europes.

In pulling the threads of our discussion together, it is suggested that in a curious way the Maastricht agenda appeared more immediately relevant to the needs of the post-communist region of Europe than to the European Community states. This can be demonstrated by reference to the central concepts of the debate on West European integration.

First, the essential *convergence in the New Europe* involves less the equalization of the discrepant economies of the 'Twelve' (such as Germany and Greece) – a precondition of economic and monetary union – than the overriding need to close the chasm in living standards between Eastern and Western Europe. Moreover, the case for monetary union as a vehicle for reintegrating economies appears at least as strong, if not stronger, in relation to the former Soviet republics as in the development of the European Community.

Plainly, the road to economic convergence on the continent is not paved with panaceas. Formal East–West treaties, such as those of December 1991 which bestowed associate EC status on Czechoslovakia, Hungary and Poland, or sector-specific agreements like the Dutch-inspired European Energy Charter (designed to develop the CIS' energy field) have a role; so, too, does trade in Western expertise, ideas and experience. But it warrants emphasis that pan-European economic integration does not necessarily entail creating legal state-level links between the two Europes. Rather, effective *de facto* integration can be achieved at lower altitudes, so to speak, by attracting Western business investment.

Second, the really significant *democratic deficit* lies less in the reputed lack of democratic control and accountability of the central decision-making organs within the political system of the EC – something particularly stressed by German Chancellor Helmut Kohl –

than in the lag in democratization between Eastern Europe and the European Economic Area (EC + EFTA) countries. In terms of democratic development, Eastern Europe has, metaphorically speaking, scarcely climbed out of the Red. The post-communist successor states have yet to achieve the stage of democratic consolidation or, in some cases, even democratic breakthrough.

In holding the fort during the transition to democracy – as the strategic contributions of president Lech Walesa in Poland and president Václav Havel of the new Czech Republic bear out – the role of responsible leadership is vital. Referring to Spain, Portugal and Greece in the 1970s, Gianfranco Pasquino has observed that 'after the demise of an authoritarian regime ... the need arises for new forms of collective identification and space is created for new types of political leadership'.[26] Yet according to L. Whitehead, democratic consolidation occurs only when 'the new regime becomes institutionalized, its framework of open and competitive expression becomes internalized and in large measure the preceding uncertainties and insecurities are overcome'.[27] This process, he insists, takes at least a generation. Plainly, the East European democracies have hardly begun to approach this stage of consolidation, nor should a successful outcome of democracy-building readily be assumed.

In any event, much of the carping about the democratic deficit and concern to check the inflated power of the European Commission stem from the myth of the domestic analogy – that is, an idealized picture of the working of parliamentary democracy in individual member-states.[28] Over the last quarter of a century, a series of protest parties ranging from Democrats '66 in Holland to New Democracy in Sweden and the Vlaams Blok in Flanders have objected at the national level to precisely the type of centralized, elitist style of decision-making which in the EC context has been the target of critics of the democratic deficit.

Put briefly, although national governments are regularly accountable to the people through general elections, the extent of effective parliamentary scrutiny over the activities of government in the wider sense – the initiation and formulation of public policy – is relatively weak. For many, increasing the powers of the domestic parliaments of the EC states is at least as relevant as the (legitimate) concern to increase the legislative powers of the European Parliament in Strasbourg. A national democratic deficit may also be said to exist in respect of the generally low electoral participation of a younger cohort of voters, apparently disillusioned with the political process and what the leader of New Democracy in Sweden, Bert Karlsson, has described as the 'crocodile politicians' – possessed of big mouths but no ears – running the affairs of state. Paradoxically, as Eastern Europe turns to the West for advice on democracy-building, political scientists in Western Europe have begun to study what they have detected as a 'crisis in democracy'.

Third, *subsidiarity* or the devolution of decision-making as close to citizens as possible, which has had a strong *prima facie* appeal to the 'unrepresented nations' and regions of the European Community, has probably its greatest immediacy in post-communist Europe. Here, as in the cases of the Albanians in Kosovo, Transylvanian Magyars, Moldovans and Tartars in Ukraine and Russians in the Baltics, it could serve as an instrument in the national integration of geographically concentrated ethnic minorities. The application of the principle of subsidiarity to cultural and linguistic minorities, in short, could provide a useful vehicle in the containment and accommodation of counter-nationalist sentiment. The question of subsidiarity or the distribution of power along a territorial–cultural axis raises the wider question of federalism.

Indeed, finally, it is suggested that the dreaded 'F' word (which was blazoned across the pages of the British press in the run-up to the Maastricht summit) has its greatest application and most powerful operational logic in Eastern Europe where federal or confederal arrangements could provide a loose institutional framework within which to achieve the urgently needed reintegration of the economies of the region. This could take the form of an EEC or *East European Community* operating either within, or as a stepping-stone towards, a pan-continental economic space. Federalism, in short, could serve as a device for harnessing the resurgence of political nationalism and containing the threat of economic nationalism in Eastern Europe, whilst also facilitating the coordination of regional affairs with the EC in Brussels. The broad Hodža rationale thus remains valid.

All in all, the case for economic (and possibly also political) union appears strongest in Eastern Europe, whilst the future of the EC probably lies along the road of functionalist, rather than federalist, integration; that is, an *ad hoc*, piecemeal, instrumentalist and, above all, sectoral course. The functionalist orientation is problem-specific rather than 'grand design' and is in tune with the history of the development of West European integration so far. There is, in any event, a risk (as Jean Monnet intimated in his *Memoirs*) of seeking to squeeze European integration into structural moulds into which it will not readily fit and, by extension, of evaluating progress by reference to established concepts which, for all their familiarity, are not without ambiguity. 'The words about which people argue – federation or confederation – are inadequate and imprecise,' Monnet insisted. 'What we are preparing, through the work of the Community, is probably without precedent.'[29] Certainly there has been division among member-states both over the meaning of federalism (best regarded as an ideology) and the distribution of power in federal systems. The Germans – presently the only federation within the EC – have been vigorous federalists, equating federalism with the decentralization of power; Britain, in contrast, has tended to view federalism as synonymous with an increased concentration of power in Brussels.

West European federalism – the European Union of Maastricht – has in any case largely failed to engage or excite political leaders, not to mention a broad public for many of whom the prospect of peace, security and an end to the long era of superpower politics is intrinsically more appealing than Delors' exhortation that 'a political superpower must emerge out of the dynamic economic and trading power which we already have'. In a post-imperialist Europe, in which, first, Third World colonies were surrendered and then Communist configurations collapsed, the prospect of a 'new imperialism' – however equitably the EC deploys its authority to defuse international crises etc. – is likely to be unappealing. Clearly, moreover, in a Europe of multiple transnational institutions, possessing complementary, indeed overlapping, functions and membership, the Community must be careful to avoid pre-emptive or bombastic action motivated by petty rivalries.

For example, the Council of Europe, the ECSC and the European Community are all committed (in the words of the provision for a common foreign and security policy formulated at Maastricht) 'to develop and consolidate democracy and the rule of law and respect for human rights and fundamental freedoms' as well as 'to preserve peace and strengthen international security'.[30] They all have a role to play – a multi-site Europe is as valid as a single-campus continent – and the EC would be wise to avoid appearing, as in its dismissive response to the Council of Europe's initial peacekeeping initiative in Yugoslavia, to want to marginalize other bodies.

Certainly the time appears ripe for the active propagation of an *ideology of Europeanism* which appeals to both head and heart and, crucially, embraces the challenges of the wider Europe beyond the EC. The risk of a two-track Community is already a real one, since it is doubtful if all member-states will meet the conditions necessary for the adoption of a single currency by 1 January 1999; accordingly, there are likely to be 'member-states with a derogation'. The risk of a three- or four-track Europe is even greater, though, with the Visegrad Triangle in track three and most of the former Soviet republics lagging well behind that. In this context, there may well be much truth in Peter Calvocoressi's conclusion that: 'The European Community will not become pan-European, since it is inconceivable that its stronger Western members will allow it to be overrun by weaker newcomers.'[31]

The Europeanism of the 21st century, however, must not (even unwittingly) reinforce the two Europes, still less a Europe *à quatre*. Rather, Europeanism should seek to embrace and extend the values of liberalism, pluralism, tolerance, rationality and human dignity and to harness, rather than erase and erode, cultural and linguistic diversity. Europeanism cannot be at the expense of nationality, in the sense of national character and identity, but just the reverse: differences in the national persona should serve to enrich the entire community of European peoples.

There is an undoubted concern, particularly in non-member states, about an acculturation process – a homogenization and levelling out of cultural variation – in which the very *volkgeist* is extinguished and a nation's creative being prostituted on the altar of an elitist EC-based Europeanism. This fear, and the cultural nationalist backlash to which it has given rise (especially on the radical left), has been admirably captured by Gúdrún Helgadóttir, a former president of the United *Allting* (parliament) in Iceland. The European Community is capital-centred, not culture-centred, firm-focused rather than folk-focused, she argues, and proceeds to defend a conception of culture in a distinctively Icelandic sense which is not sophisticated and elitist, but expresses the very identity of the people themselves. Helgadóttir, incidentally, stresses the remarkable uniformity in national culture by reference to the virtual absence of dialectical variation in the Icelandic language.[32]

Helgadóttir, though, was harsh on the intentions of European Union, which does not perforce entail cultural denationalization. Indeed, in Article 128 of the Maastricht Treaty it is stated that: 'The Community shall contribute to the flowering of the cultures of the member-states, while respecting their national and regional diversity and at the same time bringing the common cultural heritage to the fore.'[33] National diversity and the symbolism of nations will be maintained. Even within the framework of full European union (in whatever institutional form), Britain will retain her monarch, bewigged judges and bobbies' helmets! On the subject of bobbies (the police), a final word on the ineluctability of national variation in the Europe of the 21st century can perhaps be left with the Lappish writer, Jorma Etto, writing about Finns. Plainly with a body of Finns like the archetype depicted below, the risk of cultural homogenization in the New Europe remains slender indeed.

'Suomalainen on sellainen,
joka vastaa kun ei kysytä
kysyy kun ei vastata
ei vastaa kun kysytään …

eikä suomalaista erota suomalaisesta mikään

ei mikään paitsi kuolema ja poliisi'

'A Finn is somebody who answers when he is not asked
Asks when nobody answers him, but doesn't answer when he's asked.
There is nothing at all to distinguish one Finn from the next,
Only death and the police can do that!'

Notes

1 Christopher Harvie (1977), *Scotland and Nationalism*, London, George Allen & Unwin, p.58.
2 Ernest Renan (1964), 'Qu'est-ce qu'une Nation?', in Louis L. Snyder (ed.), *The Dynamics of Nationalism*, Princeton, New Jersey: Van Nostrand, pp.9–10. See also, Hans Kohn (1978), 'Nationalism', in Anthony de Crespigny and Jeremy Cronin (eds), *Ideologies of Politics*, Oxford: Oxford University Press, pp.148–60.
3 This was particularly true in France shortly after de Gaulle's accession to power when a variety of regions and linguistic minorities presented themselves as 'nations' colonized by an imperial power in order to demand (with some success under the Socialist governments of the 1980s) varying degrees of devolved power. John Loughlin (1985), 'A New Deal for France's Regions and Linguistic Minorities', *West European Politics*, 8(3), 102–13.
4 E.J. Hobsbawm (1990), *Nations and Nationalism since 1780*, Cambridge: Cambridge University Press, p.5.
5 Alfred Cobban (1969), *The Nation State and National Self-Determination*, London and Glasgow: Collins, p.66.
6 Ibid., p.68.
7 BBC television, *Heart of the Matter*, 26 July 1992.
8 E.J. Hobsbawm, 'The Return of Mitteleuropa', *The Guardian*, 11 October 1991.
9 Hobsbawm (1990), op. cit., p.30.
10 Edgar Anderson (1966), 'Towards a Baltic Union 1920–27', *Lituanus*, **12**(2), 31–2.
11 B. Chubb (1971), *The Government and Politics of Ireland*, London: Longman, p.77.
12 H.R. Kedward (1985), *Occupied France: Collaboration and Resistance 1940–44*, Oxford and New York: Basil Blackwell, p.24.
13 Tom Gallagher (1981), 'The Dimensions of Fianna Fail Rule in Ireland', *Western European Politics*, 4(1), 54–68.
14 'Czech premier announces deal', *The Guardian*, 24 July 1992, p.7.
15 H. Seton-Watson (1986), *Eastern Europe Between the Wars 1918–1941*, Boulder and London: Westview, pp.264–7.
16 European People's Party Document (1/91), *The Christian-Democratic Movement in Central and Eastern Europe* (no publication details given).
17 'Finding the Price of Freedom', *The Guardian*, 15 October 1990.
18 'Bohemians fear their new baker cooked the books', *The Guardian*, 21 October 1991.
19 Tatu Vanhanen has hypothesized that, when power resources are diffused, democracy will evolve and be maintained. In order to test his claim he calculated an Index of Power Resources (IPR) based on six variables: the size of the urban population and non-agricultural workforce; the number of students and literates; the proportion of economically active persons engaged in family farming; and the extent to which non-agricultural economic resources are decentralized. Tatu Vanhanen (1990), *The Process of Democratisation*, New York: Taylor & Francis, pp.191–7.
20 Jonathan Eyal, 'Missing the grip of an iron hand', *The Guardian*, 8 October 1991.

21   Richard C. Langworth (1990), 'Central Europe: Potential for Prosperity', *Europe*, July/August, 11–12.
22   M. Hodža (1942), *Federation in Central Europe*, London: Jarrolds, p.167.
23   Michael Kaser (1973), 'The EEC and Eastern Europe: Prospects for Trade and Finance', *International Affairs*, **49**, 411.
24   Quoted in Per Gahrton, 'All-europeiskt miljöparlament – grönt alternativ til EG', *Nordisk Kontakt*, 7/8, 1991, 14–16.
25   This seemed harsh. Jacques Delors noted that, between 1989 and 1991, the EC supplied the Visegrad Triangle of Poland, Czechoslovakia and Hungary with 70 billion ECUs – 78 per cent of its total aid. Jacques Delors, 'Ties make for peace', *The Guardian*, 13 March 1991.
26   Gianfranco Pasquino (1990), 'Political Leadership in Southern Europe: Research Problems', *West European Politics*, **13**(4), 121.
27   Geoffrey Pridham (1990), 'Political Actors, Linkages and Interactions: Democratic Consolidation in Southern Europe', *West European Politics*, **13**(4), 106.
28   Philip Lawrence (1990), 'The Domestic Analogy and the Liberal State', *Politics*, **10**(2), 20–26.
29   J. Monnet (1978), *Memoirs*, London: Collins, p.523.
30   Treaty on European Union (1992), op. cit., 123–4.
31   P. Calvocoressi (1991), *Resilient Europe 1870–2000*, London: Longman, p.255.
32   Gúdrún Helgadóttir, 'National identitet i et nyt Europa', *Nordisk Kontakt*, 7/8, 1991, 10–13.
33   Treaty on European Union (1992), op. cit., p.48.

Bibliography

Adenauer, Konrad (1966), *Memoirs 1945–53*, London: Weidenfeld & Nicolson.

Allardt, Erik and Rokkan, Stein (eds) (1970), *Mass Politics: Studies in Political Sociology*, New York: Free Press.

Allen, Hilary (1979), *Norway and Europe in the 1970s*, Oslo–Bergen–Tromsø: Universitetsforlaget.

Allison, Roy (1985), *Finland's Relations with the Soviet Union, 1944–84*, London: Macmillan.

Alperovitz, Gar (1970), *Cold War Essays*, New York: Anchor.

Amyot, Grant (1981), *The Italian Communist Party*, London: Croom Helm.

Anderson Edgar (1966), 'Towards a Baltic Union 1920–1927', *Lituanus*, **12** (2), 30–56.

Anderson, Edgar (1967), 'Towards a Baltic Union 1927–34', *Lituanus*, **13** (1), 5–28.

Aron, Raymond (1954), *The Century of Total War*, New York: Doubleday.

Arter, David (1978a) *Bumpkin Against Bigwig: The Emergence of a Green Movement in Finnish Politics*, Tampere: Tampere University.

Arter, David (1978b), 'All-Party Government for Finland?', *Parliamentary Affairs*, **XXI** (1).

Arter, David (1984), *The Nordic Parliaments: A Comparative Analysis*, London; Hurst.

Arter, David (1987), *Politics and Policy-Making in Finland*, Brighton: Wheatsheaf.

Arter, David (1989), 'A Tale of Two Carlssons: The Swedish General Election of 1988', *Parliamentary Affairs*, **42**(1), 84–101.

Arter, David (1991a), 'One *Ting* Too Many: The Shift to Unicameralism in Denmark', in L.D. Longley and D.M. Olson (eds), *Two into One*, Boulder: Westview, pp.77–142.

Arter, David (1991b), 'The Swedish Leftist Party: "Eco-Communism" or Communist Echo?', *Parliamentary Affairs*, **44**(1), 60–79.

Aubert, Jean-François (1978), 'Switzerland', in David Butler and Austin Ranney (eds), *Referendums*, Washington DC: American Enterprise Institute, pp.39–66.

Auken, Svend, Buksti, Jakob and Sørensen, Carsten Lehmann (1976),

'Denmark Joins Europe', *Journal of Common Market Studies*, **14**(1), 1–36.

Backer, John H. (1978), *The Decision to Divide Germany: American Foreign Policy in Transition*, Durham, NC: Duke University Press.

Bark, Dennis L. and Gress, David R. (1989), *From Shadow to Substance*, Oxford: Basil Blackwell.

Bell, David S. (1983), *Democratic Politics in Spain*, London, Pinter.

Beneš, Eduard (1954), *Memoirs of Dr Eduard Benes: From Munich to New War and New Victory*, translated by Godfrey Lias, London; George Allen & Unwin.

Berner, Wolfgang (1979), 'The Italian Left, 1944–1978: Patterns of Cooperation, Conflict and Compromise', in W.E. Griffith (ed.), *The European Left: Italy, France and Spain*, New York: Heath.

Birgersson, Bengt Owe, Hadenius, Stig, Molin, Björn and Wieslander, Hans (1981), *Sverige efter 1900*, Stockholm: Bonnier.

Blackmer, Donald L.M. and Tarrow, Sidney (eds) (1975), *Communism in Italy and France*, Princeton: Princeton University Press.

Borella, François (1979), *Les partis politiques dans l'Europe des Neuf*, Paris: Editions du Seuil.

Brandt, Willy (1971), *In Exile: Essays, Reflections and Letters 1933–1947*, London: Oswald Wolff.

Brandt, Willy (1978), *People and Politics: The Years 1960–1975*, London: Collins.

Brier, A.P. and Hill, A.P. (1977), 'The Estimation of Constituency and Party Voting in the British Referendum of June 1975', *Political Studies*, **25**(1), 93–102.

Brinton, William M. and Rinzler, Alan (eds) (1990), *Without Force or Lies: Voices from the Revolution of Central Europe in 1989–90*, San Francisco: Mercury House.

Bristow, Stephen L. (1975), 'Partisanship, Participation and Legitimacy in Britain's EEC Referendum', *Journal of Common Market Studies*, **14**, 297–311.

Brogan, Patrick (1990), *Eastern Europe 1939–1989: The Fifty Years War*, London: Bloomsbury.

Bromhead, Peter (1970–71), 'The British Constitution in 1970', *Parliamentary Affairs*, **24** (2), 104–11.

Brown, Archie and Gray, Jack (1977), *Political Culture and Political Change in Communist States*, Second Edition, London: Macmillan.

Brož, Alexander (1919), 'Land Reform in Czechoslovakia', *The New Europe*, **XI** (136), 22 May, 137–9.

Bruce Lockhart, Freda (1947), 'Towards a United Europe?', *The Nineteenth Century and After*, July, 12–16.

Bruneau, Thomas C. (1984), 'Continuity and Change in Portuguese Politics: Ten Years After the Revolution of 25 April 1974', in Geoffrey

Pridham (ed.), *The New Mediterranean Democracies*, London: Frank Cass, pp.72–83.

Bujack, Francis (1926), *Poland's Economic Development*, London: George Allen & Unwin.

Buksti, Jakob A. (1980), 'Corporate Structures in Danish EC Policy: Patterns of Organisational Participation and Adaptation', *Journal of Common Market Studies*, **19** (2).

Bullock, Alan (1983), *Ernest Bevin: Foreign Secretary 1945–51*, London: Heinemann.

Butler, David and Ranney, Austin (eds) (1978), *Referendums: A Comparative Study of Practice and Theory*, Washington DC: American Enterprise Institute.

Butler, W.E. (1975), 'Legal Configurations of Integration in Eastern Europe', *International Affairs*, **51** (4), 512–20.

Byrd, Peter (1975–6), 'The Labour Party and the European Community', *Journal of Common Market Studies*, **14**, 469–83.

Calvocoressi, Peter (1991), *Resilient Europe 1870–2000*, London and New York: Longman.

Camps, Miriam (1964), *Britain and the European Community, 1955–1963*, Princeton, NJ: Free Press.

Carlton, David (1981), *Anthony Eden: A Biography*, London: Allen Lane.

Carr, E.H. (1945), *Nationalism and After*, London: Macmillan.

Carsten, F.L. (1972), *Revolution in Central Europe*, London: Temple Smith.

Castle, Barbara (1980), *The Castle Diaries 1974–76*, London: Weidenfeld & Nicolson.

Castle, Barbara (1984), *The Castle Diaries 1964–70*, London: Weidenfeld & Nicolson.

Childers, Erskine (1919), 'Ireland: The International Aspect', *The New Europe*, **XI** (138), 5 June, 180–84.

Chronik der Deutschen (1982), Dortmund: Chronik Verlag.

Chubb, Basil (1982), *The Government and Politics of Ireland*, Second Edition, London: Longman.

Church, Clive H. (1989), 'Switzerland: Recent History and Politics', in *Western Europe 1989*, London: Europa, pp.446–67.

Cipolla, Carlo M. (ed.) (1976), *The Fontana Economic History of Europe: Contemporary Economics*, Part 2, Glasgow: Collins/Fontana.

Cobban, Alfred (1969), *The Nation State and National Self-Determination*, London and Glasgow: Collins.

Coombes, D. and Walkland, S. (1980), *Parliaments and Economic Affairs*, London: Heinemann.

Cooper, Duff (1954), *Old Men Forget*, London: Hart-Davis.

Cox, Geoffrey (1988), *Countdown to War: A Personal Memoir of Europe 1938–40*, London: William Kimber.

Darras, Jacques and Snowman, Daniel (1990), *Beyond the Tunnel of History*, London; Macmillan.

Deák, István (1974), 'Hungary', in Hans Rogger and Eugen Webber (eds), *The European Right*, Berkeley-Los Angeles: University of California.

De Crespigny, Anthony and Cronin, Jeremy (eds) (1978), *Ideologies of Politics*, Oxford: Oxford University Press.

De Ménil, Lois Pattison (1977), *Who Speaks for Europe? The Vision of Charles de Gaulle*, London: Weidenfeld & Nicolson.

DePorte, A.W. (1979), *Europe Between the Superpowers*, New Haven and London: Yale University Press.

Derry, T.K. (1979), *A History of Scandinavia*, London: George Allen & Unwin.

Diamandouros, P. Nikiforos (1984), 'Transition to, and Consolidation of Democratic Politics in Greece, 1974–1983: A Tentative Assessment', *West European Politics*, **7**(2), 50–71.

Diebold, William Jr. (1959), *The Schuman Plan: A Study in Economic Cooperation 1950–1959*, New York: Praeger.

Diebold, William Jr. (1988), 'The Marshall Plan in Retrospect: A Review of Recent Scholarship', *Journal of International Affairs*, **41** (2), 421–35.

Divine, Robert A. (ed.) (1969), *Causes and Consequences of World War II*, Chicago: Quadrangle Books.

Edwards, Geoffrey (1981), 'The Future Challenge: New and Potential Members', in Carol and Kenneth J. Twitchett (eds), *Building Europe: Britain's Partners in the EEC*, London: Europa Publications.

Edwards, Geoffrey (1988), 'International Relations and Defence in Western Europe', in *Western Europe 1989: A Political and Economic Survey*, London: Europa, pp.58–66.

Elcock, Howard (1972), *Portrait of a Decision*, London: Eyre Methuen.

Elder, Neil, Thomas, Alastair and Arter, David (1982), *The Consensual Democracies? The Government and Politics of the Scandinavian States*, Oxford: Martin Robertson.

Engman, Max and Kirby, David (eds) (1989), *Finland: People, Nation, State*, London: Hurst.

Fisher, Nigel (1982), *Harold Macmillan*, London: Weidenfeld & Nicolson.

Fitzmaurice, John (1976), 'National Parliaments and European Policy-Making: The Case of Denmark', *Parliamentary Affairs*, **29** (3), 281–92.

Fitzmaurice, John (1980), 'Reflections on the European Elections', *West European Politics*, **3**(2), 230–41.

Fitzmaurice, John (1981), *Politics in Denmark*, London; Hurst.

Fontaine, André (1965), *History of the Cold War*, London: Secker & Warburg.

Frei, Daniel (1973–4), 'Switzerland and the EEC: Facts and Trends', *Journal of Common Market Studies*, **12**, 248–64.

Freund, Michael (1972), *From Cold War to Ostpolitik: Germany and the New Europe*, London: Oswald Wolff.

Gallagher, Tom (1981), 'The Dimensions of Fianna Fail Rule in Ireland', *West European Politics*, **4** (1), 54–68.

Gallagher, Tom (1989), 'Recent History and Politics of Portugal', *Western Europe 1989*, London: Europa, pp.392–6.

Gallo, Max (1973), *Spain Under Franco*, London; George Allen & Unwin.

Garver, Bruce M. (1978), *The Young Czech Party 1874–1901 and the Emergence of a Multi-Party System*, New Haven and London: Yale University Press.

Garvin, Tom and Parker, Anthony (1972), 'Party Loyalty and Irish Voters: The EEC Referendum as a Case-Study', *Economic and Social Review*, **4** (1), 35–9.

George, Stephen (1990), *An Awkward Partner: Britain in the European Community*, Oxford: Oxford University Press.

Goodhart, Philip (1971), *Referendum*, London: Tom Stacy.

Graham, Malbone W. (1945), 'Parties and Politics', in Robert Kerner (ed.), *Czechoslovakia*, Berkeley: United Nations Series, pp.137–69.

Griffith, William E. (ed.) (1979), *The European Left: Italy, France and Spain*, New York: Heath.

Grosser, Alfred (1964), *The Federal Republic of Germany: A Concise History*, New York: Praeger.

Haas, Ernst B. (1968), *The Uniting of Europe: Political, Social and Economic Forces, 1950–1957*, Stanford: Stanford University Press.

Hancock, M. Donald (1972), 'Sweden, Scandinavia and the EEC', *International Affairs*, **48** (3), 420–28.

Hansen, Peter, Small, Melvin and Siune, Karen (1977), 'The Structure of the Debate in the Danish EC Campaign: A Study of an Opinion–Policy Relationship', *Journal of Common Market Studies*, **15**, 110–19.

Harvie, Christopher (1977), *Scotland and Nationalism*, London: George Allen & Unwin.

Hayward, J.E.S. and Berki, R.N. (1979), *State and Society in Contemporary Europe*, Oxford: Martin Robertson.

Heath, Edward (1970), *Old World, New Horizons: Britain, the Common Market and the Atlantic Alliance*, London: Atlantic Alliance.

Hertz, Frederick (1947), *The Economic Problems of the Danubian States: A Study in Economic Nationalism*, London: Victor Gollancz.

Hiden, John and Salmon, Patrick (1991), *The Baltic Nations and Europe: Estonia, Latvia and Lithuania in the Twentieth Century*, London and New York: Longman.

Hobsbawm, E.J. (1990), *Nations and Nationalism since 1780: Programme, Myth and Reality*, Cambridge: Cambridge University Press.

Hodža, Milan (1942), *Federation in Central Europe: Reflections and Reminiscences*, London: Jarrolds.

Holmes, Peter (1983), 'Spain and the EEC', in David S. Bell (ed.), *Democratic Politics in Spain*, London: Pinter, pp.165–79.

Horowitz, David (1967), *From Yalta to Vietnam: American Foreign Policy in the Cold War*, London: Penguin.

House, Edward Mandell and Seymour, Charles (eds) (1921), *What Really Happened at Paris*, London: Hodder & Stoughton.

Hudson, G.F. (1969), 'The Lesson of Yalta', in Robert Divine (ed.), *Causes and Consequences of World War II*, Chicago: Quadrangle Books, pp.225–36.

Hyamson, Albert M. (1919), 'National Rights in the New States', *The New Europe*, **XI** (140), 19 June, 233–4.

Information Department of the Royal Institute of International Affairs (1970), *The Baltic States: A Survey of the Political and Economic Structure and the Foreign Relations of Estonia, Latvia and Lithuania*, Westport, Conn: Greenwood.

Jászi, Oscar (1945), 'The Problem of Sub-Carpathian Ruthenia', in Robert I. Kerner (ed.), *Czechoslovakia*, Berkeley: United Nations Series, pp.193–8.

Jay, Douglas, (1980), *Change and Fortune: A Political Record*, London; Hutchinson.

Jenkins, Roy (1974), *Nine Men of Power*, London: Hamish Hamilton.

Julkunen, Martti (1975), *Talvisodan kuva: Ulkomaisten sotakirjeenvaihtajien kuvaukset suomesta 1939–40*, Helsinki: Weilin & Göös.

Kalela, Jorma (1976), 'Right-Wing Radicalism in Finland during the Inter-War Period', *Scandinavian Journal of History*, **1**, 105–24.

Karjalainen, Ahti and Tarkka, Jukka (1989), *Presidentin ministeri: Ahti Karjalaisen ura Urho Kekkosen suomessa*, Helsinki: Otava.

Kaser, Michael (1973), 'The EEC and Eastern Europe: Prospects for Trade and Finance', *International Affairs*, **49**, 402–11.

Katzenstein, Peter J. (1975), 'Trends and Oscillations in Austrian Integration Policy since 1955: Alternative Explanations', *Journal of Common Market Studies*, **14**, 171–97.

Kavka, Frantisek (1960), *An Outline of Czechoslovak History*, Prague: Orbis.

Keatinge, Patrick (1972), 'Odd Man Out? Irish Neutrality and European Security', *International Affairs*, **48** (3), 436–43.

Kedward, H.R. (1985), *Occupied France: Collaboration and Resistance 1940–1944*, Oxford: Basil Blackwell.

Kee, Robert (1976), *Ourselves Alone*, London: Quartet Books.

Kekkonen, Urho (1976a), *Kirjeitä myllystäni 1956–1967*, Keuruu: Otava.

Kekkonen, Urho (1976b), *Kirjeitä myllystäni 2, 1968–1975*, Keuruu: Otava.

Kekkonen, Urho (1980), *Tamminiemi*, Espoo: Weilin & Göös.

Kerner, Robert, J. (1945), *Czechoslovakia*, Berkeley: United Nations Series.

Kerr, Henry H. Jr. (1974), *Switzerland: Social Cleavages and Partisan Conflict*, London: Sage.

Kindleberger, Charles P. (1987), *The Marshall Plan Days*, Winchester, MA: Allen & Unwin.

Kirby, D.G. (1979), *Finland in the Twentieth Century*, London: Hurst.

Kirschbaum, Joseph M. (1960), *Slovakia: Nation at the Crossroads of Central Europe*, New York: Robert Speller.

Kitzinger, Uwe (1973), *Diplomacy and Persuasion*, London: Thames & Hudson.

Kohn, Hans (1978), 'Nationalism', in A. Crespigny and J. Cronin (eds), *Ideologies of Politics*, Oxford: Oxford University Press, pp.148–60.

Koivisto, Mauno (1978), *Väärää Politiikkaa*, Helsinki: Kirjayhtymä.

Koivisto, Mauno (1981), *Tästä lähtien*, Helsinki: Kirjayhtymä.

Lafeber, William (ed.) (1971), *The Origins of the Cold War, 1941–47*, New York-London-Sydney-Toronto: John Wiley.

Laqueur, Walter (1969), *Russia and Germany: A Century of Conflict*, London: Weidenfeld & Nicolson.

Lawrence, Philip (1990), 'The Domestic Analogy and the Liberal State', *Politics*, **10**(2), 20–26.

Leigh, Michael (1975–6), 'Linkage Politics: The French Referendum and the Paris Summit of 1972', *Journal of Common Market Studies*, **14**, 157–70.

Leslie, Peter M. (1975), 'Interest Groups and Political Integration: The 1972 EEC Decisions in Norway and Denmark', *American Political Science Review*, **69** (1), 70–75.

Lijphart, Arend (1968), *The Politics of Accommodation: Pluralism and Democracy in Divided Societies*, Berkeley: University of California.

Lindberg, Leon L. (1963), *The Political Dynamics of European Economic Integration*, Stanford; Stanford University Press.

Logue, John (1982), *Socialism and Abundance: Radical Socialism in the Danish Welfare State*, Minneapolis: University of Minnesota Press.

London, Gary (1975), *The End of an Opposition of Principle: the Case of the Finnish Socialist Workers' Party*, University of Helsinki, Institute of Political Science Research Reports No. 37.

Longley, Lawrence D. and Olson, David M. (1991), *Two into One: The Politics and Processes of National Legislative Cameral Change*, Boulder-San Francisco-Oxford: Westview.

Lord Moran (1966), *Churchill: The Struggle for Survival 1940–65*, London: Constable.

Lord, Robert Howard (1921), 'Poland', in E.M. House and C. Seymour (eds), *What Really Happened at Paris*, London: Hodder & Stoughton, pp.70–85.

Loughlin, John (1985), 'A New Deal for France's Regions and Linguistic Minorities', *West European Politics*, **8** (3), 102–13.

Luther, K.R. and Müller, W.C. (eds) (1992), *Politics in Austria: Still a Case of Consociationalism?*. London: Frank Cass.

Lyrintzis, Christos (1989), 'Greece: Recent History and Politics', in *Western Europe 1989*, London: Europa, pp.235–9.

Macartney, C.A. and Palmer, A.W. (1962), *Independent Eastern Europe*, London: Macmillan.

Macmillan, Harold (1971), *Riding the Storm 1956–59*, London: Macmillan.

Macmillan, Harold, (1973), *At the End of the Day*, London: Macmillan.

Magnússon, Sigurdur A. (1977), *Northern Sphinx: Iceland and the Icelanders from the Settlement to the Present*, London: Hurst.

Mamatey, Victor (1962), *The United States and East Central Europe 1914–1918*, London: Macmillan.

Marks, Sally (1976), *The Illusion of Peace: International Relations in Europe 1918–1933*, London: Macmillan.

Marsh, Peter (1975–6), 'The Integration Process in Eastern Europe 1968–1975', *Journal of Common Market Studies*, **14**, 311–35.

Marsh, Peter (1984), 'The European Community and East–West Economic Relations', *Journal of Common Market Studies*, **28**, 1–13.

Masaryk, T.G. (1927), *The Making of a State: Memories and Observations 1914–1918*, London: George Allen & Unwin.

Maudling, Reginald (1978), *Memoirs*, London: Sidgwick & Jackson.

Mauriac, François (1966), *De Gaulle*, London: Bodley Head.

McAleese, Dermot and Matthews, Alan (1987), 'The Single European Act and Ireland: Implications for a Small Member State', *Journal of Common Market Studies*, **26** (1), 39–60.

McNeill, Terry (1979), 'State and Nationality under Communism', in J.E.S. Hayward and R.N. Berki (eds), *State and Society in Contemporary Europe*, Oxford: Martin Robertson, pp.118–40.

Mikolayczyk, Snanislav (1948), *The Pattern of Soviet Domination*, Maston: Sampson Low.

Miljan, Toivo (1977), *The Reluctant Europeans: The Attitudes of the Nordic Countries towards European Integration*, London: Hurst.

Miller, Kenneth E. (1982), 'Policy-Making by Referendum: The Danish Experience', *West European Politics*, **5** (1), 54–67.

Monnet, Jean (1978), *Memoirs*, translated by Richard Mayne, London: Collins.

Mouritzen, Hans (1988), *Finlandisation: Towards a General Theory of Adaptive Politics*, Aldershot: Avebury.

Mylly, Juhani (1978), *Maalaisliitto ja turvallisuuspolitiikka*, Turku: Turun yliopisto.

Narkiewicz, Olga A. (1976), *The Green Flag: Polish Populist Politics 1867–1970*, London: Croom Helm.

Newhouse, John (1970), *De Gaulle and the Anglo-Saxons*, London: André Deutsch.

Newman, Karl J. (1970), *European Democracy Between the Wars*, London: George Allen & Unwin.

Newman, Michael (1983), *Socialism and European Unity: The Dilemma of the Left in Britain and France*, London.

Nicholson, Harold (1964), *Peacemaking 1919*, London: Methuen.

Nilson, Sten Sparre (1978), 'Scandinavia', in D. Butler and A. Ranney (eds), *Referendums*, Washington DC: American Enterprise Institute, pp.169–92.

Norton, Philip (1975), *Dissension in the House of Commons 1945–1974*, London: Macmillan.

Norton, Philip (1978), *Conservative Dissidents: Dissent within the Parliamentary Conservative Party 1970–74*, London: Temple Smith.

O'Brien, Conor Cruise (1972), *States of Ireland*, London: Hutchinson.

O'Corcora, Michael and Hill, Ronald J. (1982), 'The Soviet Union in Irish Foreign Policy', *International Affairs*, **58** (2), 260–68.

O'Leary, Brendan (1987), 'Towards Europeanisation and Realignment?: The Irish General Election, February 1987', *West European Politics*, **10** (3), 453–65.

Oren, Nissan (1970), 'Popular Front in the Balkans', *Journal of Contemporary History*, **5**(3), 69–82.

Orridge, Andrew (1977), 'The Irish Labour Party', in W.E. Paterson and A.H. Thomas (eds), *Social Democratic Parties in Western Europe*, London: Croom Helm, pp.153–75.

Österreichische statistik tabelle 11, Grössengliederung sämtlicher betriebe, Wien: 1909.

Parming, Tönu (1975), *The Collapse of Liberal Democracy and the Rise of Authoritarianism in Estonia*, London: Sage.

Pasquino, Gianfranco (1990), 'Political Leadership in Southern Europe: Research Problems', *West European Politics*, **13** (4), 118–30.

Paterson, William E. and Thomas, Alastair H. (eds) (1977), *Social Democratic Parties in Western Europe*, London: Croom Helm.

Payne, Stanley G. (1968), *Franco's Spain*, London: Routledge & Kegan Paul.

Pelling, Henry (1974), *Winston Churchill*, London: Macmillan.

Petersen, Nikolaj and Elklit, Jørgen (1973), 'Denmark Enters the European Community', *Scandinavian Political Studies*, **8**, 200–209.

Pollack, Benny, with Graham Hunter (1988), *The Paradox of Spanish Foreign Policy: Spain's International Relations from Franco to Democracy*, London: Pinter.

Pollard, Sidney (1974), *European Economic Integration 1815–1970*, London: Thames & Hudson.

Pollard, Sidney (1981), *The Integration of the European Economy since 1815*, London: George Allen & Unwin.

Pollard, S. and Holmes, C. (1971), *Documents of European Economic History 11: Industrial Power and National Rivalry 1870–1911*, London: Edward Arnold.

Polonsky, Antony (1975), *The Little Dictators: The History of Eastern Europe since 1918*, London and Boston: Routledge & Kegan Paul.

Preston, Paul (1986), *The Triumph of Democracy in Spain*, London and New York: Methuen.

Price, Roy (1989), 'Working Towards Integration in a Divided Continent', in *Western Europe 1989*, London: Europe, pp.1–7.

Pridham, Geoffrey (ed.) (1984), *The New Mediterranean Democracies: Regime Transition in Spain, Greece and Portugal*, London: Frank Cass.

Pridham, Geoffrey (1990), 'Political Actors, Linkages and Interactions: Democratic Consolidation in Southern Europe', *West European Politics*, **13** (4), 103–17.

Puntila, L.A. (1978), *Valtioneuvoston historia 1917–1966*, Helsinki: Valtion painatuskeskus.

Raymond, Raymond S. (1984), 'Irish Neutrality: Ideology or Pragmatism?', *International Affairs*, **60** (1), 32–42.

Renan, Ernest (1964), 'Qu'est-ce qu'une Nation?', in L.L. Snyder (ed.), *The Dynamics of Nationalism*, Princeton: Van Nostrand, pp.9–10.

Roberts, J.M. (1967), *Europe 1880–1945*, London: Longmans.

Rodgers, Hugh I. (1975), *Search for Security: A Study in Baltic Diplomacy 1920–1934*, Connecticut: Archon Books.

Rogger, Hans (1974), 'Russia', in Rogger and Weber (1974), pp.443–500.

Rogger, Hans and Weber, Eugen (eds) (1974), *The European Right: A Historical Profile*, Berkeley-Los Angeles: University of California Press.

Roucek, Joseph S. (1945), 'Czechoslovakia and her Minorities', in R.J. Kerner (ed.), *Czechoslovakia*, Berkeley: United Nations Series, pp.171–92.

Rusi, Alpo M. (1991), *After the Cold War: Europe's New Political Architecture*, New York and Prague: Macmillan.

Sainsbury, Keith (1986), *The Turning Point*, Oxford and New York: Oxford University Press.

Saint-Ouens, François (1988), 'Facing European Integration: The Case of Switzerland', *Journal of Common Market Studies*, **26** (3), 273–85.

Salmon, Trevor S. (1981), 'Ireland', in C. Twitchett and J. Kenneth (eds), *Building Europe: Britain's Partners in the EEC*, London: Europa, pp.183–93.

Salmon, Trevor (1982), 'Ireland: A Neutral in the Community', *Journal of Common Market Studies*, **15** (3), 205–27.

Scheich, Manfred (1973), 'The European Neutrals After Enlargement of the Communities: The Austrian Perspective', *Journal of Common Market Studies*, **12**, 235–47.

Schlesinger, Rudolf (1953), *Central European Democracy and Its Background*, London: Routledge & Kegan Paul.

Schmitt, Hermann (1990), 'The European Elections of June 1989', *West European Politics*, **13** (1), 116–23.

Schönbaum, Wulf (ed.) (1980), *Programm und Politik der Christlich Demokratischen Union Deutschlands seit 1945*, Bonn: CDU-Bundesgeschäftsstelle.

Schultz, D. Mark (1992), 'Austria in the International Arena: Neutrality, European Integration and Consociationalism', in K.R. Luther and W.C. Müller (eds), *Politics in Austria*, London: Frank Cass, pp.173–200.

Schultz, Gerhard (1967), *Revolutions and Peace Treaties, 1917–1920*, London: Methuen.

Serfaty, Simon (1968), *France, de Gaulle and Europe: The Policy of the Fourth and Fifth Republics Towards the Continent*, Baltimore: The Johns Hopkins Press.

Seton-Watson, Hugh (1977), *Nations and States*, London: Methuen.

Seton-Watson, Hugh (1986), *Eastern Europe Between the Wars 1918–1941*, Boulder and London: Westview.

Seton-Watson, R.W. (1943), *A History of the Czechs and Slovaks*, London-New York-Melbourne: Hutchinson.

Seymour, Charles (1921), 'The End of an Empire: Remnants of Austria-Hungary', in E.M. House and C. Seymour (eds), *What Really Happened at Paris*, London: Hodder & Stoughton, pp.89–94.

Silberschmidt, Max (1972), *The United States and Europe: Rivals and Partners*, London: Thames & Hudson.

Smith, Anthony (1986), *The Ethnic Origins of Nations*, Oxford: Basil Blackwell.

Smith, A.H. (1991), *National Identity*, London: Penguin.

Snyder, Louis L. (ed.) (1964), *The Dynamics of Nationalism*, Princeton: Van Nostrand.

Sowden, J.K. (1975), *The German Question 1945–1973: Continuity in Change*, London: Crosby Lockwood Staples.

Stridsberg, Gusti (1963), *Viisi maailmaani*, Jyväskylä: Gummerus.

Tardieu, André (1921), *The Truth about the Treaty*, London: Hodder & Houghton.

Textor, Lucy E. (1945), 'Agriculture and Agrarian Reform', in R.J. Kerner, *Czechoslovakia*, Berkeley: United Nations Series, pp.200–22.

Thomas, Alastair H. (1973), *Parliamentary Parties in Denmark 1945–1972*, University of Strathclyde Occasional Papers 13.

Thomas, Alastair H. (1975), 'Danish Social Democracy and the European Community', *Journal of Common Market Studies*, **13** (4), 454–68.

Tovias, Alfred (1984), 'The International Context of Democratic Transition', in G. Pridham (ed.), *The New Mediterranean Democracies*, London: Frank Cass, pp.158–72.

Tovias, Alfred (1991), 'EC–Eastern Europe: A Case Study of Hungary', *Journal of Common Market Studies*, **29** (3), 291–317.

Truman, Harry S (1956), *Years of Trial and Hope: Memoirs*, Volume 2, New York: Signet.

Truman, Margaret (1979), *Harry S Truman*, London: Hamish Hamilton.

Trythall, J.W.D. (1970), *Franco: A Bibliography*, London; Rupert Hart-Davis.

Tsoukalis, Loukas (1977), 'The EEC and the Mediterranean: Is "Global" Policy a Misnomer?', *International Affairs*, July, 422–38.

Tsoukalis, Loukas (1978), 'A Community of Twelve in Search of an Identity', *International Affairs*, **54** (3).

Twitchett, Carol and Kenneth, J. (eds) (1981), *Building Europe: Britain's Partners in the EEC*, London: Europa Publications.

Urwin, Derek, W. (1991), *Western Europe since 1945*, Fourth Edition, London and New York: Longman.

Urwin, Derek, W. (1992), *The Community of Europe: A History of European Integration since 1945*, London: Longman.

Uschakow, Alexander (1979), 'COMECON: Inter-State Economic Co-operation in Eastern Europe', in J.E.S. Hayward and R.N. Berki, *State and Society in Contemporary Europe*, Oxford: Martin Robertson, pp.218–36.

Vanhanen, Tatu (1990), *The Process of Democratisation*, New York: Taylor & Francis.

Vaughan, Richard (1976), *Post-War Integration in Europe*, London: Edward Arnold.

Von Rauch, Georg (1974), *The Baltic States. Estonia, Latvia, Lithuania: The Years of Independence 1917–1940*, London: Hurst.

Waite, James L. (1973), 'The Swedish Paradox: EEC and Neutrality', *Journal of Common Market Studies*, **12**, 319–36.

Watson, David Robin (1974), *Clemençeau: A Political Biography*, London: Methuen.

Watson, Richard, L. Jr. (1965), *The United States in the Contemporary World 1945–62*, New York: Free Press.

Weber, Eugen (1974), 'Romania', in H. Rogger and E. Weber (eds), *The European Right*, pp.501–74.

Western Europe 1989: A Political and Economic Survey, London; Europa.

Williams, Philip M. (1964), *Crisis and Compromise: Politics in the Fourth Republic*, London: Longman.

Wilson, Harold (1971), *The Labour Government 1964–70*, London: Weidenfeld and Nicolson.

Winnacker, Rudolph A. (1969), 'Yalta – Another Munich?', in R.A. Divine (ed.), *Causes and Consequences of World War II*, Chicago: Quadrangle, pp.237–48.

Worre, Torben (1988), 'Denmark at the Crossroads: The Danish Referendum of 28 February 1986 on the EC Reform Package', *Journal of Common Market Studies*, **26** (4), 361–88.

Wright, Vincent (1978), 'France', in D. Butler and A. Ranney (eds), *Referendums*, Washington DC: American Enterprise Institute, pp.139–67.

Zauberman, Alfred (1976), 'Russia and Eastern Europe 1920–1970', in C.M. Cipolla (ed.), *The Fontana Economic History of Europe*, Part 2, Glasgow: Collins/Fontana, pp.577–623.

Zurcher, Arnold J. (1958), *The Struggle to Unite Europe 1940–1958*, Westport, Conn.: Greenwood.

Index